SUPPLEMENT TO THE
PROCEEDINGS OF THE SEMINAR FOR ARABIAN STUDIES
VOLUME 44
2014

LANGUAGES OF SOUTHERN ARABIA

Papers from the Special Session of the Seminar for Arabian Studies held on 27 July 2013

edited by

Orhan Elmaz & Janet C.E. Watson

SEMINAR FOR ARABIAN STUDIES

ARCHAEOPRESS
OXFORD

2014

This Supplement is available with volume 44 of the *Proceedings of the Seminar for Arabian Studies* and orders should be sent to
Archaeopress, Gordon House, 276 Banbury Road, Oxford OX2 7ED, UK.
Tel +44-(0)1865-311914 Fax +44(0)1865-512231.
e-mail archaeo@archaeopress.com
http://www.archaeopress.com
For the availability of back issues see The British Foundation for the Study of Arabia's website:
http://www.thebfsa.org/content/seminar-proceedings

Seminar for Arabian Studies
c/o the Department of the Middle East, The British Museum
London, WC1B 3DG, United Kingdom
e-mail seminar.arab@durham.ac.uk
The British Foundation for the Study of Arabia: www.thebfsa.org

STEERING COMMITTEE

Dr Derek Kennet (Chair)
Dr Robert Wilson (Treasurer)
Professor Robert G. Hoyland (joint editor of PSAS)
Ms Sarah Morriss (Secretary and joint editor of PSAS)
Dr Mark Beech
Dr Rob Carter
Dr Nadia Durrani
Dr Orhan Elmaz
Dr Julian Jansen van Rensburg
Mr Michael C.A. Macdonald
Dr Harry Munt
Dr Venetia Porter
Dr St John Simpson
Dr Janet C.M. Starkey
Dr Lucy Wadeson
Professor Janet C.E. Watson

EDITORIAL COMMITTEE: ADDITIONAL MEMBERS

Prof. Alessandra Avanzini
Prof. Soumyen Bandyopadhyay
Dr Ricardo Eichmann
Prof. Clive Holes
Prof. Khalil Al-Muaikel
Prof. Daniel T. Potts
Prof. Christian Robin

Opinions expressed in papers published in the *Proceedings* are those of the authors and are not necessarily shared by the Editorial Committee.

The *Proceedings* is produced in the Times Semitic New font, which was designed by Paul Bibire for the Seminar for Arabian Studies.

© 2014 Archaeopress, Oxford, UK.
All rights reserved. No part of this publication may be reproduced, stored in a retrieval system, or transmitted, in any form or by any means, electronic, mechanical, photocopying, recording, or otherwise, without the prior permission of the publisher.
ISSN 0308-8421
ISBN 978-1-905739-81-3
ISBN 978-1-905739-55-4
Printed and bound in Great Britain by Marston Book Services Ltd, Oxfordshire

The Steering Committee of the Seminar for Arabian Studies is most grateful to the
MBI Al Jaber Foundation
for its continued generosity in making a substantial grant towards the running costs of
the Seminar and the editorial expenses of producing the *Proceedings*.

Contents

Transliteration iii

Orhan Elmaz & Janet C.E. Watson, *Languages of Southern Arabia* v

Alessandra Avanzini, *From inscriptions to grammar: notes on the grammar of non-Sabaic languages* 1

Alex Bellem & G. Rex Smith, *'Middle Arabic'? Morpho-syntactic features of clashing grammars in a thirteenth-century Arabian text* 9

Domenyk Eades, *Syncretism in the verbal morphology of the Modern South Arabian Languages* 19

Orhan Elmaz, *Investigating South Arabian words in al-Khalīl's Kitāb al-ᶜayn* 29

Richard Gravina, *The vowel system of Jibbali* 43

Leonid Kogan & Vitaly Naumkin, *The vowels of Soqotri as a phonemic system* 57

Ingo Kottsieper & Peter Stein, *Sabaic and Aramaic — a common origin?* 81

Walter W. Müller, *Sabaic lexical survivals in the Arabic language and dialects of Yemen* 89

Alessia Prioletta, *Towards a Ḥaḍramitic lexicon: lexical notes on terms relating to the formulary and rituals in expiatory inscriptions* 101

Irene Rossi, *The Minaeans beyond Maᶜīn* 111

Aaron D. Rubin, *A brief comparison of Mehri and Jibbali* 125

Christina van der Wal Anonby, *Traces of Arabian in Kumzari* 137

Janet C.E. Watson, *Southern Semitic and Arabic dialects of the south-western Arabian Peninsula* 147

Papers read in the Special Session of the Seminar for Arabian Studies on 27 July 2013 155

Transliteration

This *Supplement* to the *Proceedings of the Seminar for Arabian Studies* employs the following transliteration for Arabic, Ancient South Arabian, Modern South Arabian, and Kumzari.

Note that personal names, toponyms, and other words which have entered English in a particular form are used in that form when they occur in an English sentence, unless they are part of a quotation in the original language, or part of a correctly transliterated name or phrase.

The transliteration systems are as follows:

(a) Arabic

ء	ʾ	ج	j	ذ	dh (*dh*)	ش	sh (*sh*)	ظ	ẓ	ق	q	ن	n
ب	b	ح	ḥ	ر	r	ص	ṣ	ع	ʿ	ك	k	ه	h
ت	t	خ	kh (*kh*)	ز	z	ض	ḍ	غ	gh (*gh*)	ل	l	و	w
ث	th (*th*)	د	d	س	s	ط	ṭ	ف	f	م	m	ي	y

- Vowels: **a i u ā ī ū.**   Diphthongs **aw   ay.**
- Initial *hamzah* is omitted.
- The *lām* of the article is not assimilated before the 'sun letters', thus *al-shams* not *ash-shams*.
- The *hamzat al-waṣl* of the article should be shown after vowels except after the preposition *li-*, as in the Arabic script, e.g. *wa-ʾl-wazīr*, *fīʾl-bayt*, but *li-l-wazīr*.
- *Tāʾ marbūṭah* (ة) should be rendered *-ah*, except in a construct: e.g. *birkah*, *zakāh*, and *birkat al-sibāḥah*, *zakāt al-fiṭr*.

(b) Ancient North and South Arabian
Consonants:

ʾ	b	t	ṯ	ḥ	g	ḫ	d	ḏ	r	z	s¹	s²	s³	ṣ
ḍ	ṭ	ẓ	ʿ	ġ	f	q	k	l	m	n	h	w	y	

(c) Other Semitic languages, including Modern South Arabian, appear in the transliteration systems outlined in the *Bulletin of the American Schools of Oriental Research* 226 (1986), p. 3.

(d) Persian and Kumzari as for Arabic and Modern South Arabian, with the additional letters transliterated according to the system in the *Encyclopaedia of Islam* (Third Edition) except that *ž* is used instead of *zh*. These instructions are available online at www.brill.nl/AuthorsInstructions/EI3P.pdf with information about the transliteration of Persian, Ottoman Turkish, modern Turkish, and Urdu on p. 5 of this document.

Note on Fonts
Electronic versions of papers being submitted for publication should be submitted in **Times Semitic New** 12-point font if at all possible, with double-line spacing on A4-paper size and with 2.45 cm margins all round. This font set is available for free download from the Arabian Seminar website (www.arabianseminar.org.uk) along with the recommended Greek font set, called TimesClassicGreek (tmsrr_l.ttf).

Languages of Southern Arabia

ORHAN ELMAZ & JANET C.E. WATSON

The special session in 2013, Languages of Southern Arabia, was the fifth in the Seminar for Arabian Studies special session series, and followed 'The Palaeolithic of Arabia' in 2007, 'The Development of Arabic as a Written Language' in 2010, 'The Nabataeans in Focus' in 2011, and 'Museums in Arabia' in 2012. This was the first special session with an explicit linguistic focus to be held at the Seminar, and aimed to bring together experts on the extinct and extant languages of southern Arabia to pave the way for identifying cultural, lexical, morphological, syntactic, phonological, and phonetic links between the language families, and to discuss advances in the field and future avenues of research. Work to date had highlighted shared linguistic features across the extinct and extant languages of the region, in many cases where languages are separated by large geographical distances (e.g. Rossi 1940; Behnstedt 1988; Retsö 2000; Holes 2006; Müller 2010; Watson 2011). With papers dealing with Ancient South Arabian, the Modern South Arabian languages, and the Arabic dialects of the southern part of the Peninsula, this session examined and re-examined links within and between the language groups and further afield.

The session not only brought together established and early career scholars of the three language groups, but also experts on different types of oral and written texts — narratives, poetry and songs, and different aspects of linguistics — epigraphy, syntax, morphology, semantics, phonology, and phonetics.

The session was structured around four themed panels with each language group represented in each panel. The panels addressed the following themes:

* Semantics and lexis
* Phonology and phonetics
* Culture and language
* Morphology and syntax

We invited experts known to us in the first instance, and then put out a general call for papers. We were delighted with the response, in particular by the fact that two of the earliest participants of the Seminar for Arabian Studies were among the presenters: Professor Walter Müller and Professor Rex Smith. Presenters came from seven countries — Italy, United States, United Kingdom, Germany, the Netherlands, Russia, and France. Of the fourteen papers presented at the session, twelve have been published here. The two papers not published in this volume due to other commitments were presented by S. Naïm, *L'expression des émotions dans une perspective comparative (dialectes de la Péninsule arabique): la variation intra-langue*; and S. Liebhaber, *Intersections of Mahri Oral Poetry and Arabic Nabaṭi Poetry: The Case for Shared Cultural Inheritance.*

Within this volume, we also included Christina van de Wal Anonby's paper, delivered during the main Seminar session, since it examines Arabic and Arabian features exhibited by Kumzari, a language spoken in remote coastal villages in northern Oman. This is the only paper in the volume that examines links between a non-Semitic language and extant Semitic languages of the Peninsula.

The three papers on semantics and lexis by W.W. Müller, O. Elmaz, and A. Prioletta cover more than 100 Sabaic lexical survivals and Sabaic morphological traces in Arabic and its Yemeni dialects; the question of the actual use of thirty-six previously unnoticed words of South Arabian provenance listed in *Kitāb al-ᶜayn*, the first Classical Arabic thesaurus; and unique lexical features of Hadramitic expiatory inscriptions as compared to other Ancient South Arabian and Semitic languages as a starting point towards a Hadramitic lexicon, respectively.

J.C.E. Watson, L. Kogan, and R. Gravina contributed papers about the phonology and phonetics of southern Arabic varieties, drawing attention to commonalities between them and Ancient and Modern South Arabian as well as Ethio-Semitic languages; a first description of the vowels of Soqotri based on morphologically significant vocalic oppositions; and the vowel system of Jibbali (also known as Shahri) with comparisons to Mehri, placing it within the broader context of southern Semitic.

In the section dealing with morphology and syntax, A. Bellem and G.R. Smith introduce the term Literary Mixed Arabic in favour of Middle Arabic and define it on the basis of some morpho-syntactic variables; A. Avanzini presents insights into the grammar of the non-Sabaic Ancient South Arabian languages through orthography; D. Eades examines syncretism in the verbal morphology of the Modern South Arabian languages spoken in Oman and Yemen as compared to non-MSA languages of the wider region; and, on the basis of an initial examination of Mehri and Jibbali, A. Rubin outlines features to pave the way for a comparative study of the MSA languages.

This volume concludes with two papers about culture and language: the first, by P. Stein and I. Kottsieper, examines the relationship between Aramaic and Sabaic and raises anew the question of cultural transfer across the Arabian Peninsula; the second, by I. Rossi, presents a comparative analysis of cultural and textual features of Minaic inscriptions that were found beyond the South Arabian borders of the Minaean kingdom.

Several papers presented during the Special Session and the broader Seminar highlighted publically accessible digital archives, corpora, and websites. These include the Digital Archive for the Study of pre-Islamic Arabian Inscriptions (DASI); the King Saud University Corpus of Classical Arabic; the Mahri poetry archive; the Leeds Modern South Arabian website; the Semitic Etymology database; and the Semitic Sound Archive hosted at the University of Heidelberg. Technology often threatens minority languages, but these and further archives and corpora now present us with unprecedented tools to document, archive, disseminate, and collaborate. In terms of future research, the potential to examine and re-examine links between the languages of southern Arabia and further afield has never been greater.

Acknowledgements

We thank Miranda Morris and Michael Macdonald for ably chairing two of the panels, Venetia Porter for her support, and the Seminar for funding the publication of this volume.

References

Behnstedt P.
    1988. Lexicalisches aus dem Jemen. *Welt des Orients* 19: 142–155.

Holes C.D.
    2006. The Arabic dialects of Arabia. *Proceedings of the Seminar for Arabian Studies* 36: 25–34.

Müller W.W.
    2010. *Sabäische Inschriften nach Ären datiert. Bibliographie, Texte und Glossar.* (Akademie der Wissenschaften und der Literatur Mainz. Veröffentlichungen der Orientalischen Kommission, 53). Wiesbaden: Harrassowitz.

Retsö J.
    2000. *Kaškaša*, t-passives and the ancient dialects in Arabia. Pages 111–118 in L. Bettini (ed.), *Oriente Moderno: Studi di dialettologia Arabe*. Rome: Istituto per l'Oriente.

Rossi E.
    1940. Vocaboli sud-arabice nelle odierne parlate arabe del Yemen. *Rivista degli Studi Orientali* 18: 299–314.

Watson J.C.E.
    2011. South Arabian and Yemeni dialects. *Salford Working Papers in Linguistics* 1: 27–40; www.languages.salford.ac.uk/research/centre_applied_linguistics/salfordworkingpapers/WP%20(2011)_watson.pdf

Online resources

Digital Archive for the Study of pre-Islamic Arabian Inscriptions (DASI). 30 October 2013. http://dasi.humnet.unipi.it
King Saud University Corpus of Classical Arabic. 30 October 2013. http://ksucorpus.ksu.edu.sa
Leeds Modern South Arabian website. 30 October 2013. www.leeds.ac.uk/arts/info/125219/modern_south_arabian_languages
Mahri poetry archive. 30 October 2013. http://sites.middlebury.edu/mahripoetry
Semitic Etymology database. 30 October 2013. http://starling.rinet.ru/cgi-bin/query.cgi
Semitic Sound Archive hosted at the University of Heidelberg. 30 October 2013. www.semarch.uni-hd.de

From inscriptions to grammar: notes on the grammar of non-Sabaic languages

ALESSANDRA AVANZINI

Summary
The corpus of Sabaic inscriptions is ample and covers a broad geographical area, as well as a vast span of time. The German school of Ancient South Arabian studies, created by Professor Müller, has greatly added to our knowledge of the Sabaic language; many grammatical traits have been defined and some of their geographical and chronological variations identified. Texts written in minuscule allow us to study a different cultural and social level of the Sabaic language, not conveyed by monumental inscriptions.
A smaller number of inscriptions in the Minaic, Qatabanic, and Hadramitic languages have come down to us.
In this paper various linguistic traits and rules governing the written form of these non-Sabaic languages will be presented, including the use of the *matres lectionis* in writing vowels, and the declension of nouns.
As is always the case with dead languages, the grammatical rules that can be singled out are those transmitted by a specific writing school. Nevertheless, some of the linguistic variations that were introduced into the non-Sabaic languages over time and across geographic areas can be identified.

Keywords: South Arabia, non-Sabaic languages, epigraphy, writing school, grammar

1. Writing schools

Identifying normative grammatical rules for the ASA languages is difficult and often impossible, in particular for the non-Sabaic languages attested in smaller corpora than the Sabaic (SAB) corpus. Nevertheless, it is necessary to be cautious in shifting from text rules to language rules even in the analysis of the SAB corpus, despite the evidence attested by a large number of documents of which it is possible to identify chronologic, geographic, and partly diastratic articulations, thanks to the publication of the minuscule texts on wooden sticks. Therefore, in my opinion the compilation of an Ancient South Arabian (ASA) grammar must be considered as a completely different exercise from that of writing a Latin grammar. What can be done is to identify 'trends' towards the grammatical rules for a given language.

It might sound obvious to reiterate how the language attested in a monumental epigraphic corpus is partial, not only for what concerns the lexicon. In fact, the vocabulary of daily life, how the peoples speaking these languages viewed their world, and what they thought, are all excluded. Moreover it is well known that many morphological forms are not included in ASA monumental texts normally using the third person.

Not only is the language of the monumental inscriptions partial, but the grammatical reconstruction of the language might also be 'distorted' by the nature of the texts themselves. This last point can be illustrated by an example in Italian, where there are three past tenses, one of which — the *passato remoto* — is not frequently used and indeed has completely disappeared in many parts of Italy. Much more common are the *passato prossimo* and the *imperfetto*. If knowledge of Italian was based solely on the texts of monumental inscriptions found on buildings, however, the reconstruction of the Italian verbal system would be incomplete and distorted. It could be concluded that the only past tense in Italian is the *passato remoto*, which purpose is to inscribe an event in the past and freeze it for posterity.

The authors of the inscriptions use an obsolete and extremely formal lexicon and syntax involving complex sentences, which in the syntax of everyday spoken language would have been communicated in a much simpler manner.

In general, for all epigraphic documentation the rules identified often depend on the norms of a writing school rather than on the grammar of the language itself. A writing school imposed not only its own palaeographic style, but inserted the texts into fixed formulae, using an

FIGURE 1. *Example of an inscription with Qatabanian script style from Baynūn (BynM 201).*

extremely formal structure of the language and favouring a prescribed set of rhetorical stylemes.

One clear example of rules dictated by a writing school and not by the grammar can be found in the *matres lectionis*. It seems hard to believe that the name of the wadi Tuban written *Tbnw* in Qatabanic (QAT) and *Tbny* in SAB, for instance, constitutes proof of the existence of different realizations of the final -*w* in QAT and SAB. It may be that these represent the modes adopted by two different schools to write the final *a*, as in the parallel case of the ending of the dual construct: 0 (in Early SAB), *y* (from Middle SAB), *w* (in QAT) (Avanzini 2006: 253–260).

I believe that the hypothesis put forward by C. Robin (2001: 570–577) is more persuasive than the rigid rule proposed by P. Stein (2003: 41–43), according to whom different *matres lectionis* were always associated with different phonetic realizations.

It is also well known that the practice of marking *matres lectionis* with two consonants was a characteristic of non-SAB languages, and that the use of *matres lectionis* inside a word is attested in Minaic (MIN) and Hadramitic (HAD), but not in SAB and QAT. These practices provide yet another example of usage dictated by a writing school rather than by the phonetics of the language. Therefore it is highly probable that 'Qatabanisms' identified by P. Stein[1] in SAB inscriptions from the southern plateau — for example, the final -*hy* to indicate tens — are not dialectal traits but depend on the persistence of rules of the QAT writing school.

Various writing schools that were active in ancient southern Arabia can be identified, and it would be interesting to study their reciprocal influence.

Some interactions are obvious, such as the spread to other kingdoms of the boustrophedon style (a feature typical of Early SAB) although its acceptance was limited; or such as the spread of the 'classical' Qatabanian style beyond the borders of its own kingdom (Fig. 1).

It is interesting to note that in inscriptions written in a given ASA language by authors not originally from that linguistic region, the palaeography of texts seems to reflect the style of the writing school of the author and not of the writing school of the language in which the texts are written. Take for example the CSAI I, 72=VL 9 inscription from the city of Timnaᶜ, written in QAT by the *kabir* of Maᶜīn, which in palaeographic terms is quite similar to inscriptions written in MIN; or the RES 2999 inscription on the city wall of Barāqish, probably written by a Qatabanian community in Barāqish, whose graphic style is typical of Qatabān (see Rossi, this volume).

These examples are not trivial; on the contrary they present some interesting socio-linguistic implications.

---

[1] The Qatabanic traits of the southern middle SAB inscriptions, in particular of those belonging to the Radmanic dialect are: the use of a non-etymological *h* consonant, the particular ending of the determinate dual of nouns, the occasional use of the *s¹*-forms of the pronouns, and causative verbal stems (Stein 2003: 8).

It is therefore reasonable to assume that within an ASA community living in a nearby reign, there existed scribes able to compose an epigraphic text in a different language from their own, even though some interesting examples of language contact emerge from these texts. The palaeographic style of inscriptions from the reign they were coming from is often preserved.

2. Towards a QAT grammar

a. The -s¹ww/-s¹yw pronouns

The concepts expressed so far do not hinder the research into rules, but invite one to be cautious in the process of compiling a grammar. A profound knowledge of QAT grammar is fundamental for the interpretation of texts: it leads to the correct reading and integrations and ultimately improves translation.

Some rules that from texts lead to the definition of QAT rules can be established.

Beeston's grammars (1962: 45; 1984: 63, 65) have already identified the morphologic use, with no exceptions, of -s¹ww/-s¹yw in QAT and HAD: a singular pronoun attested after a dual or external plural. More specifically, even if the morphologic rule is clear it is harder to justify the use of such a complex writing habit.

The grammatical rule allows for the correction of some recent translations by F. Bron of the interesting dedications to the god Ḥwkm (2009: 121–126). For example, in FB-Ḥawkam 1B, 5, l-Ḥwkm w-ʾlh-s¹ww is translated by Bron as 'à Ḥwkm et à leurs dieux', but the singular long suffix -s¹ww after ʾlh refers to the god Ḥwkm, previously mentioned, and not to the authors of the text; the translation is 'for Ḥwkm and His gods'.[2]

Another phonetic rule can be detailed: before -s¹ww or -s¹yw there is no evidence of words ending in -y: ʾlh-s¹ww vs. ʾlhy ʿm w-ʾnby (BynM 421, 2). This rule applies in both QAT and HAD.

The fall of -y is clearly linked to the use of accentual patterns associated with the long pronoun.

b. The external plural and the declension of the noun

In a recent article (Avanzini, in press) some grammatical rules related to the external plural and the QAT declension have been identified. The following paragraph summarizes the conclusions drawn.

In QAT, it is possible to recognize the phonetic and grammatical principles governing the use of -hw, -hy, and -h: the endings for the external plural construct. The external plural construct -hw, attested in ASA only in QAT, is used in two nouns — ʾl and mqm — to create the forms ʾlhw and mqmhw, which are never followed by the suffix pronoun. Before the suffix pronoun there is not a single example in the entire QAT documentation of duals or plurals in w. Before the suffix pronoun we find w merging into y as a rule. The same regular use of -y before the suffix pronoun has been identified in SAB (Stein 2003: 52, 91).

-hy is employed for the external plural construct followed by plural or dual suffix pronouns. ʾlhy could be followed by a noun and, as we shall see, this form was important to specify the declension's rule in the Hoqat inscription.

Examples of -hy annexed to a singular pronoun have been found only in the case of nfs¹hy-hw. When nfs¹ is followed by the QAT singular suffix pronouns -s¹ww or -s¹yw, it appears as nfs¹h — and not nfs¹hy — according to the rule mentioned above.

-h is employed for the plural construct state, followed — as a rule — by the singular suffix pronoun -s¹ww/s¹yw or, more rarely, by a plural suffix.

Thanks to the presence of the two forms ʾlhw (nominative)/ʾlhy (accusative) for the external plural, M. Höfner (1961: 453–459) had already identified an example of declension in an inscription she had published: CSAI I, 130=Hoqat. In line 1: s¹qny ... ʾlhy bytn Bnʾ 'he dedicated to the gods of the temple Bnʾ', and in line 3: w-ʿṯtr w-ʿm w-ʾlhw bytn Bnʾ l-yrdʾwn 'and ʿAthtar and ʿAm and the gods of the temple Bnʾ might help'.

Other examples help us to specify the rule. As in SAB (see Stein 2002: 201–222), a clear example of declension is provided by the two forms bnw/bny, dual or plural of bn.

bnw in the nominative case (e.g. FB-Ḥawkam 1B, 2),[3] bnw after prepositions (CSAI I, 130=Hoqat, 9 and CSAI I, 144=MuB 409, 3), and bnw in the genitive case (five times: rbʿ byt bnw in CSAI I, 203=RES 3858).

bny in the accusative case (e.g. FB-Ḥawkam 2, 7).[4] For obvious reasons, in the examples provided bny is not followed by the suffix pronoun or there should always be the form bny + suffix pronoun also in the nominative case.

Apart from bnw/bny, in QAT it is possible to find other examples of word endings:

---

[2] For the cultural implications, see Avanzini 2013: 29–30.

[3] Further examples in CSAI I, 69=Ja 867, 1 and CSAI I, 57=RES 3963, 1.
[4] See also CSAI I, 117=Ja 852, 5; Lion 1, 3; CSAI I, 148=MuB 601, 8.

-*w* vs. -*y*.

tnw 'two' in the nominative case (CSAI I, 66=Ja 343 A, 4 and CSAI I, 67=Ja 343 B, 4); *tnw* in the genitive case (CSAI I, 203=RES 3858, 10); *tny* in the accusative case (CSAI I, 10=Ja 2362, 4 and CSAI I, 206=Thah, 8).

ḏtw plural[5] determinative pronoun in the nominative case (e.g. CSAI I, 64=AM 60.1284, 2);[6] *ḏtw* after preposition (e.g. CSAI I, 173=Ha 7, 3);[7] *ḏty* in the accusative case (e.g. FB-al-Ādī 2, 7).[8]

The ending of the QAT dual is -*w* for nouns in the nominative case or after a preposition. We find some example of duals in -*y* in the accusative case after dedication verbs (Lion 1, 1: *lbʾy*; CSAI I, 124=CIAS 47.11/o 1, 3 and CSAI I, 131=Hon 5, 3: *s²mry*; CSAI I, 118=Ja 2473, 2: *ṣlmy*).

Again, it is advisable to be cautious in applying rules. For instance, it cannot be concluded that the only example of *ḏy* in QAT is yet more evidence of *ḏw/ḏy* declension.

ḏw is the masculine dual of the determinative pronoun in the nominative case;[9] the only evidence for *ḏy* is on the border of CSAI I, 126=CIAS 47.11/p 8 no. 1 inscription in an expression that is hard to translate: 'he committed to Dhu Samawi his camel ᶜ*dwn* [name of the camel] *ḏ-ḏy-s¹*'.

The inscription that — as we shall see below — had been written on the request of a foreign community living in Timnaᶜ, presents instances of linguistic contact or, at least, it shows a lack of confidence by the authors in the use of the QAT language. *ḏ-ḏy-s¹* could mean: 'that is his own' (lit. which is among those that belong to him). *ḏy*, attested in MIN and in SAB, might be a loanword. To sum up, the examples provided so far suffice to define a declension rule in QAT.

In QAT we find the relict of a diptote declension in both the plural and the dual of the nouns in the construct state. The termination -*hy* of the external plural construct and the termination -*y* of the dual construct are regularly used when the noun is in the accusative, but they are not employed as endings for the genitive, or for nouns following a preposition.

If, in this case as well, one wanted to find isoglosses between languages, the comparison between the QAT and the Ethiopic declension would immediately catch one's attention. In Ethiopic the nominative and the genitive actually merged as grammatical categories and did so not only in their phonological representation but also as grammatical categories (Weninger 2011: 1132).

c. The correlative mark -*m*

A morpho-syntactic trait, attested in QAT and not in other ASA languages,[10] is the use on several occasions of the -*m* ending to introduce a relative clause (Nebes 1991: 148; 1997: 127; Mazzini 2006: 480–481). This rule led to the improvement of some translations such as the CSAI I, 205A=RES 4337A, 10–12: *w-ʾtrm Qtbn b-ms²ṭm w-ʾrmm w-qnym b-yḫdr w-ʾrm w-s¹s²m* 'and Qatabān has authority over the merchandise, the stock, the goods, which are in the shops, and are stocked and sold' compared to Beeston's translation 'and one who travels to Qatabān with merchandise and bales and goods shall have a trading-stall and conduct his business and sell' (1959: 12).

ḏm before the relative clause can indicate both 'the one who' and 'the thing which', *ḏtm* is the plural relative pronoun, or a correlative neutral pronoun 'the things which'.

In the formula 'what he (the dedicator) asked to the god', a stylistic trend rather than a rule can be identified: *ḏm tkrb-s¹/b-yktrb-s¹*[11] vs. *b-ḏtm tkrb-s¹/b-yktrb-s¹*.

---

[5] *ḏty* is always a plural, such that it is possible to correct the translation by Bron of FB-al-Ādī 2, 6-7: *w-ʾs¹ṭr hwrtn ḏty ḏhbm* 'l'inscription du pilier qui est en bronze'; *ḏty* is referred to the plural noun 'inscriptions (those in bronze)' and not to *hwrtn*.

[6] Other occurrences are in CSAI I, 126=CIAS 47.11/p 8 no. 1, 1; CSAI I, 156=CIAS 47.82/o 2, 2; CSAI I, 157=CIAS 95.11/o 2, 2; FB-Ḥawkam 3, 2; CSAI I, 45=Ja 119, 1; CSAI I, 66=Ja 343 A, 2; CSAI I, 67=Ja 343 B, 1; CSAI I, 54=Pi. Ḥuṣn al-Wusr, 1; CSAI I, 208=RES 3566, 20; CSAI I, 71=Ry 521, 2.

[7] Further examples in CSAI I, 208=RES 3566, 6; CSAI I, 211=RES 3879, 6.

[8] See also CSAI I, 17=MuB 659, 8; CSAI I, 206=Thah, 7.

[9] *ḏw* in CSAI I, 213=RES 4931: 'relating to the one who performed the service', is surely a *scriptio plena* for the relative pronoun (Mazzini 2006: 482). In HAD too, instead of the regular *ḏ* + the verb, in a formulary phrase, we find twice *ḏw* + the verb, in association with the personal pronoun *s¹w*. It could be a stylistic feature, a way to give force to the pronoun rather than a grammatical rule.

[10] In Early SAB, the RES 3946 inscription provides two examples that could prove a similar use of a noun with -*m* followed by a relative clause. At the very beginning, line 1: *ʾlt ʾhgrm w-ʾbḏᶜm gnʾ w-ḥftn Krbʾl* 'These are the cities and the territories which Karibil encircled with walls and took possession of'; line 6: *ʾln ʾnḫlm ᶜs¹y* 'these are the palm groves which he acquired'. Stein (2003: 230, n. 177) mentions an alternative translation with an adverbial function of -*m*: 'for what concerns', i.e. 'These, (for what concerns) the cities and the territories, Karibil encircled with walls and took possession of' and 'these, (for what concerns) the palm groves, he acquired'. But it is also plausible that -*m* + relative clause was a syntactic trait preserved from proto-ASA in QAT, with a single residual instance in Early SAB.

[11] The reading of FB-Ḥawkam 5, 3: *ḏm yktrb-s¹* is incorrect; from the photograph the reading *ḏm b-yktrb- s¹* is certain.

Indeed some exceptions can be found (e.g. CSAI I, 18=MuB 673, 5–6: *ḏtm tk[rb-s¹]*).

ḏn (singular masculine demonstrative adjective) and *ḏtn* (plural feminine and masculine demonstrative adjective) are well attested throughout the language history of QAT.

Still, *ḏn/ḏtn* as correlative pronouns substituting the 'regular' pronouns *ḏm* and *ḏtm* are present only from a specific period (a diachronic evolution within the language) and linked to a possible linguistic contact. It is also an interesting one, since it is not simply a loan from another ASA language. In SAB, for example, *ḏn* is only a demonstrative adjective, *ḏn qnyw* 'what they owned' would be incorrect in SAB. In SAB *ḏtn*, always used as a demonstrative adjective both singular and plural, is a dialectal trait specific to SAB from the southern plateau and considered by Stein to be a 'Qatabanism'.

b-ḏtn tkrb-s¹ in line 6 of the previously mentioned CSAI I, 126=CIAS 47.11/p 8 no. 1 inscription, with non-Qatabanian authors, is a linguistic 'pastiche'. The *ḏtn* pronoun does not exist in MIN,[12] neither does this syntactic use of *ḏtn* in SAB. To non-QAT authors the correlative mark -*m* must have been far from their linguistic sensibility.

d. *ʾl b-yfʿl*

As already mentioned in this paper, to know a rule means to have support in the interpretation of an inscription and sometimes also in the reading of a text.

The prefix form of the verb preceded by *b-* in QAT is always used in relative clauses preceded either by a noun with the ending -*m* (and surely in this case the noun is determinate) or by a pronoun, or by a conjunction with the ending -*m*. This rule provided very few exceptions. In CSAI I, 205=RES 4337, alongside the eleven examples that follow our rule, we find an interesting exception: the negation *ʾl* + *b* + the verb: CSAI I, 205B, 2-3: *ʾl b-yʿdwn nʿmt* 'they will not remove the privilege' and lines 18–19: *w-ʾl b-ys²tyṭ kl s²yṭm* 'no trade will be conducted'".

This construct is attested also in CSAI I, 208=RES 3566, 14: *ʾl s¹knw w-ʾl b-ys¹knwn* 'they did not validate and shall not validate', and lines 18–19: *ḏtm ʾl b-ys¹knwn* 'those which will not be validated'.

But there is also a third case of the negation *ʾl* + *b* + the verb at the end of the inscription CSAI I, 205=RES 4337. In CSAI I, 205C, 14–15 the editors read: *w-nl b-ymtʿ*.

FIGURE 2. *A new photograph of the Qatabanic text CSAI I, 205 C= RES 4337 C (M. Arbach).*

l, with the intensifying prefix *n-*, followed by *b-* before the verb, would have been too idiosyncratic a form: *l-* and *b-* followed by the verbal form *yfʿl* are mutually exclusive.

The reading had to be checked once more. Now, thanks to the new pictures of the text taken by Mounir Arbach, this verification can be made and it reads: *w-(ʾ)l b-ymtʿ* (Figs 2–3).

The overall meaning of this final part of the text that emerges with the corrected reading is: 'And no king will take away this decree'; a less moving translation indeed, but more credible from a grammatical point of view than the previous translation: 'and will safeguard this decree every king'. *mtʿ* means 'to save' in the second stem, as has been clearly demonstrated by the use of the infinitive with the suffix -*n* in SAB, but here the verb is in the first stem. The two different meanings of the two verbal forms are attested both in Arabic and in Modern South Arabian.

---

[12] While this claim does not seem quite true, *ḏtn* is attested in an unpublished MIN inscription in the Military Museum of Ṣanʿāʾ (MṢN 3560). I thank Alessia Prioletta for this remark.

Figure 3. *CSAI I, 205 C = RES 4337 C, particular of ll. 14-15 (M. Arbach).*

e. Minaean writing school

It is possible, although extremely challenging, to reflect on and try to understand the grammar of QAT, but a similar analysis of MIN poses even more difficulties.

For external plural endings, at first glance, in MIN the situation appears to be similar and we can certainly identify at least one rule: the ending of the external plural is *-hy* when it is followed by a noun or a verb whereas it is *-h* if the name is followed by a suffix pronoun. For example: *ʾbhy* (M 236, 1) vs. *ʾbh-sʲm* (Maʿīn 7, 6) or *frʿhy* (Maʿīn 1, 2) vs. *frʿh-sʲm* (M 185, 2). But in Kamna 26, 7 we find: *w-frʿh ʿttr*.

In MIN, as is well known, the ending *-h* is not only used in the case of a construct external plural preceding the suffix pronoun.

In similar contexts the ending may or may not be present: *b-kbrh* + proper name vs. *b-kbr* + proper name; *b-ywm mlkh* + proper name vs. *b-ywm mlk* + proper name. In any case, *-h* seems always attested in a noun at the construct state (Stein 2011: 1051–1052).

A further example of graphic variations in similar contexts can be found in MIN for instances of *-sʲ/-sʲw*. Where in HAD and in QAT the rule using the long writing of pronouns is easily subsumed from texts, in MIN we find *-sʲw* and *-sʲ* in perfectly similar contexts: for example *bhn-sʲw* vs. *bhn-sʲ*.

What could be considered a major weakness of the MIN writing school, which allowed several types of writing to coexist in similar contexts, should not be forgotten when shifting from texts to normative grammar. Scholars should bear in mind the weakness of the MIN writing school, which allows different writing forms to coexist in similar contexts. The definition of fixed schemes is hypothetical in all ASA languages, but this holds true especially for MIN.

f. Conclusions

In the case of languages for which the surviving documentation is fragmentary and in large part limited to monumental inscriptions, extreme caution in our methodological approach is necessary before we arrive at the point of fixing grammatical rules and exceptions to these rules.

It is not impossible to compile grammars of ASA languages, but we must remember that certain rules were imposed by the writing schools rather than reflecting grammatical rules of the language.

The temptation to systematize all the data prematurely, even when based on profound knowledge (both of monumental inscriptions and of the texts written in minuscule), as in the case of P. Stein and A. Multhoff, is in my eyes notable, but can be treacherous, particularly when broad historical conclusions are drawn on the basis of fragile hypotheses regarding the linguistic history.

Languages form an integral part of the history of a culture, but the reconstruction of this history based solely on languages has already revealed its limitations many times in the studies of 'historical grammar' since the end of the nineteenth century.

Inscriptions cited[13]

BynM 421
CSAI I, 10=Ja 2362
CSAI I, 17=MuB 659
CSAI I, 18=MuB 673
CSAI I, 45=Ja 119
CSAI I, 54=Pi. Ḥuṣn al-Wusr
CSAI I, 57=RES 3963
CSAI I, 64=AM 60.1284
CSAI I, 66=Ja 343 A

---

[13] For the bibliography of the inscriptions, please refer to their edition in DASI (http://dasi.humnet.unipi.it).

CSAI I, 67=Ja 343 B	CSAI I, 208=RES 3566
CSAI I, 69=Ja 867	CSAI I, 211=RES 3879
CSAI I, 71=Ry 521	CSAI I, 213=RES 4931
CSAI I, 117=Ja 852	DhM 201
CSAI I, 118=Ja 2473	FB-al-Ādī 2
CSAI I, 124=CIAS 47.11/o 1	FB-Ḥawkam 1B
CSAI I, 126=CIAS 47.11/p 8 n° 1	FB-Ḥawkam 2
CSAI I, 130=Hoqat	FB-Ḥawkam 3
CSAI I, 131=Hon 5	FB-Ḥawkam 5
CSAI I, 144=MuB 409	Kamna 26
CSAI I, 148=MuB 601	Lion 1
CSAI I, 156=CIAS 47.82/o 2	M 185
CSAI I, 157=CIAS 95.11/o 2	M 236
CSAI I, 173=Ha 7	Maʿīn 1
CSAI I, 203=RES 3858	Maʿīn 7
CSAI I, 205=RES 4337	RES 3946
CSAI I, 206=Thah	

References

Avanzini A.
    2006. A Fresh Look at Sabaic. *Journal of The American Oriental Society* 126/2: 253–260.
    2013. Inscriptions from museums in the region of Dhamār: Qatabanians in Baynūn and the goddess Athirat (*ʾtrtn*). Pages 27–36 in F. Briquel-Chatonnet, C. Fauveaud & I. Gajda (eds), *Entre Carthage et l'Arabie heureuse. Mélanges offerts à François Bron.* (Orient et Méditerranée, 12). Paris: De Boccard.
    (in press). The inscription CSAI I, 203=RES 3858 and some remarks on the noun declension in Qatabanic. In *Studies in honour of Christian Julien Robin*. Paris: De Boccard.

Beeston A.F.L.
    1959. *The mercantile code of Qataban. Qahtan. Studies in Old Arabian Epigraphy*. i. London: Luzac & Co.
    1962. *Descriptive Grammar of Epigraphic South Arabian*. London: Luzac & Co. Ltd.
    1984. *Sabaic Grammar*. (Journal of Semitic Studies. Monograph, 6). Manchester: University of Manchester.

Bron F.
    2009. Trois nouvelles dédicaces qatabanites à Ḥawkam. *Orientalia* 78/2: 121–126.

Höfner M.
    1961. Eine qatabanische Weihinschrift aus Timnaʿ. *Le Muséon* 74: 453–459.

Mazzini G.
    2006. A-base pronominal system in Qatabanic. Pages 475–487 in P.G. Borbone, A. Mengozzi & M. Tosco (eds), *Loquentes linguis. Linguistic and Oriental Studies in honour of Fabrizio A. Pennacchietti*. Wiesbaden: Harrassowitz Verlag.

Nebes N.
    1991. Die enklitischen Partikeln des Altsüdarabischen. Pages 133–151 in R. Richter, I. Kottsieper & M. Maraqten (eds), *Études sud-arabes. Recueil offert à Jacques Ryckmans* (Publications de l'Institut Orientaliste de Louvain, 39). Louvain-la-Neuve: Institut Orientaliste.
    1997. Stand und Aufgaben einer Grammatik des Altsüdarabischen. Pages 111–131 in R.G. Stiegner (ed.), *Aktualisierte Beiträge zum 1. Internationalen Symposion Südarabien, interdisziplinär an der Universität Graz, mit kurzen Einführungen zu Sprach- und Kulturgeschichte*. Graz: Leykam.

Robin C.J.
 2001. Les inscriptions de l'Arabie antique et les études arabes. *Arabica* 48/4: 509–577.

Rossi I.
 (this volume). The Minaeans beyond Maʿīn. *Supplement to the Proceedings of the Seminar for Arabian Studies* 44.

Stein P.
 2002. Gibt es Kasus im Sabäischen? Pages 201–222 in N. Nebes (ed.), *Neue Beiträge zur Semitistik. Erstes Arbeitstreffen der Arbeitsgemeinschaft Semitistik in der Deutschen Morgenländischen Gesellschaft vom 11. bis 13. September 2000 an der Friedrich-Schiller-Universität Jena*. Wiesbaden: Harrassowitz Verlag.
 2003. *Untersuchungen zur Phonologie und Morphologie des Sabäischen*. (Epigraphische Forschungen auf der Arabischen Halbinsel, 3). Rahden: Marie Leidorf GmbH.
 2011. Ancient South Arabian. Pages 1042–1073 in S. Weninger (ed.), *The Semitic Languages. An International Handbook*. (Handbücher zur Sprach- und Kommunikationswissenschaft, 36). Berlin/Boston: De Gruyter–Mouton.

Weninger S.
 2011. Old Ethiopic. Pages 1124–1142 in S. Weninger (ed.), *The Semitic Languages. An International Handbook*. (Handbücher zur Sprach- und Kommunikationswissenschaft, 36). Berlin/Boston: De Gruyter–Mouton.

Author's address

Prof. Alessandra Avanzini, Dipartimento di Civiltà e Forme del Sapere, University of Pisa, c/o Galvani 1, 56126 Pisa, Italy.

e-mail avanzini@sta.unipi.it

'Middle Arabic'? Morpho-syntactic features of clashing grammars in a thirteenth-century Arabian text

ALEX BELLEM & G. REX SMITH

Summary
There is a body of texts in Arabic the language of which has traditionally been called 'Middle Arabic' (MA). The term persists, although often taken to relate to chronological and historical 'middleness' rather than linguistic intermediacy.
One perhaps less well-known text composed in this style is Ibn al-Mujāwir's thirteenth-century *Tārīkh al-Mustabṣir*. As is typical of so-called 'MA' texts, Classical Arabic (CA) appears to dominate the style, with many non-CA features mixed into the CA base. Often, the non-CA features are essentially typical of Spoken Arabic (SA), so that the language is generally said to be a mix of CA and SA. There are, however, many non-CA features of *Tārīkh al-Mustabṣir* that do not conform entirely to either CA or SA, yet their use is not unsystematic. For these reasons we reject the term 'MA' in favour of 'Literary Mixed Arabic' (LMA).
This paper presents the results of the pilot study of our project, which centres on the question 'what is Literary Mixed Arabic?' Our study takes some of the morpho-syntactic variables that have been argued to differentiate CA from SA against which to test systematically the language of the text. In this context, these variables can be seen as features according to which the norms of CA and the norms of (a given variety of) SA are highly likely not to be compatible. Thus, we take such variables to reveal a systematic divergence between two grammars, or in effect, points at which they clash. We use these differential variables to explore the hypothesis that the features of the text that are not entirely compatible with the norms of CA and/or SA arise from the particular strategy employed to resolve a clash between the two grammatical systems.

Keywords: Mixed Arabic, language mixing, Middle Arabic, Ibn al-Mujāwir, morpho-syntax

1. Introduction

In the early years of the thirteenth century, a traveller from the east of the Islamic world committed to writing his experiences of his journey round the west and south of the Arabian Peninsula. Ibn al-Mujāwir's travelogue is concerned with matters of trade and commerce, agriculture, and the culture and mores of the peoples he encountered. He called it *Tārīkh al-Mustabṣir* (Ibn al-Mujāwir 1951–1954). The Arabic of the text is a mixed style, being a melange of Classical Arabic (CA), Spoken Arabic (SA), and features which are neither entirely CA nor SA (Smith 1996). It is noteworthy that Ibn al-Mujāwir's own introduction to his text is couched in an elevated CA rhymed prose (*sajʿ*) style, a feature which in all likelihood provides evidence of his competence in CA and that the mixed style was deliberate (Smith 2008: 9–10).

This language-mixing in *Tārīkh al-Mustabṣir* is characteristic of a body of texts that go back as early as the first century BCE, and which stretch across many centuries. This language has traditionally been called 'Middle Arabic' (MA). The term was initially coined by scholars of the nineteenth century and persists to this day, although it is often taken to relate to chronological and historical 'middleness' rather than linguistic intermediacy, that is, akin to 'Middle English' or 'Middle Welsh'.

We reject the term MA as being inappropriate and misleading for this style of Arabic. Our academic concern is with mixed Arabic as a literary medium, that is, as one part of the culture of literature and we therefore prefer the term Literary Mixed Arabic (LMA) in our study of *Tārīkh al-Mustabṣir* and also of the other texts which will form a part of our broader research.

An obvious feature of *Tārīkh al-Mustabṣir* is that CA appears to dominate the language style, with many non-CA features mixed into the CA base. This is typical of many LMA texts, particularly those of Muslim authors — it seems that the Judaeo-Christian LMA texts may have a greater proportion of Spoken Arabic-type features. For this reason, it is often said that so-called MA is a continuum.[1]

---
[1] Lentin 2008: 216. He also says (p. 219) that 'Middle Arabic pragmatically deal[s] with Arabic diglossia, by filling the space of the linguistic continuum between both polar varieties'. See also Zack &

In many instances, the non-CA features are clearly taken wholesale from Spoken Arabic (SA), so that the language of the text is generally said to be a mix of CA and SA, and this is particularly the case with lexical items.

However, there are many non-CA features of the text of *Tārīkh al-Mustabṣir* that do not conform entirely to either CA or SA. These are the features that have previously been called 'pseudo-corrections' or 'hyper-' and 'hypo-corrections'.[2] These are, typically, morpho-syntactic features. However, their use is *not* unsystematic, contra what has been said elsewhere,[3] and since they are not necessarily unsystematic, we disagree that such features are to be analysed as errors or categorized as types of 'pseudo-corrections'.[4] So what exactly are these features and how can we analyse them?

This paper takes some of the morpho-syntactic variables that have been argued to differentiate CA from SA[5] against which to begin to test systematically the language of Ibn al-Mujāwir's text. In this context, these variables can be seen as features according to which the norms of CA and the norms of (a given variety of) SA are highly likely not to be compatible. Thus, we take such variables to reveal a systematic divergence between two grammars, or in fact points at which they clash (since one could have either one form or the other, but not both). This paper thus uses these variables to explore the hypothesis that the features of Ibn al-Mujāwir's text that are not entirely compatible with the norms of CA and/or SA arise from the particular strategy employed to resolve a clash between the two grammatical systems.

Finally, we should add here a caveat that the earliest MS of *Tārīkh al-Mustabṣir* dates to the late sixteenth century, almost 300 years after its composition. It is not possible to know the extent to which later scribes have amended the text, but it is generally consistent with what is known about LMA from other texts.

2. The features

There are a number of features explicitly identified first by Ferguson (1959) and added to by Cohen (1970) and Versteegh (1984) which are claimed to differentiate CA from SA. As discussed by Watson (2011: 860–861), these features are not universally present in all Arabic dialects — contra CA — and there is ever increasing counter-evidence of dialects which do not adhere to one or other of these features. Nevertheless, in contradistinction to CA, very many dialects do share most of these features and they are generally seen as typical. For our purposes, since we are looking at a text which is composed in a language which is not entirely Classical and not entirely dialectal Arabic, such a list is a useful tool for investigating exactly how LMA can appear to be somehow between the two. Faced with a binary opposition (e.g. to have dual verb inflection or not to have dual verb inflection), which way does LMA swing? Or is there, rather, a third alternative which resolves this clash of two differing grammar systems, thereby creating forms unique to LMA? This latter would indicate that deviations from CA may not be entirely random in nature, but that there is something more systematic at play.

Watson (2011: 859–860) lays out these features which are likely to differentiate many dialects of Arabic from CA as a list of thirty-four variables. We focus here on some of the morpho-syntactic variables, leaving aside issues of phonology. For some of these features, we were able to perform a search of an electronic version of *Tārīkh al-Mustabṣir* which is now available online.[6] While this electronic version of the text contains differences from the original Löfgren edition (Ibn al-Mujāwir 1951–1954) from which it appears to have been copied, it was still possible to search electronically and then check against the hard copy of Löfgren. In this way, a number of interesting points have been uncovered and it is possible to identify trends. It was not really feasible to conduct a systematic search for some of the features (e.g. each occurrence of a geminate verb, as opposed to being able to search for all instances of ان- and ين- when investigating dual forms), although we had already flagged up some interesting examples arising from the list of features, which we include below.

From the list of differentiating features, those which we discuss in this paper are:

1. Duals
2. Geminate verbs (i.e. identical C_2 and C_3)
3. Form IV verbs

Schippers 2012: 113 and Smith's review, in press.
[2] Lentin (2008: 217), too, rightly disputes such analysis. See Blau 1970; also Hary 2007.
[3] E.g. Lentin (2008: 219): 'It should be kept in mind that the occurrence of these [Middle Arabic typical] features is never systematic'.
[4] Further evidence supporting the view that these are not 'errors' or 'corrections' is the *Kitāb al-Iʿtibār* of Usāmah Ibn Munqidh (1930), which is typical of (non-Judaeo-Christian) Literary Mixed Arabic.
[5] Ferguson 1959; Cohen 1970; Versteegh 1984; but see Behnstedt & Woidich 2005; Watson 2011. See also the list, and discussion and exemplification, of typical features of 'Middle Arabic' in Lentin 2008.

[6] The digitized, anonymously re-edited version was obtained from www.al-mostafa.com (accessed 22 April 2013). We are grateful to Murshed al-Hakmani for finding and sending it to the first-named author. However, as noted above, it should be treated with caution since it is not an accurate copy and contains many errors and omissions.

We also look at negation, since this was a salient feature of the text for which certain types did not concord with either CA or SA (to our knowledge).

3. The data

The Arabic examples and lexical items in the following sections are transliterated into roman orthography, as per convention, alongside the Arabic original. However, the transliteration of LMA is fraught with problems, since the Arabic script — as is usual — in *Tārīkh al-Mustabṣir* does not notate short vowels, which has the advantage for the composer of such a text that many word forms are ambiguous, with no case endings, etc. The dilemma is therefore whether to use conventional CA transliteration — thus potentially misleading the reader as to the original — or whether to attempt to mix CA transliteration with transliteration of obviously non-CA forms, for example (3) below, الرجل 'the man' as *al-rajulu* (CA) or *al-rajul* (SA/pausal form). We have therefore adopted what we consider a relatively neutral transliteration of each word with no final short vowels, that is, each word in pausal form, thus: *al-rajul*. For consistency — and to avoid assumptions as to whether a form is more CA-like or more SA-like — we apply this even to triconsonantal clusters, for example, we transliterate بنته 'his daughter' as *bint-h*. The data from *Tārīkh al-Mustabṣir* is in italics; where we discuss specifically CA forms (not data from the text), we use angle brackets, for example <hātayni> 'these two (f. obl.)'. The reader should, where possible, follow the Arabic script.

3.1. Number

Dual number is included in Ferguson's list (1959: 620–621) as a differential feature. He notes that adjectives, pronouns, and verbs do not have a dual form in the modern dialects, only singular or plural, whereas CA has dual inflection. Further, the dual is invariant, having only the form which is equivalent to the CA oblique, that is, CA <-ayni>/SA '-ayn'.

There are two issues with duals: first, in the case of an expressed dual-number-inflected noun, whether the inflectional suffix form conforms with CA grammar or not (i.e. nominative or oblique); second, whether any adjectives, verbs and so on carry dual inflectional agreement — as per CA norms — or whether they have non-CA number marking, such as plural.

A search of *Tārīkh al-Mustabṣir* reveals that the dual forms in the text are used mostly in accordance with the grammar of CA, with occasional exceptions. For instance, there are examples where a noun has the dual inflectional suffix *-ān/-ayn* in accordance with CA grammar; where the suffix is *-ayn* (for CA genitive or accusative) it is consistent with the grammar of both CA and SA. However, there are some instances of an invariant SA *-ayn*, where CA grammar norms predict *-ān. There are occasional examples which are non-CA non-SA, as in:

(1) فاذا اصبح خرج وترك نعلاه (L54.2)[7]

fa-ʾidhā ʾaṣbaḥ kharaj wa-tarak naʿlā-h

'When morning comes, he goes out and leaves behind his sandals'

In (1), *naʿlā-h* is the direct object and should thus be in the oblique form *naʿlay-h* according to both CA and SA grammar. The actual form adheres neither to CA grammar nor to the invariant SA form, yet the use of the CA nominative — clearly not SA — lends a flavour of something which feels stylistically more literary (than SA) simply by virtue of being a CA form, even though it does not accord with CA grammar here.

Agreement with dual nouns is generally as per CA, that is, a dual suffix in the same case or a dual verb form. However, there are occasional examples of usage which are unorthodox by CA standards, for example:

(2) وفيهم اثنان احدهما يسمى سيار والثانى مياس فسكنوا جدة (L43.4)

wa-fī-him ithnān aḥad-humā yusammā sayyār wa-ʾl-thānī mayyās fa-sakanū juddah

'There were two [men], one of them called Sayyār and the other Mayyās, and they settled in Jeddah'

The data in (2) is interesting because it shows CA nominative dual *ithnān* and a following (CA) dual pronominal suffix in *aḥad-humā*. However, the verb which follows is masculine plural *sakanū*, which is typically a dialectal agreement pattern. The sentence therefore displays specifically CA features and specifically SA features, so that overall the effect is somewhere between the two, as if an intermediate register.

More interesting, however, was one counter-example to this:

(3) ضفرت شعرتها دبوقتان وتشد كل دبوقة منهما ... يمسك الرجل تلك الدبوقتين ولا يزال يمدهما الى ان يقلعهما من الاصل (L56.10–13)

...ḍafarat shaʿrat-hā dabbūqatān wa-tashidd kull dabbūqah min-humā... yamsik al-rajul tilk al-dabbūqatayn wa-lā yazāl yamudd-humā ʾilā ʾan yaqlaʿ-humā min al-ʾaṣl

'...[the bride has] plaited her hair [into] two plaits, and let each of the two plaits down... the man grasps those plaits and keeps pulling until he pulls them out by the roots'

The *dabbūqatān* of the first line should be an accusative, by the norms of CA, that is, *dabbūqatayn*, which would also have concurred with the norms of SA (generally, invariant *-ayn*). However, the form used is an inappropriate CA nominative case; thus it is associated with CA but not correct by CA grammar, as in example (1) above, for *naᶜlā-h*. In (3), there are a number of pronominal suffixes which are dual form, as per CA grammar, and then another interesting form *tilk al-dabbūqatayn*, where the demonstrative pronoun is feminine singular (instead of CA feminine dual <taynika>). Meanwhile, the *dabbūqatayn* is oblique, as per CA norms.

Thus, the noun phrase (NP) *tilk al-dabbūqatayn* carries a grammatical feature which is SA and one which is CA. In the second of these instances the grammar of CA clashes with the grammar of SA, so the resolution is to use one feature of each, and this thereby mixes the two grammatical systems. The very interesting example is the first, in which *dabbūqatān* is presumably associated with CA grammar yet used in the wrong context, which avoids a form which is both CA or SA; since there are also definite CA forms *-humā*, the unexpected nominative flags up this phrase as non-SA, but also non-CA since the nominative is not grammatical. What is interesting is that this is a case where the two grammars overlap — they do not clash here. A feature is therefore changed to create a LMA intermediate form which mimics a clash resolution.

3.2. Form IV verbs

The list of features which are often thought to vary between CA and SA includes form IV verbs, that is, of the pattern <afᶜala>. It is noticeable in the text that there are many occurrences of form IV verbs, which is strikingly CA rather than (typically) SA. For instance, *ʾanfadh* is attested many times, with the meaning 'he sent':

(4) أنفذ صاحب مكة الى شيخ التجار (L45.9)

ʾanfadh ṣāḥib makkah ʾilā shaykh al-tujjār
'The lord of Mecca sent a message to the shaykh of the merchants'

It is thus very interesting to observe a form which is ungrammatical by CA norms but not an obvious SA form:

(5) فقال ما فعل الله بزبا؟ فقال بيد اى هلك فسمى البلد زب بيد (L70.11)

fa-qāl: mā faᶜal Allāh bi-zabā? fa-qāl: bīd, ayy halak, fa-summī ʾl-balad zab bīd
'[Someone] asked: "What became of [that ruler] Zabā?" He replied: "*bīd*," i.e. he was annihilated, so the area was called "Zab bīd" (for Zabīd)'

In (5), *bīd* is potentially puzzling, since it is a form I intransitive verb in CA, which therefore cannot be passivized. The internal passive is not typically SA, therefore *bīd* appears neither CA nor SA and it is not clear what it means, according to the 'rules' of either. However, with the view that there are expressions in the text which appear to be both CA and SA, that is, to carry a feature of each simultaneously, the word makes more sense. There are many attestations in LMA of form I verbs used in place of form IV verbs (which, according to the perception of what is typically SA rather than CA, as exemplified by our 'list'). This is noted by Hary (2007: 277), who notes the use of *bād* 'he destroyed' (for *ʾabād*) in a Christian LMA text. Used transitively, this verb can then undergo passivization with the CA feature of the internal passive, and the meaning 'he was annihilated/destroyed' is now clear. This means that the form is in fact a neat amalgam of a CA feature and a SA feature, therefore mixed, rather than 'neither CA nor SA'.[7]

An analogous example of an unexpected form IV verb, which ends up bearing both CA and SA features (and thus truly mixed) is as follows:

(6) الا ترى أنا قد أضرينا بهذا الرجل (L23.15)

ʾa-lā tarā ʾannā qad ʾaḍarraynā bi-hādhā ʾl-rajul
'Do you not realise that we have done this man harm?'

The verb *ʾaḍarraynā* is clearly a form IV verb, thus associated with CA rather than SA; however, it also exhibits non-CA treatment of geminate radicals, with the colloquial *-ay-* following the geminate *-rr-*. This is analogous with colloquial forms of verbs such as *marr* 'to pass', which has the CA 1st person singular perfect form <marartu> 'I passed', but the colloquial form *marrayt*.[8] In this way, the verb explicitly signals itself as an intermediate form, that is, definitely LMA because it carries both CA and SA features.

---

[7] Such forms have been categorized in the literature as 'hypocorrections', i.e. 'half corrected' to CA, but the 'correction' is not taken far enough. This view is less popular than it once was (see e.g. Lentin 2008; compare Blau 1970); it should be clear from our discussion that we disagree in the strongest terms with this analysis.
[8] In e.g. Iraqi Arabic. Cf. the well-known poem of Muẓaffar al-Nawwāb, which starts with the line *marraynā bī-kum Ḥamad* 'We passed you by, Hamad'.

3.3. Negatives

While negatives are not included specifically in the list, it is an obvious feature of dialectal Arabic that negatives differ from CA. It will suffice here to outline and exemplify briefly some of the significant aspects of negation attested in *Tārīkh al-Mustabṣir*. It should be noted that Lentin (2008: 221) discusses negation for LMA broadly. He notes that a typical feature of LMA is that verbal negation is predominantly with *mā*; *lam* is marked and is often used with perfect verbs, or to negate nominals. For Lentin this exemplifies a common LMA process, which is to borrow 'a linguistic tool' from CA, use it in a pseudo-genuine way (e.g. *lam* as negator) but without conforming to CA syntactic norms. We agree with this, but would take it a step further to say that this is an example of clash resolution, which marks LMA as a distinct linguistic variety and not just the 'no language's land'.

Several features stand out in *Tārīkh al-Mustabṣir*. Firstly, there is not a single occurrence of *lan*, the CA future negator. Further, *lam* is used as a verbal negator with past, present and future reference. It is invariably followed by an imperfect verb form (we did not find an example of *lam* + perfect, which is reportedly not uncommon in LMA, see Lentin 2008: 221); although it is often not clear from the MS whether this imperfect is in the apocopate form, where a 'weak' root follows *lam*, this is sometimes apocopate (as per CA) and sometimes not apocopate (not CA, but not SA since *lam* is not a negator generally used in most dialectal Arabic, and is thus marked). The use of *mā* as a verbal negator is frequent, but almost all instances seem to be followed by *ʾillā*, or sometimes *siwā*, thus with a limiting or exceptive meaning ('only'). *mā* is followed by both perfect and imperfect verb forms, but its function is predominantly in the *mā...ʾillā/siwā* structure, and it was very hard to find exceptions — the one exemplified below is in reported speech and to negate the main verb of the apodosis of a conditional. The other negating particle is *lā*, which is found in the text as both a verbal and a nominal negator. As a verbal negator, it negates more often imperfect verb forms, although there are a significant number of occurrences of *lā* + perfect; a notably common occurrence of *lā* is to negate *zāl* to give the meaning 'no longer, still', which appears unusual since one would probably expect CA <mā zāla/lam yazal> for past, <lā yazālu> for non-past. (Note that there are a few instances of *lam yazal* with the same meaning, and two instances of *mā zāl*.) The other use of *lā* is nominally to negate the genus (e.g.

lā shakk 'there is no doubt'[9]). Finally, *laysa*[10] is used as per CA to mean 'not to be' (e.g. with a following noun or prepositional phrase), and is additionally used on a significant number of occasions with a following verb in the imperfect, again a feature of CA.

These negative structures can be exemplified as follows:

(i) *lam*

a. past reference

(7) (L51.2) يقال انه كان فى قديم العهد لم يكن هذا بحر

yuqāl ʾinna-h kān fī qadīm al-ʿahd lam yakun hādhā baḥr

'It is said that in ancient times this [area] was not sea [but land]'

Noteworthy in (7) is that while the sentence is generally grammatical by CA norms (note especially the apocopate after *lam* and the past time reference), the nominal predicate of *yakun* is not marked for accusative case. Thus the negated verb phrase has both CA and SA features.

b. present reference

(8) (L25.4) ولم يورث احدهم بنته الدراهم

wa-lam yūrith ʾaḥad-hum bint-h al-darāhim

'but none of them bequeaths his money to his daughter'

The negation in (8) shows forms that would be expected as per CA grammatical norms, but the reference is clearly present time, which is a context in which *lam* would be disallowed in CA. This is a case where the LMA in use in this text has developed a linguistic feature which is neither CA nor SA, but it appears to be fairly systematic. That is, there appears to be a grammatical system here which is in this respect partially independent of both CA and SA.

c. future reference

(9) (L101.10) ولم تمت الى يوم القيمة

wa-lam tamut ʾilā yawm al-qiyāmah

---

[9] This is also in this text used as a pun meaning 'poking' (Smith 2008: 284).
[10] Contra the rationale outlined in section 3 above for the 'neutral' transliteration of the data in *Tārīkh al-Mustabṣir*, we notate *laysa* with the final vowel that would be expected of CA, since it is unequivocally CA, and in this lexical item it would seem actually wrong to use the form that our transliteration system would predict, i.e. *lays*.

'and she will not die until the day of resurrection'

The negation in (9) is similar to that in (8), in that the phrase is as per CA norms, with the exception that the time reference is clearly future, which is not normal CA usage.

(ii) mā

a. mā + imperfect (exceptive)

(10) ما أظن السيف أصله الا من الصاعقة التى ضربها يافث بن نوح (L28.6)

wa-mā ʾaẓunn al-sayf ʾaṣl-h ʾillā min al-ṣāʿiqah allatī ḍarab-hā Yāfiṭ bn Nūḥ

'I think the origin of this sword can only be the thunderbolt which Japheth, son of Noah, fashioned'

b. mā + perfect (exceptive)

(11) ما بقى فى الوهط من الشجر سوى شجرة توت (L28.6)

mā baqī[11] fī ʾl-waḥṭ min al-shajar siwā shajarat tūt

'Only one mulberry tree has remained in al-Waḥṭ'

c. mā + perfect

(12) ولو قتلتنى وأخذت الغنم ما نجوت (L19.4)

wa-law qatalt-nī wa-ʾaxadht al-ġanam mā najawt

'If you were to kill me and take the sheep, you would not get away with it'

The use of mā in the MS is almost always in a structure with ʾillā or siwā, with very few exceptions, such as (12). There were also two instances in the whole MS of mā zāl, with this verb otherwise co-occurring with lam or lā.

(iii) lā

a. lā + imperfect

(13) مكة لا تنصرف لانها مؤنثة (L2.12)

makkah lā tanṣarif li-ʾanna-hā muʾannathah

'The word "Mecca" cannot be fully inflected because it is feminine'

---

[11] Hypothetically, this may be read as baqā for some varieties of SA. However, here we use baqī for two reasons. Firstly, it is consistent with our transliteration scheme, which is maximally 'neutral', and this is anyway the CA form; secondly, the SA forms in this text are south Arabian, in which this form would have a final ī, as in contemporary Sanʿani Yemeni Arabic bigi 'stay, remain' (Qafisheh 1999: 44; the phonological final short i is not relevant to our treatment above).

The negator lā functions in (13) as per CA norms.

b. lā + perfect

(14) ولا زال الرجلان يعملان فى النقر والحفر (L108.7)

wa-lā zāl al-rajulān yaʿmalān fī ʾl-naqr wa-ʾl-ḥafr

'The men remained at work hewing and excavating'

Perfects occurred only rarely with lā, with the exception of lā zāl (as in 14), which occurred frequently.

(iv) laysa

a. laysa + non-verbal predicate

(15) وليس هذا الفن عندهم عار (L7.17)

wa-laysa hādhā ʾl-fann ʿind-hum ʿār

'They do not regard this practice as a shameful act'

b. laysa + verb

(16) ليس يحكم عليهم سلطان (L26.11)

laysa yaḥkum ʿalay-him sulṭān

'they are under the authority of no ruler'

The use of laysa + an imperfect verb is a CA form used as a 'strong' negative (for emphasis), and there are a number of instances in this text.

To conclude the section on negatives, the text of Tārīkh al-Mustabṣir shows negation which diverges from CA usage, yet is not SA. There is a noteworthy degree of systematicity, indicating that there is a linguistic system here which has its own unique features.

3.4. Ongoing investigation

(i) mood distinctions

Ferguson notes (1959: 622) that mood distinctions tend not to be encoded explicitly in dialectal verb forms. This is very relevant to the text in hand because there is much variation in 3rd person masculine plural imperfect verb forms. In some cases the oblique form is used where CA would have an indicative form, akin to the dialectal form. In many cases, a CA indicative form is used, in concordance with CA grammar. There are, additionally, quite a number of instances of the lam yaktubūn ('they didn't write') type, where lam in CA is followed by an apocopate verb form. An analysis of these is in preparation.

We have also conducted a preliminary search for imperative forms of verbs with a weak middle radical (such as *qām* 'get up', for instance). These forms in CA would be in the apocopate form (e.g. *qum* 'get up!'), while dialectal forms tend to retain the long vowel. So far, we have found one instance of *nām* 'sleep!' (for *nam*, L36.15).

(ii) numbers

Also on the list are number forms (Ferguson 1959: 624). Agreement in LMA is noted to be inconsistent, and we have already observed some unorthodox use of numbers.

(iii) word order (SVO/VSO)

Word order will be especially interesting (and time-consuming!) to investigate. The text is replete with instances of *kān* in the imperfect (*yakūn* etc.), in contexts which are ungrammatical in CA. A number of these instances may be a way of creating verb-initial phrases where the nominal subject is otherwise topicalized and thereby fronted. Part of this investigation will also involve looking at the use of *kān* as an auxiliary, and the use of serial/asyndetic verbs.

4. Conclusions

- The mixing exhibited in *Tārīkh al-Mustabṣir* is not entirely arbitrary. Although there is some variation (it is possible that later scribes may have contributed to this, or not), there is a considerable degree of systematicity in some aspects related to this mixing. Other aspects seem less systematic. What does seem systematic, however, is that while the text is generally towards the CA end of the spectrum, enough non-CA features are mixed into each sentence for the mixed nature of the language to dominate. Therefore, it is overall perhaps slightly 'High' LMA.
- LMA may be mixed to varying degrees, thus being a continuum, as noted by others. It can be highly variant as a whole (all the various texts which have been categorized as some form of so-called 'Middle Arabic'). There has been work on building a typology of typical LMA features (see e.g. Lentin 2008).
- The mixing of CA and SA to create an intermediate 'mixed' variety is not like mixing for example, Arabic and French, or Japanese and English, that is, two obviously very different systems. There is of course enough overlap between CA and the various other varieties of Arabic that the grammar is often perfectly compatible.
- This paper has attempted to give a snapshot of how we are approaching the question 'What is LMA?' from the flip side of the coin: primarily, by looking at what are considered to be typical indicators of SA in contradistinction to CA and to check these systematically against a given text (rather than observing 'interesting' features as one goes through a text). This is because these points are likely to be where CA grammar typically (although not always, for all features) clashes with the grammar of many or most modern dialects, so it is informative to see what the author uses to resolve the clash. Since there are two possibilities (the CA norm or the SA norm), one may expect that an author composing in LMA would choose either option depending on how much of a colloquializing or classicizing effect she/he was aiming for. In fact, what is interesting is that LMA often seems to 'invent' a third way, by using a grammatical feature of each (CA and SA) side by side, thus flagging up the particular structure as being neither CA nor SA but somehow not foreign to either because it is truly mixed.
- Since these forms are used frequently — and in some cases with a good degree of systematicity — but with not enough invariance to assume that they are simply learned and fossilized forms, we conclude that these forms are a conscious feature of LMA: thus does Ibn al-Mujāwir choose to convey his message to his audience. The idea of a 'Middle Arabic' stage in the historical development of Arabic is misleading, at best, if not simply fallacious;[12] thus we must move on from the vocabulary of error and correction and we must move on from the notion of historical middleness encoded in the term 'Middle'. The term was never appropriate in the Arabic context and the more one analyses these texts the more one becomes convinced that they are not historically middle. As we have shown, this is a specific literary form of Mixed Arabic, hence the more appropriate designation Literary Mixed Arabic.
- A final interesting question to ask is whether this intermediate code, LMA, is a distinct variety or just a style (and of what?). We have shown here for *Tārīkh al-Mustabṣir* that there are many forms

---

[12] As Owens (2006: 47) puts it, 'Middle Arabic … is primarily a style, not a historical stage.'

and structures which are not grammatical in either CA or SA (being truly mixed of features of both, simultaneously). The mixing is in this way not entirely arbitrary. This therefore begs the question, to what extent is LMA a language variety with its own linguistic system? If we think of LMA as a style, are we claiming that it does not have its own grammar? Does LMA have its own grammar?

References

Behnstedt P. & Woidich M.
    2005. *Arabische Dialektgeographie*. Leiden: Brill.

Blau J.
    1970. *On Pseudo-Corrections in Some Semitic Languages.* Jerusalem: Israel Academy of Sciences and Humanities.

Cohen D.
    1970. Koinè, langues communes et dialectes arabes. Pages 105–125 in D. Cohen (ed.), *Études de linguistique sémitique et arabe*. The Hague/Paris: Mouton.

Ferguson C.A.
    1959. The Arabic Koine. *Language* 35/4: 616–630.

Hary B.
    2007. Hypercorrection. Pages 275–279 in K. Versteegh et al. (eds), *Encyclopedia of Arabic Language and Linguistics*. ii. *Eg–Lan*. Leiden: Brill.

Ibn al-Muǧāwir/ed. O. Löfgren.
    1951–1954. *Ibn al-Muǧāwir, Descriptio Arabiae Meridionalis, Ṣifat bilād al-Yaman wa-Makkah wa-baʿḍ al-Ḥiǧāz al-musammā Taʾrīkh al-Mustabṣir*. Leiden: Brill.

Lentin J.
    2008. Middle Arabic. Pages 215–224 in K. Versteegh et al. (eds), *Encyclopedia of Arabic Language and Linguistics*. iii. *Lat–Pu*. Leiden/Boston: Brill.

Owens J.
    2006. *A Linguistic History of Arabic.* Oxford: Oxford University Press.

Qafisheh H.A.
    1999. *NTC's Yemeni Arabic-English Dictionary.* Chicago: NTC Publishing Group.

Smith G.R.
    1996. The language of Ibn al-Mujāwir's 7th/13th century guide to Arabia, *Tārīkh al-Mustabṣir*. Pages 327–351 in J.R. Smart (ed.), *Tradition and Modernity in Arabic Language and Literature*. Richmond: Curzon.
    2008. *A Traveller in Thirteenth-Century Arabia*. Ibn al-Mujāwir's Tārīkh al-Mustabṣir. (Series 3, Vol. 19). London: The Hakluyt Society.
    (in press). Review of Zack & Schippers 2012. *Journal of Semitic Studies.*

Usāmah Ibn Munqidh/ed. P.K. Hitti.
    1930. *Usāmah's Memoirs Entitled Kitāb al-Iʿtibār.* Princeton: Princeton University Press.

Versteegh K.
    1984. *Pidginization and Creolization: The Case for Arabic.* Amsterdam: Benjamin.

Watson J.C.E.
    2011. Arabic dialects (general article). Pages 851–896 in S. Weninger, G. Khan, M.P. Streck & J.C.E. Watson (eds), *The Semitic Languages: An international handbook*. Berlin: De Gruyter Mouton.

Zack L. & Schippers A.
    2012. *Middle Arabic and Mixed Arabic: Diachrony and Synchrony.* Leiden/Boston: Brill.

Authors' addresses

Dr Alex Bellem, Modern Languages & Cultures, University of Durham, DH1 3JT, UK.
e-mail alex.bellem@dur.ac.uk

Professor G. Rex Smith, Middle Eastern Studies, University of Manchester, M13 9PL, UK.
e-mail grexsmith@yahoo.co.uk

Syncretism in the verbal morphology of the Modern South Arabian Languages

DOMENYK EADES

Summary

This paper examines patterns of syncretism in the verbal morphology of the six extant Modern South Arabian Languages (MSAL) spoken in Oman and Yemen. Syncretism is a morphological phenomenon whereby a single form represents two or more contrasting morphosyntactic values, and is a common feature of languages with inflectional morphology (Baerman, Brown & Cooper 2005). In this study, patterns of syncretism in the MSAL are examined in relation to each other, and are compared with patterns in three non-MSAL Semitic varieties of the wider region: Šarqiyya Arabic (northern Oman), Rāziḥīt (north-west Yemen), and Geʻez (ancient northern Ethiopia). The study shows a wide range of patterns in the MSAL, almost all of which are unique to that family, and that within the MSAL the morphological characteristics of the varieties belonging to the 'Mehri group' (cf. Morris 2007; Simeone-Senelle 2011) differ considerably from those of the other MSAL varieties such as Shaḥri.

Keywords: Modern South Arabian, syncretism, morphology, Ḥarsūsi, Mehri

1. Syncretism

1.1. Introduction

Syncretism is a morphological phenomenon that involves 'the expression of two or more distinct morphosyntactic feature values by a single form' (Baerman 2004: 41), and is very common in inflectional languages such as those belonging to the Semitic family. For example, in Classical Arabic, verbs agree with their subject in number (singular, dual, plural), person (1/2/3), and gender (m/f), and inflect for tense/aspect, i.e. p-stem ('imperfect')/s-stem ('perfect'). In p-stem inflections, the syncretism occurs whereby 2msg and 3fsg are represented by a single phonological form, *tarkabu*. These patterns occur as a result of the neutralization of feature contrasts. The full paradigm for this verb is shown in Figure 1.

1.2. What motivates syncretism?

Baerman, Brown and Corbett (2005: 4–5) remark that syncretism has traditionally been treated in language studies as being the product of certain diachronic developments, which they exemplify with diachronic changes in verb declensions in the development of Classical Latin into Vulgar Latin. Figure 1 illustrates the process of phonological change that has resulted in the

	Sg	Dual	Pl
1	ʔarkabu 'I ride'	narkabu	narkabu
2m	**tarkabu**	tarkabāni	tarkabūna
2f	tarkabīna		tarkabna
3m	yarkabu	yarkabāni	yarkabūna
3f	**tarkabu**	tarkabāni	yarkabna

FIGURE 1. rakiba *'to ride', p-stem inflection (Classical Arabic).*

merger of the nominative and accusative singular in first declension nouns in Vulgar Latin. This is a result of the regular loss of word-final *-m*. In other declension classes, the two forms remained distinct in their formal realization (Fig. 2):

		Classical Latin	>	Vulgar Latin
first declension	Nom Sg	luna		luna
	Acc Sg	lunam		luna
second declension	Nom Sg	annus		annus
	Acc Sg	annum		anno
third declension	Nom Sg	pater		pater
	Acc Sg	patrem		patre

FIGURE 2. *Nominative/accusative in Vulgar Latin (Coleman 1976: 50–54, cited in Baerman, Brown & Corbett 2005: 5).*

With developments in linguistics in the twentieth century, syncretism was approached in primarily synchronic terms. Baerman, Brown and Corbett state in this regard: 'On this approach, syncretism involves the contrast not between an earlier stage of a language, but between an underlying system and its concrete realisation' (2005: 4). In this light, Baerman (2004) and Baerman, Brown and Corbett (2005), characterize syncretism as 'morphology failing syntax' due to the mismatch between morphosyntactic features and their morphological exponents (2005: 221). Morphology is thus a distinct structural domain that is independent from meaning.

In examining syncretism as part of a broader investigation into the typology of the world's languages, Baerman (2004) and Baerman, Brown and Corbett (2005) examined the factors that lie behind the emergence of syncretism in language. They found that syncretism emerges via two different diachronic routes. Firstly, 'natural' paradigmatic templates occur which are based on common or universal semantic or functional elements, and thus particular patterns tend to be commonly found across unrelated languages. Baerman states in this regard:

> If we choose to ascribe a semantic rationale to these patterns, it is probably significant that non-singular numbers favour syncretism, since this is precisely the context where there may be referential overlap and hence ambiguity (2004: 44).

Secondly, 'unnatural' syncretic templates occur as a result of specific phonological changes independent of semantic or functional considerations, and are therefore language-specific. These syncretisms cannot be accounted for on the basis of universal tendencies in language. Baerman, Brown and Corbett (2005) show a striking example of this in the Cushitic language Dhaasanac, spoken in Ethiopia. Dhaasanac displays a total of two person-number-gender forms, one for 1pl. (exclusive), 2f, and 3f; and one for 1sg, 1pl. inclusive, 3fpl., and 3mpl.

Figure 3 shows that two Dhaasanac morphological exponents, *sedh* and *sieti*, cut across several cells in the paradigm. These patterns do not reflect natural morphological classes based on meaning, but are a result of phonological changes that took place diachronically and are therefore language-specific. The value of each exponent can only be understood in relation to the system as a whole, as a one-to-one relationship between form and meaning does not exist. As such, the

seð 'to walk'		
	Sg	Pl
1 INCLUSIVE	------	seð
1	seð	sieti
2	sieti	sieti
3f	sieti	seð
3m	seð	seð

FIGURE 3. *Dhaasanac (Cushitic, Ethiopia) (adapted from Tosco 2001, cited in Baerman, Brown & Corbett 2005: 106).*

morphosyntactic value of the exponents can only be understood in relation to the full inflectional paradigm to which they belong.

Some features, such as case marking, show a mixture of these two tendencies. While syncretic patterns with respect to core cases show many similarities across languages, non-core cases tend to exhibit more language-specific characteristics (Baerman, Brown & Corbett 2005: 124–125). Baerman, Brown and Corbett conclude that syncretism is not a minor or insignificant morphological phenomenon, as has appeared to be the case in previous research in morphology. They remark:

> Without syncretism, the structure of inflectional morphology need be nothing more than a direct link between morphosyntactic values and forms. Syncretism, in all its variety, argues for the existence of morphological structure which is, at least in some degree, independent of meaning (2005: 221).

For the present study, focusing on syncretic patterns across the MSAL allows us to compare the morphological systems across the different varieties within this group and within the broader Semitic family, regardless of their phonological realization. Having established the importance of syncretism in establishing the notion of morphology as constituting an independent structural level between phonology and syntax, we now turn to the data and its sources.

2. Data and sources

The MSAL family can be classified into two distinct sub-groups on the basis of shared and contrasting structural characteristics (Morris 2007; Simeone-Senelle 2011).

These are: 1) a 'Mehri group', which comprises the closely related Mahri, Baṭḥari and Ḥarsūsi languages. Of these, Mahri and Ḥarsūsi are generally mutually intelligible. Ḥarsūsi oral traditions state that the Ḥarāsīs historically belonged to the Mahri tribe; 2) a second group of much less closely related languages: Shaḥri and Soqoṭri, with Hobyot falling somewhere between groups 1 and 2. In addition to the MSAL, inflectional patterns of three other Semitic languages are included in the study for the purposes of comparison. These are represented by the Ge'ez language of ancient Ethiopia, which like the MSAL is a South Semitic language; the Arabic dialect of the Šarqiyyah region in Oman; and the Arabic-based variety spoken in Rāziḥīt in Yemen. The varieties, that is, languages and dialects, are listed in the following table, and discussed in further detail in the sub-sections that follow:

South Semitic
MSAL (Eastern South Semitic)
MEHRI GROUP
Mehreyyet (Omani Mehri)
Mahriyōt (eastern Yemeni Mehri)
Ḥarsūsi
Baṭḥari
OTHER MSAL (NON-MEHRI GROUP)
Shaḥri
Soqoṭri
Hobyot
Ethio-Semitic (non-MSAL)
Ge'ez
Other Semitic varieties
Rāziḥīt (north-west Yemen)
Šarqiyya Arabic (northern Oman)

2.1. The Mehri group

Mehri is the most widely spoken language among the MSAL. It is spoken in a wide area straddling the Oman-Yemen border. Previous studies have identified three main dialects of Mehri (Simeone-Senelle 2011; Watson 2012). Two main Mehri dialect groups are spoken in Yemen: *Mehrīyət* (western Yemeni Mehri) and *Mahriyōt* (eastern Yemeni Mehri); and one in Oman: *Mehreyyet* (Omani Mehri). Mehreyyet is the most structurally conservative dialect, retaining various inflections that have been lost in Mahriyōt, such as the conditional mood on verbs. This is probably due to the more sustained contact of its speakers with Arabic-speaking communities historically. Watson's (2012) grammar of Mehri describes Mehreyyet and Mahriyōt and is the source of all of the Mehri data in this study. **Ḥarsūsi** is spoken in Jiddat Al Harasis, which is an arid desert region located in the Wusta Governorate of Oman. This is the northernmost MSAL-speaking community, and is distinguished from the other MSAL-speaking communities to the south by the fact that it is culturally assimilated to the neighbouring Arabic-speaking desert Bedouin communities. Ḥarsūsi and Mehri are largely mutually intelligible. Like Mahriyōt and unlike Mehreyyet, the conditional mood on verbs has been lost in Ḥarsūsi, most likely due to sustained contact with Arabic-speaking communities. One of the aims of this study is to examine the relationship between Ḥarsūsi and other varieties within the Mehri group with respect to patterns of syncretism. All of the Ḥarsūsi data employed in this study was collected by the author in 2012–2013. **Baṭḥari** is the most endangered of the MSAL, and is also closely related to Mehri. It was spoken by the Baṭāḥira tribe, who now live in the coastal area opposite the al-Hallaniyah islands (Morris 2007: 41), but nowadays it is only spoken by some twenty elderly speakers (Miranda Morris, personal communication). The Baṭḥari material presented here was kindly provided by Miranda Morris.

2.2. Other MSAL

Shaḥri (also known as *Jibbāli* or *Śḥerēt*) is spoken in and around the mountains of the Dhofar Governorate in Oman, and is not mutually intelligible with other MSAL. The Shaḥri data employed here is from Rubin (2014). **Soqoṭri** is spoken on the island of Soqotra off the coast of Yemen, and of all the MSAL is the most closely related to Shaḥri. The Soqoṭri data for this study is from Naumkin et al. (forthcoming). **Hobyot** was historically spoken in the border region between Yemen and Oman from the coast and into the mountains (UNESCO [2014]) and like Baṭḥari, Hobyot is now spoken by very few people. This language contains features of both Mehri and Shaḥri but is a dialect of neither, making it distinct from the other MSAL (Morris 2007: 41; UNESCO [2014]). The Hobyot material presented here was kindly provided by Miranda Morris.

2.3. Other Semitic languages

Šarqiyyah Arabic is a dialect of Arabic spoken by the mainly Bedouin communities who reside in the Šarqiyya region of northern Oman. The verbal morphological patterns of this dialect are fairly representative of Omani dialects of Arabic in general. Material representing this dialect was gathered on numerous field trips by the researcher on field trips between 2006 and 2010. **Rāziḥīt** is spoken in the mountain region of north-western Yemen, is notable for the numerous extant Ancient South Arabian features it exhibits, and is not intelligible to speakers of Yemeni Arabic in surrounding regions (Watson et al. 2006a; 2006b). While this variety has been treated in some studies as a dialect of Yemeni Arabic (e.g. Behnstedt 1987), more recently Watson et al. (cf. 2006a; 2006b; Watson 2011) have argued that Rāziḥīt could in fact be treated as a distinct language, the modern descendant of an Ancient South Arabian language. This is based on sociolinguistic factors and certain structural criteria (Watson et al. 2006a: 35). Structural features in this variety include the 2fsg. possessive suffix -š, the indeclinable relative marker *ḏī-*, and the verbal suffix -k (Arabic: -t) for 1st and 2nd person s-stem verbs (Watson 2011). The Rāziḥīt data employed in this study is drawn from Behnstedt (1987), who treats the variety he describes, which is spoken in Naḍīr as a Yemeni Arabic dialect. Rāziḥīt is included in this study in order to shed more light on the relationship between this variety and both Arabic and the MSAL with regard to their morphological structure. **Ge'ez** (Old Ethiopic) is also included as it is an ancient South Semitic language but is not a direct ancestor of the MSAL. It was spoken in northern Ethiopia and southern Eritrea, and remains in use today as the liturgical language of Christianity in Ethiopia. The Ge'ez data presented here is from Procházka (2005).

In the next section, patterns of verbal inflection are compared and contrasted in the varieties under investigation.

3. Patterns of syncretism in the data

3.1. Verbal inflection in the MSAL

The focus of this study is on patterns of syncretism in the verbal morphology of the MSAL and three other closely related Semitic varieties. The domains in which the neutralizations occur are verbal tense/aspect (p-stem/s-stem) and mood (indicative/subjunctive), and cover syncretism with respect to person, number, and gender. Figure 4 shows the Ḥarsūsi s-stem paradigm for the verb *rēkab* 'to ride' and shows a neutralization of the formal contrast between 1csg and 2msg. This pattern is common in many Semitic languages. The table also shows a neutralisation of 3msg and 3fpl (in italics):

rēkab 'to ride'			
	Sg	Dual	Pl
1c	**wrakabak**	rakōbkī	rakaban
2m	**rakabak**		rakabkam
2f w	rakabiš		rakabkin
3m	*rēkab*	arkabuh	rakabam
3f	rakbōt		*rēkab*

FIGURE 4. *Ḥarsūsi s-stem paradigm.*

The remainder of this section is divided into two parts. Syncretism in s-stem inflections is first presented and this is followed by patterns in p-stem inflections. The specific domain of inflection in which a particular pattern occurs is provided in brackets with each table.

3.2. S-stem inflection

The syncretism 1msg = 2msg (see Fig. 5), which occurs in all the MSAL as well as Šarqiyya Arabic, distinguishing these varieties from Rāziḥīt and Ge'ez because of the retained contrast in final vowels in those varieties (Rāziḥīt: -uk /-ik; Ge'ez: -ku/-ka). In the tables that follow, an asterisk marks the forms in those languages where the syncretism pattern shows other feature values in addition to those mentioned in the heading.

Another common pattern in the MSAL, which is

Ḥarsūsi	rakab-ak	'I/you rode'
Mehreyyet	rikb-ak	"
Mahriyōt	rikb-ak	"
Baṭhari	rēkəb-ək	"
Shaḥri	ḳədər-k*	'I/you can'
Soqoṭri	ʕərɔ́b-k	'I/you knew'
Hobyot	feraḥ-k	'I/you am/are happy'
Šarqiyya Ar.	rakab-t	'I/you knew'
Rāziḥīt	-	
Ge'ez	-	

FIGURE 5. *1c=2msg (person).*

shown in Figure 6, is 3msg = 3fpl. This pattern is unique to the MSAL, and does not occur in the other Semitic varieties. It is also absent from Baṭhari due to the emergence of an innovative plural suffix in that language: *rēkəb* 'he rode', *rēkəbəna* 'they f. rode' (Miranda Morris, personal communication). Nevertheless, in Ge'ez the distinction between the 3msg. and 3fpl. is minimal, being manifested only in a contrast in the length of the final vowel: *bārak-a* 'he blessed'/*bārak-ā* 'they f. blessed' (Ge'ez). These facts suggest that this pattern emerged in the MSAL due to the loss of what was originally a minor formal contrast between two inflectional exponents. This pattern is absent from the Arabic varieties and indeed other Semitic languages further afield, such as Aramaic.

Ḥarsūsi	ktōb	'he/ they f. wrote'
Mehreyyet	ktūb	"
Mahriyōt	ktōb	"
Baṭḥari	-	
Shaḥri	ḵɔdər*	'he/ they could'
Soqoṭri	ʕərɔ́b	'he /they f. knew'
Hobyot	feŕaḥ	'he was/ they f. were happy'
Šarqiyya Ar.	-	
Rāziḥīt	-	
Ge'ez	-	

FIGURE 6. *3msg = 3fpl (gender, number).*

In Shaḥri, this pattern also includes 3mpl (Fig. 7):

Shaḥri	ḵɔdər	'he was/ they are mpl./ fpl. able'

FIGURE 7. *3msg = 3mpl = 3fpl (gender, number).*

3.3. P-stem inflection

This section examines syncretisms in the p-stem inflection. In most MSAL, verbs are inflected for the indicative and subjunctive moods. Nevertheless, not all the MSAL exhibit a distinction between the indicative and the subjunctive. In those languages in which verbs are not inflected for mood, the p-stem inflection is compared alongside the indicative p-stem forms of verbs in languages that are inflected for mood.

3.3.1. Basic (non-derived) stems: indicative

The most widely occurring syncretism found in the data was 2msg = 3fsg in indicative p-stem verbs. This pattern occurs in all of the varieties investigated (Fig. 8):

Ḥarsūsi	tkōtab	'you msg. write/ she writes'
Mehreyyet	tkōtab	"
Mahriyōt	tkōtab	"
Baṭḥari	terĭkəb	'you msg. ride/ she rides'
Shaḥri	(təḵɔdər)*	
Soqoṭri	(təḵódəm)*	
Hobyot	təfoŕaḥ	'you msg. are/ she is happy'
Šarqiyya Ar.	tarkab	'you msg. ride/ she rides'
Rāziḥīt	tisraḥ	'you msg. go/ she goes'
Ge'ez	(təbārrək)*	

FIGURE 8. *2msg = 3fsg (person, gender).*

In Shaḥri and Soqoṭri, this template also includes the 2mpl (Fig. 9).

Shaḥri	təḵɔdər	'you msg./ pl./ 3fsg. can'
Soqoṭri	təḵódəm	'you msg./pl/ 3fsg. dig into'

FIGURE 9. *2msg = 2mpl = 3fsg (person, gender, number).*

In contrast with Shaḥri and Soqoṭri, this includes the 2fsg in Ge'ez (Fig. 10).

Ge'ez	təbārrək	'you msg./ fsg./ she blesses'

FIGURE 10. *2msg = 2fsg = 3fsg (person, gender, number).*

3.3.2. Derived stems: indicative

Semitic languages generally contain distinctive verbal lexico-semantic derivational patterns. A number of derived stems are distinguished by the fact that they are marked by a suffixed element -*an*/-*en* in the p-stem inflection. These constitute a declension pattern that is distinct from the basic (non-derived) pattern. Watson (2012: 83) describes this pattern as L-, B-type Š-, and B-type T-stems, and parallel patterns are also extant in the other MSAL. Only the MSAL are discussed here because of the particular syncretism patterns that occur in this family that do not occur in the other languages examined, and are centred on derivations that involve a suffixed element -*n*. This pattern is exhibited in Ḥarsūsi, Mehreyyet, and Shaḥri, but not Mahriyōt, as is shown in the table (Fig. 11). In this respect, Ḥarsūsi is more grammatically conservative than Mahriyōt. Baṭḥari and Hobyot contain a similar pattern but are distinguished from the other varieties by the fact that they have formally distinct 2fsg forms, e.g. Baṭḥari *teftekïrən* 'you fsg. think':

Ḥarsūsi	tātalīman	'you sg./pl./ she learns'
Mehreyyet	tātalīman	
Mahriyōt	-	
Shaḥri	(t)əgodəlen	'you sg./pl./ she ties, chains'
Baṭḥari	- (teftekïrən)	'you sg./pl./ she thinks'
Hobyot	- (taʕtədərən)	'you sg./pl./ she asks for forgiveness'
Soqoṭri	təsēfērən†	'you sg./pl./ she travels'

†Miranda Morris, personal communication

FIGURE 11. *2msg = 2fsg = 3fsg = 2mpl = 2fpl = 3fpl (person, number, gender).*

Baṭḥari follows a similar pattern in that it features the -*n* suffix in all cases but is distinguished from the other varieties by the fact that the 2fsg. has a distinct form *teftekirən*. This is also the case in Hobyot. In Mahriyōt, the 2/3mpl. suffix -*am* is employed with both derived and basic stems (Fig. 12). This distinguishes Mahriyōt from the other varieties in the Mehri group, and indeed all the MSAL.

Ḥarsūsi	-
Mehreyyet	-
Mahriyōt	ta-ssafr-am

FIGURE 12. *2msg = 2fsg = 3fsg = 2fpl = 3fpl (person, number, gender).*

A distinction thus exists between Ḥarsūsi and Mehreyyet on the one hand, and Mahriyōt on the other. To show this in more detail, the full paradigms for Ḥarsūsi and Mahriyōt are shown in Figures 13 and 14 below. The two different syncretic patterns are shown in bold face and italics:

	singular	*dual*	*plural*
1	ʔātalīm-an	ʔātalīm-ayan	nātalīm-an
2m	**tātalīm-an**	tātalīm-ayan	**tātalīm-an**
2f	**tātalīm-an**		**tātalīm-an**
3m	*yātalīm-an*	yātalīm-ayan	*yātalīm-an*
3f	**tātalīm-an**	tātalīm-ayan	tātalīm-an

FIGURE 13. *Ḥarsūsi.*

	singular	*dual*	*plural*
1	ʔa-ssafran	(n)a-safr-ōh	na-ssafr-an
2m	**ta-ssafr-an**	t-safr-ōh	ta-ssafr-am
2f	**ta-ssafr-an**		**ta-ssafr-an**
3m	ya-ssafr-an	ya-safr-ōh	ya-ssafr-am
3f	**ta-ssafr-an**	t-safr-ōh	ta-ssafr-an

FIGURE 14. *Mahriyōt.*

The tables (Figs 13 & 14) show that in Mahriyōt, the suffix -*am*, which marks masculine plural agreement, occurs in Ḥarsūsi and Mehreyyet only on basic stems and is also used with derived stems. In contrast, in Ḥarsūsi and Mehreyyet all verbs inflected for plural agreement are marked by the suffix -*an*, resulting in a feature neutralization that covers a greater number of cells in the paradigm than in Mahriyōt. This also means that we have a syncretism between 3msg and 3mpl in Ḥarsūsi and Mehreyyet, which does not occur in Mahriyōt. These patterns again are present due to the retention of the distinct declension pattern in these languages, which has been lost in Mahriyōt as a result of morphological levelling. This means that Ḥarsūsi and Mehreyyet are in this respect more conservative varieties. This conservatism is also evident in the dual inflection, which has a distinct suffix -*ayan* with derived stems while -*ōh* occurs with basic stems. This is in contrast with Mahriyōt, in which the suffix -*ōh* marks both basic and derived stems. Nevertheless, among younger generation Ḥarsūsi speakers, it can be observed that the patterning seen in Mahriyōt is being used. There is a collapse of the separate declension for derived verbs. Young speakers generally employ the -*am* suffix while older speakers employ -*an*.

Two pieces of evidence suggest that in those varieties in which the -*am* suffix marks 3mpl, this is a case of analogical change. Firstly, this pattern occurs in the majority of MSAL, and belonging to different branches of this family. Secondly, many young speakers of Ḥarsūsi employ the -*am* suffix while older speakers employ -*an*. This demonstrates the process of levelling across generations, which most likely occurred in other varieties.

In addition to Ḥarsūsi and Mehreyyet, the -*an* suffix has been retained on 3mpl verbs in Baṭḥari and Shaḥri, but not the other MSAL, where the -*am* prefix occurs, as in Mahriyōt (Fig. 15):

Ḥarsūsi	yātalīman	'he/ they m. learn'
Mehreyyet	ya-safr-an	'he/ they m. travel'
Mahriyōt	-	
Baṭḥari	yeftekerən	'he/ they m. think'
Shaḥri	yəgodələn	'he/ they m. tie, chain'
Hobyot	-	
Ge'ez	-	

FIGURE 15. *3msg = 3mpl (number).*

3.3.3. Basic stems: subjunctive

While most of the syncretisms in subjunctive paradigms of the varieties examined are identical to those of the indicative, some distinct patterns occur in the subjunctive mood. The subjunctive verbs are glossed here with the verb 'want', as the subjunctive form always occurs after verbs of wanting. As mood inflections do not occur in Šarqiyya Arabic and Rāziḥīt, they are not discussed with respect to the subjunctive.

The following pattern occurs in all the varieties examined (Fig. 16):

Ḥarsūsi	taktīb	'you ms. (want)/ she (wants) to write'
Mehreyyet	tsēr	'you ms. (want)/ she (wants) to go'
Mahriyōt	tasbāṭ	'you ms. (want)/ she (wants) to hit'
Baṭḥari	terĭkəb	'you ms. (want)/ she (wants) to ride'
Shaḥri	tókdər	'you ms. (want)/ she (wants) be able'
Hobyot	təfərah̬	'you ms. (want)/ she (wants) to be happy'
Ge'ez	təqtəl	'you ms. (want)/ she (want) to be happy'
Soqoṭri	təkódəm	'you ms. (want)/ she (wants) to bury'

FIGURE 16. *2ms = 3fsg (person).*

In contrast with the indicative, Shaḥri follows the same pattern as the other varieties. Soqoṭri also exhibits its own distinct pattern that does not occur in other MSAL (Fig. 17):

| Soqoṭri | yəkódəm | 'you ms. (want)/ she (wants) to bury' |

FIGURE 17. *3msg = 3mpl (person, number, gender).*

A pattern which occurs within the MSAL varieties but not Ge'ez is 2fpl = 3fpl (Fig. 18). The non-MSAL are distinguished from these by the fact that the feminine plural verb is marked by a *y*- prefix rather than *t*- (e.g. Ge'ez: *təqtəlā* 'you fpl. kill', *yəqtəlā* 'they fpl. kill').

Ḥarsūsi	taktaban	'you fs./ they fpl. (want) to write'
Mehreyyet	tsēran	'you fs./ they fpl. (want) to go'
Mahriyōt	tasbāṭan	'you fs./ they fpl. (want) to hit'
Baṭḥari	terĭkəban	'you fs./ they fpl. (want) to ride'
Shaḥri	*(təkdɛ́rən)	('you fs./ they fpl. (want) to be able')
Soqoṭri	təʕárɛbən	'you fs./ they fpl. (want) to know'
Hobyot	təfərah̬ən	'you fs./ they fpl. (want) to be happy'
Šarqiyya Ar.	-	
Rāziḥīt	-	
Ge'ez	-	

FIGURE 18. *2fpl = 3fpl (person).*

This pattern in Shaḥri also includes 2mpl (Fig. 19):

| Shaḥri | təkdɛ́rən | 'you msg/ fsg/ they fpl (want) to be able' |

FIGURE 19. *2fpl = 2mpl = 3fpl (person, gender, number).*

3.3.4. Derived stems: subjunctive

In the subjunctive mood, the template 2msg = 3fsg occurs. Only MSAL are examined in this section, as the other varieties either do not have subjunctive forms or do not have derivations that parallel those found in the MSAL with respect to suffixed derived verbs (Fig. 20).

Ḥarsūsi	tātalīm-an	'you pl./ they fpl. would learn'
Mehreyyet	tātalīm-an	'you pl./ they fpl. would learn'
Mahriyōt	-	
Baṭḥari	-	
Shaḥri	-	
Hobyot	taʕtədir-ən	'you pl./ they fpl. would ask for forgiveness'
Soqoṭri	taʕmir-in†	'you pl./ they fpl. would say'

†Miranda Morris, personal communication

FIGURE 20. *2mpl = 2fpl = 3fpl (person).*

In Shaḥri, the 2mpl does not fall into this pattern, but rather has its own distinct pattern (Fig. 21):

| Shaḥri | təftəkórən | 'you fpl./ they fpl. (want to) be able' |

FIGURE 21. *2fpl = 3fpl (person).*

4. Summary and discussion

This study examined patterns of syncretism in seven varieties of MSAL and in three other Semitic languages for the purposes of comparison. It was found that the patterns that occurred in the MSAL are largely absent from the other Semitic languages investigated. A substantial number of patterns occurred across the entire MSAL, which are unique to this family, and the proportion of shared patterning of syncretisms between the MSAL varieties roughly divide the varieties belonging to the Mehri group from the other MSAL. The MSAL variety, which is the most distinctive with regard to the syncretisms it exhibits, is Shaḥri. The results are summarized in Figure 22.

In sum, the results of the study show that only two patterns of syncretism in the data are common to all or almost all the varieties examined: 1) p-stem *1csg=2msg*; 2) p-stem *2msg = 3fsg*. The other patterns are unique to the MSAL, six occurring widely among these varieties. Shaḥri, and to a lesser extent Soqoṭri and Hobyot, have a number of distinct patterns that are unique to those languages. For Rāziḥīt, it was observed that in spite of the fact that the language exhibits numerous Ancient

Patterns	MSAL (= 7)	Other (= 3)
s-stem, basic stems:		
1csg = 2msg (person)	7: Hs, Mht, Mōt, B, Sh, Sq, Hb,	3: Rz, Gz, ŠAr
3msg = 3fpl (gender, number)	1: Hs, Mht, Mōt, Sq, Hb, Sh	-
3msg = 3mpl = 3fpl = (gender, number)	1: Sh	-
p-stem basic stems:		
2msg = 3fsg (person, gender)	7: Hs, Mt, Mōt, B, (Sh*), (Sq*), Hb	4: ŠAr, Rz, (Gz*)
2msg = 2fsg = 3fsg (person, gender, number)	-	1: Gz
2msg = 2mpl = 3fsg (person, gender, number)	2: Sh, Sq	-
2fpl = 3fpl (person)	6: Hs, Mt, Mōt, J, Sq, Hb	-
2mpl = 3fpl (person)	1: B	-
3msg = 3mpl (number)	2: Sh, Sq	-
p-stem, derived stems:	MSAL (= 6)	Other
2msg = 2fsg = 3fsg = 2mpl = 2fpl = 3fpl (person, number, gender)	5: Hs, Mōt, B, Sh, Sq, Hb	-
2msg = 2fsg = 3fsg = 2fpl = 3fpl (person, number, gender)	1: Mōt	-
3msg = 3mpl (number)	4: Hs, Mt, B, Sh	-
p-stem subjunctive basic stems:		
2ms = 3fs (person)	6: Hs, Mt, Mōt, B, Sh, Sq, Hb	-
2fs = 3mpl (person, number, gender)	1: Sq	-
2fpl = 3fpl (person)	6: Hs, Mt, Mōt, B, Sh, Sq, Hb	-
2fpl = 2mpl = 3fpl (person, gender, number)	1: Sh	-
p-stem subjunctive derived stems:		
2mpl = 2fpl = 3fpl (person)	3: Hs, Mt, Hb	-
2fpl = 3fpl (person)	1: Sh	-

(Key: **Mt** = Mehreyyet; **Mōt** = Mahriyōt; **Hs** = Ḥarsūsi; **B** = Baṭḥari; **Sh** = Shaḥri; **Sq** = Soqoṭri; **Hb** = Hobyot; **ŠAr** = Šarqiyya Arabic; **Rz** = Rāziḥīt; **Gz** = Ge'ez)

FIGURE 22. *A summary of patterns in the data.*

South Arabian phonological and morphological features (cf. Watson 2011; Watson et al. 2006a), its morphological structure with respect to patterns of syncretism almost entirely resembles Arabic and is unlike those of the MSAL.

All the languages of the Mehri group share a common patterning, with the exception of the derived p-stem forms. It was shown that Ḥarsūsi and Mehreyyet retain a distinct declension pattern with derived stems, which has been lost in Mahriyōt, and in this regard the Omani varieties are more conservative than the Yemeni variety. This pattern is being lost, however, among younger speakers of Ḥarsūsi due to contact-induced morphological levelling. This tendency is also manifested in the loss of other features such as the conditional mood inflection in both Mahriyōt and Ḥarsūsi, which is retained in the more conservative Mehreyyet variety. Baṭḥari resembles the other varieties in the Mehri group in most respects, but has been subject to the development of the innovative *-an* suffix in feminine s-stem forms.

References

Baerman M.
    2004. Typology and the formal modelling of syncretism. Pages 41–72 in G. Booij & J. van Marle (eds), *Yearbook of Morphology*. Dordrecht: Kluwer Academic Publishers.

Baerman M., Brown D. & Corbett G.
    2005. *The Syntax-Morphology Interface: A Study of Syncretism*. Cambridge: Cambridge University Press.

Behnstedt P.
    1987. *Dialekte der Gegend von Ṣaʿdah (Nord-Jemen)*. Wiesbaden: Harrassowitz.

Coleman, R.
    1976. Patterns of Syncretism in Latin. Pages 47-56 in A. M. Davies & W. Meid (eds.) *Studies in Greek, Italic and Indo-European Linguistics Offered to Leonard R. Palmer*. Innsbruck: Institut für Sprachwissenschaft der Universität Innsbruck.

Johnstone T.M.
    1977. *Ḥarsūsi Lexicon and English–Ḥarsūsi Word List*. London: Oxford University Press.

Morris M.
    2007. The pre-literate, non-Arabic languages of Oman and Yemen: Their Current Situation and Uncertain Future. *The British-Yemeni Society Journal* 15: 39–53.

Naumkin V., Bulakh M., Cherkashin D., Kogan L. et al.
    (forthcoming). Studies in the verbal morphology of Soqoṭri I/1: Strong triconsonantal roots in the basic stems (the analysis). *Zeitschrift für Arabische Linguistik*. Wiesbaden: Harrassowitz.

Procházka S.
    2005. *Altäthiopische Studiengrammatik*. (Orbis Biblicus Et Orientalis – Subsidia Linguistica, 2). Göttingen: Vandenhoeck & Ruprecht Verlag.

Rubin A.
    2014. *The Jibbali (Shaḥri) Language of Oman*. Leiden: Brill.

Simeone-Senelle M-C.
    2011. Modern South Arabian. Pages 1073–1113 in S. Weninger, G. Khan, M. Streck & J.C.E. Watson (eds), *Handbook of Semitic Languages*. Berlin: Walter de Gruyter.

Tosco M.
    2001. *The Dhaasanac language*. Cologne: Rüdiger Köppe.

UNESCO.
    [2014]. *The UNESCO Atlas of the World's Languages in Danger (online)*. www.unesco.org/culture/languages-atlas/. [Accessed 23 January 2014.]

Watson J.C.E.
    2011. South Arabian and Yemeni dialects. *Salford Working Papers in Linguistics and Applied Linguistics* 1: 27–40.
    2012. *The Structure of Mehri*. Wiesbaden: Harrassowitz.

Watson J.C.E., Glover Stalls B., Al-Razihi K. & Weir S.
    2006a. The Language of Jabal Rāziḥ. Arabic or something else? *Proceedings of the Seminar for Arabian Studies* 36: 35–41.
    2006b. Two texts from Jabal Rāziḥ. Pages 40–63 in L. Edzard & J. Retsö (eds), *Current Issues in the Analysis of Semitic Grammar and Lexicon*. ii. Wiesbaden: Harrassowitz.

Author's address

Domenyk Eades, School of Humanities, Languages and Social Sciences, University of Salford, Salford, Greater Manchester, M5 4WT

e-mail: *d.eades@salford.ac.uk*

Investigating South Arabian words in al-Khalīl's *Kitāb al-ʿayn*

ORHAN ELMAZ

Summary
This modest contribution attempts to demonstrate the problems related to diachronic research into South Arabian vocabulary. The first Arabic thesaurus, *Kitāb al-ʿayn*, is said to have been compiled by Omani-born al-Khalīl b. Aḥmad by the end of the eighth century AD; in it he mentions fifty-seven words of supposed South Arabian provenance, thirty-six of which have not been dealt with elsewhere. In this paper these words are studied while searching for further corroboration for them and commenting upon their provenance and use. Overall, the paper demonstrates how Classical Arabic lexicography can add to our knowledge of Old Arabic dialects while contributing interesting input for debates on the emergence and development of Modern South Arabian languages and sharpening their history if research is furthered along the lines indicated here.

Keywords: southern Arabia, Classical Arabic lexicography, corpus linguistics, multilingualism, Modern South Arabian Languages

Approaching the conference theme with a background in Arabic studies, and having mentioned words of proposed South Arabian origin in al-Khalīl's (d. 789 in Basra) *Kitāb al-ʿayn* in an article about ʿarim (Elmaz, forthcoming), I decided to have a closer look at these words as to their origin and actual occurrence. Although I am inclined to trust al-Khalīl's judgement because of his Omani Azd background, I especially wanted to study the context and use of these words. Throughout this paper of limited scope, I will refer to al-Khalīl as the author and not deal with the question of *Kitāb al-ʿayn*'s authorship since this has been dealt with elsewhere (Wild 1965: 13–21; Haywood 1965: 24–27).

I managed to extract fifty-seven words from a digitized edition of *Kitāb al-ʿayn* (al-Farāhidī [2013]). Al-Khalīl gives thirty-eight words as Yemenite (*yamāniyyah*, *lughat ahl al-Yaman*), sixteen as Himyarite (*ḥimyariyyah*, *lughat Ḥimyar*), one in the idiom of Balḥārith, which denotes the dialect of the tribe of the same name, two of Jawfi, four of Shiḥri, one of Jawfi and Shiḥri, and seven of Omani provenance. Aiming at showing in which context and how often these words occur in Early and Classical Arabic literature, at first I tried to locate similar, unvocalized forms of the word in question in the Digital Archive for the Study of pre-Islamic Arabian Inscriptions (DASI) in order to see whether it could be a loan from an Ancient South Arabian language. I then looked for the word in the digitized library of Classical Arabic, *al-War[r]aq*, and the source files of the *King Saud University Corpus of Classical Arabic* (50 million words) compiled by Maha al-Rabiah. In order to include previous scholarship, I searched each word on Google and JSTOR in various forms, even using wildcards.

Two scholars have dealt with some of these words, al-Selwi (twenty-one words) and Ghūl (three words), and some of them have made their way into Arabic dictionaries, specifically Lane's *Lexicon* and Wahrmund's *Handwörterbuch*. For the sake of completeness, I will list these with short references to the edition of *Kitāb al-ʿayn* by al-Makhzūmī and al-Sāmirrāʾī (al-Farāhidī 1980–1985) with capitalized Roman numbers giving the number of the volume and Arabic numbers indicating page numbers, while adding comments wherever there is something to add.

1. Words documented in al-Selwi 1987

As words in the language of Yemen (*lughat ahl al-Yaman*) one finds *kaḥb* (III, 65; al-Selwi, 187 'unreife Weintraube'; Lane 1863: 191a 'a certain kind of plant which camels do not feed upon except in cases of necessity'), *mikhlāf* (IV, 267; al-Selwi, 78 'Provinz, Region'), *jafn* (VI, 146; al-Selwi, 63 'Weinstock'), *daẓẓ* (VIII, 5; al-Selwi, 172 'Überwältigung'), *burt* (VIII, 118; al-Selwi, 41 'Axt; Kandiszucker?'), and *talam* (VIII, 126; al-Selwi, 51 *tilm* 'Ackerfurche'). As Yamani (*yamānī*) words, there are *qillawb* (V, 171; al-Selwi, 183–184 'Schakalwolf') and *wīj* (VI, 197; al-Selwi, 222 *wayj* 'Balken, Deichsel des Pfluges', 'plough beam'; cf. Varisco 2004: 124).

The last word *wayj*, is also given as an Omani word by al-Khalīl, together with *ḥays* (IV, 72; al-Selwi, 215

'Pflug', 'plough'; cf. Varisco 2004: 122). Relying upon al-Khalīl's Omani origins and his specification of *hays* as an Omani word, Varisco's assumption of an underlying copyist's error in Ibn Durayd's *Jamharah*, which turned the word's provenance from Omani to Yamani, makes even more sense since the word is virtually absent from especially northern Yemeni dialects.

There are eight words which are categorized as Himyarite: ʿ*uksūm* = *kusʿūm* (II, 305; al-Selwi, 189–190 'Esel'), *jaḥmah* (III, 88 *ḥajmah* [*sic*]: ʿ*ayn* 'eye'; 'menschliches Auge', see al-Selwi, 57), ʿ*illawḍ* (I, 279; al-Selwi, 162 'Schakal'), *qabābah* (V, 229; al-Selwi, 175 'Bitterkeit'), *habayyakhah* (III, 359 with a verb in form XIII; al-Selwi, 211 'zarte Dienerin'), *shantarah* (VI, 301; al-Selwi, 125f. *shuntur*, pl. *shanātir* 'Finger'), *thib* (VIII, 247; al-Selwi, 216f. 'setz dich'), and *withāb* (VIII, 247; al-Selwi, 216 'Matte').

As to seven words from Jawf and Shiḥr, al-Selwi has treated *ḥawf* (III, 307; al-Selwi, 75 'eine Art Kamelsänfte').

2. Words documented in Ghūl

For another three of the remaining thirty-six words we find explanations given by Ghūl — for *muballat* (VIII, 125 *mahr maḍmūn* 'assured dowry', cf. Ghūl 1993: 94–96), *bill* (VIII, 319 *mubāḥ* 'allowable, lawful', see Lane 1863: 244a; Ghūl 1993: 97–100), and *barkh* (IV, 256 *rakhīṣ* 'cheap'). I cannot add anything to the explanation of *muballat* or propose an ostensibly missing link between notions of 'free for use, unrestricted' and 'removing restrictions, making free; (later:) trespass, laxity, immorality' (Ar. *mubāḥ*, *ibāḥah*), and 'sins, faults' and 'abundant, bountiful' (ASA *bllm*), respectively (Ghūl 1993: 99), or their linkage.

I note, however, that Ghūl approves of Ibn Durayd when he assumed that Omani *barkh* is of Syriac or Hebrew origin and is from the same sense as Arabic *barakah* 'blessing' (Ghūl 1993: 208). This might be true for related contexts like the *shahīd* of Ruʾba given by al-Khalīl: 'When I say give blessings (*barrikhū*) they gave blessings (*barrakhū*) | for the Holy Sergius (*Mār Sarjīs*)'. Yet, it is to be questioned whether it is right to understand *barkh* as a blessing in Old Omani Arabic since according to *Kitāb al-ʿayn* the people of Oman say, 'How are the prices with you?' and the answering person says, '*barkh*'.

One can question whether it is likely that a Syriac or — in the words of al-Khalīl — a Nabataean word makes sense for notions of blessings (likewise in Ibn Sīdah 2000, v: 182) and could possibly have been used in Oman as a word for 'cheap'. Bearing in mind that there are Aramaic-influenced words in contemporary Omani Arabic — for example, *habbar* 'to set bones' (cf. Mandaic *hbr* 'join, associate, fasten, be fastened', see Holes 2002: 278) — but also that present-day Oman was ruled or at least influenced by Persian empires for nearly a millennium before the emergence of Islam, we should not rule out an Iranian etymology for the meaning 'share' as suggested by al-Azharī (1964–1976, vii: 362). We can strengthen this with Middle-Persian *bahr* 'part, portion, share, lot' (MacKenzie 1986: 16; New Persian *bahr* or *barx*, from Old Persian **baxtra-* and Avestan **baxðra-*, see Hübschmann 1895: 33) and New Persian *barxé* 'fraction' (see Heydari-Malayeri [2005-2014]) as a more plausible origin of *barkh* for 'cheap'.

3. Words documented in Lane and Wahrmund

Some of the remaining thirty-three words can be found in bilingual dictionaries. The Yemeni words to be found include: *ḥifrāh* (III, 213 *khashabah dhāt aṣābiʿ tudharrā bihā l-kudūs al-madūsah wa-yunaqqā bihā al-burr*, cf. Lane 1863: 965b s.v. *midhrāh* 'a wooden implement having prongs, with which one winnows wheat and with which the heaps of grain are cleared'; apparently related to ḤFR 'to dig'), *qunfuʿah* (II, 302 = *furquʿah* = *{a,u}st* [*sic*] 'anus', see Lane 1863: 2387b with variant *qurfuʿah* [*sic*]), *injār* (VI, 107 < *ijjār* 'flat top, roof of a house', see Lane 1863: 24), *shirnāf* (VI, 302 'the leaves of seed-produce that have become so long and abundant that one fears its becoming marred; wherefore they are cut off', see Lane 1863: 1538b).

Al-Khalīl's explanation of *ḥifrāh*, a pronged tool to separate the chaff and straw from the grain, sounds like a synonym of *midhrāh* 'a winnower' which in fact cannot be found in his dictionary (for synonyms see ʿAlī 1993, vii: 51–53). Three possible items may come to one's mind from this explanation: a winnower, a pitchfork, and a flail, but the prongs do not admit an interpretation either as winnower (in form of a fan) or as flail (a wooden staff with a short heavy stick swinging from it); thus, it should be 'a winnowing fork'. In this context it is very interesting to look at various interpretations of disputed Greek *ptýon* in Matt 3: 12 and Luke 3: 17 ('pitchfork', 'winnowing shovel', 'winnowing fork', and 'fan', see Bibleapps), which was translated in the Syriac NT as *rapshā* in Luke 3: 17 (see Dukhrana [2013], from Akkadian *rapshu* 'winnowing shovel', see Kaufman 1974: 88) and rather unsurprisingly as *rafsh* in the Arabic NT (see Van Dyck

[2013]), which according to al-Khalīl was of southern Iraqi provenance (*sawādiyyah*).

I could not find the word *qunfuʿah* 'anus' anywhere else than a single verse of poetry cited by al-Khalīl (II, 302) in which the colour of the bottom and the breasts of a short woman is described as pink (*qafraniyyah ka-anna bi-ṭabṭabayhā | wa-qunfuʿihā ṭilāʾa l-urjuwāni*) since in Classical Arabic, *ʾist* and *sath* are used which reflect Proto-West Semitic **šit-* for 'buttocks' just as in MSAL. In Mehri, for instance, the word used is *šīt* (cf. Kogan 2011a: 218). We find *furquʿah* and (through metathesis) *qurfuʿah*, however, as meaning 'anus' in Yemeni Arabic based on Lane (Piamenta 1990–1991, ii: 373), while the supposedly related (and onomatopoeic) verb *farqaʿa* is actually a dissimilation of *faqqaʿa* 'to crack fingers' (Landberg 1920–1942, iii: 2412f.). It is even more confusing that Ghūl listed *funquʿah* (*sic*) in his appendix (1993: 336), but we can locate *farqaʿah* meaning 'cracking' in Ibn al-Jawzī's historiographical work *al-Muntaẓam* (1992–1993, xxiii: 283) where the cracking of a piece of kohl — when thrown into fire — is explained as a severe cracking (*fa-tafarqaʿa farqaʿatan shadīdatan*).

Al-Khalīl explained *ʾajjār* to be a Yemenite word indicating the flat roof of a house (*saṭḥ*) or a roof chamber (*ḥujrah*) (VI, 107): it is a flat, uncovered (*laysa ḥawālayh sutra*) roof and has two plurals: *ajājīr* and *ajājirah*, with *injār* being an ugly variant (*lughah qabīḥah*) of *ijjār* (VI, 174). This word and its variant with *–nj–* instead of *–jj–* was also used by the people of Homs who pronounced *ḥaẓẓ* 'luck, prosperity' as *ḥanẓ*, too (III, 22). Quite possibly therefore, Ibn Fāris (1979, i: 63) holds *ʾijjār* to be Levantine (*lughah shāmiyyah*) — or Syriac (Barsoum 1950: 365) — and possibly Hijāzī Arabic but he disapproves of its usage for not being genuinely Arabic (*laysat min kalām al-bādiyyah*).

We can find *ʾinjār* or *ʾijjār* and *ʾajjār* in a hadith by the Prophet Muḥammad: 'If anyone spends the night on a flat roof (without walls; *ʾinjār*) and then falls off of it and dies, no one bears any responsibility for him' (al-Bukhārī 2000: 436, #1194). In the *Musnad* of Aḥmad b. Ḥanbal there are three versions of this with *ʾijjār* (Ibn Ḥanbal 1995–2001, xxxiv: 351f. #20748 and #20749; xxxvii: 23 #22333), and there we also find a more deliberate usage of *ʾijjār*: Muḥammad b. Maslamah, one of the first Muslims of Medina, wanted to marry Buthaynah bt. al-Ḍaḥḥāk and examined her (*yuṭārid*, Ibn Ḥanbal 1995–2001, xxv: 410f. #16028; xxix: 492 #17976) while she was on her parental *ʾijjār* (1995–2001, xxix: 492 #17977).

We find another occurrence in the narration about the people in Medina going into the streets and on top of their roofs (*ʾanājīr* or *ʾajājīr*) when they received the Prophet in Medina for the first time (see Ibn Ḥanbal 1995–2001, i: 181 [#3]) and started singing the most famous chant *ṭalaʿa l-badru ʿalaynā* 'the full/white moon rose over us' (Ibn Ḥibbān 1973, i: 131). These traditions are also to be found — among other related literature — in Ibn al-Athīr's *Nihāyah* (1963, i: 26) and al-Muṭarrizī's book about Arabicized words (1979: 30).

Bearing these quotations in mind, we can compare *ʾijjār* to Aramaic *ʾeggārā* (cf. Fraenkel 1886: 25; occurs in the Syriac Mark 2: 4, Luke 5: 19, and Acts 10: 9) and Akkadian *igāru* (< Sumerian *egar* [e₂-gar₈] 'wall', see ePSD and CAD I & J, 34b; see also Zimmern 1917: 31; Krebernik 2008: 250) and its cognates in Ethiopic languages (see Semitic etymology database [2013]). The dissimilation of Aramaic /gg/ to /ng/ is also to be found in Mandaic in the same word: *engaria* denoting 'roofs' (Burtea 2011: 674; Drower & Macuch 1963: 25a) and 'roof demons' (Kwasman 2007). The closest word we can point to in Sabaic is *ngr* 'erzählen' in X.BSB 111/2 interpreted on the basis of Ethiopic (Stein 2010: 392), which does not seem to be related.

It is not clear why al-Khalīl categorized it as a Yemeni word and why he did not quote the related traditions. Although we cannot prove that the word in question was not used in Yemen, we may note that it is an Aramaic loanword, which was definitely used in Hijāzī Arabic. While the actual usage of this word seems to have been quite restricted in Arabic, its Aramaic cognate is quite well documented, especially in incantations, magic bowls, and amulets.

As to *shirnāf*, its corresponding verb *sharnafa* points to its actual usage in Yemeni Arabic (al-Selwi 1987: 121). Some lexicographers have doubted this form, however, and held the original to be *shiryāf* and *sharyafa* (al-Jawharī 1990, iv: 1381a; al-Ṣāḥib 1994, vii: 322 *sharrafū arḍahum, sharyafa z-zarʿ*; al-Ṣāghānī 1981: 316). In al-Farābī's *Dīwān al-adab* (1974, ii: 488a) we find *sharyafa* as an example of a /y/-augmented verb (*faʿyala*). The intransitive verb is held to mean that crops' leaves are getting overlong (*sharyafa z-zarʿ*) while when used as a transitive verb, it means that overlong leaves are cut (*sharyaftu z-zarʿ*).

We cannot quote any occurrences in literature and Ghūl did not find any comparable word in South Arabian inscriptions either (1993: 331) but we can refer to two videos on YouTube which reveal that *shiryāf* is used in Yemen to this day (see Video 1; Video 2). In these videos one can see how the leaves are cut off from reed crops, which is exactly how Landberg explains *shiryāf* 'feuilles de roseau = *rīfʿ* (1920–1942, ii: 2048); but it seems very far-fetched to think of *shiryāf* as an infinitive of the causative stem formed with a *sh-*prefix of the verb RYF with the basic meaning 'to make the land abundant with herbage' in Classical Arabic (see Lane 1863: 1202c for *ʾarāfat al-arḍ*). It is much more likely that *shiryāf* is a noun (cf. *jiryāl, kiryās, tiryāq* and *siryāḥ*, see al-Raffāʾ 1986, iv: 57, although not listed as *fiʿyāl* in Ibn Durayd 1987, ii: 1204a) and probably related to SRF: *sarifati s-surfatu sh-shajarata* 'the *surfah* eats the tree's leaves' with *surfah* being a bagworm that builds quadrilateral bags (*Amicta quadrangularis*, see Abivardi 2001, i: 473).

4. Proper names

Easy things come first. There is one single proper noun in our list: MNŠM. According to al-Khalīl, Mansh{a,i}m was the name of 'a female seller of perfume of the Himyar or Hamdān; when they applied her perfumes, it caused violent wars between them, hence she became a proverb signifying evil' (VI, 270). Indeed, this name occurs a lot in Arabic literature (113 times in sixty-three digitized books on al-Warrāq [2013]) and it did develop into the proverb *ashʾam min ʿiṭri Mansham* 'more ill-omened than the perfume of Mansham' (al-Ḥarīrī 1867–1898, ii: 287, for which Steingass cites Freytag's classic *Arabum proverbia*; see Freytag 1838, i: 692–694 'infaustior quam aroma Manschimi'). The locus classicus for 'Mansham' is the *muʿallaqah* of Zuhayr for it describes that men would apply the perfume of Mansham when going to war: 'You alone mended the rift between Abs and Dhubán after long slaughter, and much grinding of the perfume of Manshim' (Arberry 1957: 115). This indicates that in pre-Islamic Arabia perfume was applied to the shroud of the deceased and their clothes, a rite which is continued in Islam (ʿAlī 1993, iv: 626; v: 162).

5. Particles

Al-Khalīl mentions two particles: *ʾam* (VIII, 435 *mubtadaʾ al-kalām fī l-khabar* 'marker of the (beginning of the) predicate'), and *yaʿzī* (II, 206). Bearing in mind that al-Khalīl must have considered spoken varieties of his time, corroboration for them comes solely from al-Khalīl. The first is in any case difficult to search for since it looks like Arabic *ʾam* 'or' (also in Sabaic *ʾm*, see Stein 2010: 89/5) and in fact seems to be a Yemenite variant of Arabic *ʾan* 'that, whether', while Shiḥri *yaʿzī* equals Classical Arabic *la-ʿamrī* 'by my life'.

6. Metatheses

We can explain two Yemenite words through metatheses: *Yanam* for *Yaman* 'Yemen' (VIII, 388 *naẓīr al-barakah* 'felicity'), and *madd* for *ḍamd* (VII, 24), which Ghūl did not deal with as they do not occur in Ancient South Arabian inscriptions known to us (1993: 339). Al-Khalīl explained both words as generated through metatheses. Varisco (2004: 105) explained *ḍamd* (still in use) rightly as a 'yoked team of oxen' and sheds further light on the word.

7. Vowel change

A total of four words show one different vowel compared to their Classical Arabic equivalents: Yemenite *jirīn* for *jarīn* 'threshing floor' (VI, 104) and *qiryah* for *qaryah* 'village, town' (V, 203, cf. Rabin 1951: 122 n. 7), and Shiḥri *shihida* for *shahida* 'to witness' (VII, 317) and *kithīr* for *kathīr* 'lot, many' (VII, 175).

It is not necessary in a paper of this size to bring in other Semitic languages here to discuss the origins of *qiryah* (cf. Smith 2012: 111–113, esp. 112 n. 29) and *jarīn* (cf. Sabaic *grn* 'threshing floor', see MAFY-dhī-aṣ-Ṣawlaʿ 1 A+B/2 in Robin 1991: 171–173, figs 7–10; Stein 2010: 35/9f.; for Geez *gʷərn* 'threshing floor' and comparative references see Leslau 1991: 203a) since, when comparing them to their Classical Arabic counterparts, there seems to be a shared feature between these words, namely, the change of the word initial syllable C_1aC_2- (followed by /y/, /i/, and /ī/) into C_1iC_2- which might have been a general feature in some forms of Old Arabic (cf. al-Farāhīdī 1980–1985, vii: 317) and is still common; for example, regarding the Shiḥri verb *shihid*, compare contemporary Meccan *simiʿ* 'to hear' (see Schreiber 1970: 37) and for *kithīr*, contemporary Cairene *kitīr* (Woidich 2006: 92).

8. Semantic variation

Al-Khalīl gives six lemmas that have a different meaning in Arabic or that are related to Arabic words. He lists Yemeni *junbukhah* 'big louse' (IV, 328, cf. ǦNBḤ 'big' and Geez *gunbāḥ*, see Leslau 1991: 3), *zubb* 'beard' (VII, 353, uncommented by Ghūl 1993: 329; cf. ZBB 'to be hairy', Syriac *zbābā* 'hairiness' is probably an Arabism, see CAL), *qaḥbah* 'old woman' (III, 53; uncommented by Ghūl 1993: 337, cf. QḤB 'fornication' — *qaḥbah* 'prostitute' well known in pre-Islamic Arabia, see ʿAlī 1993, v: 131; cf. Mehri *ḵeḥbēt* 'whore, harlot', see Johnstone 1987a: 227 s.r. *ḵḥb* [*sic*]), *hibrizī* 'good camel' (IV, 123 *al-khuff al-jayyid* 'a good camel (toe)/horseman/shoe [*khuff*?]', cf. HBRZ 'good, handsome'), Jawfi *qushᶜur* 'cucumber' (II, 287, uncommented by Ghūl 1993: 337; cf. QŠᶜR 'gooseflesh', the verb *iqshaᶜarra* occurs in Qurʾān 39. 23), and Omani *bazkh* 'cliff' [= *jurf*] (IV, 211, cf. BZḪ '(a.o.) to have a prominent breast and hollow back').

I could only find occurrences of Old Yemeni Arabic *zubb* meaning 'beard' in an anonymous but definitely Yemeni verse given by al-Khalīl (VII, 353): 'and the tears of the eyes overflowed without the sound of weeping over the beard until the beard was dipping into water' (*fa-fāḍat dumūᶜu l-jaḥmatayni bi-ᶜabratin | ᶜalā z-zubbi ḥattā z-zubbu fī l-māʾi ghāmis*), and in trivializing context (see below).

9. Old Vernacular Arabic

There are five Yemeni and Omani Arabic words that seem to have been used in particular regions of Yemen and Oman of that time. I have already dealt with Yemeni *ḥifrāh* and *qunfuᶜah* above. As to the Omani words, they are *zifn* (VII, 372 *ẓullah yattakhidhūnahā fawq suṭūḥihim taqīhim wamad al-baḥr ay ḥarrahū wa-nadāhu* 'a covering which they make over their flat house-tops to protect them from the heat and dew of the sea', see Lane 1863: 1237c), *suᶜn* (I, 338 *ẓullah yattakhidhuhā ahl ᶜUmān fawq suṭūḥihim min ajl nadā al-wamadah* 'Schattendach' [shading roof in sticky nights], see Wahrmund 1887, i: 902, and *suᶜnah* in Steingass 1884: 494b) and *qadf* (V, 119; 'Wasser mit der Hand ausschöpfen, Wasser ausschütten', see Wahrmund 1887, ii: 464). Omani *suᶜnah* 'roof for shade, baldachin' can also be found in Steingass's dictionary (1884: 494b), and there is a verb related to *zifn* 'palm frond sheeting' ('roof for protection' in Steingass 1884: 458b), *zefen, yizfin, iz-zufūn* 'to tie clipped palm fronds into sheets' (see Holes 2001–2005, i: 222b; Dévényi 2001: 43).

10. Emendation of copy errors

There are four Yemeni and Himyari words that might have been miscopied over the ages. I have already mentioned Yemeni *shirnāf* above. As for Yemeni *minzam* 'tooth' (VII, 376), we can emend that to documented Yemeni *mibzam* 'tooth' and cite Ibn Ḥamdūn's *Tadhkarah* (1996, iii: 411f.; cf. Hämeen-Anttila 1994: 109–112) in which a man of the Kindah and a man of the Tamīm try to impress the Abbasid caliph Abū al-ᶜAbbās al-Saffāḥ (r. 749–754) with the achievements of Yemenis and Muḍar Arabs respectively. Khālid b. Ṣafwān ridiculed Ibrāhīm b. Makhramah and Yemeni Arabic in one version of the account by choosing three clauses from the Qurʾān where the vocabulary of Yemeni Arabic differs significantly: Q 5. 45 ('eye for eye': Yemeni *jaḥmah* for *ᶜayn*, and 'tooth for tooth': Yemeni *mibzam* for *sinn*) and, well aware of the fact that *zubb* in Arabic mostly means 'penis', quite obviously climaxing in Q 20. 94 (*lā taʾkhudh bi-liḥyatī wa-lā bi-raʾsī* 'do not seize [me] by my beard nor my head' with Yemeni *zubb* for *liḥyah*). *Zubb* and *mibzam*, however, seem to be obsolete in present-day Yemeni Arabic and are not used in Modern South Arabian languages, either (for 'beard', see Nakano 1986: 5; for 'penis'; 1986: 8; for 'tooth' Kogan 2011a: 223f.; Nakano 1986: 3).

As to the Himyarite words *khamīt* and *shashqalah*, both are easily explained. The former was explained as a name of *samīn* (IV, 242), which could be plausible since morphologically both look like adjectives. This seems to be an error, however, since *khamīt* should be 'butter' proper and not an adjective meaning 'flobby, fat'. Sima (2000: 240) explains Sabaic *khmʾt* in CIH 540 — an inscription that Ghūl (1993: 320) might not have had access to — very plausibly as present-day Yemeni *samn* 'Butterschmalz' (clarified butter). The word also occurs in a minuscule inscription with the same meaning (Stein 2010: 138/7). Taking into account Proto-Semitic **khimʾ-at-* to which Akkadian *khimētu*, Aramaic *ḥewtā*, Ugaritic *khmʾat*, Hebrew *ḥāmʾā*, Harsusi *ḥāmi*, and Soqotri *ḥámi* go back (Kogan 2011a: 240; Nakano 1986: 19; in non-eastern dialects of Soqotri *xaymi* [see Morris, forthcoming, a], *maxəmi* 'clarified butter' and *xəmɔ́ yəxīm yəxēm* 'to clarify butter' in Hobyot [see Morris, forthcoming, b]), we must assume that a copyist overcorrected the gloss from *khamīt = samn* to *khamīt = samīn* if this supposed error were not to be traced back to al-Khalīl himself. It is therefore strange that *khamīt* occurs in a poem by Sīdī b. al-Mukhtār b. al-Hībah (1776–1867) from Mauritania as a rhyme-word obviously meaning *samīn* (see al-Shaykh Sīdī al-Kabīr [2013]: l.35; on him see Ibn al-Hībah [2013]), and that the Egyptian writer and poet ᶜAlī al-Jārim (1881–1949) accepts the hyper-corrected equalization of *khamīt = samīn* and bases on this hypothetical verbs of ḪMT (see al-Jārim 1990: 175; completely theoretical and not even listed in al-Zabīdī's [1732–1791] *Tāj al-ᶜarūs*, 1965–2001) in his proposal to extend the vocabulary of Arabic. Still, in the light of its cognates, I think *khamīt* is actually non-Arabic and cannot be derived from **ḪMT.

As to *shashqalah* (V, 245 *taᶜyīr* 'weighing coins'), al-Khalīl classifies it as Himyarī slave-speak (*ḥimyariyyah ᶜibādiyyah*) which was used by Iraqi bullion dealers/money changers (*ṣayārifah*) when weighing dinars, an idea expressed by derivatives of similar roots across the Semitic language family: Arabic ṬQL, Hebrew ŠQL, Aramaic TQL, and Geʿez SQL. For 'we weighed them [i.e. dinars]' they would say *shashqalnāhā*. Al-Suyūṭī ([n.d.], i: 287) gives a varying explanation of *shashqalah*: 'it means that you weigh dinars against each other to see which of them is heavier'. Ghūl listed it in his appendix as incomparable to the vocabulary of Ancient South Arabian inscriptions (1993: 321) while al-Sāmirrāʾī listed it together with *shāqūl* but only explained the latter (al-Sāmirrāʾī 1985: 142f.).

The closest we can get to *shashqalah* in Aramaic dialects is the Mandaic verb *shashqil* meaning 'to raise up high' which is an example of the rare causative ša-stem (Nöldeke 1875: 212; Macuch 1965: 248; Voigt 2007: 161; Burtea 2011: 678). The Aramaic variants of ŠQL, however, might be influenced by the Akkadian verb *shaqālu* (Kaufman 1974: 100) means 'darwägen, zahlen lassen' in the Š-stem (AHW III 1981: 1178) and which might also explain the Mandaic shift to 'to raise up high', if we imagine the process of paying as lifting a scale with coins or metals. Fraenkel (1886: 197) doubted the actual existence of this word and unfortunately, we cannot provide any corroboration except for the sample given by al-Khalīl.

Yet, among the permutations of Q, Š, and L, the only lemma that is not marked as foreign is *shāqūl* which al-Sāmirrāʾī considers a Syriac instrumental noun. Related to our word in question, the verb *shaqaltu d-danānīra* 'I weighed the dinars' is given as slave-speak from al-Ḥīrah (*ḥīriyyah ʿibādiyyah*). Hence the verb and the supposed verbal noun *shashqalah* were used in southern Mesopotamia. Therefore, we can at least suggest changing the reading of *kalimah himyariyyah ʿibādiyyah* in the explanation of *shashqalah* in both editions of *Kitāb al-ʿayn* (al-Farāhīdī 1980–1985, v: 245; 2003, ii: 330) to the more likely *kalimah ḥīriyah ʿibādiyyah*, which links the word to the ancient city al-Ḥīrah in southern Mesopotamia instead of the Ḥimyar. Derivations of the Arabicized root ŠQL with different meanings are still in use in Bahrain and the Levant (Holes 2002: 276f.) and in Yemen (see al-Iryānī 1996: 509b).

11. Unsupported words

There are five words for which corroboration only comes from al-Khalīl. The Omani word *barkh* was dealt with above and we cannot say anything about Shiḥri *khasf* (IV, 202 *jawr* 'deviating, acting wrongfully', see Lane 1863: 838c; for construction-related *binā al-khasf* and *makhsūf*, see Piamenta 1990–1991, i: 128; for *khasaf* as 'beating' in modern Yemeni Arabic, see Behnstedt 1993: 66; perhaps Mehri and Ḥarsusi are comparable, see Johnstone 1987a: 449 s.r. *xsf*).

An interesting word is Jawfi *shalṭ* = *sikkīn* (VI, 236) 'slaughtering knife'. The closest word to compare it to is Jewish Literary Aramaic and Syriac *shlāṭā* 'quiver; (Syr.) weapon' (see CAL; cf. Arabic *shalṭah* [pl. *shilaṭ*] 'arrow' in al-Ṣāḥib 1994, vii: 293). If we look for the closest word by place and manner of articulation within Arabic, however, *jalaṭa raʾsah* 'he shaved his head' (cf. Abū al-Ṭayyib 1961, i: 226–229 for the interchanging of /j/ and /sh/) would make better sense than 'quiver' but there is no variant **jalṭ*. To make things even worse, in present-day Yemeni Arabic *shalṭ* means 'a stealing' and is interchangeable with *malṭ* (see al-Iryānī 1996: 513b; cf. Abū Ṭayyib 1961, ii: 234–236 for the interchanging of /sh/ and /m/). We may join al-Azharī (1964–1976, xi: 311b) and admit that we neither know *shalṭ* nor deem it to be Arabic and that only God knows everything.

As to Himyarite *baydakhah* (IV, 234 *tārrah* 'plump', cf. Lane 1863: 300a; Ghūl 1993: 320 uncommented), it is an adjective for women while Baydakh is a female name, which occurs in a verse. Bearing in mind the very closest Semitic word *baṭ(ṭ)īkhah* 'watermelon' and representations of fertility goddesses, especially Venus figurines, I would still suggest viewing *baydakhah* as a probable loanword from Persian *bēduxt* 'Venus (< daughter of God)' (see Dehkhodā [2013]: s.v. *beydokht*), feminine par excellence.

The last Himyari word, *shikhāf* 'milk' (IV, 172 *laban* 'milk'), was not treated by Ghūl (1993: 321, 331) but commented upon as *shakhf* to which it is indeed related and which denotes the 'sound of milking' (related to ŠḤB). This onomatopoeic aetiology as an etymology does not seem to have been considered as such but it becomes manifest in a verse that compares the sound of milking to that of a hissing snake and was passed on by many Arab lexicographers: *ka-ʾanna ṣawta shakhbihā dhī sh-shakhfi | kashīshu afʿā fī yabīsi quffi*.

It is most striking that cognates of this word still denote 'milk' in MSAL: Harsusi *śkhōf* (see Johnstone 1977: 122 s.r. *śxf*; 2004: 12 l.34), Baṭḥari and Hobyot *śxāf* (Morris, forthcoming, *b*; forthcoming, *c*) Mehri *śxōf*, and Soqotri *śḥ̣Ʌƒ*, while the related verb denotes 'to drink fresh milk' in various MSAL (see Morris 2002: 60; Kogan 2011a: 240; Diakonoff 1981: 60; Johnstone 1987b: 389 s.r. *śxf*).

12. Non-Arabic words

Al-Khalīl lists a word that cannot be Arabic by force of rule since a /sh/ must not follow a /l/ as a root literal:

ʿillawsh (I, 256 *dhiʾb* 'wolf'; cf. ʿillawḍ in al-Selwi 1987: 162, cf. Eisenstein 2009: 22; uncommented in Ghūl 1993: 322, 334). There is a quotation for this word other than an infamous poem of al-Suyūṭī's, which consists of about seventy synonyms of 'dog' in which he ridicules the poet and philosopher al-Maʿarrī. Since it relies heavily on lexicography, we want to disregard it for our purpose along with the other verse that is related to us by al-Khalīl: ʾa-yā jaḥmatī bakkī ʿalā ʾummi wāhibin | {qatīlati, akīlati} ʿillawshin bi-ʾiḥdā dh-dhanāʾibi. Although clearly Yemeni in its style with *jaḥmah* for ʿayn, this verse has also come down to us in at least one other variant, including a Yemeni synonym for the word in question! In Ibn Manẓūr's recension (1981: 553c, quoting Ibn Barrī for adjacent verses), the verse goes: ʾa-yā jaḥmatā bakkī ʿalā ʾummi mālikin | akīlati qillawbin bi-ʾaʿlā l-madhānibi and overall, we learn that the poet orders his eyes to weep for the mother of Wāhib or Mālik because she was killed or eaten by a jackal (ʿillawsh or qillawb) at the highest or just one of the canyons, but we should disregard this evidence.

There seems to be a lexical doublet, ʿillawḍ (cf. al-Selwi 1987: 162), however, and if ʿillawsh can be mistaken for qillawb, what about changing ʿillawsh to ʿillawḍ or vice versa? The existence of this supposedly Himyari pair has attracted much attention and together with other examples showing an alternation of /sh/ and /ḍ/, it is used in theories about the delateralization of /ḍ/ in Arabic (cf. Rabin 1951: 33; Lipiński 2001: 138; Kogan 2011b: 75f) but we cannot prove its actual existence and use except for the doubtful verse given by al-Khalīl and al-Suyūṭī's poem where ʿillawsh is the sixtieth synonym for 'dog' (al-Suyūṭī 2009: 25).

13. Kulturwort

Lastly there is *baʾlah* = *qārūrah* 'bottle' (VIII, 342) in the dialect of Balḥārith, and al-Khalīl's only hint is that its 'Nabataean' form ends on a /t/ although the word does occur in Early Arabic poetry. Looking for the origin of *baʾlah* in al-Jawālīqī's compendium (1990: 163f. 'flask, falcon, etc.'), we find Persian <bʾlh>. However unhelpful this was, in Middle Persian there is *paygāl* for New Persian *payghāla* and *piyāla* meaning 'cup, goblet', which makes it a plausible origin and moreover, this is the same word as Modern English *phial* from Greek *phiálē* (non-Indo-European pre-Greek, cf. Beekes 2010, ii: 1571). The same word is also attested in Aramaic *pyly*, *pylyʾ* ({p,f}īalē) meaning 'flat bowl' and Syriac *ballətā* meaning 'perfume flask'. Crossing many cultures and languages up to the present, this word was also used by the tribe of Balḥārith.

Conclusion

What started as a curious look into the South Arabian words in al-Khalīl b. Aḥmad's *Kitāb al-ʿayn*, unfortunately ended up being a modest study — at least in our limited assessment of Early and Classical Arabic literature — of mostly unattested words. We have, however, no proof against believing that they were dialectal Arabic words in the eighth century AD (*terminus ad quem*) since some of the words are documented in bilingual dictionaries and some of these words are still used in southern Arabia.

Indeed, we can plausibly explain many of the unstudied words of southern provenance in *Kitāb al-ʿayn* through Classical Arabic by metatheses (2: *maḍd* < *ḍamd*, *Yanam* < *Yaman*), vowel change (4: *jirīn*, *qiryah*, *shihida*, *kithīr*), and semantic variation (6: *junbukhah*, *zubb*, *qaḥbah*, *hibrizī*, *qushʿur*, *bazkh*). There is one proper noun (MNŠM) and two particles (ʾam, yaʿzī), four (out of five) dialectal words that can be found in bilingual dictionaries (*qunfuʿah*, *zifn*, *suʿn*, *qadf*; *ḥifrāh*), and four words that have fallen victim to copy-editing errors (dotting: *shirnāf* [recte *shiryāf*], *minzam* [recte *mibzam*]; explanation: *khamīt*, *shashqalah*). There are one Kulturwort (*baʾlah*) and one loanword from Aramaic (*ijjār*), which can be traced back to Sumerian, and one supposed ghost word (ʿillawsh), while for five words there was almost no corroboration (*shalṭ*, *khasf*, *baydakhah*, *shikhāf*, *barkh*).

While the proper name MNŠM developed into a still common phrase in MSA, from among the words that can be explained through Classical Arabic, there is only corroboration for *zubb* meaning 'beard' in Old Yemeni Arabic in prose and poetry. The usage of the two particles in Old Yemeni Arabic is explained by al-Khalīl. As for the five words in Old Vernacular Arabic, we can find the three Omani ones in early modern dictionaries (*zifn*, *suʿnah*, *qadf*), while *qunfuʿah* is exemplified in an anonymous verse in *Kitāb al-ʿayn* and *ḥifrāh* might still be in use (cf. ʿAlī 1993, vii: 51–53, although not listed in Baʿlbakī 1995: 477a).

Among the four words which involve copy-editing errors, *shashqalah* turned out to be of South Mesopotamian instead of Himyarī provenance, while for *minzam* (recte *mibzam*) there is corroboration from prose, *shiryāf* is still common in Yemeni Arabic, and reflexes of possibly Sabaic *khamīt* still denote 'clarified butter' in Modern South Arabian languages.

The Kulturwort *baʾlah* testified among others in the old dialect of Balḥārith might have entered Arabic from

Category	#	Poetry	Prose	Colloquialism	Living
Proper names	1	MNŠM	MNŠM	MNŠM	(MSA) MNŠM
Particles	2			ʾam, yaʿzī	
Metatheses	2				
Vowel change	4				(YA) jirīn
Semantic variation	6	zubb	zubb		
Vernacular Arabic	5	qunfuʿah			(OA) zifn, suʿnah, qadf
Copy error	4	khamīt	mibzam	shashqalah	(YA) shiryāf (MSAL) khamīt
Kulturwort	1	baʾlah			
Loanword	1		ijjār		
Ghost word/doublet	1	ʿillawsh			
Unsupported word	5	shikhāf		barkh	(MSAL) shikhāf

FIGURE 1. *Analysis of the South Arabian material in* Kitāb al-ʿayn.

Middle Persian. We could locate the Aramaic loan *ijjār* in Hadith literature, and it was a common word during the time of the Prophet Muḥammad who used it too. Very strange is the case of *ʿillawsh* that has been said to be a doublet of *ʿillawḍ*, but we could not locate it anywhere else than in two doubtful verses, which raises suspicion about the actual existence of the word if it was not used in a specific dialect of that time.

As to 'unsupported words', the Old Omani Arabic word *barkh* 'cheap' must have an Iranian etymology and is unlikely to be of Aramaic origin. The only word for which there is corroboration is *shikhāf*, which is explained as an onomatopoeic word describing the sound of 'milk squirting from the udder' in one verse given by al-Khalīl and the reflexes of which still denote 'milk' in MSAL.

Although these results might seem very meagre at first, one should remember that we have only dealt with thirty-six words here, but this set was more than large enough to demonstrate the intertwined relation of Arabic (and its old and modern dialects) and ASA and MSAL. We could not only retrieve a Himyaritic name for a female that turned into a phrase still common in Media Arabic (MNŠM) but also show that, for example, three Old Omani Arabic words testify to dialectal continuity as they are still used in modern Omani. As the most significant results, there are two non-Arabic 'Ḥimyarī' words that were collected about 1200 years ago and are part of some of MSAL's basic vocabulary. Indeed, it is this way that we can demonstrate how Classical Arabic lexicography can help further our understanding of the emergence and development of the languages of southern Arabia in past and modern times.

Sigla

AHW III	Akkadisches Handwörterbuch 1981.
CAD	Chicago Assyrian Dictionary [2013].
CAL	Comprehensive Aramaic Lexicon [2013].
CIH 540	Inscription in *Corpus Inscriptionum Semiticarum*. Pars IV. *Inscriptiones Ḥimyariticas et Sabaeas continens*. Paris: Reipublicae Typographeo, 1889–1932.
DASI	Digital Archive for the Study of pre-Islamic Arabian Inscriptions, http://dasi.humnet.unipi.it/
ePSD	Pennsylvania Sumerian Dictionary [2013].

References

Arabic sources

Abū al-Ṭayyib, ᶜAbd al-Wāḥid b. ᶜAlī al-Lughawī al-Ḥalabī/ed. I. al-Tannūkhī.
    1961. *Kitāb al-ibdāl*. (2 volumes). Damascus: Majmaᶜ al-lughah al-ᶜarabiyyah.

ᶜAlī J.
    1993. *Al-mufaṣṣal fī tārīkh al-ᶜarab qabl al-islām*. (10 volumes). (Second edition). Baghdad: Jāmiᶜat Baghdād.

al-Azharī, Abū Manṣūr Muḥammad b. Aḥmad/ed. A.S. Hārūn, M.A. al-Najjār, A.H. al-Najjār, A.A.A. al-Bardūnī et al.
    1964–1976. *Tahdhīb al-lughah*. (15 volumes). Cairo: Al-Dār al-miṣriyyah li-l-taʾlīf wa-l-tarjamah.

Barsoum I.A.
    1950. Dhayl. Al-alfāẓ al-suryāniyyah fī al-maᶜājim al-ᶜarabiyyah. *Majallat al-majmaᶜ al-ᶜilmī al-ᶜarabī bi-Dimashq* 25/3: 364–398.

al-Bukhārī, Muḥammad b. Ismāᶜīl/ed. N. al-Albānī.
    2000. *Al-Adab al-mufrad.* Jubail: Dār al-ṣadīq.

al-Fārābī, Abū Ibrāhīm Isḥāq b. Ibrāhīm/ed. A.M. ᶜUmar & I. Anīs.
    1974. *Dīwān al-adab*. (2 volumes). Cairo: Majmaᶜ al-lughah al-ᶜarabiyyah.

al-Farāhidī, Ibn ᶜAbd al-Raḥman al-Khalīl b. Aḥmad/ed. M. al-Makhzūmī & I. al-Sāmirrāʾī.
    1980–1985. *Kitāb al-ᶜayn*. (8 volumes). Baghdad: Dār al-Rashīd.

al-Farāhidī, Ibn ᶜAbd al-Raḥman al-Khalīl b. Aḥmad/ed. A. Hindāwī.
    2003. *Kitāb al-ᶜayn*. (4 volumes). Beirut: Dār al-kutub al-ᶜilmiyyah.

al-Farāhidī, Ibn ᶜAbd al-Raḥmān al-Khalīl b. Aḥmad.
    [2013]. *Kitāb al-ᶜayn*. (Digitized edition). 30 October 2013. www.almeshkat.net/books/archive/books/alfrahedi.zip; http://ar.lib.eshia.ir/20006/1/1.

al-Ḥarīrī, Qāsim b. ᶜAlī/transl. F.J. Steingass.
    1867–1898. *Al-Maqāmāt. The assemblies of al-Harîri.* (2 volumes). London: Williams and Northgate.

Ibn al-Athīr, Majd al-Dīn Abū al-Saᶜādāt al-Mubārak b. Muḥammad al-Jazarī/ed. Ṭ.A. al-Zāwī & M.M. al-Ṭanājī.
    1963. *Al-Nihāyah fī gharīb al-ḥadīth wa-l-athar*. (5 volumes). Beirut: Dār iḥyāʾ al-turāth al-ᶜarabī.

Ibn Durayd, Abū Bakr Muḥammad b. al-Ḥasan/ed. R.M. Baᶜlbakī.
    1987. *Jamharat al-lughah*. Beirut: Dār al-ᶜilm li-l-malāyīn.

Ibn Fāris, Abū al-Ḥusayn, Aḥmad b. Fāris b. Zakariyya/ed. A.M. Hārūn.
    1979. *Muᶜjam maqāyīs al-lughah*. (6 volumes). Beirut: Dār al-fikr.

Ibn Ḥamdūn, Muḥammad b. al-Ḥasan b. Muḥammad b. ᶜAlī/ed. I. ᶜAbbās & B. ᶜAbbās.
    1996. *Al-Tadhkarah al-ḥamdūniyyah*. (10 volumes). Beirut: Dār ṣādir.

Ibn Ḥanbal, Ahmad/ed. Sh. al-Arnaʾūṭ, M.N. al-ᶜIrqsūsī, A. Murshid, I. al-Zaybaq et al.
    1995–2001. *Musnad al-Imām Aḥmad b. Ḥanbal*. (50 volumes). Beirut: Muʾassasat al-risālah.

Ibn al-Hība.
    [2013]. *Aᶜlām Mūrītāniyā*. Quotation from *Kitāb tarājim al-aᶜlām al-mūrītānīyīn*. i. (ed. Ibrāhīm b. Ismāᶜīl b. al-Shaykh Sīdī & Sīdī Aḥmad b. Aḥmad Sālim, Nouakchott, 1997). 30 October 2013. http://assahwa.com/index.php/2013-04-24-01-46-29/193----1.

Ibn Ḥibbān, Muḥammad Abū Ḥātim al-Tamīmī/ed. M. ᶜAbd al-Muᶜīd Khān.
    1973. *Al-Thiqāt.* (10 volumes). Dāʾirat al-maᶜārif al-ᶜuthmāniyya.

Ibn al-Jawzī, Abū al-Faraj ᶜAbd al-Raḥmān b. ᶜAlī b. Muḥammad/ed. M.A. ᶜAṭā & M.A. ᶜAṭā.
    1992–1993. *al-Muntaẓam fī tārīkh al-umam*. (19 volumes including index). Beirut: Dār al-kutub al-ᶜilmiyyah.

Ibn Manẓūr, Jamāl al-Dīn Abū al-Faḍl Muḥammad b. Mukarram/ed. A.A. Kabīr, M.A. Ḥasaballāh & H.M. al-Shādhilī.
    1981. *Lisān al-ᶜarab*. Cairo: Dār al-Maᶜārif.

Ibn Sīdah, Abū al-Ḥasan ᶜAlī/ed. A. Hindāwī.
    2000. *Al-Muḥkam wa-l-muḥīṭ al-aᶜẓam*. (11 volumes). Beirut: Dār al-kutub al-ᶜilmiyyah.

al-Iryānī M.
    1996. *Al-Muʿjam al-yamanī fī al-lughah wa-l-turāth ḥawl mufradāt khāṣṣah min al-lahjāt al-yamaniyyah.* Damascus: Dār al-fikr al-muʿāṣir.

al-Jārim, ʿAlī/ed. A.A. al-Jārim.
    1990. *Jārimiyyāt. Buḥūth wa-maqālāt al-shāʿir wa-l-adīb al-lughawī.* Cairo: Dār al-shurūq.

al-Jawālīqī, Abū Manṣūr Mawhūb b. Aḥmad/ed. F. ʿAbd al-Raḥīm.
    1990. *al-Muʿarrab min al-kalām al-aʿjamī ʿalā ḥurūf al-muʿjam.* Damascus: Dār al-qalam.

al-Jawharī, Ismāʿīl b. Ḥammād/ed. A.A. ʿAṭṭār.
    1990. *Al-ṣiḥāḥ. Tāj al-lughah wa-ṣiḥāḥ al-ʿarabiyyah.* (7 volumes). Beirut: Dār al-ʿilm li-l-malāyīn.

al-Muṭarrizī, Abū al-Fatḥ Nāṣir al-Dīn/ed. M. Fākhūrī & ʿA. Mukhtār.
    1979. *Al-Mughrib fī tartīb al-muʿrib.* Aleppo: Maktabat Usāmah b. Zayd.

al-Raffāʾ, al-Sarī b. Aḥmad/ed. M. Ghalāwanjī & M.Ḥ. al-Dhahabī.
    1986. *Al-muḥibb wa-l-maḥbūb wa-l-mashmūm wa-l-mashrūb.* Damascus: Maṭbūʿāt majmaʿ al-lughah al-ʿarabiyyah.

al-Ṣāghānī, al-Ḥasan b. Muḥammad b. al-Ḥasan/ed. M.H. Āl Yāsīn.
    1981. *Al-ʿubāb al-zākhir wa-l-lubāb al-fākhir. Ḥarf al-fāʾ.* Baghdad: Dār al-rashīd li-l-nashr.

al-Ṣāḥib. Ismāʿīl b. ʿAbbād/ed. M.Ḥ. Āl Yāsīn.
    1994. *Al-muḥīṭ fī al-lughah.* (11 volumes). Beirut: ʿĀlam al-kutub.

al-Sāmirrāʾī I.
    1985. *Dirāsāt fī al-lughatayn al-suryāniyyah wa-l-ʿarabiyyah.* Beirut: Dār al-jīl.

al-Shaykh Sīdī al-Kabīr.
    [2013]. *Al-Qaṣīdah al-Isisqāʾīyah.* 30 October 2013. http://alinaratou.blogspot.co.uk/2009/06/blog-post_3868.html.

al-Suyūṭī, ʿAbd al-Raḥmān Jalāl al-Dīn/ed. A. al-Mālikī.
    2009. *al-Tabarrī min maʿarrat al-Maʿarrī.* Wajdah [?]: Maktabat nūr.

al-Suyūṭī, ʿAbd al-Raḥmān Jalāl al-Dīn/ed. M.A.J. al-Mawlā Bak, M.A. Ibrāhīm & A.M. al-Bajāwī.
    [n.d.]. *al-Muzhir fī al-lughah wa-anwāʿihā.* (2 volumes). (Third edition). Cairo: Dār al-turāth.

al-Warrāq.
    [2013]. 30 October 2013. www.alwaraq.net/Core/index.jsp?option=1.

al-Zabīdī, Muḥammad Murtaḍā al-Ḥusaynī/ed. A.A. Farrāj, A.M. Ḥulw, A.M. ʿUmar & Kh.A. Jumʿah.
    1965–2001. *Tāj al-ʿarūs min jawhar al-qāmūs.* (40 volumes). Kuwait: Maṭbaʿat ḥukūmat al-Kuwayt.

Western sources

Abivardi C.
    2001. *Iranian Entomology — An Introduction.* (2 volumes). Heidelberg: Springer.

Akkadisches Handwörterbuch.
    1981. *Akkadisches Handwörterbuch: unter Benutzung des lexikalischen Nachlasses von Bruno Meissner.* iii. S–Z. Berichtigungen und Nachträge. (Ed. Wolfram von Soden. 2., um Hinweise auf die Nachträge verm. Auflage). Wiesbaden: Harrassowitz.

Arberry A.J.
    1957. *The Seven Odes.* London: George Allen & Unwin Ltd.

Baʿlbakī R.
    1995. *Al-Mawrid. A Modern Arabic-English Dictionary.* (Seventh edition). Beirut: Dār al-ʿilm li-l-malāyīn.

Beekes R.
    2010. *Etymological Dictionary of Greek.* (2 volumes). Leiden: Brill.

Behnstedt P.
    1993. *Glossar der jemenitischen Dialektwörter in Eduard Glasers Tagebüchern (II, III, VI, VII, VIII, X).* (Veröffentlichungen der Arabischen Kommission, 6). (Österreichische Akademie der Wissenschaften, Philosophisch-Historische Klasse, Sitzungsberichte, 594). Vienna: Österreichische Akademie der Wissenschaften.

Bibleapps.
    [2013]. *Strong's Greek: 4425 (ptýon)* etc. 30 October 2013. http://bibleapps.com/greek/4425.htm.

Burtea B.
    2011. Mandaic. Pages 670–685 in S. Weninger et al. (eds), *The Semitic Languages. An International Handbook*. Berlin/Boston: De Gruyter.

Chicago Assyrian Dictionary
    [2013]. *The Assyrian Dictionary of the Oriental Institute of the University of Chicago*. 30 October 2013. http://oi.uchicago.edu/research/pubs/catalog/cad/.

Comprehensive Aramaic Lexicon
    [2013]. *The Comprehensive Aramaic Lexicon at the Hebrew Union College Jewish Institute of Religion*. Cincinnati, USA. 30 October 2013. http://cal1.cn.huc.edu

Dehkhodā A.A.
    [2013]. *Loghatnāmeh-e Dehkhodā*. 30 October 2013. www.loghatnaameh.org

Dévényi K.
    2001. Omani Proverbs: Date Palms and Dates. Pages 29–46 in *al-Mustaʿrib. Essays In Honour of Alexander Fodor on His Sixtieth Birthday*. (The Arabist: Budapest Studies in Arabic, 23). Budapest: Eotvos Lorand University.

Diakonoff I.
    1981. Earliest Semites in Asia. Agriculture and Animal Husbandry According to Linguistic Data (VIIIth–IVth Millennia B.C.). *Altorientalische Forschungen* 8: 23–74.

Drower E.S. & Macuch R.
    1963. *A Mandaic Dictionary*. Oxford: Clarendon Press.

Dukhrana
    [2013]. Analytical Lexicon of the Syriac New Testament. 30 October 2013. www.dukhrana.com

Eisenstein H.
    2009. *Klassisch-arabische Kunya-Bezeichnungen für Tiere*. (Neue Beihefte zur Wiener Zeitschrift für die Kunde des Morgenlandes, 5). Vienna: Lit-Verlag.

Elmaz O.
    (forthcoming). ʿarim — A Sabaic word in the Qurʾān? Pages 227-261 in R.G. Stiegner (ed.), *South Arabia. A Great 'Lost Corridor' of Mankind. A collection of papers dedicated to the Re-establishment of South Arabian Studies in Austria (2008–2013)*. i. (Wiener Offene Orientalistik, 10). Vienna: Lit-Verlag.

Fraenkel S.
    1886. *Die aramäischen Fremdwörter im Arabischen*. Leiden: Brill.

Freytag G.W.
    1838. *Arabum proverbia*. Pars prior. Bonna ad Rhenum: A. Marcus.

Ghūl M.A.
    1993. *Early southern Arabian languages and classical Arabic sources. A critical examination of literary and lexicographical sources by comparison with the inscriptions*. Irbid: Yarmouk University.

Hämeen-Anttila J.
    1994. Khālid ibn Ṣafwān. The man and the legend. *Studia orientalia* 73: 69–166.

Haywood J.A.
    1965. *Arabic Lexicography*. Leiden: Brill.

Heydari-Malayeri M.
    [2005–2014]. *An Etymological Dictionary of Astronomy and Astrophysics English-French-Persian*. Paris Observatory. 30 October 2013. http://aramis2.obspm.fr/~heydari/dictionary/index.ormSearchTextfield=fraction&&page=5

Holes C.
    2001–2005. *Dialect, culture, and society in Eastern Arabia*. (2 volumes). Leiden: Brill.
    2002. Non-Arabic Semitic elements in the Arabic dialects of Eastern Arabia. Pages 269–280 in W. Arnold

& H. Bobzin (eds), *'Sprich Doch Mit Deinen Knechten Aramäisch, Wir Verstehen Es!' Festschrift für Otto Jastrow zum 60. Geburtstag*. Wiesbaden: Harrassowitz.

Hübschmann H.
    1895. *Persische Studien*. Strassburg: Karl J. Trübner.

Johnstone T.M.
    1977. *Harsusi lexicon and English-Harsusi word-list*. London: Oxford University Press.
    1987*a*. *Mehri lexicon and English-Mehri word-list*. London: School of Oriental & African Studies.
    1987*b*. *Ḥarsūsi Lexicon*. London: Oxford University Press.

Kaufman S.A.
    1974. *The Akkadian Influences on Aramaic*. Chicago: The University of Chicago Press.

King Saud University Corpus of Classical Arabic.
    [2013]. Compiled by Maha Al-Rabiah. 30 October 2013. http://ksucorpus.ksu.edu.sa/?p=43

Kogan L.
    2011*a*. Proto-Semitic Lexicon. Pages 179–258 in S. Weninger et al. (eds), *The Semitic Languages. An International Handbook*. Berlin/Boston: De Gruyter.
    2011*b*. Proto-Semitic Phonetics and Phonology. Pages 54–151 in S. Weninger et al. (eds), *The Semitic Languages. An International Handbook*. Berlin/Boston: De Gruyter.

Krebernik M.
    2008. Von Gindibu bis Muḥammad. Stand, Probleme und Aufgaben altorientalistischarabistischer Philologie. Pages 247–279 in O. Jastrow, S. Talay & H. Hafenrichter (eds), *Studien zur Semitistik und Arabistik. Festschrift für Hartmut Bobzin zum 60. Geburtstag*. Wiesbaden: Harrassowitz.

Kwasman T.
    2007. The Demon of the Roof. Pages 160–186 in L. Finkel & M.J. Geller (eds), *Disease in Babylonia*. Leiden: Brill.

Landberg C.
    1920–1942. *Glossaire daṯînois*. (3 volumes). Leiden: Brill.

Lane E.W.
    1863. *An Arabic-English Lexicon*. London: Williams and Norgate.

Leslau W.
    1991. *Comparative Dictionary of Gəʿəz*. Wiesbaden: Harrassowitz.

Lipiński E.
    2001. *Semitic languages. Outline of a comparative grammar*. (Second edition). Leuven: Peeters.

MacKenzie D.N.
    1986. *A Concise Pahlavi Dictionary*. London: Oxford University Press. [Reprinted with corrections.]

Macuch R.
    1965. *Handbook of Classical and Modern Mandaic*. Berlin: De Gruyter.

Morris M.
    2002. Plant names in Dhofar and the Soqotra Archipelago. *Proceedings of the Seminar for Arabian Studies* 32: 47–61.
    (forthcoming, *a*). Soqoṭri Lexicon.
    (forthcoming, *b*). Hobyot Lexicon.
    (forthcoming, *c*). Baṭḥari Lexicon.

Nakano A.
    1986. *Comparative vocabulary of Southern Arabic: Mahri, Gibbali and Soqotri*. Tokyo: Institute for the Study of Languages and Cultures of Asia and Africa, Tokyo University of Foreign Studies.

Nöldeke T.
    1875. *Mandäische Grammatik*. Halle: Waisenhaus.

Pennsylvania Sumerian Dictionary.
    [2013]. *The Pennsylvania Sumerian Dictionary*. 30 October 2013. http://psd.museum.upenn.edu/epsd

Piamenta M.
   1990–1991. *Dictionary of post-classical Yemeni Arabic*. Leiden: Brill.

Rabin C.
   1951. *Ancient West-Arabian*. London: Taylor's Foreign Press.

Robin C.J.
   1991. ᶜAmdān Bayyin Yuhaqbid, roi de Sabaʾ et de ḏū-Raydān. Pages 167–205 in C.J. Robin (ed.), *Études sud-arabes. Recueil offert à Jacques Ryckmans*. (Publications de l'Institut Orientaliste de Louvain, 39). Louvain-la-Neuve: Université Catholique de Louvain, Institut Orientaliste.

Schreiber G.
   1970. *Der arabische Dialekt von Mekka. Abriß der Grammatik mit Texten und Glossar*. Dissertation, Westfälische Wilhelms-Universität Münster. http://menadoc.bibliothek.uni-halle.de/iud/content/titleinfo/305137

al-Selwi I.
   1987. *Jemenitische Wörter in den Werken von al-Hamdānī und Nashwān und ihre Parallelen in den semitischen Sprachen*. Berlin: Reimer.

Semitic etymology database.
   [2013]. *The Tower of Babel*. Sergei Starostin's homepage. 30 October 2013. http://starling.rinet.ru/cgi-bin/query.cgi?basename=\data\semham\semet&root=config&morpho=0

Sima A.
   2000. *Tiere, Pflanzen, Steine und Metalle in den altsüdarabischen Inschriften. Eine lexikalische und realienkundliche Untersuchung*. (Veröffentlichungen der Orientalischen Kommission der Akademie der Wissenschaften und der Literatur Mainz, 46). Wiesbaden: Harrassowitz.

Smith M.
   2012. The Concept of the 'City' ('Town') in Ugarit. Pages 107–146 in A. Schart & J. Krispenz (eds), *Die Stadt im Zwölfprophetenbuch*. (Beihefte zur Zeitschrift für die alttestamentliche Wissenschaft, 428). Berlin: de Gruyter.

Stein P.
   2010. *Die altsüdarabischen Minuskelinschriften auf Holzstäbchen aus der Bayerischen Staatsbibliothek in München. i. Die Inschriften der mittel- und spätsabäischen Periode. Part 1: Text*. (Epigraphische Forschungen auf der Arabischen Halbinsel, 5). Tübingen/Berlin: Wasmuth.

Steingass F.J.
   1884. *Arabic-English Dictionary*. London: Crosby Lockwood.

Stroomer H.
   2004. *Ḥarsūsi texts from Oman. Based on the field materials of T.M. Johnstone*. Wiesbaden: Harrassowitz.

Van Dyck, C.
   [2013]. *Arabic New Testament*. 30 October 2013. www.injeel.com/Read.3&t=2&b=42&c=3&svn=1&btp=3&stp=0

Varisco D.M.
   2004. Terminology for plough cultivation in Yemeni Arabic. *Journal of Semitic Studies* 49/1: 71–129.

Video 1.
   [2013]. *Min qalb al-ḥadath mawsim al-shiryāf fī Banī Bakr 2011*. 30 October 2013. www.youtube.com/watch?v=oitq4b8qkQ4

Video 2.
   [2013]. *Madīnat Juban (mawsim al-shiryāf) 2010*. 30 October 2013. www.youtube.com/watch?v=MbRTMZLa5wI

Voigt R.
   2007. Mandaic. Pages 149–166 in A.S. Kaye (ed.), *Morphologies of Asia and Africa*. i. Winona Lake, IN: Eisenbrauns.

Wahrmund A.
   1887. *Handwörterbuch der neu-arabischen und deutschen Sprache*. (Second edition). Giessen: J. Riecker'sche Buchhandlung.

Wild S.
    1965. *Das Kitāb al-'Ain und die arabische Lexikographie*. Wiesbaden: Harrassowitz.

Woidich M.
    2006. *Das Kairenisch-Arabische: eine Grammatik*. Wiesbaden: Harrassowitz.

Zimmern H.
    1917. *Akkadische Fremdwörter als Beweis für babylonischen Kultureinfluß*. (2., durch vollständige Wörterverzeichnisse vermehrte Ausgabe). Leipzig: Hinrichs.

Author's address

Orhan Elmaz, Department of Arabic, School of Modern Languages, University of St Andrews, Buchanan Building, Union Street, St Andrews, Fife, KY16 9PH, UK.

e-mail oe2@st-andrews.ac.uk

The vowel system of Jibbali

RICHARD GRAVINA

Summary
Jibbali (also known as Śhehri) has an interesting and unusual vowel system. It is described by Johnstone (1981a) as having a system of eight vowels: /i/, /e/, /ɛ/, /a/, /ɔ/, /o/, /u/, and /ə/. All of the vowels except ə have both long and nasalized equivalents. This compares with the vowel system of Mehri, for example, which is analysed by Watson (2012) and Rubin (2010) as having five long vowels /ī/, /ē/, /ā/, /ō/, /ū/ (with a marginal sixth vowel /ɛ̄/) and, depending on the dialect, either two or three short vowels: /i/~/ə/, /a/, (/u/).
Here we analyse Jibbali with a similar vowel system to Mehri, consisting of four full vowels /i/, /ɛ/, /ɔ/, and /o/, along with two reduced vowels /e/ and /ə/. We will describe the phonological processes affecting these vowels, including those that result in long or nasalized vowels, and propose ordered rules for the processes. We will also place this vowel system in the context of the vowel systems in other South Semitic languages.

Keywords: Jibbali, Mehri, phonology, vowels, reconstruction

1. Introduction

Jibbali, or Shehri, is spoken in the Dhofar Mountains of southern Oman. The number of speakers was given as 25,000 in the 1993 census (Lewis 2009). It is classified in the *Ethnologue* (2009) as Afroasiatic: Semitic: South: South Arabian (Fig. 1).

The main studies to date are a reference grammar (Rubin 2014), a Jibbali lexicon (Johnstone 1981a), a study of Jibbali syntax (Hofstede 1998), and papers on a variety of topics (Johnstone 1980; Hayward, Hayward & Al-Tabūki 1988; Testen 1992). Of these, only Rubin and Hayward, Hayward and Al-Tabūki address questions about the interpretation of vowels.

1.1. Methodology

This paper will present an analysis of the vowel system, describing the underlying vowel phonemes and the processes that lead to the wide range of phonetic vowels in the language. The data is taken from Johnstone's lexicon (1981a). While this is not an ideal method of studying a language, the consistency of the data gives confidence for its reliability. Where the data appears inconsistent, no conclusions are drawn.

Standard methods of studying vowels, such as looking for pairs of lexemes that show contrast or conditioning, are not suitable for Jibbali, due to the complexity of the processes involved and the large degree of overlap in the

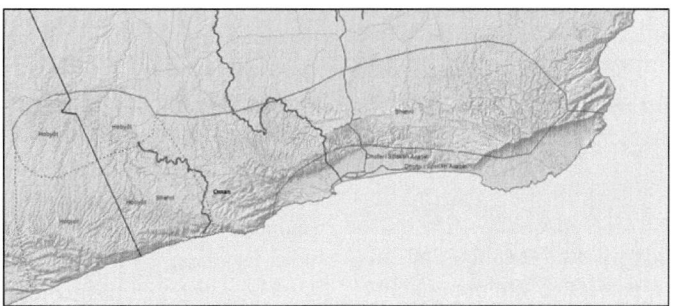

FIGURE 1. *The Jibbali language area (Lewis 2009).*

realizations of the different phonemes. The methodology used here is based on the verb forms. Firstly, the underlying vocalization pattern for a particular verb form is determined. Secondly, the root consonants are determined for the different verbs, by comparing different verb forms. Thirdly, the variant vocalization patterns are investigated to determine the causes of the variations. Finally, the vowels in the data from nouns and other lexical categories are inspected to see if the surface forms conform to the rules established for verbs.

1.2. Vowel terminology

In this paper we shall distinguish four different categories of vowel. Firstly there are 'intrusive' vowels — non-phonemic vowels that are inserted at a phonetic level in order to make a word pronounceable. Secondly there are the 'reduced' vowels — vowels that are affected by a number of phonological processes, including deletion, and have a large variety of overlapping realizations. These vowels are the equivalent of the short vowels in Mehri. Thirdly there are the 'full' vowels — vowels with largely stable realizations. These are equivalent to the long vowels in Mehri. Finally there are the 'long' vowels — the vowels in Jibbali with phonetic length.

The term 'intrusive' is used following Hall (2006), and it distinguishes these vowels from the reduced vowel /ə/. While the intrusive vowels may have the same phonetic value as /ə/, they do not constitute phonological units. /ə/ is a phonological unit and could be analysed as an epenthetic vowel according to Hall's definition.

The distinction between reduced and full vowels reflects a general distinction in the other South Arabian languages between short and long vowels. The short vowels commonly have a wider range of realizations than the long vowels, and the realizations overlap. In Jibbali there is no distinction in phonetic length between reduced and full vowels, but the pattern of realizations follows that of the short vowels in other South Arabian languages. The distinction between reduced and full vowels is kept in this analysis in order to make clear the relationship between the Jibbali vowel system and the other South Arabian vowel systems.

1.3. Verb forms

In the data, the verb forms that are cited are almost all 3ms. There are two main aspects, perfective and imperfective, with the imperfective 3ms being marked by a prefix /j-/. Also marked with a prefix /j-/ is the subjunctive form. The verb stems cited in this paper are denoted as G-stem, C-stem, T-stem, and L-stem. These correspond to Johnstone's simple, causative, reflexive and intensive-conative stem types. The unmarked vocalization patterns for some of the different verb forms for three-consonant verbs are as follows:

(1)   G-stem perfective   CeCəC, CɔCɔC
         G-stem imperfective   jCeCəC, jCɔCəC
         G-stem subjunctive   jɔCCəC, jəCCɔC
         C-stem perfective   eCCeC
         C-stem imperfective   jCeCəC, jCɔCəC
         C-stem subjunctive   jɛCCəC
         L-stem perfective   eCoCəC
         T-stem perfective   CɔtCəC, əCteCeC
         T-stem imperfective   jəCteCəC, jəCteCeC
         T-stem subjunctive   jəCtɔCəC, jəCteCəC

2. Overview

The vowel system of Jibbali consists of six vowels (Fig. 2). There are four 'full' vowels: /i/, /ɛ/, /ɔ/, /o/, and two 'reduced' vowels /e/ and /ə/. Surprisingly, there is no */a/. The full vowels are largely stable, but the two reduced vowels have a wide range of surface forms. The vowel system is represented schematically as follows:

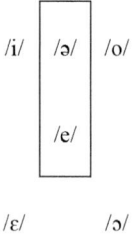

FIGURE 2. *Jibbali vowel phonemes.*

These six vowels are affected by local conditioning, raising processes, vowel harmony, and lengthening and nasalization processes due to the deletion of certain consonants. The result is a surface system of eight vowels [i], [e], [ɛ], [a], [ɔ], [o], [u], and [ə], most of which have corresponding long and nasalized forms. The total phonetic vowel inventory covers around twenty-two vowel sounds.

The consonant phonemes (Fig. 3), the study of which falls outside the scope of this paper, are provisionally as follows:

	Labial	Interdental	Alveolar	Grooved Alveolar	Labialized Alveolar	Palatal	Velar	Uvular	Glottal
Voiceless plosive			t				k		π
Voiced plosive	b		d				g		
Emphatic plosive			t'				k'		
Voiceless fricative	f	ẓ	τ	s	sʷ	ï	x	ħ	h
Voiced fricative		ð	ɮ	z	zʷ		ŕ	ρ	
Emphatic fricative		ðˤ	τ'	s'	s'ʷ				
Nasal	m		n						
Approximant	w		r, l			j			

FIGURE 3. *Jibbali consonant phonemes.*

3. Conditioning, raising, and vowel harmony

In this section we shall look at each of the six vowel phonemes and describe some of the processes that affect them. The processes are of three types. Firstly there are conditioning processes, where the quality of a vowel is affected by an adjacent consonant. The consonants that are most relevant here are the back fricatives /x/, /ɣ/, /ħ/, and /ʕ/. Secondly there are raising processes, where certain vowels are raised by nasals and approximants. Thirdly there are vowel harmony processes, where back-rounding can spread through a back fricative consonant or /h/ right-to-left to affect one other vowel.

3.1. Full vowels

The four full vowels /i/, /ɛ/, /ɔ/, and /o/ are largely stable. There are few environments where they take a different realization.

3.1.1. /i/

There are no known environments where /i/ is affected by any of these processes.

3.1.2. /ɛ/

The vowel /ɛ/ is largely stable. There is only one known environment where conditioning takes place: /ɛ/→ [a]/ j_ʕ.

The 3ms subjunctive of C-stem verbs has the form jɛCCəC, as exemplified by the first three items in (2) below. The last three items have /ʕ/ as C1, and the /ɛ/ is realized as [a].

(2) to return from town up the mountain kbr jɛkbər
    to take food off the fire   xtr jɛxtər
    to escape   flt jɛflət
    to repair   ʕbl jaʕbəl
    to kindle   ʕlk' jaʕlək'
    to sacrifice   ʕtk' jaʕtək'

3.1.3. /ɔ/

The vowel /ɔ/ is also largely stable. It is raised, however, when it is adjacent to a nasal consonant. The resultant surface form varies between [o] and [u]. In addition, a final nasal consonant causes the raising of /ɔ/ even when the vowel is not adjacent to the nasal.

The 3ms perfective of one class of G-stem verbs has the form CɔCɔC. Again, the first three items in (3) below show the unmarked case. The next two items show the raising of /ɔ/ by an adjacent nasal. The final two items show the raising of /ɔ/ whether the nasal is adjacent or not.

(3) to leave something   bðl bɔðɔl
    to be hunch-backed   ħdb hɔdɔb

	to mince	xs´l	xɔs´ɔl
	to be rotten	mzr	mozɔr
	to taste	fnk´	fonuk´
	to bury	dfn	dufun
	to be grim-faced	zrm	zorum

The 3ms perfective of T-stem verbs also shows the raising of /ɔ/→[u] when the last consonant is /j/. The unmarked form of the verb is CɔtCəC.

(4)	to collect together	gbj	gutbi
	to be delirious	hðj	hutði
	to have enough	kfj	kutfi
	to be skinned	ɬrj	ɬutri

3.1.4. /o/

The vowel /o/ may be realized as [u] or [o]. When there is an adjacent nasal, the realization is always [u] due to raising. The form given is the 3ms L-stem eCoCəC.

(5)	to spoil	fsd	efusəd
	to look down	dhg	edohəg
	to undo	nkɬ	enukəɬ

In other environments, the vowel is stable.

3.2. Reduced vowels

In contrast to the stability of the full vowels, the two reduced vowels give rise to many different surface forms. In many environments the contrast between the two vowels are neutralized.

3.2.1. /e/

The vowel /e/ is lowered to [ɛ] before /h/, and to [a] before the back fricatives /x/, /ɣ/, /ħ/, /ʕ/. The 3ms perfective form for C-stem verbs is eCCeC.

(6)	to make kneel	brk	ebrek
	to make someone disgusted	ɬxl	eɬxel
	to squander	hdr	ɛhder
	to insult	sfh	esfɛh
	to put someone in a dangerous position	hlk	ɛhlek
	to make bad	xbž	axbež
	to leave food to burn	hlk´	aħlek´
	to dye	sbɣ	esbaɣ
	to make greedy	t´mʕ	et´maʕ

The vowel /e/ is raised to [i] following a nasal. The unmarked 3ms perfective form of one class of G-stem verbs is CeCəC.

(7)	to be abundant	kžr	kežər
	to chew	k´ɬ´b	k´eɬ´əb
	to be like someone	mžl	mižəl
	to be finished	nɬk´	niɬək´

Preceding a nasal there is no change, unless the nasal is the final consonant. The 3ms perfective form for C-stem verbs eCCeC illustrates this.

(8)	to blow on a fire	dfr	edfer
	to make a stone wall	gdr	egder
	to turn aside	mjl	emjel
	to cut down	nfl	enfel
	to spoil	dmr	edmir
	to have pleurisy	gnb	egnib
	to get plump	bdn	ebdin
	to keep someone quiet	zgm	ezgim

When /e/ is followed by a back fricative (or /h/) then a back vowel, /e/ harmonizes with the back vowel. The form of the L-stem 3ms perfective is eCoCəC. If C1 is a back fricative or /h/, the initial /e/ is realized as [o]. If /o/ is raised to [u] by an adjacent nasal, /e/ remains as [o].

(9)	to turn around	hdr	ohodər
	to trip someone	ɣfg	oɣofəg
	to rip	xdk´	oxodək´
	to have problems	ʕðʕl	oʕoðʕəl
	to ponder	hgs	ohogəs
	to feel drowsy	hnd	ohund

The 3ms imperfective C-stem form jCeCəC shows /e/ harmonizing to [ɔ] if C2 is a back fricative or /h/. Where /ɔ/ is raised to [u] by a final nasal, the /e/ is realized as [o]. If the /e/ is itself adjacent to a nasal, the result is [u].

(10)	to lean on	dhr	jdɔhɔr
	to put down	gʕr	jgɔʕɔr
	to foreswear	dxl	jdɔxɔl
	to have bad breath and flatulence	dxm	idoxum
	to give people a little food	t´ʕm	it´oʕum
	to anger one's wife	nɣm	jnuɣum

3.2.2. /ə/

The vowel /ə/ undergoes some, but not all, of the same conditioning processes as /e/.

Before /ʔ/, /ə/ is realized as [e] or [ɛ]. In the following

table the 3ms perfective G-stem form CeCəC is given.

(11) to begin   bdʔ   bedeʔ
     to push animals into a pen hlʔ   heleʔ
     to become rusty   dsʔ   desɛʔ

Before /h/, /ə/ is realized as [ɛ]. The data cited is the 3ms perfective T-stem, which has the form əCteCeC.

(12) to be destroyed   hdm   ɛhtedim
     to ponder   hgs   ɛhteges
     to try to avoid   hrb   ɛhtereb

The vowel /ə/ is realized as [a] adjacent to a back fricative. Note that /e/ is only conditioned by a following back fricative, but /ə/ is conditioned by both preceding and following back fricatives. The 3ms perfective G-stem CeCəC is given.

(13) to swallow   blʕ   belaʕ
     to embarrass   fɬˤh   feɬˤah
     to sprout   bɣl   baɣal
     to have a pain sxb   saxab

/ə/ is deleted between identical consonants, or between certain consonant sequences, where the first is one of /r/, /l/, /s/, /f/. The 3ms perfective G-stem CeCəC is given.

(14) to tie tightly   sʷtʼtʼ   sʷetʼtʼ
     to run swiftly   bðð   beðð
     to dream   hlm   helm
     to wait   slb   selb
     to produce fruit xrf   xerf

The vowel /ə/ is not affected by any raising processes. It may also be unaffected by vowel harmony, although there are occasional instances of sporadic harmonization. In the 3ms L-stem perfective, with unmarked form eCoCəC, the final /ə/ is sometimes realized as [u].

(15) to shiver   rgf   erogəf
     to be brave rfd   erofud

3.2.3. Comparison of /e/ and /ə/

There is considerable overlap in the realizations of /e/ and /ə/ (Fig. 4). In particular, before back consonants both are lowered to [ɛ] or [a]. In most environments, however, there is a clear contrast between the two phonemes.

It is worth highlighting some of the differences in behaviour.

- /ə/ is not affected by an adjacent nasal, whereas /e/ is raised to [i].
- /e/ is never deleted, whereas /ə/ is deleted in certain environments.
- /e/ harmonizes with back vowels in the environment _XO, where X is a back fricative or /h/ and O is a back vowel. It has not been possible to find verb forms where /ə/ can be tested to see if it also harmonizes systematically.

Environment	/e/	/ə/
Before /h/, /ʔ/	ɛ	ɛ
Adjacent to back fricative	a	a
Following a nasal	i	ə
Between identical consonants	e	zero
Between some C_C#	e	zero
_Xo	o	?
_Xɔ	ɔ	?

FIGURE 4. *A comparison of /e/ and /ə/.*

3.2.4. Is /ə/ epenthetic?

There are some occasions where [ə] has been inserted to break up awkward CC clusters. For example, in 3ms T-stem forms the default pattern is əCteCeC. If C1 is /kʼ/, however, a [ə] is inserted.

(16) to escape   blsʼ   əbtelesʼ
     to be detached   ndr   ənteder
     to dare   kʼdr   əkʼəteder
     to go thin (hair) kʼrɬʼ   əkʼəterɬʼ

These examples show that [ə] can be epenthetic or at least exist as a phonetic intrusive vowel. The initial [ə] in the last two items, however, cannot be epenthetic in the same way since forms such as [*kʼəteder] are allowable.

Furthermore, there are numerous examples of [ə] occurring in the environment VC_CV. Again, the combinations VCCV would be allowable. In (17), an example with VCəCV is followed by an example with VCCV containing the same consonants.

(17) ball of dates   kəzərɛt
     sickly   məzrɔt

good news	bəɬərɛt	
happy at good news	bəɬrun	
noose	gədəlɛt	
plump	gədlun	

The conclusion must therefore be that /ə/ exists as a phoneme, and that the examples of deletion cited in section 3.2.2. are indeed deletion and not epenthesis.

4. Nasalization and lengthening

One of the most noticeable features of Jibbali phonology is the existence of long and nasalized vowels due to the deletion of /b/, /m/, /w/, and /j/. These consonants are always deleted inter-vocalically, and /w/ and /j/ are also deleted in word-initial and word-final positions.

In intervocalic position, /b/, /w/, and /j/ often, but not always, behave in the same manner, producing identical surface forms. Where one of the two vowels is stressed and the other is not, it is the stressed vowel that gives the surface form of the resultant vowel.

The phoneme /w/ is particularly interesting. It has two primary allophones, adjacent to a consonant and [j] elsewhere. /w/ is never realized as [w], and this sound only exists in Jibbali in loanwords. In spite of this, it is necessary to include /w/ as a phoneme in order to explain the surface forms of the different forms of verbs with /w/ as one of their root consonants.

4.1. /m/

As we have already seen, the phoneme /m/, along with /n/, causes adjacent /ɔ/ to be raised to [o]~[u] and a following /e/ to be raised to [i]. In addition, when /m/ is in intervocalic position, it combines with the adjacent vowels, resulting in the creation of a single nasalized vowel. The raising process takes place before /m/ is deleted.

The sequence /emo/ results in either [õ] or [ũ]. The data given is for 3ms L-stem perfective, with the unmarked form eCoCəC. When C1 is /m/, the nasalized vowel is created.

(18)	to send	mtl	emotəl→õtəl
	to rinse the mouth with water	mgʕ	emogəʕ→õgəʕ
	to put gravy on food	mrk´	emorək´→õrək´
	to chat	mžl	emožəl→ũžəl

When C2 is /m/ the same verb form shows the sequence /omə/ resulting in [õ] or [ũ].

(19)	to put one's hand into food	dms	edoməs→edũs
	to finish	kml	ekoməl→ekũl
	to keep bumping into something	s´md	es´oməd→es´õd
	to make someone win	k´mr	ek´omər→ek´õr

The sequence /ɔmə/ results in [ũ]. Note that /ɔ/ is raised to [o] or [u] adjacent to a nasal (see section 3.1.3.). The form cited is 3ms imperfective with unmarked form jCɔCəC.

(20)	to guide	ðmr	jðũr
	to keep someone quiet	kmh	jkũh
	to become fat	ʃmn	jʃũn

The sequence /ɔmɔ/ also results in [õ] or [ũ]. The data given is for 3ms perfective G-stem form of type CɔCɔC.

(21)	to guide	ðmr	jðũr
	to be finished	kml	kõl
	to roll in ashes	rmd	rõd
	to prosper	žmr	žõr

The 3ms perfective G-stem form of type CeCəC shows that the sequence /emə/ results in [ĩ].

(22)	to be destroyed	dmr	dĩr
	to become solid	gmd	gĩd
	to begin turning into butter	hmɬ´	hĩɬ´

The sequence /eme/ also results in [ĩ]. The data is for 3ms perfective T-stem verbs, with underlying form əCteCeC.

(23)	to do a favour	gml	əgtĩl
	to become fat	ʃmn	əʃtĩn
	to be fit and prosperous	zmn	əztĩn

The sequence /əme/ results in [ẽ]. The data given is the 3ms imperfective, jəCeCɔC.

(24)	to give a husband possession of a wife	mlk	jẽlɔk
	to be ill	mrɬ´	jẽrəɬ´

The sequence /əmɛ/ results in [ɛ̃]. The data is from four-consonant 3ms subjunctive forms, with the pattern jəCɛCCəC.

(25)	to clear up	mrk´h	jɛ̃rk´ah
	to welcome (Ar.)	mrhb	jɛ̃rhəb

The sequence /emɔ/ results in [jũ]. The form given is 3ms imperfective, jCeCɔC.

(26)	to ripen	žmr	jžjũr
	to dip (bread in gravy)	dms	jdjũs
	to become solid	gmd	jgjũd

4.2. /b/

When /b/ occurs inter-vocalically it is deleted, and the adjacent vowels combine, resulting in a long vowel.

The sequence /ebo/ results in [oː]. The form given is the 3ms perfective L-stem, eCoCəC.

(27) to change   bdl   oːdəl
     to give good news bɫr   oːɫər
     to make grieve   bxs   oːxəs

Similarly, the same verb form shows that the sequence /obə/ results in [oː].

(28) to finish   kˈbɫˈ   ekˈoːɫˈ
     to dress   lbs   eloːs
     to grumble zbd   ezoːd

The sequence /ɔbə/ results in [ɔː]. The form cited is 3ms perfective T-stem, əCtɔCəC.

(29) to become blunt   gbh   əgtɔːh
     to do things in an odd way   rbʕ   ərtɔːʕ
     to look alike   ɫbh   əɫtɔːh

The sequence /ɔbɔ/ results in [ɔː]. The form cited is 3ms perfective G-stem of type CɔCɔC.

(30) to collect honey   dbʃ   dɔːʃ
     to sew together   hbk   hɔːk
     to come back at night   kˈbr kˈɔːr
     to dig up   nbž   nɔːž

The sequence /ebə/ results in [eː]. The form cited is 3ms perfective G-stem of type CeCəC.

(31) to step   ɫbðˤ   ɫeːðˤ
     to accept   kˈbl   kˈeːl
     to be thirsty xbt   xeːt
     to be cowardly gbn   giːn

The sequence /ebe/ results in [eː]. The form cited is 3ms perfective T-stem, əCteCeC.

(32) to panic   kbl   əkteːl
     to get bigger (wound) sbb   əsteːb
     to hang on to   ɫbž   əɫteːž
     to be healthy   zbn   əztiːn

The sequence /əbe/ results in [eː]. The form cited is 3ms imperfective, jəCeCɔC.

(33) to make kneel   brk   jeːrɔk
     to see well   bsˈr   jeːsˈɔr
     to be emptied (pimple) bzg   jeːzɔg

The same verb form shows that the sequence /ebɔ/ results in [jɔ].

(34) to get cold   hbr   jhjɔr
     to become cold   ɫˈbl   jɫˈjɔl
     to be given a liability tˈbkˈ jtˈjɔkˈ

The passive G-stem shows that the sequence /ibi/ results in [iː].

(35) to be hung   ɫnkˈ   ɫinikˈ
     to be sent away   tˈrd   tˈirid
     to be passed   sbkˈ   siːkˈ
     to have patience   sˈbr   sˈiːr

4.3. /j/

The phoneme /j/ is deleted in word initial position before /e/. The form cited is the 3ms perfective G-stem, CeCəC.

(36) to become an orphan   jtm   etəm

/j/ is retained, however, before /ə/. The form cited is the 3ms imperfective of T-stem verbs, with form jəCteCəC.

(37) to burst, split   fgr   jəftegər
     to chat   klž   jəkteləž

The sequence /ejo/ results in [oː]. The form given is the 3ms perfective L-stem, eCoCəC.

(38) to become an orphan   jtm   oːtəm

Similarly, the sequence /ojə/ results in [oː].

(39) to flatter   zjg   ezoːg
     to redeem   xjž   oxoːž

The sequence /ɔjə/ results in [ɔː]. The form cited is 3ms imperfective G-stem, jCɔCəC.

(40) to melt   ðjb   jðɔːb
     to win   fjz   jfɔːz
     to give a measure kjl   jkɔːl

The sequence /ejə/ results in [ɛː]. The form cited is 3ms perfective, simple form, CeCəC.

(41) to melt   ðjb   ðɛːb
     to be of benefit fjd   fɛːd
     to be fed up   ɫˈjk' ɫˈɛːkˈ

The sequence /eje/ results in [eː]. The form cited is 3ms perfective, T-stem verbs, əCteCeC.

(42)	to gain an advantage	fjd	əfte:d	
	to feel flattered	zjg	əzte:g	
	to be disappointed	xjb	axte:b	
	to have a debt	djn	ədti:n	(raised by the following /n/)

The sequence /ejɔ/ results in [jɔ]. The form cited is 3ms imperfective, jCeCɔC.

| (43) | to melt | ðjb | iðjɔb |
| | to change | ɣjr | jɣjɔr |

In word-final position we have /ej/→e and /əj/→i. The form cited for the first case is the 3ms perfective C-stem form, eCCeC.

(44)	to cause to weep	bkj	ebke	
	to collect	gbj	egbe	
	to amuse	slj	esle	
	to make pregnant	dnj	edni	(with /e/ raised by /n/)

For /əj/→i we use the 3ms perfective of T-stem verbs, CətCəC. Note that the presence of a final /j/ causes the /ə/ to be raised to [u].

(45)	to collect together	gbj	gutbi
	to come loose	rxj	rutxi
	to be irrigated	ʃkʼj	ʃutkʼi

The 3ms perfective passive of H-stem verbs has the form eCCiC. From this we can see that the sequence /ij/ results in [i].

(46)	to be lost (animal)	ɬrh	eɬrih
	to be acceptable	rɬʼj	ɛrɬʼi
	to be able to climb easily	lfj	ɛlfi

4.4. /w/

The phoneme /w/ follows the realizations of /b/ adjacent to a consonant and the realizations of /j/ elsewhere. It is never realized as [w]. As the following data shows, however, it is necessary to include /w/ as a phoneme, since /b/ exhibits different behaviour.

(47)	/wgh/	G-stem	/wegəh/	[egah]	'he entered'
		C-stem	/ewgeh/	[ebgah]	'he inserted'
	/bʃl/	G-stem	/beʃəl/	[beʃəl]	'it is cooked'
		C-stem	/ebʃel/	[ebʃel]	'he cooked'

/w/ is lost in word initial position before /e/. The form cited is the 3ms perfective G-stem, CeCəC.

(48)	to be suitable	wfkʼ	efəkʼ
	to give resin	wgs	egəs
	to be fed up	wɬh	eɬʼah

The same applies before /ɔ/ and /o/.

(49)	to become a duty	wgb	/wɔtgəb/	ɔtgəb
	to be startled	wkd	/wɔtkəd/	ɔtkəd
	to move aside	wzj	/wɔtzəj/→wutzi	utzi
	to be pestered	wðj	/wɔtðəj/→wutði	utði

The sequence /ewo/ results in [o:]. The form given is the 3ms perfective L-stem, eCoCəC.

(50)	to look for something	wfd	o:fəd
	to have prominent cheekbones	wgn	o:gən
	to chew the cud	wlkʼ	o:ləkʼ

Similarly, the sequence /owə/ results in [o:]. The same verb form is used.

(51)	to fan someone	rwh	ero:h
	to provision	zwd	ezo:d
	to have many calves	nwtʼ	eno:tʼ

The sequence /ɔwə/ results in [ɔ:]. The form cited is 3ms imperfective, jCɔCəC.

(52)	to be finished	gwz	jgɔ:z
	to be distant	ʕwr	jʕɔ:r
	to turn a corner	lwtʼ	ilɔ:tʼ

The sequence /ewə/ results in [ɛ:]. The form cited is 3ms perfective G-stem, CeCəC.

(53)	to wander around	dwr	dɛ:r
	to blame	lwm	lɛ:m
	to repeat	twb	tɛ:b

The sequence /ewe/ results in [e:]. The form cited is 3ms perfective T-stem, əCteCeC.

| (54) | to get provisions | zwd | əzte:d |
| | to move aside | xwz | axte:z |

The sequence /ewɔ/ results in [e]. The form cited is 3ms imperfective, jCeCɔC.

(55)	to take by force	hwɬ	jheɬ
	to clean one's teeth	ɬwsʼ	jɬesʼ
	to visit (a sick person)	tʼwf	jtʼef

In word-final position we have /ew/→e and /ɔw/→i. The form cited for the first case is the 3ms perfective C-stem, eCCeC.

(56) to give lunch   fɬw   efɬe
      to be in winter   ɬtw   eɬte
      to postpone   rgw   erge
      to encourage   zhw   ezhe

For /əw/→[i] we use the 3ms perfective of T-stem verbs, CɔtCəC. Note that the presence of a final /w/ causes the /ɔ/ to be raised to [u]; this is the same behaviour noted for verbs with final /j/. It is worth noting that the changes described here only make phonological sense if /w/ first becomes realized as /j/ before the deletion and lengthening processes take place.

(57) to be stitched   ɬfw   ɬutfi
      to wait   rgw   rutgi
      to be loose   ʃxw   ʃutxi

We also have /iw/→[i], corresponding to the related process for /j/. The 3ms perfective passive of H-stem verbs has the form eCCiC.

(58) to spoil (a child) rɣd   erɣid
      to throw   rdw   ɛrdi

4.5. Summary

The consonants /w/ and /j/ are only retained adjacent to a consonant, albeit with /w/ having the realization /b/. In almost all other cases, the behaviour of /j/ is identical to /w/, implying that /w/ is realized as /j/ in all environments where it is not realized as /b/. /b/ and /m/ are only lost inter-vocalically.

Figure 5 gives a summary of the nasalization and lengthening processes that are known. For a full description we need to be able to give the surface form for each of the thirty-six possible combinations of preceding and following vowels, not to mention the initial and final cases involving /w/ and /j/, and the different possibilities for the placement of stress. So far the data only covers around ten of these combinations.

5. Finding the underlying form

From the rules that we have looked at, given the underlying form we can determine what the surface form will be, but we need to be able to determine the underlying form of a word based on the surface form. In this section we will take each surface vowel and give the different phonemes and environments that can lead to each phonetic form.

	/b/	/w/	/j/	/m/
#_e	#be→be	#we→e	#je→e	#me→mi
#_ə			#jə→jə	
e_o	ebo→o:	ewo→o:	ejo→o:	emo→õ
e_ə	ebə→e:	ewə→ɛ:	ejə→ɛ:	emə→ĩ
o_ə	obə→o:	owə→o:	ojə→o:	omə→ũ
ɔ_o	ɔbo→ɔ:	ɔwo→ɔ:, ɔ		ɔmo→ũ
ɔ_ə	ɔbə→ɔ:		ɔjə→ɔ:	ɔmə→jũ
e_e	ebe→e:	ewe→e:	eje→e:	eme→ĩ
ə_e	əbe→e:	əwe→e		əme→ẽ
ə_ɔ	əbɔ→ɔ:	əwɔ→ɔ:		
ə_ɛ				əmɛ→ɛ̃
e_ɔ	ebɔ→jɔ	ewɔ→e	ejɔ→jɔ	emɔ→jũ
i_i	ibi→i:			
e_#		ew#→e	ej#→e	
ə_#		əw#→i	əj#→i	
i_#		iw#→i	ij#→i	

FIGURE 5. A *summary of nasalization and lengthening processes.*

5.1. Short vowels

[i]	/i/	All environments
	/e/	Following a nasal
	/əj/	əj→i/_#
	/əw/	əw→i/_#
[e]	/e/	Unmarked cases
	/ə/	Before /ʔ/
	/je/	je→[e]/#_
	/ej/	ej→[e]/_#
	/we/	we→[e]/#_
	/ew/	ew→[e]/_#
	/ewɔ/	
	/ejɔ/	
[ɛ]	/ɛ/	Unmarked cases
	/e/	Before /h/
	/ə/	Before /h/
	/ə/	Before /ʔ/
[a]	/ɛ/	j_ʕ
	/e/	Before back fricatives
	/ə/	Adjacent to back fricatives
[ɔ]	/ɔ/	Unmarked cases
	/e/	_Xɔ (and no adjacent nasals)
	/ebɔ/	The surface form is [jɔ]
	/ejɔ/	The surface form is [jɔ]
	/wɔ/	wɔ→ɔ/#_
[o]~[u]	/o/	All environments
	/ɔ/	Adjacent to a nasal
	/ɔ/	When final C is /j/
	/e/	_Xo
	/wɔ/	Word initial, when final C is /j/
[ə]	/ə/	Unmarked cases
	zero	Intrusive vowel

5.2. Long vowels

Long vowels result from the loss of /b/, /w/, or /j/ when occurring inter-vocalically. With six underlying vowels, this gives thirty-six possible sequences for each consonant that would result in a long vowel. When looking at long vowels in verb forms, it was only possible to find data to cover at most ten of these cases. Almost all the cases had either /e/ or /ə/ as one of the two vowels and the vowels /ɛ/ and /i/ barely feature. This leaves a large number of holes to be filled before the analysis of long vowels in Jibbali is complete.

In many cases it is possible to determine the underlying consonant from another form of the word. For the surrounding vowels, there are often different combinations that result in the same surface form. In these cases, the underlying vowels can only be deduced if the underlying vowel pattern is known from the grammar.

The following tables give the environments that can result in each of the long vowel sounds.

[i:]	[e:] next to a nasal
[e:]	/ebə/
	/ebe/
	/əbe/
	/eje/
	/ewe/
[ɛ:]	/ejə/
	/ewə/
[a:]	[e:] next to a back fricative
[ɔ:]	/ɔbə/
	/ɔbɔ/
	/ɔjə/
	/ɔwə/
	/ɔwɔ/
[o:]	/ebo/
	/obə/
	/ejo/
	/ojə/
	/ewo/
	/owə/
[u:]	[o:] next to a nasal

5.3. Nasalized vowels

The nasalized vowels result from the loss of /m/ in intervocalic position. The following tables give the environments for each of the phonetic nasalized vowels so far attested.

[ĩ]	/emə/
	/eme/
[ẽ]	/əme/
[ɛ̃]	/əmɛ/
[ã]	Found occasionally where a nasal vowel occurs next to a back fricative
[õ]	/emo/
[ũ]	/omə/
	/ɔmə/

/ɔmə/   The surface form is [jũ]
/emɔ/   The surface form is [jũ]

6. Proving contrast

With the methodology that we have been using, we have been able to analyse the data from the verb morphology using just six underlying vowels. This methodology, however, does not enable us properly to establish that these six vowels are contrastive or to eliminate the existence of other vowel phonemes. To do that, we need to examine other word categories.

6.1. Contrast

6.1.1. /i/

(59) /i/-/ɛ/ hit   'you (fs)'   hɛt   'you (ms)'
     /i/-/ɔ/ hadid 'iron'   ħadɔd 'blacksmith'
     /i/-/o/ ɬikˈi 'troublesome'   eɬ:okˈi 'to do something tiring'

6.1.2. /ɛ/

(60) /ɛ/-/ɔ/ kfɛs 'asthma' kfɔs 'to give someone limited freedom'
     /ɛ/-/o/ tˈɛl 'dew'   tˈol 'length'

6.1.3. /ɔ/

(61) /ɔ/-/o/ tfɔl 'to spit' tfol 'spit (noun)'

6.1.4. /o/

The contrasts with /i/, /ɛ/, and /ɔ/ have already been established, but it is necessary to show that there is no contrast between [o] and [u].

In some environments [u] and [o] are in free variation and are not contrastive. Some L-stem verbs have [u] in place of [o], without a conditioning environment.

(62) ekofəl 'to guarantee'   ekuɬ   'to hurry someone up'
     eɬ:ors 'to have long hooves'   eɬ:urk 'to share with someone'
     efols   'to split'   efult 'to get something away'

Other occurrences of [u] are due to raising processes, either by nasals or final /j/ (see sections 3.1.3. and 3.1.4.).

7. Rule ordering

There are several phonological processes that take place in Jibbali. In this section we will look at the order in which the processes take place in the derivation of the surface forms from the underlying forms.

The order of the processes is as follows:

- Application of vowel melody from the grammar
- Schwa deletion; nasal raising
- Vowel harmony; nasalization and lengthening
- Back consonant conditioning
- Final /j/ raising
- Intrusive schwa

7.1. Schwa deletion before lengthening and nasalization

Schwa deletion takes place before the lengthening and nasalization processes.

(63) /sbb/ 'to insult' sebəb→seb: 'he insulted' not *se:b
     /smm/ 'to poison' seməm→sem:→sim: 'he poisoned' not *se:m→si:m

It is not possible to determine whether schwa deletion takes place before or after nasal raising.

(64) /smm/ 'to poison' seməm→sem:→sim: or seməm→siməm→sim: 'he poisoned'

7.2. Nasal raising before lengthening and nasalization

Nasal consonants cause adjacent vowels (except /ə/) to be raised. This process takes place before the nasalization and lengthening processes.

(65) /kmh/ 'to keep someone quiet' kemə h→kimə h→kĩh 'he kept s.o. quiet' *kemə h→kẽh
     /dmr/ 'to be destroyed'   demər→dimər→dĩr   'he was destroyed'   *dwemər→dẽr

7.3. Vowel harmony before back consonant conditioning

Vowel harmony precedes conditioning by back fricatives. In the L-stem forms with pattern eCoCəC, if C1 is a back fricative then we would expect the initial /e/ to be conditioned by the back fricative and lowered to [a]. With a back vowel following the back fricative, however, we also expect the /e/ to harmonize to [o]. In the data, it is the vowel harmony process that takes place, showing that it precedes the process of conditioning by the back fricative.

(66) /ħsn/ 'to shave'   eħosən   'he shaved' *eħosən
                        →oħosən   →aħosən
     /xzr/ 'to make   exozər   'he made   *exozər
           butter'   →oxozər   butter'   →axozər

7.4. Nasalization, lengthening, and vowel harmony

The data does not permit us to determine whether nasalization and lengthening processes precede or follow the vowel harmony processes. In the L-stem 3ms perfective the vocalization pattern is eCoCəC. When C1 is a back fricative, the initial /e/ harmonizes to [o] due to the presence of a back vowel following the back fricative. When C2 is one of /b/, /m/, /w/, and /j/, then the sequence /oCə/ becomes [o:] or [õ]. Whether the nasalization or lengthening process has already taken place, there will always be a back vowel present to trigger the vowel harmony.

(67) /ħms/ 'to grind   eħoməs   eħoməs   'he ground'
           (coffee)'   →eħõs   →oħoməs
                       →oħõs   →oħõs
     /ʕbl/ 'to tend   eʕobəl   eʕobəl   'he tended'
           (animal)'   →eʕo:l   →oʕobəl
                       →oʕo:l   →oʕo:l

7.5. Lengthening before back fricative conditioning

In the following data (68) we have the 3ms G-stem forms of the type CeCəC. Item a. shows the unmarked form, and b. shows the form which results from lengthening when C2 is /b/. Item c. shows the lowering of /ə/ to by the following back fricative. Item d. shows the situation when there is lengthening and a final back fricative. There is no change in vowel quality from b., implying that the lowering process has been bled by the lengthening process.

(68) a. to itch   ðrf   ðerəf
     b. to be   žbr   žebər
        broken   →že:r
     c. to twist   ʃlh   ʃeləh
                               →ʃelah

     d. to be   ɬbʕ   ɬebəʕ   (not *ɬebəh
        satisfied   →ɬe:ʕ   →ɬebah→ɬe:h)
     e. to be red   mrt   merət
        hot   →mirət
     f. to succeed   ngh   negəh
                               →nigəh
                               →nigah
     g. to bark   nbh   nebəh   (not *nebəh
                               →nibəh   →nibah
                               →ni:h   →nibah→ni:h)

Item e. shows the raising effect of an initial nasal, and item f. combines this with a final back fricative. In item g., where the second consonant is /b/, the result of the lengthening process is [i:]. This is more naturally the result of the process applying to /ibə/ than to /iba/, implying again that the lowering process has been bled by the lengthening process.

The conclusion is that the lengthening process precedes back fricative lowering.

7.6. Final /j/ raising

When /j/ or /w/ occurs as the final consonant, preceded by /ə/, the result is [i]. In this environment, a /ə/ earlier in the word is raised to [u]. If the penultimate consonant is a back fricative, however, this can lower /ə/ to [a], taking away the environment. In the majority of the data, the /əj#/→[i] process takes precedence over the back fricative lowering, as in the third item below, but there are two examples — the fourth and fifth items — where the back fricative lowering can take place before the /j/ loss process.

(69) to collect together   gbj   /gətbəj/   [gutbi]
     to be stitched   ɬfw   /ɬətfəj/   [lutfi]
     to come loose   rxj   /rətxəj/   [rutxi]
     to go to pasture   rʕw   /rətʕəj/   [rutʕi]~[rətʕa]
     to curse one another dʕw   /dətʕəj/   [dətʕa]

This data reinforces the conclusion of the previous section that the lengthening processes, including the word-final /j/-loss process, precede the back fricative lowering process. In addition, the data shows that the final /j/ raising process must follow these processes, as the output of these processes must produce a final [i] for the raising to take place.

8. A comparative perspective

In this section we shall look at the Jibbali vowel system in relation to the vowel systems of related languages.

8.1. Modern South Arabian

The most closely related languages to Jibbali are the other Modern South Arabian languages. Of these, the best studied is Mehri (Rubin 2010; Watson 2012). Both studies describe Mehri as having six long vowels /iː/, /eː/, /aː/, /oː/, /uː/, and /ɛː/, although /ɛː/ has limited functional load. These long vowels are equivalent to the 'full' vowels in Jibbali. There are also two or three short vowels in Mehri (according to the dialect), /a/, /i/ (or /ə/) and also /u/ in Mahriyyot. These are equivalent to the 'reduced' vowels in Jibbali.

Harsusi (Johnstone 1981*b*) has a similar system to Mehri. There are five long vowels /iː/, /eː/, /aː/, /oː/, /uː/, and two short vowels /a/ and /e/.

Soqotri (Kogan & Naumkin, this volume) has a similar system to Jibbali, although it is analysed with only one reduced vowel, with allophones conditioned by stress.

There is a common system of five long or 'full' vowels and two short or 'reduced' vowels, although in some languages the full vowel /a/ has been lost. The phonetic forms of the two 'reduced' vowels are varied, both from one language to another and within an individual language.

8.2. South Semitic

The Modern South Arabian languages are classified within the South Semitic branch of Semitic (Lewis 2009), alongside the Ethiopian Semitic languages.

Many of the Ethiopian Semitic languages have a system of seven vowels /i/, /e/, /a/, /o/, /u/, /ɨ/, and /ɜ/. These include Ge'ez (Bender et al. 1976), Tigrinya (1976) and Amharic (Bender & Fulass 1978). This system is comparable to the systems found in the Modern South Arabian languages. /i/, /e/, /a/, /o/, and /u/ correspond to the Modern South Arabian 'full' vowels, and /ɨ/ and /ɜ/ correspond to the two 'reduced' vowels.

Other Ethiopian Semitic languages have a different vowel system, in particular the languages referred to as Gujarge languages. This vowel system may be the result of contact with Cushitic languages (Gutt 1983).

8.3. Summary

At this point we can only speculate that there may be a common seven-vowel system within South Semitic, or that this system was inherited from an ancestor of today's South Semitic languages. Detailed reconstructions of individual lexical items are needed before this can be established.

9. Further questions

There are many further questions to be answered about Jibbali vowels and the relationship between the Jibbali system and the vowel systems of other South Semitic languages. Among these are the following:

- Why does /a/ appear to be missing in Jibbali?
- Is it possible to find correspondences between the vowels in the different Modern South Arabian languages?
- Is it possible to reconstruct the proto-Modern South Arabian vowels for individual lexical items?

Jibbali is a fascinating language, and it is hoped that future research in Jibbali will bring understanding not just to Jibbali itself, but to the Modern South Arabian languages in general.

References

Bender M.L. & Fulass H.
    1978. *Amharic verb morphology: A generative approach.* East Lansing, MI: African studies Center, Michigan State University.

Bender M.L., J.D. Bowen, R.L.Cooper & C.A. Ferguson
    1976. *Language in Ethiopia.* London: Oxford University Press.Gutt E-A.

Gutt E-A.
    1983. Studies in the phonology of Silti. *Journal of Ethiopian Studies* 16: 37–73.

Hall N.
    2006. Cross-linguistic patterns of vowel intrusion. *Phonology* 23/3: 387–429.

Hayward K.M., Hayward R.J. & Al-Tabūki S.B.
    1988. Vowels in Jibbali verbs. *Bulletin of the School of Oriental and African Studies* 51/2: 240–250.

Hofstede A.I.
    1998. Syntax of Jibbali. PhD thesis, University of Manchester. [Unpublished.]

Johnstone T.M.
    1980. The non-occurrence of a t- prefix in certain Jibbāli verbal forms. *Bulletin of the School of Oriental and African Studies* 43/03: 466–470.
    1981*a*. *Jibbāli lexicon.* London: Oxford University Press.
    1981*b*. *Harsusi lexicon and English–Harsusi word-list.* London: Oxford University Press.

Kogan L. & Naumkin V.
    (this volume). The vowels of Soqotri as a phonemic system. *Supplement to the Proceedings of the Seminar for Arabian Studies* 44.

Lewis M.P.
    2009. *Ethnologue: languagues of the world.* Dallas: SIL International.

Rubin A.
    2010. *The Mehri language of Oman.* Leiden: Brill.
    2014. *The Jibbali (Shaḥri) language of Oman.* Leiden: Brill.

Testen D.
    1992. The loss of the person-marker t- in Jibbali and Socotri. *Bulletin of the School of Oriental and African Studies* 55/03: 445–450.

Watson, J.C.E.
    2012. *The structure of Mehri.* Wiesbaden: Harrassowitz.

Author's address

Richard Gravina, 11 Hillary Close, High Wycombe, HP13 7RP, UK.

e-mail richardgravina@btinternet.com

The vowels of Soqotri as a phonemic system

LEONID KOGAN & VITALY NAUMKIN

Summary
The article is the first attempt at describing the vowels of the Modern South Arabian language Soqotri (island of Soqotra, Yemen) in strictly phonemic terms, mostly on the basis of morphologically significant vocalic oppositions in the domain of inflectional verbal morphology. Contrary to common opinion, the ensuing system is quite simple and consists of five members only.

Keywords: Modern South Arabian languages, Soqotri, phonology, vocalic phonemes, verbal morphology

1. Introduction

The aim of this article is to present the vocalic phones of Soqotri as a system of phonemic oppositions.

Our investigation has been performed in the framework of the Russian-Yemeni research project carried out since 2010.[1] In many respects, it is a by-product of the forthcoming first volume of our *Corpus of Soqotri Oral Literature*, more concretely, of its 200-page Soqotri–English–Arabic glossary. The Russian part of the team includes Vitaly Naumkin, Leonid Kogan, Maria Bulakh, and Dmitry Cherkashin. Our Soqotri collaborators are ʿĪsā Gumʿān al-Daʿarhī and Aḥmad ʿĪsā al-Daʿarhī. The description is restricted to the dialect of the Daʿarho tribe in the central-eastern inland part of the island.

Since no systematic description of the Soqotri vowels has been published so far, there is little research history behind our study. In the existing scholarly literature, the vowels of Soqotri have been usually embedded into summary descriptions of the MSA group as a whole (Johnstone 1975: 10–11; Simeone-Senelle 1997: 385; Lonnet & Simeone-Senelle 1997: 351), which is a serious methodological oversight. But even within this approach, the remarks pertinent to our subject hardly ever occupy more than one or two short paragraphs, with no proper distinction between phonetics and phonology[2] and without any lexical examples, let alone minimal pairs or any similar instruments of phonemic analysis.

The main output of our study is that, in strictly phonemic terms, the vocalic system of Soqotri is very simple and consists of five essential elements: *a*, *e*, *o*, *i*, and *u* (length non-phonemic).[3] Since the phoneme *u* is comparatively rare, the core of the system comprises just four elements. All this contrasts sharply with the bewildering array of vocalic symbols found in the majority of the Soqotri texts published so far as well as in the pertinent sections of the grammatical descriptions.[4]

While few in number, the Soqotri vowels play an important role in the morphological system of the language, particularly in the verbal domain where, differently from most other Semitic languages, not only derivational, but also purely inflectional categories such as gender and especially number are regularly expressed by internal vocalic alternations.

The verbal morphology of Soqotri thus provides an ideal starting point for describing its vocalic system, and it is in this way that our presentation will be

---

[1] More details on this project can be found in Naumkin et al. 2013: 61–68.

[2] This has rarely been acknowledged explicitly. Thus, it is only as recently as 2011 that M-C. Simeone-Senelle (2011: 1081) makes it clear that 'a very large range of vocalic timbers' is observed exclusively 'on the phonetic level', with no implications for the hypothetic phonological system. Cf. also Johnstone 1968: 518: 'In a phonological system it will not be necessary to distinguish as many vowel qualities as are distinguished here'.

[3] Contrast Lonnet & Simeone-Senelle 1997: 367 ('L'opposition de longueur n'apparaît qu'exceptionnellement dans les dialectes connus et avec un rendement infime'); Simeone-Senelle 2011: 1081 ('In S[oqotri] the contrast between long and short vowels is not always phonological'). Both statements apparently mean that the length *can* be phonemic at least on some occasions. Rather ambiguous is Lonnet 1998: 72: 'Le socotri a perdu ultérieurement l'opposition phonologique de durée. Les voyelles longues d'aujourd'hui sont sans rapport et, dans la plupart des dialectes, non phonologiques'. Cf. Johnstone's remarks (1968: 518) making clear that he considered the length as a purely phonetic feature (more explicitly in 1975: 11: 'It would seem that length here is a phonetic rather than a phonological feature').

[4] Johnstone 1975: 11 (*a, e, ɛ, ə, i, o, ɔ, u*); 1968: 517 (*i, u, ɪ, e, ə, ɛ, ɔ, a*); Simeone-Senelle 1996a: 313; 1996b: 810 (*a, e, ɛ, ə, i, o, ɔ, u*, 'in certain dialects' also *ö* and *œ*); Lonnet & Simeone-Senelle 1997: 351 ('y figurent toujours les voyelles *a, i, u, o, e, ɛ, ə*).

arranged: for each vocalic phoneme, the characteristic morphological environments within the subsystem of the verbal morphology will be established and analysed. The verbal evidence (which we have tried to make nearly exhaustive) will be supplemented by more fragmentary pieces of material from nominal morphology.

To define the functional value of the vocalic phones in the morphological system is by far the most reliable way to assure their phonemic status, as it practically amounts to building a network of systematic, 'morphological' minimal pairs. Further research into the nominal morphology of Soqotri, side by side with a closer attention to what one may label 'lexical vocalism', may bring about some amendments to our present vision of the subject, but no truly serious changes are expected.

The Arabic-based Soqotri writing, originally designed by ʿĪsā Gumʿān and then improved and refined by the joint efforts of the team (particularly by Dmitry Cherkashin), has played a key role in our understanding of the Soqotri vocalism. In today's conditions, a sufficiently developed Arabic-based writing system is the only possibility of guaranteeing a fully fledged, creative participation of the native speakers in the linguistic analysis of their mother tongue. For this reason, Arabic-based Soqotri renderings will be provided for every grammatical form appearing in the article.[5]

2. The phoneme *a/ɛ*

The first phoneme to be discussed is realized in two main allophones: the open front [a] ('average European *a*') and the open mid-front [ɛ] (in certain environments, rather a near-open front [æ]). In terms of acoustic perception, the two realizations [a] and [ɛ] differ considerably from each other, and it is not surprising that most researchers, particularly those with no mid-front vowels in their native languages, did not recognize them as representing one and the same phoneme, but rather associated the latter with their own *e*-vowel.[6]

Yet a closer inspection of the Soqotri verbal paradigms makes patent the predominantly allophonic relationship between [ɛ] and [a]: the first is the basic allophone appearing in neutral environments, the second is conditioned by the proximity of emphatics and pharyngeals. Below in this section, each table illustrating the distribution of this phoneme is divided into six columns (rather than three as elsewhere in the article): the first three represent the 'neutral' ɛ-examples, whereas the second three provide the corresponding forms with *a*.

2.1. Strong verb, basic stem

In the basic stem, *a/ɛ* characterizes the second syllable of the perfect base in 3 sg. f., both active and inactive types (Fig. 1), the first syllable of the imperfect base in the inactive type (Fig. 2), which coincides with the corresponding form of the causative stem. It appears in both syllables of the dual base of the imperfect (Fig. 3), a feature also shared by the causative stem. It is the thematic vowel of the jussive in the active type (Fig. 4), as well as in the 'old imperative', whose very existence has been unfoundedly denied in the majority of the grammatical descriptions of Soqotri.[7] In the passive voice, it appears in the second syllable of 3 sg. m. form (Fig. 5).

ḳedéro	قْدَارو	'she cooked'	ʿeṭášo	عْطَاشو	'she sneezed'
netéro	نْتَارو	'she recited'	rebáẑo	رْبَاضو	'she robbed'
ḥibéro	حيبَارو	'she suffered from cold'	ḥiṭáro	حيطَارو	'she fainted'

FIGURE 1. *Active voice, active and inactive types, second syllable of 3 sg. f. of the perfect.*

Similarly, *bébɛ* 'father' appears as *bāba* in Müller 1902: 76₁₅, but *bébe* in Müller 1905: 5₁₁. In the former case, both variants are taken from one and the same informant. It may be not too daring to suppose that the rather consistent use of ɛ in T.M. Johnstone's Soqotri transcriptions is due to the high prominence of this vowel in his native tongue, English.
[7] Bittner 1918*a*: 73, 1918*b*: 14; 1917–1918: 349; Simeone-Senelle 1996*b*: 810 ('the jussive [*sic*] is expressed by the imperfect indicative'); 1997: 404; 2011: 1095–1096; and, most explicitly, Lonnet 1993: 74 ('Le soqotri n'a pas d'impératif'). Johnstone 1968: 516 is only slightly more cautious: 'In Socotri there is no imperative, the imperfect performing this function. One or two forms raise doubts as to whether this was always so ... but the general principle cannot be doubted'. While it is true that the imperfect is the neutral and most common exponent of the imperative meaning, the 'old' imperative is far from being completely obliterated. According to our informants, it is used when an especially polite command is intended. For a lucid exposition of the facts from the Vienna corpus see Wagner 1953: 11–12 (overlooked in Lonnet 1993: 74).

---

[5] The simplicity of the vocalic system of Soqotri as established in the present article means that its written representation with the help of the Arabic letters and vocalic signs is by no means a difficult exercise, *contra* Lonnet and Simeone-Senelle (1997: 341) who believe that 'le soqotri noté en lettres arabes nécessite une *scriptio plena* très lourde; les (nombreuses) voyelles doivent être notées'.
[6] For example, the inability to recognize [ɛ] as a separate phone(me) different from *e* is the only major flaw of David Heinrich Müller's Soqotri transcriptions in his masterly, pioneering edition of Soqotri texts (esp. Müller 1905). In fact, variant transcriptions with ɛ rendered as *a* do crop up here and there in Müller's texts, side by side with the much more common *e*-renderings. For example, *sérɛd* 'mature goat kid' can be rendered as both *séred* (Müller 1905: 114₂₇) and *sárad* (1905: 192₉).

yedékor	يَذاكُر	'he remembers'	ya'ágob	يَعَاجُب	'he wants'
yedérof	يَدَارُف	'he itches'	ya'áḳob	يَعَاقُب	'he turns into'
yenɛ́gof	يَنَاجُف	'it is poured'	yeḳárom	يَقَارُم	'he craves'

FIGURE 2. *Active voice, inactive type, first syllable of the imperfect base.*

yenɛbéto	يَنَبَاتُو	'they pollinate'	yekaréšo	يَقَارَاشُو	'they peel'
tekɛtébo	تَكَاتَبُو	'you write'	teṭaréfo	تَطَارَافُو	'you fold'
etɛbéro	أَتَبَارُو	'we break'	efaṣáro	أَفَاصَارُو	'we squash'

FIGURE 3. *Both syllables of the imperfect base, active voice, active and inactive types, all dual forms.*

lifréd	لِفرَاد	'may he flee'	liḳrá'	لِقرَاع	'may he kindle'
lirgém	لِرجَام	'may he cover'	lifnáḳ	لِفنَاق	'may he wait'
ligsér	لِجسَار	'may he be able'	lišṭár	لِشطَار	'may he split'
eblég	أَبلَاج	'send!'	ešrá'	أَشرَاع	'hang!'

FIGURE 4. *Active voice, active type, the thematic vowel of the jussive and the imperative.*

sírɛk	سيرَك	'it was tethered'	hímaẓ̂	هيمَض	'it was shaken'
'ígɛb	عيجَب	'it was wanted'	šíṭar	شيطَر	'it was torn'
tígɛr	تيجَر	'it was bought'	šíra'	شيرَع	'it was hung'

FIGURE 5. *Passive voice, second syllable of the perfect base.*

2.2. Strong verb, intensive (II), causative-reflexive intensive (X$_{II}$) and reflexive intensive (V) stems, quadriradical verb intensive stem (Q$_{II}$)

In the intensive-based stems (Fig. 6), a/ɛ appears before the second radical in each of the three conjugational types (perfect, imperfect, jussive). A curious, still enigmatic exception is the intensive stem proper, where about half of the verbs display o rather than a/ɛ in the perfect and the imperfect (but only a/ɛ in the jussive). The origin of this split, almost certainly conditioned by the surrounding consonants, remains to be established.

féniŝ	فَانِيس	'to breathe'	ḥálil	حَالِيل	'to turn'
yefɛníŝin	يَفَانِيسِين		yeḥalílin	يَحَالِيلِين	
lifénɛŝ	لِفَانَس		liḥálɛl	لِحَالَل	
šéfit	شَافِيت	'to try to leave behind'	ḳábit	قَابِيت	'to teach'
yešɛfítin	يَشَافِيتِين		yeḳabítin	يَقَابِيتِين	
lišéfɛt	لِشَافَت		liḳábɛt	لِقَابَت	
tébil	تَابِيل	'to collect'	ṭábir	طَابِير	'to reproach'
yetɛbílin	يَتَابِيلِين		yeṭabírin	يَطَابِيرِين	
litébɛl	لِتَابَل		liṭábɛr	لِطَابَر	
ŝólik	شُالِيك	'to fasten'	ḳólib	قَالِيب	'to inspect'
yeŝolíkin	يَشُالِيكِين		yeḳólibin	يَقَالِيبِين	
liŝélɛk	لِشَالَك		liḳálɛb	لِقَالَب	
sóbir	سُابِير	'to begin'	ḥórig	حُارِيج	'to prevent'
yesobírin	يَسُابِيرِين		yeḥorígin	يَحُارِيجِين	
lisébɛr	لِسَابَر		liḥárɛg	لِحَارَج	

bórik yeboríkin libérek	بَارِيك يُبَارِيكِين لِبَارَك	'to congratulate'	ḥódir yeḥodírin liḥáder	حَادِير يُحَادِيرِين لِحَادَر	'to top a stone wall with prickly branches'
šenêŝif yešnêŝifin lišnêŝef	شْنَاشِيف يَشْنَاشِيفِين لِشْنَاشَف	'to sip from a vessel (one after another)'	šeṭálim yešṭalímin lišṭálem	شْطَالِيم يَشْطَالِيمِين لِشْطَالَم	'to eat one's dinner'
šemɛlík yešmɛlíkin lišmɛ́lek	شْمَالِيك يَشْمَالِيكِين لِشْمَالَك	'to be in front of'	šekábit yeškabítin liškábet	شْقَابِيت يَشْقَابِيتِين لِشْقَابَت	'to learn'
šeʔɛbíd yešʔɛbídin lišʔɛ́bed	شْآبِيد يَشْآبِيدِين لِشْآبَد	'to lie flat'	šekádim yeškadímin liškádem	شْقَادِيم يَشْقَادِيمِين لِشْقَادَم	'to wait'
entɛ́gif yentɛgífin lintɛ́gef	أنْتَاجِيف يَنْتَاجِيفِين لِنْتَاجَف	'to wave'	aʕtákib yaʕtakíbin laʕtákeb	أعْتَاقِيب يَعْتَاقِيبِين لَعْتَاقَب	'to pour from one vessel into another'
demɛ́dim yedemɛdímin lidemɛ́dem	دْمَادِيم يَدْمَادِيمِين لِدْمَادَم	'to rock repeatedly'	ẑafáẑif yeẑafaẑífin liẑafáẑef	ضْفَاضِيف يَضْفَاضِيفِين لِضْفَاضَف	'to blink repeatedly'
ḥarɛ́sim yeḥarɛsímin liḥarɛ́sem	حَرَاسِيم يَحَرَاسِيمِين لِحَرَاسَم	'to sneak'	kasákis yekasakísin likasákes	قَسَاقِيس يَقَسَاقِيسِين لِقَسَاقَس	'to gnaw repeatedly'
temɛ́til yetemɛtílin litemɛ́tel	تْمَاتِيل يَتْمَاتِيلِين لِتْمَاتَل	'to recite a poem'	ṭabáṭib yeṭabaṭíbin liṭabáṭeb	طْبَاطِيب يَطْبَاطِيبِين لِطْبَاطَب	'to clap repeatedly'

FIGURE 6. *Active voice, second syllable of the base, all forms.*

In the passive voice of the intensive stem, a/ɛ is the feature of the second syllable (Fig. 7).

ḥérɛg	حَارَج	'it was prevented'	nékaḷ	نَاقَل	'it was selected'
ḳéḷɛb	قَالْب	'it was inspected'	tékab	تَاقَب	'it was collected'
tégɛŝ	تَاجَش	'it was collected'	tékaf	تَاقَف	'it was prepared'

FIGURE 7. *Passive voice, second syllable of the perfect.*

2.3. Strong verb, causative (IV) and causative-reflexive (X) stems

In the causative and causative-reflexive stems, the imperfect base (Fig. 8) can be supplemented by the prefix vowel of the jussive (Fig. 9, causative stem only) and the second syllable of the passive perfect (Fig. 10).

yegézoṃ	يْجَازِمْ	'he makes swear'	yeḳádom	يْقَادُمْ	'he sees'
yenédoḳ	يْنَادُق	'he gives'	yeʿároẓ	يْعَارُض	'he lends'
yerékob	يْرَاكُب	'he puts over'	yeṣárom	يْصَارُمْ	'it brings cold'
yešnékor	يْشْنَاكُر	'he is surprised'	yešʿárok	يْشْعَارُكْ	'he fishes'
yešmétoḷ	يْشْمَاتْلِ	'he talks'	yešḥálof	يْشْحَالْفْ	'he leaves in the morning'
yešrébon	يْشْرَابُنْ	'he obeys'	yešʿábor	يْشْعَابُرْ	'he reacts'

FIGURE 8. *First syllable of the imperfect base.*

létrɛf	لْتْرَفْ	'may he cure'	láḳdɛm	لْقْدَمْ	'may he see'
lédmɛs	لْدْمَسْ	'may he plant'	láʿbɛr	لْعْبَرْ	'may he deliver'
lékbɛr	لْكْبَرْ	'may he visit'	lášyɛr	لْضْيَرْ	'may he diminish'

FIGURE 9. *The prefix vowel of the jussive.*

iʿbɛr	إعْبَرْ	'it was offered'	ígdaḥ	إجْدَحْ	'it was brought'
íḳdɛm	إقْدَمْ	'he was seen'	índaḳ	إنْدَقْ	'it was given'
iʿšɛr	إعْشَرْ	'it was added'	írḳaḥ	إرْقَحْ	'it was taken out'

FIGURE 10. *Second syllable of the perfect, passive voice.*

2.4. Strong verb, reflexive stem (VIII)

The vowel a/ɛ is the thematic vowel of the jussive in the reflexive stem (Fig. 11).

liŝténɛz	لِسْتَانَزْ	'may it be slanted'	lintéṣar	لِنْتَاصَرْ	'may it burst'
liftérɛk	لِفْتَارَكْ	'may he become poor'	lintébaʿ	لِنْتَابَعْ	'may it get a crack'
laʿtébɛr	لَعْتَابَرْ	'may he watch'	likténaḥ	لِكْتَانَحْ	'may he return'

FIGURE 11. *Second syllable of the jussive base.*

2.5. Reduplicated quadriradical verbs

The vowel a/ɛ is a stable feature of the first syllable of the base in each of the three conjugational forms of the reduplicated quadriradical verb (Fig. 12).

bérber yebérber libérber	بَرْبَر يَبَرْبَر لِبَرْبَر	'to be in rut (a camel)'	ḳáskes yeḳáskes liḳáskes	قَسْقَس يَقَسْقَس لِقَسْقَس	'to knock'
démdem yedémdem lidémdem	دَمْدَم يَدَمْدَم لِدَمْدَم	'to rock'	ṭábṭeb yeṭábṭeb liṭábṭeb	طَبْطَب يَطَبْطَب لِطَبْطَب	'to clap'
zégzeg yezégzeg lizégzeg	زَجْزَج يَزَجْزَج لِزَجْزَج	'to run calmly'	ẑáfẑef yeẑáfẑef liẑáfẑef	ضَفْضَف يَضَفْضَف لِضَفْضَف	'to blink'

FIGURE 12. *First syllable of all conjugational forms.*

2.6. Verbs IIIy

Among the weak verbal classes, the passive imperfect of the basic and causative stems has to be mentioned (Fig. 13), where a/ɛ is present in the last syllable instead of o in the regular verb.

yebóunɛ	يْبونَى	'it is built'	yeḳóuʕa	يْقوعَى	'it is opened'
yebóurɛ	يْبورَى	'it is born'	yeḳóuṣa	يْقوصَى	'it is cut off'
yeḥóurɛ	يْحورَى	'it is looked for'	yeróuʕa	يْروعَى	'it is pastured'
yenóubɛ	يْنوبَى	'it is called'	yeróuẑa	يْروضَى	'he is appeased'
yeśóunɛ	يْسونَى	'it is shown'	yeḥóuṣa	يْحوصَى	'it is known'
yegóuzɛ	يْجوزَى	'it is granted'	yemóuṭa	يْموطَى	'he is instructed'

FIGURE 13. *Last syllable of the imperfect base, basic and causative stems, passive voice.*

2.7. Verbal classes with *a* conditioned by the presence of gutturals and emphatics among the radicals

In a few verbal classes with emphatics and pharyngeals as root consonants, the vowel *a* corresponds to *o* or *e* in a neutral consonantal environment (Figs 14–19). In such cases, the variant ɛ cannot usually appear: what we are dealing with is thus not the allophonic alternation ɛ ~ a, but rather the phonemic (or, better, morphophonemic) shift *o, *e > a.[8]

méraṭ	مَارَط	'he instructed'
yemáraṭ	يْمَارَط	'he instructs'
fénaḳ	فَانَق	'he waited'
yefánaḳ	يْفَانَق	'he waits'
méšar	مَاضَر	'he sipped'
yemášar	يْمَاضَر	'he sips'

FIGURE 14. *Second or third radical emphatic, basic stem, active type, active voice, perfect and imperfect.*

déḷaḳ	ذَالْق	'it was much'
ḥéṭar	حَاطَر	'it fainted'
ḳéšaʕ	قَاسِع	'it became dry'

FIGURE 15. *Second or third radical emphatic or third radical guttural, basic stem, inactive type, active voice, second syllable of the perfect base.*

nátaʕ	نَاتَع	'he pulled out'
yenátaʕ	يْنَاتَع	'he pulls out'
ẑálaʕ	ضَالِع	'he told'
yeẑálaʕ	يْضَالِع	'he tells'
sábaḥ	سَابَح	'he swam'
yesábaḥ	يْسَابَح	'he swims'

FIGURE 16. *Third radical guttural, basic stem, active type, active voice, perfect and imperfect.*

yeḳáber	يْقَابَر	'he buries'
yeṣáleb	يْصَالْب	'he slaughters'
yeṭáreb	يْطَارْب	'he goes down'

FIGURE 17. *First radical emphatic, basic stem, active type, active voice, imperfect.*

---

[8] A full account of this phenomenon can be found in Naumkin et al., forthcoming, *a*; forthcoming, *b*.

béḥɛl	بَاهَلْ	'it was cooked'
báˤal	بَاعَلْ	'he married'
ráḥab	رَاحَبْ	'it was broad'

*Note the different behaviour of the laryngeal h (+ ɛ) and the pharyngeals ˤ and ḥ (+ a).

FIGURE 18. *Second radical guttural, basic stem, active voice, perfect*.*

yenáḥag	يْنَاحَج	'he plays'
yeṭáḥan	يْطَاحَنْ	'he grinds'
yeṭáˤan	يْطَاعَنْ	'he transhumes'

FIGURE 19. *Second radical guttural, basic stem, active voice, imperfect.*

2.8. Gender opposition in adjectives

The vowel a/ɛ is the feature of the masculine form of quadriliteral adjectives (often substantivized), mostly with partial reduplication. The corresponding feminine forms display e or i (Fig. 20).[9]

fídɛd/fídid	فِيدَد فِيدِيد	'hornless'
ṣáˤbɛb/ṣáˤbeb	صَعْبَب صَعْبَب	'brown-skinned, tawny'
ŝíbɛb/ŝíbib	سِيبَب سِيبِيب	'old'
ṭáḥrɛr/ṭáḥrer*	طَحْرَر طَحْرَر	'semi-wild goat'

*The opposition ṭáḥrər (masculine)/ṭáḥrer (feminine) as presented in Simeone-Senelle & Lonnet 1997: 353; Lonnet 2008: 128 and Simeone-Senelle 2011: 1084 is in all respects the opposite of the true picture.

FIGURE 20. *Gender opposition in adjectives.*

2.9. The broken plural pattern $C_1iC_2(h)\varepsilon C_3$

The vowel a/ɛ is the main element of the widespread pattern $C_1iC_2(h)\varepsilon C_3$ (Fig. 21).

---

[9] For a detailed treatment of this phenomenon see Müller 1909 and Lonnet 2008 (cf. also Johnstone 1975: 22). In Lonnet's transcriptions, a/ɛ in the masculine forms is variously rendered as e, a, or ɛ, whereas Müller vacillates between e and a.

žirɛ́me > žírhɛm	چِيرَامَه چِرْهَم	'dom berry'	ẑalˤ > ẑílaˤ	ضَلْع ضِيلَع	'rib'
šébde > šíbɛd	شَبْدَه شِيبَد	'liver'	nékbe > níkab	نَقْبَه نِيقَب	'niche in a mountain'
kíme > kíhɛm	كِيمَه كِيهَم	'sweat'	ríḥo > ríyaḥ	رِيحُو رِييَح	'palm of the hand'

FIGURE 21. *The broken plural pattern $C_1iC_2(h)\varepsilon C_3$.*

2.10. Lexical items

Figure 22 displays a few non-verbal lexemes where the phoneme a/ɛ occurs.

tɛ	تَاه	'meat'	ṭa	طَاه	'thus'
kɛn	گَان	'colour'	ṭaḥ	طَاح	'seashore'
mɛr	مَار	'belly'	ḳay	قَاي	'vomiting'
sɛk	سَاك	'roof'	ˤaf	عَاف	'until'
fɛ́ne	فَانَى	'face'	ṣáre	صَارَه	'knife'
kɛ́fe	كَافَى	'beestings'	ˤále	عَالِه	'tooth'
mɛ́se	مَاسَى	'rain'	kánе	قَانَه	'inside'
šɛ́hɛm	شَاهَم	'heat'	náṣar	نَاصَر	'cheek'
ŝɛ́her	سَاهَر	'month'	métaḷ	مَاتِلِ	'speech'
bɛrk	بَرْك	'knee'	fakḥ	فَقْح	'part'

FIGURE 22. *Lexical items with a/ɛ.*

2.11. a vs. ɛ as a phonemic opposition?

To the best of our knowledge, there is not a single position in the verbal paradigms where the relationship between a and ɛ could not be described in terms of conditional distribution. The picture turns out more complicated, however, if non-verbal lexemes are brought into discussion: as one can see from the examples in Figure 23, there may be a few minimal pairs opposing a and ɛ as independent distinctive entities. As far as one can see, such cases are exceedingly rare and do not seriously disrupt the essentially allophonic nature of the a/ɛ opposition. We are nevertheless forced to acknowledge the existence of a as a separate phoneme, even with a very restricted distinctive load.

bεr	بَار	'son of'	bar	بَار	'strength'
nέfaʕ	نَافَع	'work'	náfaʕ	نَافَع	'he worked'
ḥέdeb	حَاذْب	'a person well acquainted with a certain place, guide'	ḥádeb	حَاذْب	'ground, area'

*In the first pair, only the first member is attested in the Vienna corpus, variously rendered as *bar* or *ber* by Müller (see references in Leslau 1938: 95). In the second pair, the two elements are opposed as *néfaḥ* vs. *náfaḥ* (1938: 271). In the third pair, both elements are uniformly rendered as *ḥádib* (1938: 163).

FIGURE 23. *Minimal pairs involving the contrast a vs. ε*.*

3. The phoneme *o*

3.1. Strong verb, basic stem

In the basic stem, the phoneme *o* appears in the second syllable of 3 sg. of the perfect of the active type (Fig. 24). In the imperfect, it is the feature of the first syllable of the base in the active type (Fig. 25) and the second syllable in the inactive type (Fig. 26). It is the thematic vowel of the jussive and the imperative in the inactive type (Fig. 27). In the passive voice, it is the vowel of the second syllable of the imperfect base (Fig. 28) and the thematic vowel of the jussive (Fig. 27).

dékof	ذَاكْف	'he pushed'
gésor	جَاسُر	'he was able'
zénog	زْاَنْج	'he carried on his shoulders'

FIGURE 24. *Active type, active voice, second syllable of the perfect base.*

yegóref	يْجَارْف	'he gathers'
yefóred	يْفَارْد	'he flees'
yenóteg	يْنَاتْج	'he removes from fire'

FIGURE 25. *Active type, active voice, first syllable of the imperfect base.*

yelέbok	يَلَابْك	'it is thick'
yebédoḷ	يَبَادْلِ	'it is dirty'
yaʕáḵob	يَعَاقْب	'he turns into'

FIGURE 26. *Inactive type, active voice, second syllable of the imperfect base.*

laʕgób	لَعْجَاب	'may he want'
lidróf	لِدْرَاف	'may he itch'
liŝróm	لِسْرَام	'may he be harsh'
lirbóẑ	لِرْبَاض	'may it be stolen'
libḷóg	لِبْلَاج	'may he be sent'
litgór	لِتْجَار	'may it be bought'
ebʕóḷ	أَبْعَالِ	'marry!'

FIGURE 27. *Inactive type, active voice, the thematic vowel of the jussive and the imperative; passive voice, the thematic vowel of the jussive.*

yeróugom	يْروجُم	'it is covered'
yebóuḷog	يْبولِج	'it is sent'
yeḵóudor	يْقودُر	'it is cooked'

FIGURE 28. *Passive voice, second syllable of the imperfect base.*

3.2. Strong verb, intensive stem (II)

In the intensive stem, *o* appears after the first radical of the perfect and the imperfect bases of a large group of verbs (Fig. 29); it is also the vowel of the second syllable of the imperfect in the passive voice, for all verbs of this stem (Fig. 30).

nóḳil	ناقِيل	'he selected'
yenoḳílin	يُناقِيلين	'he selects'
ʕódib	عادِيب	'he pestered'
yeʕodíbin	يَعادِيبين	'he pesters'
fóḳiḥ	فاقِيح	'he reached the middle'
yefoḳíḥin	يَفاقِيحين	'he reaches the middle'

FIGURE 29. *Active voice, first syllable of the perfect and the imperfect bases.*

liḥéḷoḷ	لِحالِل	'may it be turned'
liḥéšom	لِحاشِم	'may he be honoured'
liṭébor	لِطابِر	'may he be blamed'

FIGURE 30. *Passive voice, second syllable of the jussive base.*

3.3. Causative (IV) and causative-reflexive (X) stems; quadriradical reduplicated verb

In the causative and causative reflexive stems, *o* replaces *e* in those forms of the perfect, which display consonant-initial suffixes (Fig. 31) (cf. Bittner 1918a: 74); the same feature characterizes the corresponding forms of the quadriradical verb (Fig. 32). The vowel *o* appears before the third radical in the imperfect (Fig. 33); it is also the feature of the last syllable of the imperfect and the jussive of the passive voice (Figs 34 & 35).

ézʕomk	أَزْعُمْك	'I sat down'
éghomk	أَجْهُمْك	'I brought the animals into the pen'
éntork	أَنْتُرْك	'I released'
šémtoḷk	شَمْتُلْك	'I spoke'
šérbonk	شَرْبُنْك	'I obeyed'
šáʕroẓk	شَعْرُضْك	'I borrowed'

FIGURE 31. *Active voice, second syllable of the perfect, forms with consonant-initial suffixes.*

mégmogk	مَجْمُجْك	'I hooked from beneath'
démdomk	دَمْدُمْك	'I rocked gently'
ẓáfẓofk	ضَفْضُفْك	'I blinked'

FIGURE 32. *Quadriradical verbs, second syllable of the perfect, forms with consonant-initial suffixes.*

yegézom	يَجازِم	'he makes swear'
yenéšor	يَنايِسْر	'he brings forward'
yaʕámod	يَعامِد	'he spends the night'
yešḥárof	يَشْحارُف	'he becomes a friend'
yešḥáboḷ	يَشْحابِل	'he notices'
yešʕémon	يَشامَن	'he believes'

FIGURE 33. *Active voice, second syllable of the imperfect base.*

yeḳóudom	يَقودُم	'it is seen'
yegóuhom	يَجوهُم	'it is brought into the pen'
yeṭóurob	يَطورُب	'it is brought down'

FIGURE 34. *Passive voice, second syllable of the imperfect base.*

liḳdóm	لِقْدام	'may it be seen'
limrót	لِمْرات	'may it be boiled'
ligdóḥ	لِجْداح	'may it be brought'

FIGURE 35. *Passive voice, the thematic vowel of the jussive.*

3.4. The reflexive stem (VIII)

In the reflexive stem, *o* is the vowel of the first syllable of the perfect (Fig. 36)[10] and the last syllable of the imperfect (Fig. 37).

---

[10] Cf. Bittner 1918a: 75. Some speakers prefer to reserve the ʕotéber-like shape for 3 pl. m. (as opposed to ʕatéber in 3 sg. m.), admitting the other variant as fully grammatical.

gotéʔer	جُتَّائِر	'it was destroyed'
ʕotéber	عُتَّابَر	'he watched'
notéʔeḷ	نُتَّائَلْ	'it slipped away'

FIGURE 36. *The first syllable of the perfect base.*

yaʕtébor	يَعْتَّابَر	'he watches'
yeftérok	يَفْتَّارُك	'he becomes poor'
yaʕtégom	يَعْتَّاجُم	'he becomes dumb'

FIGURE 37. *The second syllable of the imperfect base.*

3.5. Verbs IIIy

The vowel *o* appears in two morphological positions specific to verbs IIIy: the first syllable of the perfect base with consonant-initial suffixes (Fig. 38) (cf. Bittner 1918a: 80) and the prefix vowel of the jussive of the causative stem (Fig. 39).

dómik	دَامِيك	'I slept'
yʰóšik	يهَاضِيك	'I watered'
sófik	سَافِيك	'I cleansed'

FIGURE 38. *Basic stem, active type, active voice, first syllable of the perfect, forms with consonant-initial suffixes.*

lódim	لَاديم	'may he lull to sleep'
lóliz	لَاليز	'may he be inclined'
lómiṭ	لَاميط	'may he instruct'

FIGURE 39. *Causative stem, the prefix vowel of the jussive.*

3.6. Verbs IIH

The vowel *o* features in both syllables of the imperfect base of verbs with the second radical guttural (Fig. 40).

yeḳóʕod	يِقَاعُد	'he goes down'
yegóʔor	يَجَاوُر	'he destroys'
yegóḥob	يَجَاحُب	'he drags a boat ashore'

FIGURE 40. *Verbs with second radical guttural, both syllables of the imperfect base.*

3.7. Patterns of broken plural

The vowel *o* replaces *e* or *i* in the last syllable in the broken plural of (mostly) quadriliteral substantives (Fig. 41), a feature inherited from proto-MSA (Ratcliffe 1998: 193, 200; cf. Bittner 1918a: 66). A few other, mutually related patterns of broken plural also display *o* in the last syllable (Fig. 42).[11]

ʕifef > ʕifof	عيفف > عيفف	'goat-kid'
áʕreb > áʕrob	أَعْرَب > أَعْرُب	'raven'
édbher > édbhor	أَدْبَهَر > أَدْبَهُر	'bee'
ṣáfrer > ṣáfror	صَفْرَر > صَفْرُر	'flower'
déftem > déftom	دَفْتَم > دَفْتُم	'ant'
máḥber > máḥbor	مَحْبَر > مَحْبُر	'hundred'
menféyreher > menféyrohor	مَنْفَيْرَهَر > مَنْفَيْرُهُر	'placenta (of women)'
ṣélhel > ṣólhoḷ	صَلْهَل > صُلْهُل	'little wadi'
záʕadhim > záʕadhom	زَعَدْهيم > زَعَدْهُم	'mouse'
mézred > mézrod	مَجْرَد > مَجْرُد	'palm-rib'
míʕšer > médkor	مَأْشَر > مَدْكُر	'he-goat'
mísher > mákhor	مِضْهَر > مَقْهُر	'pen'
ḳeḥílhin > ḳaḥéḷhon	قَحْلِهين > قَحْلِهُن	'egg'

FIGURE 41. *Broken plural of nouns with* e *and* i *in the last syllable.*

berk > bírok	بَرْك > بيرُك	'knee'
ḥalf > ḥílof	حَلْف > حيلف	'place'
ḥádeb > ḥídob	حَادَب > حيدُب	'land, area'
gášaḷ > géshoḷ	جَاشَل > جَشْهُل	'piece'
ḳarišo > káryoš	قَرِيشو > قَرْيُش	'peel'
ʕáṣar > ʕíṣhor	عَاصَر > عصْهُر	'time'
fákam > fíkhom	فَاقَم > فِقْهُم	'lower jaw'
bédo > bíyyod	بَادو > بيُّد	'path between two mountain slopes'

---

[11] For a cognate pattern in Jibbali see Ratcliffe 1998: 196.

tébo > tíyyob	تَابو < تِيُّب	'portion'
áṭab > iṭob	أطَب < إيطَب	'teat'
óben > óbhon	أبْن < أبْهُن	'stone'
ḳáber > ḳóbhor	قَابَر < قَبْهُر	'tomb'
kónem > kénhom	كَانَم < كَنْهُم	'louse'
šɛm > šóhom	شَام < شَاهُم	'name'
ṣ́ádher > ékdhor	ضَدْهَر < أقْدْهُر	'cooking pot'

FIGURE 42. *Other patterns of broken plural with o in the last syllable.*

3.8. The nominal pattern móC₁C₂iC₃

In the sphere of nominal derivation, the rather common pattern $móC_1C_2iC_3$ is to be singled out (Fig. 43).

mórkit	مُرْكِيت	'rimmed mat for trampling dates'
móṣḥir	مُصْحِير	'cauterizing instrument'
móṣriˁ	مُصْرِيع	'liquid dung'
móhdid	مُهْدِيد	'a door-wing'

FIGURE 43. *The nominal pattern* $móC_1C_2iC_3$.

3.9. Lexical items

A few lexical items with *o* are listed in Figure 44.

órem	أَرْم	'road'
ˁob	عَاب	'dung'
dor	دَار	'blood'
fólhi	فَلْهِي	'calf'
fóti	فَاتِي	'clay vessel'
kobŝ	كُبْس	'ram'
ŝorṭ	شُرْط	'street'
nóyʰer	نَيْهَر	'bird'

FIGURE 44. *Lexical items with* o.

3.10. *o* vs. *a/ɛ*: a restricted opposition?

Within the subsystem of verbal morphology, it is difficult to find a minimal pair opposing *o* to *a/ɛ*. Pertinent examples typically involve non-neutral, consonant-specific verbal classes, such as *yeṣáleb* 'he slaughters' vs. *yeṣóleb* 'they slaughter' (first radical emphatic) or *dáˁar* 'it flowed' vs. *dóˁor* 'he spilled' (second radical pharyngeal). This restrictive trend is not accidental and must be conditioned by diachronic factors: since Soqotri (and proto-MSA) *o* normally reflects an earlier stressed *a* (or *ā*), it is natural for *a/ɛ* to avoid this position. However, in view of the paradigmatic oppositions mentioned above, side by side with reliable minimal pairs provided by non-verbal lexemes (such as *dómi* 'she lulls to sleep' vs. *démi* 'sleep$_{noun}$'), the synchronically valid phonemic contrast between *o* to *a/ɛ* is not in doubt.

4. The phoneme *i*

4.1. Strong verb, basic stem

In the basic and causative stems, a prominent position of *i* is the passive of the perfect, first syllable in 3 sg. m. and first and second syllables in 3 sg. f. (Fig. 49). It is the vowel of the first syllable of the perfect in the inactive type (Fig. 45) and the stem vowel of the dual forms of the jussive and the imperative (Fig. 47). The ending $-iC_3in$ marks the conditional (energetic), allegedly non-existent in Soqotri according to most modern descriptions (Johnstone 1975: 18; Lonnet 1994: 247–248; Simeone-Senelle 2011: 1092, 1096), but plainly attested in the Vienna corpus and correctly identified as such in Ewald Wagner's classic study on the MSA syntax (1953: 152)[12] (see Fig. 48).

Throughout the verbal paradigm, the vowel *i* marks the 2 sg. f. forms of the imperfect, the jussive, and the imperative (Fig. 46) (see Müller 1909: 448; Bittner 1917–1918: 354; Lonnet 2008: 122).

bizégo	بيزَاجو	'it got a cut'
ḥiṭáro	حيطَارو	'she fainted'
ḳiŝóˁo	قيشَاعو	'it became dry'

FIGURE 45. *Inactive type, active voice, first syllable of 3 sg. f. of the perfect.*

---

[12] From Wagner's 'in den Gedichten' one may infer that we are faced with an archaic feature restricted to poetry, but in reality *n*-forms are normal (even if not very common) in the ordinary speech of our informants.

tóurit	توريت	'you inherit'
toʕózil	تُعَازيل	'you spin'
téshiṭ	تَسْحيط	'you brush'
tekóli	تَكَّالي	'you turn'
tíʕid	تِيعيد	'you walk'
nédik	نَاديق	'you give'
ḳádim	قَاديم	'you see'
tid	تيد	'you wait'
ṭif	طيف	'you give'
teblíg	تَبْليج	'may you send'
teṭhír	تَطْهير	'may you go'
terẓ́i	تَرْضي	'may you become glad'
esfír	أَسْفير	'travel!'
ebʕíl	أَبْعيل	'marry!'

*Not only in the basic stem but in the verbal paradigm as a whole (Lonnet 2008: 122).

FIGURE 46. *Last syllable of 2 sg. f. of the imperfect, the jussive and the imperative*.

liktíbo	لَكْتيبو	'may they write'
tesfíro	تَسْفيرو	'may you travel'
leblígo	لَبْليجو	'may we send'
eṭhíro	أَطْهيرو	'go!'

FIGURE 47. *The dual of the jussive and the imperative.*

taʕmírin	تَعْميرين	'perhaps you say'
ligdíhin	لَجْديحين	'perhaps he comes'
leṭhírin	لَطْهيرين	'perhaps he goes'

FIGURE 48. *The conditional (energetic).*

bílɛg	بيلَج	'he was sent'
bilígo	بيليجو	'she was sent'
ʕígɛb	عيجَب	'he was wanted'
ʕigíbo	عيجيبو	'she was wanted'
ḳíder	قيدَر	'it_m. was cooked'
ḳidíro	قيديرو	'it_f. was cooked'
íʕber	إِعْبَر	'he was offered'
iʕbíro	إِعْبيرو	'she was offered'
ígdaḥ	إِجْدَح	'he was brought'
igdíḥo	إِجْديحو	'she was brought'
íṭrɛb	إِطْرَب	'he was brought down'
iṭríbo	إِطْريبو	'she was brought down'

FIGURE 49. *Passive voice, the perfect (also in the causative stem).*

4.2. Strong verb, intensive-based stems

A most conspicuous morphological environment of *i* is provided by the intensive-based verbal stems, where it is the key distinctive feature in both the perfect and the imperfect (Fig. 50).

fɛ́niŝ	فَانيش	'he breathed'
yefɛníŝin	يَفَانيشين	'he breathes'
tɛ́rir	تَارير	'he brought near'
yeterírin	يَتَّارِيرين	'he brings near'
ʕógil	عَاجيل	'he met'
yeʕogílin	يَعَاجيلين	'he meets'
šeḳádim	شَقَاديم	'he waited'
yešḳadímin	يَشْقَاديمين	'he waits'
šerákis	شَرَاقيس	'he leaned'
yešrakísin	يَشْرَاقيسين	'he leans'
šeʕásir	شَعَاسير	'he spent the afternoon'
yešʕasírin	يَشْعَاسيرين	'he spends the afternoon'
entɛ́gif	أَنْتَاجيف	'he waved'
yentɛgífin	يَنْتَاجيفين	'he waves'
aʕtáḳib	أَعْتَاقيب	'he poured from one vessel to another'
yaʕtaḳíbin	يَعْتَاقيبين	'he pours from one vessel to another'
demɛ́dim	دَمَاديم	'he rocked gently'
yedemɛdímin	يَدَمَاديمين	'he rocks gently'
ḥarɛ́sim	حَرَاسيم	'he sneaked'
yeḥarɛsímin	يَحَرَاسيمين	'he sneaks'

FIGURE 50. *Intensive (**II**), causative-reflexive intensive (X_{II}) and reflexive intensive (**V**) stems, quadriradical intensive stem (Q_{II}), perfect and imperfect.*

4.3. Verbs IIIy

The vowel *i* is, predictably, an important element in the conjugation of verbs III*y*: basic stem, active type, first syllable of the perfect with consonant-initial suffixes (Fig. 51); both syllables of the perfect in the inactive type (Fig. 52); the last vowel in 2/3 pl. forms of the imperfect of the basic stem (Fig. 53); imperfect and jussive of the causative, causative-reflexive and reflexive stems (Figs 54 & 55).

bódik	بُاديك	'I told lies'
dómik	دُاميك	'I slept'
sófik	سُافيك	'I cleansed'

FIGURE 51. *Basic stem, active type, active voice, forms of the perfect with consonant-initial suffixes.*

fíni	فيني	'he turned towards'
mídi	ميدي	'he was tired'
míli	ميلي	'it was full'

FIGURE 52. *Basic stem, inactive type, the perfect.*

tebórin	تَبارين	'you/they give birth'
tefónin	تَفانين	'you/they face'
tedómin	تَدامين	'you/they sleep'

FIGURE 53. *Basic stem, 2/3 pl. f. of the imperfect.*

yedómi lódmi (lódim)	يُدامي لُدمي (لُاديم)	'he lulls to sleep' 'may he lull to sleep'
yefóti lófti (lófit)	يَفاتي لُفتي (لُافيت)	'he loses in a game' 'may he lose in a game'
yenóbi lónbi (lónib)	يُنابي لُنبي (لُانيب)	'he calls' 'may he call'
yešʔóki lišéʔik	يَشاكي لشائيك	'he approaches' 'may he approach'
yešbóni lišóbin	يَشباني لشابين	'it is suitable for building' 'may it be suitable for building'
yešnóti lišónit	يَشناتي لشانيت	'he calls his cow' 'may he call his cow'

FIGURE 54. *Causative (IV) and causative-reflexive (X) stems, imperfect and jussive.*

yaʕtíri laʕtír	يَعْتيري لَعْتير	'he talks' 'may he talk'
yektíni liktín	يَقْتيني لِقْتين	'he eats' 'may he eat'
yemtíni limtín	يَمْتيني لِمْتين	'he desires' 'may he desire'

FIGURE 55. *Reflexive stem (VIII), imperfect and jussive.*

4.4. Nominal patterns

The vowel *i* is found in a few widespread patterns of nominal derivation (Figs 56–60).

mešáʕrik	مَشَعْريك	'fisher'
mešáḥsil	مَشَحْسيل	'wise man'
mešómtil	مَشْمْتيل	'interpreter'

FIGURE 56. *The pattern* mešáC_1C_2iC_3.

maʕmído	مَعْميدو	'pillow'
maʕrízo	مَعْريزو	'fold of the garment'
maʕtíro	مَعْطيرو	'small of the back'
maʕṭíṭo	مَعْطيطو	'lid'
menŝíʕo	مَنْسيعو	'thumb'
mešḥíro	مَصْحيرو	'cauterization'
mešḥímo	مَيشْحيمو	'scratch, abrasion'
mezhíro	مَزْهيرو	'seasonal transhumance to lower areas'

FIGURE 57. *The pattern* meC_1C_2íC_3o.

móḫlib	مُحْليب	'milking place of large cattle'
móndik	مُنْديك	'placenta (of animals)'
mónḥiṣ	مُنْحيص	'small of the back'

FIGURE 58. *The pattern* móC_1C_2iC_3.

temtílo	تَمتيلُو	'poem'
tentíro	تَنْتيرُو	'poem'
toukíʕo	تو قيعُو	'riddle'

FIGURE 59. *The pattern* teC_1C_2iC_3o.

ebtíḳo	أَبْتِيقِو	'step'
edbíbo	أَدْبِيبِو	'fly'
edmíʕo	أَدْمِيعِو	'tear'
emʕíro	أَمْعِيرِو	'frankincense tree'
enṭífo	أَنْطِيفِو	'drip'
eṣḥíro	أَصْحِيرِو	'bread'
eṣlíʕo	أَصْلِيعِو	'aloe leaf'
esṭíʕo	أَصْطِيعِو	'spark'
eṭlífo	أَطْلِيفِو	'skin on milk'

Figure 60. *The pattern* $eC_1C_2iC_3o$.

4.5. Patterns of broken plural

The vowel *i* features in the first syllable of two common patterns of broken plural: $C_1iC_2(h)\varepsilon C_3$ and $C_1iC_2(h)oC_3$ (Fig. 61).

ṣárfe > ṣíref	صَرْفَه / صِيرَف	'waterfall'
ŝégre > ŝígher	پَنْجْرَه / پِيجْهَر	'mountain pass'
káŝre > kíŝer	قَپْرَه / قِيپَر	'stony surface with sharp edges'
ḥágeb > ḥígob	حَاجَب / حِيجُب	'palm sapling'
náṣar > níṣhor	نَاصَر / نِصْهُر	'cheek'
ḥank > ḥínoḳ	حَنَقْ / حِينُقْ	'necklace'

Figure 61. *The broken plural patterns* $C_1iC_2(h)\varepsilon C_3$ *and* $C_1iC_2(h)oC_3$.

4.6. The diminutive

In spite of the pioneering efforts of M. Bittner (1918*a*: 59–60) and T.M. Johnstone (1973), the morphology of the Soqotri diminutive remains understudied. Yet it is clear that at least one type of diminutive formation displays the *i*-vocalism as its key feature (Fig. 62).[13]

---

[13] For further examples see Bittner 1918*a*: 60. This type does not seem

ʕafífhin	ʕífef	عَفِفهِين	'kid'
ʕafírrhin	ʕáfer	عَفَرْرهِين	'red'
ḥourírhin	ḥáher	حورِيرهِين	'black'

*In the second column, the basic form of the corresponding noun or adjective is provided.

Figure 62. *The diminutive**.

4.7. Lexical items

A few lexical items with *i* are listed in Figure 63.

ídhɛn	إِدْهَن	'ear'
íno	إِينو	'there is'
bíle	بِيلَه	'thing'
bíŝi	بِيشِي	'there is not'
ḥiẑáre	حِيضَارَه	'goat staying in the living compound'
žiréme	چِيرَامَه	'*dom*-berry'
líšin	لِيشِين	'tongue'
níhaḥ	نِيهَح	'joy'
ŝkímo	شكِيمو	'seed, grain'

Figure 63. *Lexical items with* i.

5. The phoneme *u*

The phoneme *u*, in the speech of our informants mostly realized as a falling diphthong [ou], is the least common vowel in Soqotri, although one can hardly say that this sound is 'exceedingly rare'.[14]

The use of *u* is restricted to several well-defined morphological environments: the imperfect of the passive voice in the basic and causative stems (Fig. 64),[15] the juncture between the prefix and the base in the imperfect of verbs Iʔ, active and passive voice of the basic stem and passive voice of the causative stem (Fig. 65) (cf. Bittner 1918*a*: 77), dual forms of the perfect and the imperfect of doubly weak verbs (Fig. 66), and a few other, less important positions (Fig. 67). In the nominal domain, it is the vowel of the first syllable of the two common types of the diminutive formation (Fig. 68).[16] In

---

to be considered in Johnstone's article (1973).

[14] 'Le timbre *u* est rarissime en soqotri' (Lonnet 1994: 246).

[15] The only morphological position of *u* recognized in Lonnet & Simeone-Senelle 1997: 367.

[16] The morphologically simple 'type I' and the *n*-extended 'type II' of Johnstone 1973 (see also Bittner 1918*a*: 59–60).

t-prefixed nous from roots I⁽ʔ⁾, *u* appears after *t*- (Fig. 69). Lexical items involving *u* are very rare (Fig. 70).

In spite of its relative rarity, the phonemic status of *u* is not in doubt. For a minimal pair with *o* cf. *yeṣóʕof* 'he cleans the date clusters of dead fruit' vs. *yeṣúʕof* 'it is being cleaned'.

yebóuloɡ	يَبولِج	'it is sent'
yeḥóuton	يَحوتَن	'he is circumcised'
yeʕóuraẓ̂	يَعورَض	'it is weaned'
yegóuhom	يَجوهُم	'it is brought into the pen'
yemóurot	يَمورُت	'it is boiled'
yeróukaḥ	يَروكَح	'it is taken out'
yeḳetóunɛ	يَقْتونى	'it is eaten, consumed'

FIGURE 64. *Strong verb, basic, causative (IV) and reflexive (VIII) stems, passive voice, first (or second in VIII) syllable of the imperfect base.*

yóudof	يودُف	'he seizes'
ouḳáro	أوقَارو	'we two will come in the evening'
yóuḳaf	يوقَف	'he keeps silence'
yóutom	يوتَم	'it is shared'
yóurom	يورُم	'(leather) is steeped before tanning'
yóukob	يوكُب	'it is entered'
yóuḳar	يوقَر	'it is brought into the pen'
yóudaḥ	يودَح	'it is put'
yóuraḥ	يورَح	'it is brought'

FIGURE 65. *Verbs I⁽ʔ⁾, basic stem active and passive voice, causative stem (IV) passive voice, imperfect, juncture between the prefix and the base.*

ḷóuyo	لُويو	'they caught'
yeḷóuyo	يَلُويو	'they catch'
tóuyo	تويو	'they ate'
yetóuyo	يَتويو	'they eat'
yʰúyo	يهويو	'they put in'
yeyʰúyo	يَيهويو	'they put in'

FIGURE 66. *Doubly weak verbs, dual forms of the perfect and the imperfect.*

šeḳóuwɛš	شَقووَش	'to be inquired about'
yešóuḳaš	يَشوقَش	
lišóuḳaš	لِشوقَش	
entóuho	أنتوحو	'to fight'
yentóuhon	يَنتوحون	
lintóuho	لِنتوحو	
ẓ̂óuwɛf	ضووَف	'it was slaughtered for a feast'

FIGURE 67. *Forms of verbs IIy.*

óuṭab	áṭab	أوطَب	'teat, nipple'
ḥóunak	ḥank	حونَق	'necklace'
bóukɛr	békɛr	بوكَر	'a goat who has given birth only once'
ḳouhér-i		قوهَاري	'two minutes, a little while'
ouḳásɛn	aḳs	أوقَاسَن	'wind raising dust and pebbles'
ouyʰéḷhɛn		أويهَلهَن	'work, affair'
ʕouyéghɛn	ʕag	عويَجهَن	'boy'
ʕougéno		عوجَانو	'girl'
souʕído		سوعيدو	'Egyptian vulture'
ketoutéyhin	kóte	كتوتيهين	'inflammation'
ḥóulehel		حولَهَل	'finger-ring; canine tooth'
ṣóuʕehɛr		صوأهَر	*Ocimum forskolei*
ŝóukɛher		ڛوقَهَر	'morning'

*The second column indicates the basic form of the corresponding lexeme (if extant).

FIGURE 68. *The diminutive*.*

toutéyo	توتَايو	'story'
touḳíʕo	توقيعو	'riddle'

FIGURE 69. *t-prefixed nouns from verbs I⁽ʔ⁾.*

ḥóuro	حورو	'black_f'
ʕóuhɛr	عوهَر	'blind'

FIGURE 70. *Lexical items.*

6. The phoneme *e*

The phoneme *e* has two basic allophones, a close mid-front *e* ('average European *e*') and mid-central *ə* ('schwa'). The positional distribution between them has not yet been studied systematically but what one can say now is that [e] tends to appear in stressed syllables (particularly the open ones) whereas [ə] is found elsewhere.[17] *Contra* many modern descriptions, the two entities are certainly not opposed to each other on the phonemic level, being perceived as fully identical by native speakers.

As far as the written representation of *e* is concerned, our informants have quickly realized that the standard graphemic inventory of Arabic does not provide an adequate means for rendering this phoneme and have chosen ڤ to represent it in their Arabic-based Soqotri writing system.

The nature of the *e*-phoneme can best be described through an analysis of vocalic alternations in which it participates. Indeed, what can be labelled 'the *e*-shift' is one of the key features of the prominently internalized Soqotri morphology: each of the three remaining common vowels can be replaced by *e* in order to express certain morphological categories.[18]

6.1. The shift *o* > *e*

The shift *o* > *e* is the primary marker of the third (in the prefix conjugations, also second) person plural masculine in numerous areas of the verbal paradigm: basic stem, active type, the perfect (Fig. 71); basic stem, inactive type, the jussive (Fig. 72, same in the passive voice of the basic and causative stems); basic stem, inactive type, the imperfect (Fig. 73, same in the causative stem); basic and causative stems, passive voice, the imperfect (Fig. 74); reflexive stem, the imperfect (Fig. 75). The shift affects both syllables of the imperfect base of verbs with the second radical guttural (Fig. 76).

ḳénom	قَانُم	'he fed his livestock'
ḳénem	قَانِم	'they fed their livestock'
zégod	زَاجُد	'he lifted'
zéged	زَاجِد	'they lifted'
rékot	رَاكُت	'he trampled the dates'
réket	رَاكِت	'they trampled the dates'

FIGURE 71. *Basic stem, active type, active voice, 3 pl. m. of the perfect.*

lilbóḳ	لِلْبَاك	'may it be thick'
lilbéḳ	لِلْبَاك	'may they be thick'
lišróm	لِشرَام	'may he be harsh'
lišrém	لِشرَام	'may they be harsh'
lisnóm	لِسنَام	'may it be rotten'
lisném	لِسنَام	'may they be rotten'
liʕbór	لِعبَار	'may it be handed over'
liʕbér	لِعبَار	'may they be handed over'
lighóm	لِجهَام	'may it be brought into the pen'
lighém	لِجهَام	'may they be brought into the pen'
liḳdóm	لِقدَام	'may it be seen'
liḳdém	لِقدَام	'may they be seen'

FIGURE 72. *Basic stem, inactive type, active voice and basic/causative (IV) stem, passive voice, 2/3 pl. m. of the jussive.*

yedéloḳ	يَدَالُق	'it is much'
yedéleḳ	يَدَالِق	'they are numerous'
yegéšol	يَجَاشُل	'it is broken'
yegéšel	يَجَاشِل	'they are broken'
tenédor	تَنَادُر	'you_sg. pay attention'
tenéder	تَنَادِر	'you_pl. pay attention'
yaʕároẓ̂	يَعَارُض	'he lends'
yaʕáreẓ̂	يَعَارِض	'they lend'
yedémos	يَدَامُس	'he plants'
yedémes	يَدَامِس	'they plant'
yeméloḳ	يَمَالُك	'he tames'
yeméleḳ	يَمَالِك	'they tame'

FIGURE 73. *Basic stem, inactive type, active voice and causative stem (IV), active voice, 2/3 pl. m. of the imperfect.*

---

[17] Our impressions at this point appear to be quite similar to Johnstone's remarks about *e* in Harsusi (1977: xiv–xv).

[18] For a deeply original account of this phenomenon see Bittner 1917–1918: 353–355 (and cf. Bittner 1918*a*: 72). Less detailed is Lonnet & Simeone-Senelle 1997: 353.

yeʕúmor	يَعومُر	'it is done'
yeʕúmer	يَعومِّر	'they are done'
yekúnom	يَقونُم	'is is foddered'
yekúnem	يَقونِّم	'they are foddered'
yeṣóuḷob	يَصوﻠُب	'it is slaughtered'
yeṣóuḷeb	يَصوﻠِّب	'they are slaughtered'
yeʕúbor	يَعوبُر	'it is delivered'
yeʕúber	يَعوبِّر	'they are delivered'
yeṭóurob	يَطورُب	'it is brought down'
yeṭóureb	يَطورِّب	'they are brought down'
yekúdom	يَقودُم	'is is seen'
yekúdem	يَقودِّم	'they are seen'

FIGURE 74. *Basic and causative (IV) stems, passive voice, imperfect 2/3 pl. m.*

yaʕtébor	يَعتَابُر	'he watches'
yaʕtéber	يَعتَابِّر	'they watch'
yaḥténok	يَحتَانُك	'he takes his first food'
yaḥtének	يَحتَانِّك	'they take their first food'
yaʕtégom	يَعتَاجُم	'he becomes dumb'
yaʕtégem	يَعتَاجِّم	'they become dumb'

FIGURE 75. *Reflexive stem (VIII), 2/3 pl. m. of the imperfect.*

yeḷóhom	يَلاهُم	'he touches'
yeḷéhem	يَلاهِّم	'they touch'
yeŝóʔom	يَسْاؤُم	'he sells'
yeŝéʔem	يَسْائِّم	'they sell'
yemóḥoŝ	يَماحُس	'he tears off'
yeméḥeŝ	يَماحِّس	'they tear off'

FIGURE 76. *Basic stem, second radical guttural, imperfect 2/3 pl. m.*

6.2. The shift ɛ/a > e

The shift ɛ/a > e typically occurs when *a* appears in the positions where, in neutral environments, *o* or *e* would be expected, that is, in roots with pharyngeals and emphatics as root consonants (see above, section 2.7). The corresponding examples are to be found in Figures 78–83. Elsewhere, this alternation is regularly attested in

the jussive of the basic stem, active type (Fig. 77) and the reflexive stem (Fig. 84).[19]

linŝér	لِنِسَار	'may he go ahead'	limráṭ	لِمرَاط	'may he instruct'
linŝér	لِنِسَّار	'may they go ahead'	limréṭ	لِمرِّاط	'may they instruct'
ligzém	لِجزَام	'may he swear'	lirbáẓ̂	لِربَاض	'may he rob'
ligzém	لِجزِّام	'may they swear'	lirbéẓ̂	لِربِّاض	'may they rob'
lisfér	لِسفَار	'may he travel'	lifnák	لِفنَاق	'may he wait'
lisfér	لِسفِّار	'may they travel'	lifnék	لِفنِّاق	'may they wait'

FIGURE 77. *Basic stem, active type, active voice, 2/3 pl. m. of the jussive.*

ḥéḷaṭ	حَاﻠَط	'he visited unexpectedly'
ḥéḷeṭ	حَاﻠِّط	'they visited unexpectedly'
yeḥáḷaṭ	يَحَاﻠَط	'he visits unexpectedly'
yeḥóḷeṭ	يَحُاﻠِّط	'they visit unexpectedly'
zéḷak	زَاﻠِق	'he drew water'
zéḷek	زَاﻠِّق	'they drew water'
yezáḷak	يَزَاﻠَق	'he draws water'
yezóḷek	يَزُاﻠِّق	'they draw water'
ḥékan	حَاقَن	'he embraced'
ḥéken	حَاقِّن	'they embraced'
yeḥákan	يَحَاقَن	'he embraces'
yeḥóken	يَحُاقِّن	'they embrace'

FIGURE 78. *Basic stem, active type, active voice, second or third radical emphatic, 3 pl. m. of the perfect, 2/3 pl. m. of the imperfect.*

---

[19] In the speech of some informants, also in other derived stems, such as intensive (lifɛrer 'may he dismember' vs. liférer 'may they dismember') or causative (láɣhɛm 'may he bring into the pen' vs. láɣhem 'may they bring into the pen'). Other speakers pronounce *e* throughout, so that the corresponding forms are to be attributed to the non-alternating classes discussed in section 6.5.

béẓar	بَاضَر	'it was cut'
béẓer	بَاضَر	'they were cut'
hérak̠	حَارَك̠	'it was little'
hérek̠	حَارَك̠	'there were few'
ʕék̠ab	عَاقَب	'he turned into'
ʕék̠eb	عَاقَب	'they turned into'

FIGURE 79. *Basic stem, inactive type, active voice, second or third radical emphatic, 3 pl. m. of the perfect.*

gámaḥ	جَامَح	'he caught'
gémeḥ	جَامَح	'they caught'
yegámaḥ	يَجَامَح	'he catches'
yegómeḥ	يَجُامَح	'they catch'
náfaḥ	نَافَح	'he blew'
néfeḥ	نَافَح	'they blew'
yenáfaḥ	يَنَافَح	'he blows'
yenófeḥ	يُنَافَح	'they blow'
sáka ʕ	سَاكَع	'he crossed the wadi'
séke ʕ	سَاكَع	'they crossed the wadi'
yesáka ʕ	يَسَاكَع	'he crosses the wadi'
yesóke ʕ	يَسُاكَع	'they cross the wadi'

FIGURE 80. *Basic stem, active type, active voice, third radical guttural, 3 pl. m. of the perfect, 2/3 pl. m. of the imperfect.*

déra ʕ	دَارَع	'he wore'
dére ʕ	دَارَع	'they wore'
yedára ʕ	يَدَارَع	'he wears'
yedóre ʕ	يَدَارَع	'they wear'
k̠éŝa ʕ	قَايَِع	'it was dry'
k̠éŝe ʕ	قَايَِع	'they were dry'
yek̠áŝa ʕ	يَقَايَِع	'it is dry'
yek̠óŝe ʕ	يُقَايَِع	'they are dry'
béga ʕ	بَاجَع	'he was able'
bége ʕ	بَاجَع	'they were able'
yebága ʕ	يَبَاجَع	'he is able'
yebóge ʕ	يَبُاجَع	'they are able'

FIGURE 81. *Basic stem, inactive type, active voice, third radical guttural, 3 pl. m. of the perfect.*

géhɛm	جَاهَم	'he came at noon'
géhem	جَاهَم	'they came at noon'
ráḥaẑ	رَاحَض	'he washed himself'
réḥeẑ	رَاحَض	'they washed themselves'
ṭáʕan	طَاعَن	'he transhumed'
ṭéʕen	طَاعَن	'they transhumed'

FIGURE 82. *Basic stem, active voice, second radical guttural, 3 pl. m. of the perfect.*

yeḷáʕam	يَلَاعَم	'he spits'
yeḷéʕem	يَلَاعَم	'they spit'
yeḷáḥag	يَلَاحَج	'it gets stuck'
yeḷéḥeg	يَلَاحَج	'they get stuck'
yenéhɛr	يَنَاهَر	'he passes by'
yenéher	يَنَاهَر	'they pass by'

FIGURE 83. *Basic stem, active voice, second radical guttural, 2/3 pl. m. of the imperfect.*

laḥtéšɛm	لَحْتَاشَم	'may he faint'
laḥtéšem	لَحْتَاشَم	'may they faint'
lintéfeš	لِنْتَافَش	'may it splash'
lintéfeš	لِنْتَافَش	'may they splash'
liftérɛk	لِفْتَارَك	'may he become poor'
liftérek	لِفْتَارَك	'may they become poor'

FIGURE 84. *Reflexive stem (VIII), 2/3 pl. m. of the jussive.*

6.3. The shift *i* > *e*

A remarkable, morphologically varied phenomenon is the shift *i* > *e*, whose primary domain are the intensive-based stems. Here it affects the last syllable of 3 pl. m. of the perfect (Fig. 85) (cf. Bittner 1918a: 74) and the two last syllables of the imperfect (Fig. 86) (cf. Bittner 1918a: 74).

An interesting case of the *i* > *e* shift is the correlation between 3 sg. f. and 3 sg. m. of the perfect in the basic stem, inactive type: the etymological vowel *i* in the first syllable does not surface in the masculine form, but reappears in the feminine (Fig. 87).

The $i > e$ alternation is an important conjugational feature of verbs IIIy. Thus, in the basic stem, inactive type both *i*-vowels of the 3 sg. m. base of the perfect are replaced by *e* in 3 pl. m. (Fig. 88). In the active type, the 3 sg. m. base of the perfect is characterized by two *e*-vowels in 3 sg. m. but *i* reappears in the second syllable before the consonant-initial suffixes (Fig. 89).

tébil	تَابِيل	'he collected'
tébeḷ	تَابْلَ	'they collected'
ʿógil	عُاجِيل	'he met'
ʿógeḷ	عُاجْلَ	'they met'
ḥósib	حَاسِيب	'he counted'
ḥóseb	حَاسْبَ	'they counted'
šeḳádim	شَقَادِيم	'he waited'
šeḳádem	شَقَادْمَ	'they waited'
šeṭálim	شَطَالِيم	'he ate his dinner'
šeṭáḷem	شَطَاِلْمَ	'they ate their dinner'
šemélik	شَمَاِليك	'he was in front'
šemélek	شَمَاِلْكَ	'they were in front'
aʿtákib	أَعْتَاقِيب	'he poured from one vessel to another'
aʿtákeb	أَعْتَاقْبَ	'they poured from one vessel to another'
entégif	أَنْتَاجِيف	'he brandished'
entégef	أَنْتَاجْفَ	'they brandished'

FIGURE 85. *Intensive (II), causative-reflexive intensive (X_{II}) and reflexive intensive (V) stems, 3 pl. m. of the perfect.*

yehoṣírin	يُحَاصِيرِين	'he pours broth on rice'
yehoṣéren	يُحَاصْارَن	'they pour broth on rice'
yeʿoṭíbin	يُعَاطِيبِين	'he leads away an animal'
yeʿoṭében	يُعَاطْابَن	'they lead away an animal'
yebɛgíʿin	يَبَاجِيعِين	'he tries'
yebɛgéʿen	يَبَاجَاعَن	'they try'
yešḥabírin	يَشْحَابِيرِين	'he inquires'
yešḥabéren	يَشْحَابَارَن	'they inquire'

yešṭaḥímin	يَشْطَاحِيمِين	'he voids excrements'
yešṭaḥémen	يَشْطَاحَامَن	'they void excrements'
yešẓaḥíkin	يَشْضَاحِيكِين	'he mocks'
yešẓaḥéken	يَشْضَاحَاكَن	'they mock'
yentɛgífin	يَنْتَاجِيفِين	'he waves'
yentɛgéfen	يَنْتَاجَافَن	'they wave'
yaʿtakíbin	يَعْتَاقِيبِين	'he pours from one vessel into another'
yaʿtakében	يَعْتَاقَابَن	'they pour from one vessel into another'

FIGURE 86. *Intensive (II), causative-reflexive intensive (X_{II}) and reflexive intensive (V) stems, 2/3 pl. m. of the imperfect.*

éret	آرَت	'he inherited'
iréto	إيرَاتو	'she inherited'
déker	ذَاكِر	'he remembered'
dikéro	ديكَارو	'she remembered'
néker	نَاكِر	'he was nostalgic'
nikéro	نيكَارو	'she was nostalgic'

FIGURE 87. *Basic stem, inactive type, 3 sg. m. and f. of the perfect.*

mídi	ميدي	'he was tired'
méde	مَاذَى	'they were tired'
míli	ميلي	'it was full'
méle	مَالَى	'they were full'
gízi	جيزي	'he was in despair'
géze	جَازَى	'they were in despair'

FIGURE 88. *Verbs IIIy, inactive type, 3 pl. m. of the perfect.*

gébe	جَابَى	'he was able'
góbik	جُابِيك	'I was able'
béše	بَاشَى	'he wept'
bóšik	بُاشِيك	'I wept'
déme	ذَامَى	'he slept'
dómik	ذَاميك	'I slept'

FIGURE 89. *Verbs IIIy, active type, 3 sg. m. of the perfect vs. forms with consonant-initial suffixes.*

6.4. Multiple *e*-shifts within one form

Different types of the *e*-shift can be simultaneously attested within a single verbal form. Prominent examples of such multi-faced *e*-replacement are provided by the passive of the intensive stem (the imperfect and 3 sg. f. of the perfect) as represented in Figure 90.

yeṭabírin	يَطَابِيرِين	'he blames'
yeṭebéren	يَطَابَارَن	'he is blamed'
ṭabíro	طَابِيرو	'she blamed'
ṭebéro	طَابَارو	'she was blamed'
yetɛgíšin	يَتَاجِيبِين	'he collects'
yetegéšen	يَتَاجَابِّن	'it is collected'
tɛgíšo	تَاجِيبو	'she collected'
tegéšo	تَاجَابو	'it_f. was collected'
yehošímin	يَحَاشِيمِين	'he honours'
yehešémen	يَحَاشَامَن	'he is honoured'
ḥašímo	حَاشِيمو	'she honoured'
ḥešémo	حَاشَامو	'she was honoured'

FIGURE 90. *The alternations* i > e, ɛ/a > e *and* o > e *within one form: intensive stem (II), passive voice, the imperfect and 3 sg. f. of the perfect.*

6.5. Non-alternating types

Since *e* cannot replace itself, there emerge a substantial amount of non-alternating verbal classes which do not distinguish between singular and plural of the masculine: both types of forms are characterized by *e* as their thematic vowel(s) (Fig. 91).

déker	ذَاكِر	'he/they remembered'
yenóter	يَنَاتَر	'he/they speak(s) in verse'
ḥére	حَارَى	'he/they looked for'
fer	فَار	'he/they flew'
yéfrer	يَفْرَر	'he/they fly'
égzem	أَجْزَم	'he/they made swear'
frer	فرَّار	'he/they woke'
yefrér	يَفْرَار	'he/they will wake'
šénker	شَنكَّر	'he/they was/were surprised'
hotének	حُتَانَك	'he/they was/were given the first food'

FIGURE 91. *Non-alternating types.*

7. Other phones

As we have seen above (section 2.11), a closer look at the Soqotri vocabulary outside the verbal paradigms allows one to broaden the inventory of the vocalic phonemes by splitting the duo ɛ/a into two independent entities (even with quite a restricted distribution). Are there any other candidates to be added to the list?

7.1. The phone *ö*

Many modern descriptions of Soqotri include the close mid-front rounded *ø* and/or the open mid-front rounded *œ* in their vocalic inventories. While a mid-front rounded vowel is certainly a prominent feature of the Soqotri vocalic landscape, its phonemic status is open to serious doubt.

In most cases, *ö* is a positional variant of *e*, labialization being occasioned by the presence of *o* in the following syllable or, more rarely, by the following *w*. Within the verbal paradigm, it occurs in several well-defined environments (Fig. 92). By far the most prominent one is the 3 sg. m. of the perfect of the active type in the basic stem: as one can see from the examples adduced in Figure 93, whenever the vowel of the second syllable shifts to *e* in 3 pl. m. the labialization also disappears. The other two conspicuous *ö*-environments include the prefix vowel of the imperfect of verbs IIIy, active type, and the perfect of the passive voice of the same verbal type. Not infrequently, this vowel is attested in individual nominal lexemes.

In a great majority of cases, the presence of labialization is facultative: non-labialized forms are admitted as fully grammatical by the native speakers who normally do not distinguish the labialized variant from the ordinary *ḥaraka* (ْ).

As established by Maria Bulakh, however (see Naumkin et al., forthcoming, *a*; forthcoming, *b*), the complete picture is less straightforward. In roots with the second or third radical emphatic, the 3 sg. m. of the perfect should, in principle, be identical in both the active and inactive types: *e* in the first syllable, *a* in the second. Due to the unstable character of the labialization as outlined

benṓwe	بَنَاوَى	'it was built'
berṓwe	بَرَّاوَى	'he was born'
egzṓwe	أجْزَاوَى	'it was spent freely'
enbṓwe	أنْبَاوَى	'it was called'
ʕṓwag	عَاوَج	'it was born (an animal)'
ṓbon	أبْن	'I build'
ṓfoŝ	أفْس	'I eat the lunch'
tṓboš	تَابْش	'she weeps'
kṓbo	كَابو	'she made enter'
ʕṓbhor	عَبْهُر	'well_n.'
ḥṓbhor	حَبْهُر	'cold_n.'
ḳṓsho	قَصْهُو	'grass'
ṣṓhlo	صَحْلُو	'bone'
ṣṓbhor	صَبْهُر	'tamarind'
ṓbhon	أبْهُن	'stones'
ḳṓbhor	قَبْهُر	'tombs'
fḥṓmo	فَحَامُو	'coal'

FIGURE 92. *The typical environments where ö appears.*

ḳṓbor	قَابْر	'he buried'
kḗber	قَابْر	'they buried'
nṓbot	نَابْت	'he pollinated'
nḗbot	نَابْت	'they pollinated'
ṣṓlob	صَالْب	'he slaughtered'
sḗleb	صَالْب	'they slaughtered'

FIGURE 93. *The shift ö > e in the first syllable of the perfect, strong verb, active type, basic stem, 3 sg. and pl. m.*

fṓṣar	فَاصَر	'he squashed'	fḗṣar	فَاصَر	'it got squashed'
nṓḳaṣ	نَاقَص	'he reduced'	nḗḳaṣ	نَاقَص	'it decreased'
ḳṓṣam	قَاصَم	'he ate his breakfast'	ḳḗṣam	قَاصَم	'it cooled down'

FIGURE 94. *The opposition ö vs. e in the first syllable of the perfect, strong verb, basic stem, active vs. inactive type, 3 sg. m.*

7.2. The phone ɔ

There remains the open mid-back rounded ɔ. The status of this phone, clearly audible in certain words and forms (Fig. 95), is still uncertain to us. As far as one can see, ɔ is never opposed to o and, in most cases, is likely to be considered as a positional allophone of this phoneme. The labials *f* and *m* as well as the nasal *n* appear to be among the chief conditional factors of its emergence, but further research is needed to gain more certainty about this. In any case, ɔ is unlikely to turn out to be a fully fledged phonemic entity.

fɔ́ne	فَانى	'formerly'
fɔnŝ	فَنْس	'breath'
šfɔ́niŝ	شفَانيس	'animal'
megɔ́še	مَجَاشى	'boys'
hɔ	هَا	'eh' (particle for attracting one's attention)
kɔn	كَان	'he was'
mɔ́ʕa	مَاعه	'grand-father'
mɔn	مَان	'who?'
šɔm	شَام	'sun; day'
ŝɔb	سَاب	'foot'
tɔ́mer	تَامَر	'dates'
trɔ	ترو	'two'

FIGURE 95. *Lexical illustrations for the phone ɔ.*

above, this is often indeed the case. When such pairs are produced from one and the same consonantal root, however, the morphological and/or lexical homonymy can be avoided: the speakers tend to produce the labialized variant in the active type, reserving the neutral *e* for the inactive. The minimal pairs adduced in Figure 94 may provide *ö* with a certain phonemic load, although it is clearly not to be treated on the same level as the basic five vowels dealt with in the main part of this article.

Acknowledgements

The present study owes much to the other members of our team, and our indebtedness to them is immense. Dr

Bulakh's meticulous scrutiny of the morphology of the basic stem of the Soqotri verb (for which see Naumkin et al., forthcoming, *a*; forthcoming, *b*) is to be particularly singled out. The article has been written in the framework of the project 12-06-00182a supported by FRBR/РФФИ and the projects 14-01-18048, 14-04-00277 supported by RFH/РГНФ. It is a pleasant duty to extend our gratitude to these institutions.

References

Bittner M.
   1917–1918. Einige Besonderheiten aus der Sprache der Insel Soqoṭra. *Wiener Zeitschrift für die Kunde des Morgenlandes* 30: 347–358.
   1918*a*. Charakteristik der Sprache der Insel Soqoṭra. *Anzeiger der pilosophisch-historischen Klasse der kais. Akademie der Wissenschaften in Wien* 55: 48–83.
   1918*b*. *Vorstudien zur Grammatik und zum Wörterbuche der Soqoṭri-Sprache II*. Vienna: Hölder.

Johnstone T.M.
   1968. The non-occurrence of a *t*-prefix in certain Socotri verbal forms. *Bulletin of the School of Oriental and African Studies* 31: 515–525.
   1973. Diminutive Patterns in Modern South Arabian Languages. *Journal of Semitic Studies* 18: 98–107.
   1975. The Modern South Arabian languages. *Afroasiatic Linguistics* 1/5: 93–121.
   1977. *Ḥarsūsi Lexicon*. London: Oxford University Press.

Leslau W.
   1938. *Lexique Soqoṭri*. Paris: Klincksieck.

Lonnet A.
   1993. Quelques résultats en linguistique sudarabique moderne. *Quaderni di studi arabi* 11: 37–81.
   1994. Le verbe sudarabique moderne: hypothèses sur des tendences. *Matériaux arabes et sudarabiques*, N.S. 6: 213–255.
   1998. Le socotri: une métamorphose contrariée. Pages 69–85 in M. el-Medlaoui et al. (eds), *Actes du 1er congrès Chamito-Sémitique de Fès*. Fès: L'Média.
   2008. La marque -*i* de féminin en (chamito-)sémitique et son développement en sudarabique moderne oriental. *Aula Orientalis* 26: 117–134.

Lonnet A. & Simeone-Senelle M-C.
   1997. La phonologie des langues sudarabiques modernes. Pages 337–372 in A. Kaye (ed.), *Phonologies of Asia and Africa*. Winona Lake, IN: Eisenbrauns.

Müller D.H.
   1902. *Die Mehri- und Soqoṭri-Sprache*. i. *Texte*. Vienna: Hölder.
   1905. *Die Mehri- und Soqoṭri-Sprache*. ii. *Soqoṭri-Texte*. Vienna: Hölder.
   1909. Die Formen *qátlal* und *qátlil* in der Soqoṭri-Sprache. Pages 445–455 in G. Maspero (ed.), *Florilegium Melchior de Vogüé*. Paris: Imprimerie nationale.

Naumkin V., Kogan L., Cherkashin D., ad-Daʿrhi A.I. & ad-Daʿrhi I.G.
   2013. Soqotri lexical archive: the 2010 fieldwork season. *Zeitschrift der Deutschen Morgenländischen Gesellschaft* 163: 61–95.

Naumkin V., Bulakh M., Kogan L., Cherkashin D., ad-Daʿrhi A.I. & ad-Daʿrhi I.G.
   (forthcoming, *a*). Studies in the verbal morphology of Soqotri I/1: Strong triconsonantal roots in the basic stem (the analysis). *Zeitschrift für arabische Linguistik*.
   (forthcoming, *b*). Studies in the Verbal Morphology of Soqotri I/1: Strong triconsonantal roots in the basic stem (the lexical data). *Zeitschrift für arabische Linguistik*.

Ratcliffe R.
   1998. *The 'broken' plural problem in Arabic and Comparative Semitic*. Amsterdam/Philadelphia: Benjamins.

Simeone-Senelle M-C.
    1996*a*. The Soqotri language. Pages 309–321 in H.J. Dumont (ed.), *Proceedings of the First International Symposium on Soqotra Island: Present and Future*. New York: United Nations Publications.
    1996*b*. Suḵuṭra. 3. Language. Pages 809–811 in *Encyclopedia of Islam*. (New edition). ix. Leiden: Brill.
    1997. The Modern South Arabian languages. Pages 378–423 in R. Hetzron (ed.), *The Semitic Languages*. London: Routledge.
    2011. Modern South Arabian. Pages 1073–1113 in S. Weninger et al. (eds), *The Semitic Languages. An International Handbook*. Berlin/Boston: De Gruyter.

Wagner E.
    1953. *Syntax der Mehri-Sprache, unter Berücksichtigung auch der anderen neusüdarabischen Sprachen*. Berlin: Akademie.

Authors' addresses

Leonid Kogan, Russian State University for the Humanities, Institute of Oriental and Classical Studies, Miusskaya sq. 6, 125993, Moscow, Russia.
e-mail: lkog@rggu.ru

Vitaly Naumkin, Institute of Oriental Studies, Russian Academy of Sciences, Rozhdestvenka 12, 103753, Moscow, Russia.
e-mail: vinaumkin@yandex.ru

Sabaic and Aramaic — a common origin?

INGO KOTTSIEPER & PETER STEIN

Summary
The origin of civilization in pre-Islamic South Arabia is closely connected with the linguistic affiliation of the Ancient South Arabian languages. That these languages have some particularities in common with the North-west Semitic language realm has been known for a long time. Recent investigations, however, allow us to confine these isoglosses in particular to the Aramaic and the Sabaic branches of both language groups, suggesting a fairly close linguistic relationship between these two languages. Since these isoglosses are definitely not shared by other South Arabian languages such as Minaic and Hadramitic, the traditional picture of a linguistic continuity of the so-called Ancient South Arabian language group gets broken up. Consequently, the question of a cultural transfer across the Arabian Peninsula arises anew. On the other hand, the assumption of Aramaic as a member of an alleged North-west Semitic language group should also be questioned on the basis of these isoglosses. The linguistic evidence and its historical implications are examined from an Aramaist's and a Sabaist's perspective.

Keywords: Sabaic, Aramaic, Ancient South Arabian language history, Arabian Peninsula

Traditionally, Aramaic has been connected with the Canaanite languages as part of an alleged North-west Semitic branch of West Semitic. This classification has been questioned especially by the works of Robert Hetzron who argues for the existence of a Central Semitic branch to which Aramaic would belong as a separate sub-branch side by side with Arabo-Canaanite. Rainer Voigt has modified this picture by proposing that Hetzron's Central Semitic together with languages like Ugaritic would in fact form a special North-west Semitic sub-branch of a Central Semitic branch, the latter including also Ancient (also Old or Epigraphic) South Arabian. Most recently, John Huehnergard and Aaron Rubin argued again to include Aramaic side by side with Canaanite and Ugaritic into a north-western sub-branch of Central Semitic, while Arabic and the Ancient South Arabian languages ('Ṣayhadic') should be considered a corresponding southern group, influenced by, but not emerging from, the South Semitic realm.[1] All in all, there is a tendency to see a connection between Arabic and Ancient South Arabian on the one hand and the languages of the north-west on the other— abandoning their traditional genetic sub-grouping with the so-called South Semitic branch as represented by Modern South Arabian and Ethiopian.

What all these approaches have in common is that Ancient South Arabian is always treated as a distinct group or, more traditionally, even as one common language split up into a number of dialects. But this presupposition is, as will been shown in the second part of this paper, by no means certain and thus only simplifies an obviously more complex picture.

The same is true in respect of Aramaic. The question is, what are the essential features of Aramaic? Several scholars who deal mainly with the ancient languages of Syro-Palestine tend to define Aramaic implicitly, but sometimes even explicitly, in a negative way: every dialect in Syro-Palestine found in the inscriptions of the first millennium BC is deemed Aramaic if it is not Canaanite, as explicitly expressed by Josef Tropper (2001: 213). Consequently, the dialects of Samʾal and Deir ʿAlla, which exhibit some non-Canaanite features, as in the word *br* for 'son', which can also be found in Aramaic, are classified as Aramaic. On the other hand these two dialects lack the definite article and exhibit the verbal N-stem. Consequently, the postponed article and the absence of N-stems, which had been commonly accepted peculiarities of Aramaic, are interpreted as secondary developments and thus not as essential features of Aramaic on the basis of those particular texts (Tropper 1993: 307–311). Thus, one would have to assume the

---

[1] See Huehnergard & Rubin 2011, with a summary of the previous approaches.

existence of a proto-Aramaic still used in the eighth century at the fringes of the area of Aramaic dialects, which in fact would be very similar to the Canaanite dialects,² leaving the question of when and why those later peculiarities were developed. Such an assumption, however, presupposes that this proto-Aramaic had already been used as a common language in the vast area from the very north-east in Zincirli down to Deir ᶜAlla located east of the river Jordan before those innovations had been spread throughout this vast area — apart from its very fringes — leaving the questions, through which media and for what reasons could this have happened?

These questions lead us to the problem of the prehistory of Aramaic and the Aramaeans in general.

Traditionally, scholars suppose their cradle to be somewhere in north Syria because in the first millennium the Jazira was an Aramaean centre and even the Bible connects Haran with the early Aramaeans. But a critical survey of the earliest sources about the Aramaeans and Aramaic does not foster such an assumption.³ According to the extant sources, the Aramaeans first appeared in Mesopotamia at the end of the second millennium into which they intruded as a new element of the so-called Aḫlamu groups. Those Aramaic elements were located in the Jebel Bishri area and only gradually infiltrated Mesopotamia especially along the rivers. Obviously, they first gained a leading role among the Aḫlamu, then among the rural people outside the cities in Mesopotamia, and finally in the evolving minor states at the fringes of the area of Assyrian influence. Thus, not only two states called Aram developed at the beginning of the first millennium — one in north Syria in the area west of the Euphrates and one south-west of Jebel Bishri in the vicinity of Damascus — but also the language of this new elite gained the status of a trans-regional literary lingua franca used also in other areas throughout Syria and was later adopted even by the neo-Assyrian empire apart from Akkadian. Since, on the other hand, there is no hint of any Aramaic — be it proto or not — used in Syria before the tenth century BC, one has to conclude that both the Aramaeans and their language are new elements of the Syrian-Mesopotamian society, which arrived there only at the end of the second millennium and probably originated from an area south of Mesopotamia somewhere at the eastern fringes of Syria-Palestine or even further south.

These observations fit very well the linguistic observation that Aramaic differs in several aspects from all other languages found in its later area:

1. The best-known distinctive feature of Aramaic is the postponed article. Since in all old texts it is always written with ʾ and never with *h* and since, in the older texts, ʾ is not used as *mater lectionis*, this article was not a mere -[ā] but had a consonantal value.
2. The system of verbal stems in Aramaic is quite simple and follows strict rules. There are only three stems — G, D, and H — and all these stems were obviously used in the active and the passive voice, and each accompanied by a t-stem. In contrast to tD and tH, originally the t-stem of G was realized with an infixed *t*, thus Gt. This is found, however, only in the earliest Aramaic inscription from T. Fekheriye (*ygtzr*, KAI 309: 23). Thus, in this case, Aramaic switched very early to the pattern most common in Syria-Palestine, which preferred the prefixed *t*-element. This illustrates the influence of the regional language traditions, which of course did start to affect Aramaic at the very moment it began to be used in this region.
3. Typically, Aramaic also keeps the /h/ of the H-stem in all forms (thus *hqtl*, *yhqtl*, etc.) whereas in the other so-called North-west Semitic languages it would not appear in forms with prefixes (thus *hqtl*, *yqtl*).
4. The adaptation of the Phoenician script blurred the fact that Aramaic exhibited twenty-nine consonantal phonemes. That Aramaic originally used /ḍ/, /ḏ/, /ẓ/, /ṭ/, and /ś/ is well known by the orthographic change in regard to these phonemes, but Pap. Amherst 63, a spoken Aramaic text transcribed in the fourth century BC into Demotic script, attests that /ḥ/ and /ḫ/ and /ᶜ/ and /ġ/ were also phonetically distinguished (Kottsieper 1990: 27–31; Tropper 1993: 307; Fales 2011: 566). Although other dialects in Syria-Palestine may also have used more phonemes than expressed by the Phoenician script adapted throughout this area, there exists no hint that any of them exhibited all those now clearly attested for Aramaic.⁴
5. Together with the Phoenician script, the scribes also took over Canaanite features as mere orthographic conventions. Since in Canaanite languages [n]

---

² Cf. Tropper 1993: 309: 'Die linguistischen Differenzen zwischen dem Uraramäischen und dem Urkanaanäischen sind nicht so ausgeprägt, wie traditionell angenommen wird.'
³ See Kottsieper 2009: 393–404 for a more detailed analysis of the sources and a sketch of the early history of the Aramaeans.

⁴ Cf. the overview given by Gzella 2011: 433.

assimilated to a consonant following directly and thus such a [n] never appears in writing, most scribes of Old Aramaic texts followed this custom, leaving the impression that Old Aramaic also fully assimilated [n]. Wolfram von Soden has already observed, however, that in many Aramaic names and words written in cuneiform, the original [n] appears, although not written in alphabetic script (see Soden 1968: 175–176). Consequently, such a [n] must still have been pronounced in some way. Moreover, texts from the seventh century onwards start to write [n] in such positions although the scribes, especially in the later Persian period, sometimes had severe problems in doing this correctly. On the basis of this observation, Rainer Degen also doubted the assumption that [n] assimilated in earlier Aramaic and proposed to explain the missing *n* in the Old Aramaic inscriptions as a mere orthographic feature (Degen 1969: 39–40). This is corroborated not only by the oldest Aramaic inscription published after Degen's Grammar which in fact does write [n] before consonant (cf. *mhnḫt*, KAI 309: 2), but also by an analysis of the dialect of the Proverbs of Aḥiqar which goes back to eighth-century sources. In this text each etymological /n/ is written correctly and no etymologically incorrect *n* appears (Kottsieper 1990: 50–62). Thus we can be quite sure that in the older Aramaic dialects /n/ was pronounced even before a consonant in some way — perhaps not as a full [n] but at least as a clear discernible nasalization.

6. Aramaic also preserved the difference between roots ending with /y/ and those with /w/ — a feature completely unknown in Canaanite languages. Thus, the forms without endings of the short prefix-conjugation of G-stem of III-*y* were originally pronounced with -[ī] at the end (written with -*y*) while those of III-*w* had -[ē] instead (written with -*h*) (Kottsieper 1990: 158–177). The difference between those roots is also kept in the later dialects in nouns according to the /qvtl/-pattern in which the original third consonant reappears.

To sum up this section: the Aramaeans appeared at the northern fringe of the Syrian Desert only at the end of the second millennium BC, probably from the south; and since the Syrian world underwent a dramatic cultural change just at this time, caused by the decline of the city-states, these Aramaic groups were able to gain enormous influence on the new elites evolving in Syria. Consequently, their language became the main trans-regional language of the western Near East. The foreign (i.e. not Syrian) origin of the Aramaeans, however, is reflected by several peculiarities of the Aramaic language, which separate it clearly from the older languages of Syria-Palestine. That some of these differences got lost during the first millennium, a period in which Aramaic was now used in its new linguistic environment, is what any linguist would expect. Since all these peculiarities are to be found in languages from the Arabian Peninsula,[5] the question arises as to whether the cradle of the Aramaeans and their language can be found there — or at least some relatives.

Let us therefore turn to the other end of the Arabian Peninsula: the linguistic area of so-called Ancient South Arabian. As has been stated above, this language group has been put in close connection with the languages of Syria-Palestine (and also Arabic) by recent scholars under the label 'Central Semitic'. A number of characteristic features clearly distinguish this group from the languages of Ethiopia (and Modern South Arabian). Among these features are the formation of the imperfect indicative with a basis /qtVl/ (thus *yaqtulu* vs. Ethiopic *yəqattəl*) and the feminine plural of prefix conjugation ending in /-na/ (vs. Ethiopic /-ā/). Some other peculiarities of Ancient South Arabian, which seem to link it closely with the South Semitic family, such as the suffix conjugation of 1st and 2nd persons in -*k* and the extensive use of broken plurals, could well be considered areal phenomena rather than traces of a common genetic origin.[6] We have thus a rather clear picture of a firm embodiment of Ancient South Arabian in the Central Semitic language realm.[7]

What is the problem with this? The problem is to be able to explain how and when these Central Semitic

---

[5] One may add also the use of *br* 'son' or *tryn* 'two' which Aramaic shares with Modern South Arabian dialects, but *br* is also found in all written dialects used in Zincirli and in Deir ʿAlla although possibly under Aramaic influence. Perhaps a further connection between Old Aramaic and Sabaic can also be found in the use of short performative conjugation without copula to express progress (cf. Kottsieper 1999; Nebes 1994).

[6] Thus e.g. Huehnergard & Rubin 2011: 271–274, referring to the parallel situation of perfect formation in -*k* in present-day Yemeni Arabic, which can only be seen as influenced by, but not originally shared with, the pre-Arabic language in the area.

[7] One has to admit that this simple view is mainly held by scholars of comparative Semitics, while some specialists in the ASA languages draw a more complex picture, laying more importance on the South Semitic connections and warning against any hasty conclusion (e.g. Mazzini 2005: esp. 222–223).

languages found their way to South Arabia. This question has evolved a long controversy between adherents of any kind of migration model, explaining the 'Central Semitic' impact in Ancient South Arabian as input from abroad,[8] and the defenders of an endogenous origin in the southern Peninsula.[9] Two main arguments are put forward in favour of the endogenous theory: 1) the archaeological continuity in South Arabia far beyond the late second millennium BC;[10] and 2) the improbability of an exodus of probably tens of thousands of people through the Arabian Desert to become the inhabitants of a future 'Arabia Felix'.[11] Indeed, both arguments are plausible but could seriously be questioned, if not refuted.

We now come back to Aramaic. When we recall the particular features that distinguish Aramaic from other languages of the north-west, we can easily see that the same features are found in Sabaic as well:[12] we have a postponed article (-n, paralleled by /-āʾ/ in Aramaic) (cf. also Voigt 1998: 242–243), the verbal stem system is exactly the same in both languages (three base stems G, D, and H, and three corresponding reflexives, formed by infixed or prefixed t, as well as passive forms, but no lengthened stems[13] and no N-stems); we have the same morphological treatment of the causative stem, retaining its /h/ in all forms (thus hqtl, yhqtl, etc.); and we can proceed from a comparable inventory of consonants. As for the assimilation of /n/, we seem to observe a development similar to Aramaic: while the early Sabaic inscriptions (from the so-called early Sabaic period, c. tenth–third centuries BC) exhibit the n in all positions as a rule, defectively written (and thus assimilated) forms start to appear in early Middle Sabaic times, consequently prevailing during the following centuries. Finally, roots III-y and III-w are well distinguished in Sabaic, consequently spelled with respective endings -y and -w (thus ybny 'he shall build' as opposed to yʾtw 'he shall come').

To sum up, we find that these phonological and morphological essentials are shared by both languages — Aramaic and Sabaic — as opposed to the other languages of Syria-Palestine. The question now is: do we find a similar distinction in the south of the Peninsula as well? In other words, are the other Ancient South Arabian languages part of this picture, or not? In truth, we cannot yet give a definite answer, as the grammatical evidence in those other languages is far less complete than that of Sabaic. If we compose a combined picture of those fragmentary languages, however, we can pick out a certain tendency that reveals some striking differences from the Aramaeo-Sabaic picture shown above. Regarding the four main features in question, the picture appears as follows:

1. The postpositive article is indeed shared by all four ASA languages.
2. As for verbal stem formation, the most complex pattern is found in Minaic.[14] Besides the three common base stems and the corresponding reflexives, we have a system of reduplicating stems, showing the second radical twice in the script and thus probably to be distinguished from the regular geminating (D-)stems.[15] Such reduplicating stems have recently been established not only for the base stem, but also for all other derivations, such as S, T, and ST (thus, $f^{cc}l$, $sf^{cc}l$, $ft^{cc}l$, and $stf^{cc}l$, besides the corresponding base stems f^cl, sf^cl, ft^cl, and stf^cl). This system of sub-derivations from derived (and even T-)stems is completely unknown in the Central Semitic languages,[16] but characteristic for Ethiopian and thus for the South Semitic language group.[17]

---

[8] See most recently Nebes 2001, with mainly linguistic arguments of Sabaic-Canaanite isoglosses that could support a migration of 'Proto-South Arabians' from Syria-Palestine through the Peninsula during the second millennium BC. In contrast to this, the repeated attempts by Giovanni Garbini (see most recently Garbini 2004) to establish a sophisticated theory of proto-South Arabians wandering from southern Mesopotamia via the Levant and finally to Yemen have been criticized, for good reason, because of their historical inconsistencies.
[9] Thus mainly Mazzini 2005; Avanzini 2009. According to their argumentation, the isoglosses with the north-western languages originate from common linguistic connections in the 'proto' phase of the second millennium (cf. Mazzini 2005: 226–227).
[10] Cf. Avanzini 2009: 206–207. Although there seems to be no unbroken continuity from the late Bronze Age to the first millennium in Yemen, we have no reason to assume an 'empty' country in the second millennium which was only awaiting migrants coming from the north and bringing along their Semitic language and script.
[11] See, again, the critical remarks by Mazzini 2005: 224–225.
[12] Cf. already Stein 2012a, with focus on verbal morphology, and Kottsieper 2009: 405–406.
[13] According to the Arabic and Ethiopian pattern /fāʿala/; cf. Huehnergard & Rubin 2011: L-stem.

[14] While the verbal stem formation in Qatabanic seems to follow the Sabaic pattern, the Hadramitic system is not yet clearly established due to its still poor documentation; at present, however, no instances for reduplicating stems (as in Minaic) have been observed.
[15] These D-stems are, of course, not graphically distinguished from the corresponding base stems but can only be determined by semantic arguments (cf. Multhoff, forthcoming).
[16] A particular case is, of course, Classical Arabic, which preserves traces of this system in its derived themes V and VI. These remains, however, can easily be interpreted as pre- (or extra-)Sabaic substrate influence. The exact position of Arabic in the linguistic history of the Ancient Near East remains a question of its own.
[17] Note that the particular characteristic is not the reduplicated second radical but rather the system of sub-derivation by different means of lengthening, resulting in a sequence of (at least) three sub-categories for

3. Another, well-known feature which separates all other South Arabian languages from Sabaic is the formation of the causative stem (and the 3rd person pronouns) with a sibilant (traditionally spelled $s = s_1$, but pronounced like [š]), not with /h/. This feature links these languages with the ancient representative of East Semitic, Akkadian, but separates them from Central Semitic.
4. The last striking phenomenon is the number of consonants. While the immediately neighbouring languages, Minaic and Qatabanic, like Sabaic have preserved the full consonantal inventory, the most remote language, Hadramitic, shows remarkable deficiencies: not only does it lack the fricative interdentals /ḏ/ and /ṯ/ (being merged with the corresponding sibilants /z/ and /ś/, respectively),[18] but it also confuses the emphatics /ṣ/ and /ẓ/, thus strongly recalling the consonantal system of Ethiopic.[19]

What do we learn from this picture? Sabaic appears to be linguistically much closer to Aramaic than to any of its neighbouring languages from the so-called Ancient South Arabian group. If we took only the grammatical evidence without knowing the historic-geographical background of the languages, we would certainly be inclined to connect Sabaic with Aramaic, and not with Minaic or Hadramitic. As a result, this means that the origin of the Sabaic language is in all probability to be looked for not in South Arabia, in the area of South Semitic, but further northwards, in the environment that also gave birth to Aramaic.

This proto-Aramaic was, as we have seen, probably not located in Syria (which became the heartland of that language only in the early first millennium) but rather somewhere further to the south. Here, on the north-western fringes of the Arabian Peninsula, we may imagine some folk settling there during the second millennium and speaking some kind of proto-Aramaeo-Sabaic dialects. At some time towards the end of the millennium, perhaps evoked by dramatic climatic changes causing severe drought in Syria-Palestine (cf. e.g. Litt et al. 2012; Kaniewski et al. 2013), a group of these folk could have set out for a new home — along the international trade route — finally to settle at the end of that route in South Arabia. This travelling group encountered a Semitic-speaking people there — the ancestors of what shortly later appeared as Minaeans, Qatabanians, and Hadramites. During a process of mutual integration and assimilation, the newcomers quickly took over political leadership — in parallel with the progress of Aramaean elites in Syria shortly after.[20] A remembrance of the migrating roots of this people could even be seen in their name, Sabaʾ. The root behind this name (SBʾ) simply means 'to travel' in Sabaic, and broad use is made of it in the Sabaean inscriptions!

The seeming paradox of a continuity of South Arabian civilization during the second millennium along with a clearly Central (or North-west) Semitic setting of some parts of this culture could well be solved by assuming migration, not of entire civilizations but of a rather small group, the Sabaeans. Together with their language, this group introduced the use of script in their new homeland and thus laid the basis for a common writing culture of peoples speaking completely different languages, as the Aramaeans did a couple of generations later in the north.[21]

Siglum

KAI   Inscription in Donner & Röllig 2002.

---

each base stem (thus 0_1, 0_2, 0_3; S_1, S_2, S_3, and so on). The combination of causative and reflexive morphemes with $0_2/0_3$ patterns is indeed a characteristic of South Semitic (see most recently Weninger 2011: 1116), most largely developed in Old Ethiopic (Geʿez) with a system of twelve verbal stems quite similar to Minaic. Indeed, verbal stems with reduplicated second radical are found not in Geʿez, but rather in other Ethio-Semitic languages such as Amharic (see Leslau 2000: 92–94).

[18] Since the Hadramites used the same script as the Sabaeans, the particular letters of the missing consonants (ḏ, ṯ) actually occur in the texts but are mixed up with the corresponding letters z and ś, and often even in etymologically the wrong position.

[19] For the evidence, see Stein 2011: 1047–1048 with references.

[20] The particular prestige the Sabaeans enjoyed among their new neighbours is evident in the epigraphic documentation: other people made broad use of Sabaic phrases in their inscriptions and gave their children Sabaean names, despite the completely different structure of their own languages (cf. Stein 2012b: 44–51).

[21] It is hardly necessary to stress that similar developments can be found all over the world. The common acceptance of Latin language and script in Medieval Europe, or the advance of English in the former colonies of the British Empire may suffice as examples. In all these cases, the original population continues to speak completely different languages, adapting not only the script but also borrowing words, phrases, and formal aspects of the foreign language.

References

Avanzini A.
    2009. Origin and classification of the Ancient South Arabian languages. *Journal of Semitic Studies* 54: 205–220.

Degen R.
    1969. *Altaramäische Grammatik der Inschriften des 10.–8. Jh. v. Chr.* (Abhandlungen für die Kunde des Morgenlandes, XXXIII/3). Wiesbaden: Franz Steiner.

Donner H. & Rölling W.
    2002. *Kanaanäische und aramäische Inschriften.* i. (5th edition). Wiesbaden: Harrassowitz.

Fales F.M.
    2011. Old Aramaic. Pages 555–573 in Weninger et al. 2011.

Garbini G.
    2004. The origins of South Arabians. Pages 203–209 in A.V. Sedov (ed.), *Scripta Yemenica. Issledovanija po Južnoj Aravii. Sbornik naučnych statej v čest' 60-letija M.B. Piotrovskogo.* Moscow: Vostočnaja literatura, RAN.

Gzella H.
    2011. Northwest Semitic in General. Pages 425–451 in Weninger et al. 2011.

Huehnergard J. & Rubin A.D.
    2011. Phyla and waves: Models of classification of the Semitic Languages. Pages 259–278 in Weninger et al. 2011.

Kaniewski D., Van Campo E., Guiot J., Le Burel S. et al.
    2013. Environmental roots of the Late Bronze Age crisis. PLoS ONE 8(8): e71004. doi:10.1371/journal.pone.0071004.

Kottsieper I.
    1990. *Die Sprache der Aḥiqarsprüche.* (Beihefte zur Zeitschrift für die alttestamentliche Wissenschaft, 194). Berlin/New York: De Gruyter.
    1999. '... und mein Vater zog hinauf ...': Aspekte des älteren aramäischen Verbalsystems und seiner Entwicklung. Pages 55–76 in N. Nebes (ed.), *Tempus und Aspekt in den semitischen Sprachen.* (Jenaer Beiträge zum Vorderen Orient, 1). Wiesbaden: Harrassowitz.
    2009. Aramaic Literature. Pages 393–444, 487–492 in C.S. Ehrlich (ed.), *From an Antique Land: An Introduction to Ancient Near Eastern Literature.* Lanham, MD: Rowman & Littlefield.

Leslau W.
    2000. *Introductory Grammar of Amharic.* (Porta linguarum orientalium N.S. 21). Wiesbaden: Harrassowitz.

Litt T., Ohlwein C., Neuman F.H., Hense A. & Stein M.
    2012. Holocene climate variability in the Levant from the Dead Sea pollen record. *Quaterny Science reviews* 49: 95–105.

Mazzini G.
    2005. Ancient South Arabian documentation and the reconstruction of Semitic. Pages 215–238 in P. Fronzaroli & P. Marrassini (eds), *Proceedings of the 10th Meeting of Hamito-Semitic (Afroasiatic) Linguistics, Firenze, 18–20 April 2001.* (Quaderni di Semitistica 25). Florence: Dept. of Linguistics, University of Florence.

Multhoff A.
    (forthcoming). Neue Perspektiven der altsüdarabischen Grammatik. In R.G. Stiegner (ed.), *South Arabia. A Great Lost Corridor of Mankind.* (Wiener Offene Orientalistik, 10). Münster: LIT.

Nebes N.
    1994. Verwendung und Funktion der Präfixkonjugation im Sabäischen. Pages 191–211 in N. Nebes (ed.), *Arabia felix. Beiträge zur Sprache und Kultur des vorislamischen Arabien.* Wiesbaden: Harrassowitz.
    2001. Zur Genese der altsüdarabischen Kultur. Eine Arbeitshypothese. Pages 427–435 in R. Eichmann & H. Parzinger (eds), *Migration und Kulturtransfer. Der Wandel vorder- und zentralasiatischer Kulturen im*

Umbruch vom 2. zum 1. vorchristlichen Jahrtausend. Akten des internationalen Kolloquiums Berlin, 23. bis 26. November 1999 (Kolloquien zur Vor- und Frühgeschichte 6). Bonn: Habelt.

Soden W. von
- 1968. *n* als Wurzelaugment im Semitischen. Pages 175–184 in M. Fleischhammer (ed.), *Studia Orientalia in memoriam Caroli Brockelmann*. (Wissenschaftliche Zeitschrift der Universität Halle, 17). Halle: Martin-Luther-Universität.

Stein P.
- 2011. Ancient South Arabian. Pages 1042–1073 in Weninger et al. 2011.
- 2012*a*. Sabaica-Aramaica (1). Pages 503–522 in T. Polański (ed.), *Studia Andreae Zaborski dedicata*. (Folia Orientalia 49). Cracow: Polish Academy of Sciences.
- 2012*b*. Aspekte von Sprachbewusstsein im antiken Südarabien. Pages 29–59 in J. Thon, G. Veltri & E-J. Waschke (eds), *Sprachbewusstsein und Sprachkonzepte im Alten Orient, Alten Testament und Rabbinischen Judentum*. (Orientwissenschaftliche Hefte, 30). Halle: Zentrum für Interdisziplinäre Regionalstudien.

Tropper J.
- 1993. *Die Inschriften von Zincirli*. (Abhandlungen zur Literatur Alt-Syrien-Palästinas, 6). Münster: Ugarit-Verlag.
- 2001. Dialektvielfalt und Sprachwandel im frühen Aramäischen. Soziolinguistische Überlegungen. Pages 213–222 in M. Daviau, J.W. Wevers & M. Weigl (eds), *The World of the Arameans* III. (Journal for the Study of the Old Testament Supplement Series 326). Sheffield: Sheffield Academic Press.

Voigt R.
- 1998. Der Artikel im Semitischen. *Journal of Semitic Studies* 43: 221–258.

Weninger S.
- 2011. Ethio-Semitic in general. Pages 1114–1123 in Weninger et al. 2011.

Weninger S. in collaboration with G. Khan, M.P. Streck & J.C.E. Watson (eds).
- 2011. *The Semitic Languages. An International Handbook*. (Handbücher zur Sprach- und Kommunikationswissenschaft, 36). Berlin/New York: De Gruyter Mouton.

Authors' addresses

Ingo Kottsieper, Akademie der Wissenschaften zu Göttingen, Forschungsstelle Qumran-Wörterbuch, c/o Theologische Fakultät der Georg-August-Universität, Platz der Göttinger Sieben 2/HBK 5, 37073 Göttingen, Germany.
e-mail Ingo.Kottsieper@mail.uni-goettingen.de

Peter Stein, Friedrich-Schiller-Universität Jena, Theologische Fakultät, Fürstengraben 6, 07743 Jena, Germany.
e-mail Peter.Stein@uni-jena.de

Sabaic lexical survivals in the Arabic language and dialects of Yemen

WALTER W. MÜLLER

Summary

At the beginning of Sabaean studies in the last quarter of the nineteenth century scholars noticed words in the inscriptions, which had parallels not in Classical Arabic but in the dialects of Yemen. Experts including David Heinrich Müller, Eduard Glaser, and Carlo de Landberg paid special attention to lexical links between the extinct and extant languages of southern Arabia. Ettore Rossi checked the glossary in Carolus Conti Rossini's *Chrestomathia Arabica Meridionalis Epigraphica* (1931) and provided numerous lemmata with words taken from Yemeni dialects. The authors of the Sabaic Dictionary (1982) marked some entries with the Arabic letter *yāʾ* to denote the modern Yemeni usage of that word. It was Ibrahim Al-Selwi's aim in his doctoral dissertation (1987) to collect Yemeni words from the writings of the two medieval South Arabian authors, Al-Hamdānī and Nashwān al-Ḥimyarī, many of which go back to pre-Islamic times. In the three parts of his glossary of northern Yemeni Arabic dialects (1992–2006), Peter Behnstedt indicated etymological correspondences in Epigraphic South Arabian for a number of words, which he had found in the Sabaic Dictionary. Muṭahhar al-Iryānī occasionally pointed to parallels in the ancient inscriptions in the two editions of his Muʿjam al-Yamanī (1996; 2012). Janet Watson (2004) noted the problem of lexical survivals and listed a number of words from ancient South Arabian roots that retained their original Sabaic meaning. Finally it can be recorded that the quantity of old attestations has been considerably increased since the publications of wooden sticks with texts in minuscule script. The Sabaic lexical survivals in the Arabic language and dialects of Yemen, which are dealt with in this article, amount to more than 100. Words that have survived from Sabaic belong mainly to the semantic fields of geographical features, agriculture, irrigation, architecture, building materials, cultural history, and local foodstuffs. Apart from elements of archaic vocabulary the Sabaic substratum also left traces in the morphology, that is, in prepositions and negations and in the so-called k-perfect of some Yemeni dialects.

Keywords: Ancient South Arabia, lexicography, Sabaic inscriptions, al-Hamdānī, Yemeni Arabic dialects

In the summer semester of 1970, Muṭahhar al-Iryānī, a nephew of the then president of the Republic of Yemen, ʿAbdarraḥmān al-Iryānī, spent some months at the University of Tübingen to study Ancient South Arabian inscriptions with me. It happened that at the time the building inscription of King Shuraḥbiʾil Yaʿfur's royal palace of Hargab in the Himyarite capital Ẓafār had just been published (Garbini 1969). This fully preserved inscription is a very difficult text consisting of fourteen lines to which the siglum ZM 1 (Ẓafār Museum 1) was later given (Müller 2010: 75–76). Muṭahhar and I tried to read and understand this inscription. When we came, in line 5, across the plural form ʾlhg, which was left untranslated by the editor who ignored an earlier reference (Landberg 1920–1942: 2648), Muṭahhar said that he knew this word and that the meaning of *lahj* in Yemeni Arabic is 'upper window' (Beeston et al. 1982: 82). I gave this as an example to explain the need of a comprehensive dictionary of all words occurring in the Yemeni Arabic dialects, which are not attested in Classical Arabic. In the introduction to his Yemeni Arabic dictionary, a book of more than 1000 pages (al-Iryānī 1996), Muṭahhar al-Iryānī wrote that I had encouraged him to compile this immense work, of which a second enlarged and revised edition in two volumes appeared not long ago (al-Iryānī 2012). The word *lahj* is as a Yemenism also attested in the eighth book of the *Iklīl* (al-Hamdānī 1979: 61, line 2), where al-Hamdānī writes in his description of the castle of Ghumdān in Ṣanʿāʾ that at the top of the palace there was a room which had upper windows, *luhuj*, which he explains by *kuwā* 'small windows, skylights'.

Besides ʾlhg the inscription ZM 1 contains a number of further Yemenisms. The name of the king, who was the dedicator of the text, is Shuraḥbiʾil; the vocalization of this name is confirmed by the fact that many South Arabians in pre-Islamic and early Islamic times bore the name Shuraḥbīl (Caskel 1966: 532). The meaning of the name is 'protected by God', showing the passive form of the Sabaic verb *šrḥ* 'to preserve, to protect' (Beeston et al. 1982: 134), which has survived in Yemeni Arabic *sharaḥ* 'to guard, to watch' (al-Iryānī 2012: 600). The building activities began with the laying of the foundations of the house, expressed in Sabaic by the verb *hwṯr* and the noun *mwṯr* (Beeston et al. 1982: 166), which corresponds to the Yemeni Arabic verb *waththar* and the noun *mawthar* (Behnstedt 1992–2006: 1281). Apart from being rectangular blocks of stone, the building materials were 'smooth dressed, polished stones', Sabaic *mnhmt* (pl.) (Beeston et al. 1982: 94), which we encounter as *munhamāt* 'hewn stones' (Al-Selwi 1987: 209) in several passages in the eighth volume of the *Iklīl*, where al-Hamdānī describes the castles and public buildings of the Himyarites. The guards who were posted in the royal palace Hargab were alarmed by *mᶜhrtm/ḏhbm*, bronze bells (Müller 2010: 135). In his description of Ẓafār, al-Hamdānī mentions that *maᶜāhirah* were attached to one of the nine gates of the town, which would be heard from afar whenever the gate was opened or closed; the plural form *maᶜāhirah* is explained by Arabic *ajrās* bells (al-Hamdānī 1979: 70, lines 2–3). In line 10 to 12 of inscription ZM 1 a report is given on the restoration of the ᶜ*rm* 'dam' (Beeston et al. 1982: 19) in Mārib; ᶜ*arim* and ᶜ*arīm* are Yemeni Arabic words for dike, dam, wall (Behnstedt 1992–2006: 822) and the *sayl al-*ᶜ*arim* in the Sūrat Sabaʾ of the Qurʾān (34. 16) testifies to the catastrophic flood which destroyed the dam of the Sabaeans. The workers repaired the dam by the activities of *msrm* and *šṣnm*; *msrm* signifies either the clearing away of silt behind the dam (Beeston et al. 1982: 87) or, more probably, the heaping up of embankments of earth (Müller 2010: 187), while *šṣnm* signifies the revetting or facing of the dam wall in stones (Beeston et al. 1982: 135). The first can be compared with the Yemeni Arabic verb *masar*, 'to clean a well, cistern or canal from deposits' (al-Iryānī 2012: 976), the second with the noun *mashṣan* 'dam, parapet or low wall of stones to distribute the water' (Landberg 1905–1913: 1142). Furthermore, the workers renewed the *rthm* 'stone supports' (Müller 2010: 202) at the lower part of the dam; the meaning of *rth* is given in al-Iryānī's Yemeni Arabic dictionary, where the verb *ratah* is explained by 'to support and underpin something, to give strength to something' (al-Iryānī 2012: 452). In ZM 2, the fragmentary parallel version of inscription ZM 1 (Müller 2010: 77), we encounter among the building activities at the dam in Mārib the plural ᶜ*glmn* of the noun ᶜ*glmt* 'diversion mole' (Beeston et al. 1982: 14); in Yemeni Arabic ᶜ*ijlamah* is a mole or low wall of stones built up to deviate water into the cultivated fields (Piamenta 1990–1991: 317). The dating formula at the end of the inscription begins with the Sabaic word *wrh* 'month, date' (Beeston et al. 1982: 162). Chaim Rabin and other scholars before him (Nöldeke 1904: 11 n. 3) have argued that the derivation of Arabic *taʾrīkh* 'date', from South Arabian is plausible because the word *warkh* 'moon, month', does not exist in Arabic. The Arabic form *taʾrīkh* may represent South Arabian *tawrīkh* 'dating'; this less-attested form and the plural *tawārīkh* point to an original form *warkh* (Rabin 1984: 127–128).

At the beginning of Sabaean studies in the last quarter of the nineteenth century, scholars noticed words in the inscriptions, which had parallels not in Classical Arabic but in the dialects of Yemen. Experts including David Heinrich Müller, Eduard Glaser, and Carlo de Landberg paid special attention to the problem of lexical links between the extinct and extant languages of southern Arabia. Ettore Rossi checked the glossary in Carolus Conti Rossini's *Chrestomathia Arabica Meridionalis Epigraphica* (pub. Rome 1931) and provided numerous lemmata with words taken from the Yemeni Arabic dialects and with place names of present-day southern Arabia (Rossi 1940: 299–314). The authors of the Sabaic Dictionary (Beeston et al. 1982) marked some lexical entries with the Arabic letter *yāʾ* to denote the modern Yemeni usage of the same word. It was Ibrahim al-Selwi's aim in his doctoral dissertation (1987) to collect Yemeni words from the writings of the two medieval South Arabian authors, al-Hamdānī and Nashwān, many of which likewise go back to pre-Islamic times. In the three parts of his glossary of the North Yemeni dialects Peter Behnstedt (1992–2006) indicated etymological correspondences in Epigraphic South Arabian for a number of lexical roots and words, which he had found in the Sabaic Dictionary. He also undertook the task of extracting the words from Yemeni dialects as contained in the diaries of Eduard Glaser (Behnstedt 1993), who had already pointed to parallels in the ancient inscriptions. Likewise Muṭahhar al-Iryānī in the two editions of his *Muᶜjam al-Yamānī* (1996; 2012) sometimes indicated words from Yemeni dialects, which are also attested in Sabaic. In an article published in the *Proceedings of the Seminar for Arabian Studies* Janet C.E. Watson (2004) noted the problem of lexical attestations and listed a number of words from ancient South Arabian roots that retained their original Sabaic meaning. The importance of the Yemeni Arabic vocabulary for research in the inscriptions of ancient South Arabia was also stressed by Anna Belova in three small articles, the latest of which appeared in the *Proceedings of the 15th Rencontre sabéenne* held 2011 in Moscow (Belova 2012). Finally it can be recorded that the quantity of Sabaic attestations has been considerably increased since the publications of wooden sticks with texts in minuscule script. Words that have survived from Sabaic belong mainly to the semantic fields of geographical features, agriculture, irrigation, architecture, building materials, cultural history, and local foodstuffs. Apart from elements of archaic vocabulary the Sabaic substratum also left traces in the phonology, such as the total regressive assimilation of *n* to a following consonant in Middle and Late Sabaic, for example *bt* (for *bnt*) 'daughter' (Stein 2011: 1048), Yemeni Arabic *bitt* 'girl, daughter' (instead of *bint*), in the whole of the Tihāmah and elsewhere (Behnstedt 1992–2006: 57); further in the morphology, that is in prepositions, for example Sabaic *s* ' towards, to, near' (Stein 2003: 214), Yemeni Arabic *sī* 'towards, until, to (local)' (Behnstedt 1992–2006: 600); in negations, for example Sabaic *dʾ* 'not' (Müller 2010: 151), Yemeni Arabic *daʾ*, *dāʾ*, *dā*, *dawʾ* 'no' (al-Iryānī 2012: 369); and in the so-called *k*-perfect of some Yemeni Arabic dialects, which is to say that the 1st person and the 2nd person singular have, like Sabaic *fʿlk* (Stein 2011: 1060), the forms *katabku* 'I wrote', *katabk* 'you (masc.) wrote', and *katabki* 'you (fem.) wrote' (Diem 1973: 95) instead of *katabtu*, *katabt*, and *katabti*.

It is not the intention of this article to enumerate *all* probable Sabaic lexical survivals in the Arabic language and dialects of Yemen. Let us start with the most important thing in daily life, food, especially local foodstuffs, with vegetable matter and medical plants, and including verbs and nouns pertaining to cooking and baking. Most of the Sabaic words in this category are found in minuscule texts. Sabaic *bkrm*, a kind of grain (Stein 2010: 519), may be explained by Yemeni Arabic *bukr*, a variety of red sorghum or durra (Varisco 1994: 168), and Sabaic *wkrm*, a kind of sorghum or durra (Weninger 2001: 241) used as fodder cereal, corresponds to Yemeni Arabic *wakīrī*, a variety of sorghum (Piamenta 1990–1991: 531). Sabaic *qšm* 'vegetable' (Stein 2010: 316) is Yemeni Arabic *qushm* 'vegetable' (al-Iryānī 2012: 857), and Sabaic *qšmt* 'vegetable plot' (Beeston et al. 1982: 108) is Yemeni Arabic *maqshamah* 'vegetable plot' (Behnstedt 1992–2006: 997). Sabaic *blśnm* 'lentils' (Sima 2000: 196–197), are the small South Arabian lentils named *bilsin* (Behnstedt 1992–2006: 107); the word is explained by Arabic ʿ*adas*. Another leguminous plant is Sabaic ʿ*trm* 'peas' (ʿAbdallāh 1986: 11), Yemeni Arabic ʿ*atar* 'peas' (al-Hamdānī 1884–1891, i: 123, line 2), and ʿ*atar akhḍar* 'green peas' (Varisco 1994: 183). A typical Yemenism is also Sabaic *glglnm* 'sesame' (Ryckmans, Müller & Abdallāh 1994: 54 and 65), in Yemeni Arabic *juljulān* or *jiljilān* 'sesame' (al-Iryānī 2012: 214), which is interpreted by Arabic *simsim*. According to Pliny in his *Naturalis Historia* (Plinius Secundus 1995: 18.22.96) the product, *Sesamum indicum* L., came from India, and from the report about the expedition of Aelius Gallus we learn that the South Arabians, like the Indians, pressed oil from sesame (Plinius Secundus 1996: 6.32.161). Sabaic *ḥmrm* (ʿAbdallāh 1986: 11) is the Yemeni Arabic term *ḥumar* (Behnstedt 1992–2006: 284) for *tamar hindī*, the tamarind or, more precisely, the fruit of the tamarind tree. Sabaic ʿ*lb* (pl. ʾ*lb*), is the ʿ*ilb* tree or plantation of ʿ*ilb* trees (Beeston et al. 1982: 15), which is Christ's thorn or, to give its botanical name, *Ziziphus spina Christi*, the ripe and dried fruits (*dawm*) of which are a favourite food (Schopen 1983: 111–113); since the name of this tree is a typical Yemenism, ʿ*ilb* is explained by Arabic *sidr*, which is encountered among the trees in the garden of the Sabaeans after the catastrophe of the *sayl al-ʿarim* as described in Sūrat Sabaʾ of the Qurʾān (34. 16). The Sabaic name for *Lepidium sativum* L. is *ḥlfm* (ʿAbdallāh 1986: 11), in Yemeni Arabic *ḥilf* 'seeds of water cress' (Schopen 1983: 38–39), explained by Arabic *ḥabb ar-rashād* and a Yemeni variant of North Arabic *ḥurf*. Epigraphically as well as archaeologically attested is linseed or flax seed, Sabaic *mmtm* (Drewes & Ryckmans 1997: 226), Yemeni Arabic *mūmah* or *ṣīb al-mūmah* (Schopen 1983: 100–101), which is synonymous with *bizr al-kattān*. Among the provisions for the workers who repaired the dam in Mārib *mzrm*/*ḍtmrm* is mentioned in CIH 540 (Müller 2010: 71), a kind of fermented drink made from dates or date-wine, while Nashwān in his dictionary gives under the entry *mizr* (1999: 6286) the explanation 'drink made from barley or durrah'. Sabaic *hbslt* 'cooked' (Stein 2010: 581) and *mbsl* 'cooking-place' (Beeston et al. 1982: 32) can be compared to the Yemeni Arabic verb *bassal* 'to cook (in the transitive meaning)' (Behnstedt 1992–2006: 85). Sabaic ʾ*fym*, 'a sort of foodstuff' (Beeston et al. 1982: 3), probably baked food, is to be linked with Yemeni Arabic *mawfe*, *mōfī*, *mawfaʾ*, or *māfī* 'baking oven' (Behnstedt 1992–2006: 1309).

Let us now continue with some words belonging to the semantic field of geographical features in the wider sense of this term. Sabaic *ḫlf* means 'region; the vicinity of a town' (Beeston et al. 1982: 60); its counterpart seems to be Yemeni Arabic *mikhlāf* 'province, region' (Al-Selwi 1987: 78), which is explained by Arabic *nāḥiyah* 'region, (administrative) district'. In some Sabaic warfare inscriptions we encounter the plural noun ʾ*dyr* or ʾ*dwr*, denoting 'settlements in the Tihāmah' (Beeston et al. 1982: 37); still today we find not infrequently *dayr* 'village' (al-Maqḥafī 2002: 636), as the first element of composed place names in the northern part of the Tihāmah. Sabaic *kwr* 'hill, mountain' (Beeston et al. 1982: 80) is in Yemeni Arabic, especially in Ḥaḍramawt and Dathīnah, *kawr* or *kōr* 'mountain' (Landberg 1920–1942: 2543); the noun *kur 'mountain' is a genuine, well-attested Hamito-Semitic root, for example in Lowland East Cushitic and Central Chadic (Orel & Stolbova 1995: 328). The frequent Sabaic ᶜ*r* 'mountain, citadel, castle-hill' (Beeston et al. 1982: 20) and Yemeni Arabic ᶜ*urr*, which is described by al-Hamdānī (1884–1891, i: 67, lines 22–23) as an isolated mountain and explained by the Arabic word *jabal*, has survived until the present time in South Arabia, mainly in place names. The term *sr* (pl. ᵓ*srr*), which often occurs in Sabaic inscriptions, is a valley, more precisely the cultivated land beside the flood-bed (Beeston et al. 1982: 128); in al-Hamdānī's *Geography sirr* (pl. *asrār*) is a synonym of Arabic *wādī*, as for example in his description of the *asrār* Najrān 'the valleys of Najrān' (al-Hamdānī 1884–1891, i: 169, line 2). Another typical Yemenism is the Yemeni Arabic word *jirbah* (pl. *jirab*) 'terraced field' (al-Iryānī 2012: 191–197), which is attested in the Sabaic verb *grb* 'to lay out fields in terraces' (Beeston et al. 1982: 50), and in *tgrb* (pl. *tgrbt*) 'laying out of terraced fields' (Müller 2010: 160), while in Qatabanic we also find the nouns *grbt* (pl. *grwb*) 'terraced field' (Ricks 1989: 40). Terms which are related to *grbt* and *grb* are Sabaic ᶜ*br*, ᶜ*brt* 'wadi-side cultivation, terraced fields' (Beeston et al. 1982: 11), in Yemeni Arabic ᶜ*abr*, ᶜ*ubr* 'terraced cultivated land' (Landberg 1920–1942: 2261), Sabaic *ḫyf* 'to terrace (fields at the foot of a hill)' (Beeston et al. 1982: 74), and Yemeni Arabic *ḫayfah* 'field, arable land' (Behnstedt 1992–2006: 305). The Sabaic plural *ḫblt* 'vineyards, cultivations of vine' (Sima 2000: 210–211) has an exact parallel in Yemeni Arabic *ḫablah* 'grapevine, vineyard' (Behnstedt 1992–2006: 232). Sabaic ᶜ*qr* 'land watered by rain' (Beeston et al. 1982: 18) corresponds to Yemeni Arabic ᶜ*qr*, cultivated land dependent on rain rather than irrigation (Behnstedt 1992–2006: 850). Sabaic *ḏhb* is an 'alluvial valley' (Beeston et al. 1982: 38), an oasis, and the southern half of the oasis of Mārib is called *ḏhbn/ysrn* 'the oasis (named) Yasrān' in the inscription CIH 540,26 (Müller 2010: 69); Yemeni Arabic *dhahb* 'field, piece of land' (al-Iryānī 2012: 441), with the variant *zahb* (Behnstedt 1992–2006: 232), is perhaps a remnant of this old noun. A homonym of *ḏhb* 'oasis' is Sabaic *ḏhb* (pl. ᵓ*ḏhb*) a measure of capacity (Stein 2010: 113), which is often found in the miniscule texts and can be compared to Yemeni Arabic *dhahb*, a dry measure of capacity for corn (Al-Selwi 1987: 94). Yemeni Arabic *ghayl*, continually flowing water, water coming from the ground, also *qanāt* (ᶜAṣlān 2000), is likewise a characteristic Yemenism known since antiquity in Sabaic *ġyl* 'water-course, conduit, covered canal' (Beeston et al. 1982: 54–55). The Sabaic *hapax legomenon mqṭṭ/šmsn* in the inscription Ja 649, 32–33 'setting of the sun' (Beeston et al. 1982: 87) may be compared to Yemeni Arabic *maqṭ at-turāb* in the second volume of the *Iklīl* 'the end of the land' (al-Hamdānī 1966: 270, line 2), that is, the place where the continent ends and the sea begins. From the Sabaic inscription Iryānī 28 we learn that the god Almaqah restrained and kept under control *nd-n* 'the wind' (Beeston et al. 1982: 101), the violent wind on the Red Sea, which is dangerous to ships; in Yemeni Arabic *nawd* is also the name of a strong and cold blowing wind (al-Iryānī 2012: 1036).

Since antiquity Yemen has been known as a country of master builders, therefore it is not surprising that we find in the field of architecture and building materials lexical survivals from ancient times, as already demonstrated earlier in the case of inscription ZM 1. Sabaic *mḥfd* is a tower or a projecting element of a wall (Beeston et al. 1982: 66), a bastion; the Yemeni Arabic *maḥfid* means 'tower, fortress' (Nashwān 1999: 1510), and al-Hamdānī writes in the subtitle of the eighth book of his *Iklīl* that in it he deals with the castles of Yemen, *fī maḥāfid* al-Yaman. Sabaic *mnẓr* (Beeston et al. 1982: 102) is perhaps 'a watch-tower, a high building' and Yemeni Arabic *manẓar* (pl. *manāẓir*) 'high building, multi-storey house, palace', is attested several times in the various books of *al-Iklīl* (al-Hamdānī 1966: 118, line 4), and confirmed also by Jewish sources (Piamenta 1990–1991: 489). Eduard Glaser recorded in the Mashriq the Yemeni Arabic *mikrāb* for a pagan or heathen temple of the ancients (Behnstedt 1993: 182); this word is a survival of late Sabaic *mkrb*, which is used in the inscriptions for a shrine, temple, or synagogue (Beeston et al. 1982: 78). Sabaic *mṣnᶜt* (pl. *mṣnᶜ*) is a fortification, fortress, or castle (Müller 2010: 221), and in Yemeni Arabic *maṣnaᶜah* (pl. *maṣāniᶜ*) is also a fortress or fortified building or settlement (al-Hamdānī 1884–1891, i: 90, line 23). 'Maṣnaᶜat' occurs as the first part of names of ancient ruins or villages which are situated on mountains and therefore naturally fortified, for example Maṣnaᶜat Māriyah or Maṣnaᶜat Ānis; the *maṣāniᶜ*, which are associated in the Sūrat al-Shuᶜarāʾ of the Qurʾān (26. 129) with the ᶜĀd, point likewise to South Arabia (Grimme 1912: 159–160). Sabaic *mḫrb* is an upper or separated room (Müller 2010: 170) and Yemeni Arabic *miḫrāb* (pl. *maḫārīb*) is in the works of al-Hamdānī, likewise attested in the special meaning 'upper room' (al-Hamdānī 1968: 297, line 19). Another

Yemenism is Sabaic *mdfn* 'corn-storage pit' (Beeston et al. 1982: 35) and Yemeni Arabic *madfan*, an underground grain silo outside the house (Behnstedt 1992–2006: 381). Sabaic *ḫlt* 'funeral chamber' (Beeston et al. 1982: 60) may be compared with Yemeni Arabic *khalwah* 'an upper or small room, store room, chamber' (Behnstedt 1992–2006: 341–342), and Sabaic *ḥwd* 'recess excavated in hill side' (Beeston et al. 1982: 73) with Yemeni Arabic *ḥūd* 'small gap, tiny hole' (Behnstedt 1992–2006: 295). Yemeni Arabic *ṣalalah*, collective *ṣalal*, 'paving stone, flat stone, slab, flagstone' (al-Iryānī 2012: 676) suggests the translation of Sabaic *ṣll* by 'covering of flat stones' (Beeston et al. 1982: 142) and *ṣlt* by 'pavement' (Müller 2010: 220). The Sabaic plural *mᶜrbt* (Müller 2010: 139) has the same meaning as Yemeni Arabic *maᶜrib* (pl. *maᶜārib*) 'hewn, oblong stone blocks' (Al-Selwi 1987: 149–150), and the Sabaic plural *grb* (Müller 2010: 160) may be Yemeni Arabic *jurūb* (al-Hamdānī 1979: 36, line 8) or *jurub* 'dressed stones, building stones' (Behnstedt 1993: 43); from this noun is derived the Sabaic profession *grby*, 'stonemason' (Beeston et al. 1982: 50). To the north of the great dam of Mārib is the Jabal Balaq al-Qiblī, to the south of it the Jabal Balaq al-Awsaṭ (Glaser 1913: Blatt 4); *balaq* is the Yemeni Arabic word for limestone, as a rule white or yellowish in colour (Behnstedt 1992–2006: 109); not only in Sabaic, but also in Minaic and Qatabanic inscriptions *blq* 'limestone' is frequently mentioned (Sima 2000: 289–291), since it was used as a building material and for the manufacture of votive objects. Sabaic *ḥbl* is 'a course of stones in a wall' (Beeston et al. 1982: 65), like Yemeni Arabic *ḥabl* 'a course of stones' (Piamenta 1990–1991: 82). In the late Sabaic inscription CIH 540 we encounter five times the noun *kʾbt*, in the singular, or *kʾbtn* in the dual respectively, describing a structure consisting of either one pillar or two pillars as part of the dam of Mārib (Müller 2010: 69–72); in Yemeni Arabic *kābah* (pl. *kawāb*) is a doorpost or, according to Eduard Glaser, more precisely the two outer vertical stone doorposts (Behnstedt 1993: 185). Sabaic *mᶜqm* 'spill-ledge' at the dam of Mārib (Müller 2010: 139) can be compared with Yemeni Arabic *maᶜqam* 'threshold, door sill', also with the meaning 'dike, barrage' (Al-Selwi 1987: 159–160). The Sabaic terms *qyf*, *qf*, and *mqf* are used to denote 'stelae, cult-stones of any kind and boundary stones' (Beeston et al. 1982: 111); Ettore Rossi noted for eastern Khawlān the Yemeni Arabic *muqwaf* 'upright stone put up to support vines' (Rossi 1940: 311). Sabaic *wqr* is a stone, a building stone, an inscribed stone (Beeston et al. 1982: 161), and a document carved in stone (Stein 2010: 215–216); in Yemeni Arabic the verb *waqqar* has the meaning 'to hew', 'to cut stones', and 'to carve with a chisel' (Behnstedt 1992–2006: 1311). It has long been known that the isolated Classical Arabic noun *wathan* 'idol, image of a deity' is a loan-word (Wellhausen 1897: 102), precisely from Sabaic *wṯn* 'stela, boundary stone, boundary mark' (Beeston et al. 1982 166); in Yemeni Arabic the word has survived in *wathan* 'borderstone in a field' (Behnstedt 1992–2006: 1281). Yemeni Arabic *ḥabash* (Habshush 1941: 83) or *ḥabāsh* (Rossi 1939: 171) 'dark hewn stones' helps to interpret Sabaic *ḥbš* in CIH 325, which is a term for building stones (Müller 2010: 123). The Sabaic noun *lbt*, which occurs three times in CIH 540 and which has been left untranslated in the Sabaic dictionary (Beeston et al. 1982: 81), was interpreted by 'bolt, wedge, peg' (Müller 2010: 69–72), following Yemeni Arabic *libbah*, which is explained by Arabic *isfīn* 'wedge of wood or iron' (al-Iryānī 2012: 931). The Sabaic plural *gᶜwr* in Grjaznevič 3 (Beeston et al. 1982: 48), hitherto unsatisfactorily translated by 'in total', may be compared to the singular *jaᶜīr* in a Musnad text in the second volume of Hamdānī's *Iklīl*, for which the explanation *khashabah*, 'wooden beam' (al-Hamdānī 1966: 354, lines 9–12) is given; the rendering of the passage ᶜšry/ʾʾblm/gᶜwrm is consequently 'twenty camel-loads of wooden beams'. The Sabaic verb *zbr* 'to erect a construction' (Beeston et al. 1982: 170) is perhaps to be understood in the sense of Yemeni Arabic *zabar* 'to build a wall of mud' (Piamenta 1990–1991: 195), consisting of *zābūr*, compact layers of clay (al-Iryānī 2012: 499). Sabaic *ṣhr* is the coating with stones of the Mārib dam (Müller 2010: 113) in the Abraha inscription (CIH 541,60), while the Yemeni Arabic *ṣhār* is a plaster for walls (Behnstedt 1993: 127). Sabaic *mḏḥ* 'to sieve (burnt lime)' (Stein 2010: 495–496) may correctly be compared with Yemeni Arabic *madhaḥ* 'to winnow (grain)' (Behnstedt 1992–2006: 1150). The verb *madhaḥ* for the agricultural activity of winnowing grain as a typical Yemenism leads us to the next topic.

A number of lexical terms from ancient times are also found to belong to the semantic field of agriculture and irrigation. I shall start with two words that will be familiar to those who have spent some time in the rural areas of Yemen. Sabaic *krf* is a basin or cistern (Beeston et al. 1982: 79) and Yemeni Arabic *karīf* is a large water hole cut in the rocks (Al-Selwi 1987: 189); the only references to this term which are listed in the *Wörterbuch der Klassischen Arabischen Sprache* (Ullmann 1970: 135) are taken from the works of al-Hamdānī (e.g. 1884–1891, i: 78, line 20). The second word is Sabaic *mʾgl* 'tank, cistern' (Beeston et al. 1982: 3) and Yemeni Arabic *maʾjil*, *mājil*, *mawjil* 'reservoir, open cistern for collecting rain water' (Al-Selwi 1987: 33–34). In the following is a list of terms comparing Sabaic with the Yemeni Arabic words:

Sabaic mʾḫḏ 'control dyke' (Beeston et al. 1982: 3) — Yemeni Arabic maʾkhadh 'dam' (al-Hamdānī 1966: 352, line 9);
Sabaic mḥwl 'water reservoir' (Müller 2010: 122) — Yemeni Arabic maḥwal 'water reservoir near a well' (Behnstedt 1992–2006: 299);
Sabaic mṭbr 'damage, rupture (of a dam)' (Beeston et al. 1982: 149) — Yemeni Arabic mithbir 'damage of a dam (by heavy rainfalls)' (Behnstedt 1992–2006: 147);
Sabaic mḍrf 'retaining wall, water-container' (Müller 2010: 156) — Yemeni Arabic maḍraf 'dam (in the wadi-bed)' (Goitein 1934: 87);
Sabaic mʾtw 'inlet/outlet channel' (Beeston et al. 1982: 9) — Yemeni Arabic maʾtā 'inflow (of water), feeder river' (al-Hamdānī 1884–1891, i: 71, line 11);
Sabaic mzf (pl. mzff) 'outflow channel of a dam' (Beeston et al. 1982: 170) — Yemeni Arabic mazaff 'wooden pipe used for conducting water into a basin' (Piamenta 1990–1991: 201);
Sabaic nḍḥ 'irrigation' (Stein 2010: 87) — Yemeni Arabic naḍḍāḥa 'well, irrigation system' (al-Hamdānī 1966: 73, line 2);
Sabaic šrg 'water-course' (Beeston et al. 1982: 134) — Yemeni Arabic sharīj 'water-course, channel' Behnstedt 1992–2006: 634);
Sabaic fnwt 'secondary canal' (Beeston et al. 1982: 45) — Yemeni Arabic fāniyah 'canal' (Behnstedt 1992–2006: 956);
Sabaic ḫrt 'irrigation canal; bund' (Beeston et al. 1982: 71), 'main canal; deflecting dam' — Yemeni Arabic ḫarrah, 'stone dam to protect the fields against flood, wall around a field (Behnstedt 1992–2006: 244–245), 'trench; build up erosion barrier or drainage' (Piamenta 1990–1991: 87);
Sabaic qlḥ 'raised water-channel' (Beeston et al. 1982: 104) — Yemeni Arabic qalḥ 'water-channel through which water is conducted to high-lying fields' (Behnstedt 1992–2006: 1022);
Sabaic mḥmy 'field irrigated by a dam-canal' (Beeston et al. 1082: 69) — Yemeni Arabic maḥmā 'area irrigated by a dam-canal' (al-Hamdānī 1990: 40,6);
Sabaic mtʿd 'irrigated land' (Müller 2010: 223) — Yemeni Arabic mathʿad 'place where the water for irrigation is divided between two properties' (Rossi 1940: 313);

Sabaic mṭr 'rain-watered field' (Beeston et al. 1982: 88) — Yemeni Arabic maṭīrah 'irrigated plot of land' (Piamenta 1990–1991: 468–469);
Sabaic qrf (pl. qwrf) 'ploughed field' (Stein 2010: 346–348) — Yemeni Arabic qarrafa 'to loosen the soil with the plough' (Goitein 1934: 31);
Sabaic plural ʾklʾ 'pastureland, open country' (Beeston et al. 1982: 77) — Yemeni Arabic kilāʾ 'uncultivated land' (Rossi 1940: 306);
Sabaic nšʾ 'to take out water from a canal' (Beeston et al. 1982: 92) — Yemeni Arabic nāshiʾ 'point of distribution of water dammed up by a dike' (Rossi 1940: 308);
Sabaic bqr 'to dig up, level (fields)' (Beeston et al. 1982: 30) — Yemeni Arabic baqar 'to work the soil' (Varisco 2004: 76);
Sabaic wdn 'to prepare fields for flood irrigation' (Beeston et al. 1982: 156) — Yemeni Arabic wadīn 'small ditch for irrigation' (Behnstedt 1992–2006: 1290);
Sabaic ʿfr 'sowing land before rain' (Beeston et al. 1982: 13–14), ʿfr 'first irrigation of the seedlings' (Bron & Ryckmans 1999: 164–166) — Yemeni Arabic ʿafar 'sowing land before rain' (Behnstedt 1992–2006: 845), taʿfīr 'first irrigation after sowing' (Nashwān 1999: 4638);
Sabaic fql 'to reap crops'; fql (pl. ʾfql) '(cereal) crops' (Beeston et al. 1982: 45) — Yemeni Arabic faqal 'to winnow (grain), to ventilate corn'; fiqlah 'threshed corn, corn on the threshing ground' (Behnstedt 1992–2006: 949); faqal (pl. afqāl) 'harvest products' (Landberg 1920–1942: 2427);
Sabaic šrk 'to make a crop-sharing agreement; crop sharing' (Beeston et al. 1982: 134), 'participation, share' (Stein 2010: 350–351) — Yemeni Arabic shirk 'crop-sharing; agreement by which the crop is divided in equal shares between landlord and tenant' (Piamenta 1990–1991: 254);
Sabaic dtʾ 'spring season; spring crops' (Beeston et al. 1982: 36) — Yemeni Arabic dithāʾ 'crops which are harvested in early summer (ṣayf)' (al-Iryānī 2012: 372–385);
Sabaic ṣrb 'harvest; harvest season' (Beeston et al. 1982: 144) — Yemeni Arabic ṣirāb/ṣurāb 'harvest (of cereal crops), harvest season in autumn' (Piamenta 1990–1991: 280). The late Sabaic or so-called Himyaritic month name ḏ-ṣrbn corresponds to our October (Müller 2010: 221).

Sabaic qwl, qyl (pl. ʾqwl) are the members of the leading clan in a šʿb (Beeston et al. 1982: 110), the leaders and speakers of a tribe (Müller 2010: 197); in literary Yemeni sources one finds *qayl* (pl. *aqyāl, aqwāl*) as a designation of South Arabian princes and noblemen, for example Nashwān's Himyarite ode, *Al-Qaṣīdah al-ḥimyariyyah*, bears the title Mulūk Ḥimyar wa-aqyāl al-Yaman 'The kings of Himyar and the princes of Yemen' (Nashwān 1958). Sabaic plural *ṯbnt* 'proprietor, landlord' (Beeston et al. 1982: 152) has a parallel in Yemeni Arabic *ṯabīn* 'patron', recorded for Ḥaḍramawt (Landberg 1920–1942: 2193). The Late Sabaic collective *qbḍ* 'troop, gendarmes' (Müller 2010: 193) is probably the same as the Yemeni Arabic plural *aqbāḍ* 'troops, detachments', which occurs in three of al-Hamdānī's works (Al-Selwi 1987: 175). Sabaic *šf, šwf* 'to look after, protect, defend', *šwft* 'protection' (Beeston et al. 1982: 136); in Yemeni Arabic the verbal noun *tashwīf* retains the sense of 'protection (of women)', while *shawfah* has the specific sense of 'woman, wife (i.e. someone who is protected or under protection)' (Watson 2004: 407). The Sabaic term *ršw* 'title of holder of a religious function' (Beeston et al. 1982: 118), 'priest', for which so far no satisfactory etymology has been proposed, may be connected with the Yemeni Arabic verb *trāshā* (VI. stem) 'to reconcile, to appease' (Goitein 1934: 59), 'to request something, to beg for something' (Behnstedt 1992–2006: 446). Sabaic *mśnd* is an inscription or an inscribed votive tablet (Beeston et al. 1982: 138), while the Yemeni Arab word *musnad* (pl. *masānid*) is the term for the Himyarite inscriptions and the Himyarite script (Al-Selwi 1987: 114). In the Sabaic inscription Miᶜsāl 2, Abyssinians are mentioned wearing rings and bracelets of gold and silver (Müller 2010: 26); gold, *ṭyb*, and more frequently silver, *ṣrf* (Beeston et al.1982: 144) are well known from Sabaic texts. In his *Kitāb al-Jawharatain al-ᶜatīqatayn*, about the two precious metals gold and silver, in the chapter of the names of gold and silver al-Hamdānī lists the Himyaritic word *ṭīb* for gold (1968: 79, line 10) and the ancient term *ṣarīf*, which Nashwān in his dictionary explains by the Arabic *fiḍḍa* 'silver' (Nashwān 1999: 3721). In the just quoted Sabaic inscription Miᶜsāl 2 the Abyssinians are characterized as bearing lances, shields, and bows ᵓ*qsd* (Müller 2010: 26) as weapons; in the second book of his *Iklīl* al-Hamdānī writes that *qasd* is the Himyaritic word for bow (as a weapon), which he explains by Arabic *qaws* (1966: 142, line 1). The Sabaic, Minaic, and Hadramitic noun *mfḥm* 'incense burner' (Maraqten 1994: 168), is formed on the basis of the root *fḥm* (cf. Arabic *faḥm* 'charcoal'); in the same way the etymology of the Sabaic *mswdt* 'incense burner, fire-pan' (Lichtenstadter & Heinrichs 1987: 82–83) is based on the synonymous Yemeni Arabic *sawd* 'charcoal' (al-Hamdānī 1968: 271, lines 5–7; al-Iryānī 2012: 576).

The following list offers further verbs and nouns derived from verbal roots, which are found both in Sabaic and in Yemeni Arabic. Only in minuscule texts do the Sabaic verb *zbr* 'to write, sign' (Ryckmans, Müller & Abdallah 1994: 83) and the noun *zbr* 'document, something written' (Stein 2010: 545–546) occur; when the verb *zabara* 'to write' (al-Hamdānī 1966: 73, line 13), and the noun *zabūr* (al-Hamdānī 1954–1965: 51, line 19), pl. *zubur* 'script, writing, inscription' (1954–1965: 5, line 15), are used in the works of al-Hamdānī and other Arab historians and lexicographers, they occur, as I have demonstrated in my article 'L'écriture zabūr du Yémen pré-islamique dans la tradition arabe' (Ryckmans, Müller & Abdallah 1994: 35–39), almost exclusively in connection with Himyar or with the pre-Islamic era in Yemen. A variant of the verb *zbr* with a change of the initial consonant is *ḏbr*, attested in Sabaic *ḏbr* 'to write, sign' (Stein 2010: 239–241), as well as in Yemeni Arabic *dhabara* 'to write' (Nashwān 1999: 2244). The Sabaic verb *hmr* 'to grant, bestow' (Beeston et al. 1982: 61) occurs mainly in votive texts, Yemeni Arabic *khamara* has the meaning 'to give (a present)' (al-Hamdānī 1966: 389, line 14; Landberg 1920–1944: 643), and in the *Arabic–English Lexicon* the verb *akhmara* 'he gave him the thing, or put him in possession of it' (Lane 1863–1874: 808) is marked as a Yemenism. The root *šyṭ* which is well attested in the Qatabanic inscriptions on the market stela of Timnaᶜ, for example in the verbal forms *šyṭ* 'to trade, sell', and *štyṭ* 'to buy' and in the nominal form *šyṭ* 'merchandise' (Mazzini 2009: 157–161), has now also been found in minuscule texts in the Sabaic verb *šyṭ* 'to trade' (Stein 2010: 313–314) and in the Sabaic noun *šyṭ* 'commercial value, price' (Stein 2010: 239–240); in Yemeni Arabic the root *šyṭ* has survived with specialized meanings in the verb *shāṭ, yashīṭ* 'to sell cereals (wholesale)', and *shtāṭ* 'to buy cereals (wholesale)' (Piamenta 1990–1991: 273). The Sabaic verb *stᵓb* 'to draw water' (Müller 2010: 22) can be compared with the Yemeni Arabic verb *siᵓib* 'to draw water, to carry water home' (Behnstedt 1992–2006: 525), and the Sabaic verb ᵓ*sy* 'to find, be present' (Beeston et al. 1982: 7–8) with the Yemeni verb *asā, yaᵓsī* 'to find, meet, see' (al-Iryānī 2012: 37–38; Behnstedt 1992–2006: 23). The Sabaic nouns *zhd* (Stein 2010: 158), plural ᵓ*zhd* (Stein 2010: 126) 'estimate, fixing of taxes, taxes on yields' are to be explained by the Yemeni Arabic verbs *zahada* 'to estimate the yield of the not yet harvested cereals' (Nashwān 1999: 2861–2862) and *zahad* 'to estimate, suppose' (Behnstedt 1992–

2006: 513). Sabaic *ḫrš* 'to destroy (e.g. a monument)' (Beeston et al. 1982: 62) has its equivalent in Yemeni Arabic *kharrash* 'to break' (Piamenta 1990–1991: 124). In warfare inscriptions we encounter the Sabaic verb *sbṭ* 'to beat, defeat (an enemy)', in other contexts the noun *sbṭ* 'stroke, blow (as punishment)' (Beeston et al. 1982: 123); in Yemeni Arabic the verb *sabaṭ* has survived with the special meaning 'to pound limestone' (al-Iryānī 2012: 542). The Sabaic idiomatic expression *ḏkwn/kwnhmw* was interpreted by A.F.L. Beeston as 'to give support to' (Beeston et al. 1982: 80), comparing Yemeni Arabic *kāwana* 'to join forces with, be on the side of, support', a term which is according to the editor of Ibn Ḥātim's *Kitāb al-Simṭ*, G. Rex Smith, not infrequently used in this work in the given meaning (Smith 1978: 127). The last Yemenism to mention is the verb *wathaba*: Sabaic *wṯb* 'to sit, reside, settle' with many derivations (Beeston et al. 1982: 165), Yemeni Arabic *withāb*, in the language of the Himyar an equivalent to Arabic *firāsh*, a thing which is spread on the floor to sit on (Nashwān 1999: 7063), and *twaththab* 'to sit on the floor with crossed legs' (Landberg 1920–1942: 2901–2902). According to the *Arabic–English Lexicon* the verb *wathaba* signifies in the language of the Himyar 'he sat, sat down' (Lane 1863–1874: 2919), adding the following, often reported story: a man of the Banū Dārim came to the king of al-Yaman in Ẓafār and found him outside the city seated on the edge of a precipice. When the king saw him and had learned that he was an envoy he said to him: *Thib ʿalā l-fināʾ* 'sit down on the ground'. The man understood the king to have said 'jump over the cliff'; so he leaped from the mountain and lost his life (al-Hamdānī 1966: 78, lines 1–4). This story was the cause of the proverb *Man dakhala Ẓafāri taḥammara*, in Yemeni Arabic *man dakhal Ẓafār tiḥammar*, 'Whoever comes to Ẓafār should master the Himyaritic language' (al-Akwaʿ 1984: 1210).

It goes without saying that many towns, villages, mountains, and rivers in Yemen have preserved their ancient names, which they already had at the time of the Sabaeans and Himyarites and which can only be understood and explained with reference to the Epigraphic South Arabian languages, for example names such as Ṣanʿāʾ, Ṣirwāḥ, Jabal Riyām, and Wādī al-Sirr; furthermore, the well-known tribal name Bakīl has its origin in the Sabaic collective noun *bkl* 'settlers, colonists' (Beeston et al. 1982: 28).

References

ʿAbdallāh Y.M.
    1986. Khaṭṭ al-musnad wal-nuqūsh al-yamaniyyah al-qadīmah manqūshah ʿalā l-khashab. Al-ḥalqah al-thāniyah. *Al-Yaman al-jadīd* 15/6: 10–28.
al-Akwaʿ I. b. ʿA.
    1984. *Al-Amthāl al-yamaniyyah*. (2 volumes). Ṣanʿāʾ: Al-Jīl al-Jadīd.
ʿAṣlān ʿA.M.
    2000. *Ghuyūl Ṣanʿāʾ. Dirāsah taʾrīkhiyya, athariyya, wathāʾiqiyya*. Dimashq: Dār al-Fikr.
Beeston A.F.L., Ghul M.A., Müller W.W. & Ryckmans J.
    1982. *Sabaic Dictionary (English, French, Arabic)*. Louvain-la-Neuve: Peeters.
Behnstedt P.
    1992–2006. *Die nordjemenitischen Dialekte*. Teil 2: *Glossar*. Wiesbaden: Reichert.
    1993. *Glossar der jemenitischen Dialektwörter in Eduard Glasers Tagebüchern*. (Österreichische Akademie der Wissenschaften, Philosophisch-historische Klasse, Sitzungsberichte, 594. Veröffentlichungen der Arabischen Kommission, 6). Vienna: Österreichische Akademie der Wissenschaften.
Belova A.
    2012. Importance du lexique arabo-yéménite aux recherches sudarabiques. Pages 69–74 in A. Sedov (ed.), *New research in archaeology and epigraphy of South Arabia and its neighbors*. Moscow: The State Museum of Oriental Art.
Bron F. & Ryckmans J.
    1999. Une inscription sabéenne sur bronze provenant du Maḥram Bilqīs à Mārib. *Semitica* 49: 161–169.
Caskel W.
    1966. *Ǧamharat an-nasab. Das genealogische Werk des Hišām Ibn Muḥammad al-Kalbī*. ii. *Das Register*. Leiden: Brill.

Diem W.
    1973. *Skizzen jemenitischer Dialekte.* (Beiruter Texte und Studien, 13). Wiesbaden: Steiner.
Drewes A.J. & Ryckmans J.
    1997. Un pétiole de palme inscrit en sabéen, no 14 de la collection de l'Oosters Instituut à Leyde. *Proceedings of the Seminar for Arabian Studies* 27: 225–230.
Garbini G.
    1969. Una nuova iscrizione di Šaraḥbiʾil Yaʿfur. *Annali dell'Istituto Orientale di Napoli* 29: 559–566.
Glaser E.
    1913. *Eduard Glasers Reise nach Mârib.* (ed. D.H. v. Müller & N. Rhodokanakis). (Sammlung Eduard Glaser I). Vienna: Hölder.
Goitein S.D.F.
    1934. *Jemenica. Sprichwörter und Redensarten aus Zentral-Jemen.* Leiden: Brill.
Grimme H.
    1912. Über einige Klassen südarabischer Lehnwörter im Koran. *Zeitschrift für Assyriologie* 26: 158–168.
Habshush H.
    1941. *Travels in Yemen. An account of Joseph Halévy's journey to Najran in the year 1870 written in Sanʿani Arabic by his guide Hayyim Habshush.* (ed. S.D. Goitein). Jerusalem: Hebrew University Press.
al-Hamdānī, Abū Muḥammad al-Ḥasan b. Aḥmad/ed. D.H. Müller.
    1884–1891. *Ṣifat jazīrat al-ʿarab. Al-Hamdânî's Geographie der Arabischen Halbinsel.* (2 volumes). Leiden: Brill.
al-Hamdānī, Abū Muḥammad al-Ḥasan b. Aḥmad/ed. O. Löfgren.
    1954–1965. *Al-Iklīl. Erstes Buch.* (Bibliotheca Ekmaniana Universitatis Regiae Upsalensia, 58/1.2). Uppsala: Almqvist & Wiksell.
al-Hamdānī, Abū Muḥammad al-Ḥasan b. Aḥmad/ed. M. b. ʿA. al-Akwaʿ.
    1966. *Kitāb al-Iklīl. Al-Juzʾ al-thānī.* Al-Qāhira: Al-Sunna al-Muḥammadiyya.
al-Hamdānī, Abū Muḥammad al-Ḥasan b. Aḥmad/ed. and transl. C. Toll.
    1968. *Kitāb al-Jawharatayn al-ʿatīqatayn. Die beiden Edelmetalle Gold und Silber.* (Acta Universitatis Upsalensis Studia Semitica Upsalensia, 1). Uppsala: Almqvist & Wiksell.
al-Hamdānī, Abū Muḥammad al-Ḥasan b. Aḥmad/ed. M. b. ʿA. al-Akwaʿ.
    1979. *Kitāb al-Iklīl. Al-Juzʾ al-thāmin.* Dimasq: Al-Kātib al-ʿArabī.
    1990. *Kitāb al-Iklīl. Al-Kitāb al-ʿāšir.* Ṣanʿāʾ: Al-Jīl al-Jadīd.
al-Iryānī M.ʿA.
    1996. *Al-Muʿjam al-yamanī fī l-lughah wal-turāth ḥawla mufradāt khāṣṣah min al-lahajāt al-yamaniyyah.* Dimasq: Dār al-Fikr.
    2012. *Al-Muʿjam al-yamanī fī l-lughah wal-turāth ḥawla mufradāt khāṣṣah min al-lahajāt al-yamaniyyah.* (Al-ṭabʿah al-thāniyah muzayyadah wa-munaqqaḥah). Ṣanʿāʾ: Al-Mīthāq.
Landberg C. de.
    1905–1913. *Études sur les dialectes de l'Arabie Méridionale.* ii. *Daṯīnah.* Leiden: Brill.
    1920–1942. *Glossaire Daṯînois.* (3 volumes). (Troisième volume publié par K.V. Zetterstéen). Leiden: Brill.
Lane E.W.
    1863–1874. *An Arabic–English Lexicon derived from the best and most copious eastern sources.* Parts 1–5. London: Williams and Norgate.
Lichtenstadter I. & Heinrichs W.
    1987. A South-Arabian bronze vessel. *Jerusalem Studies in Arabic and Islam* 9: 76–86.
al-Maqḥafī I.A.
    2002. *Muʿjam al-buldān wal-qabāʾil al-yamaniyyah.* Ṣanʿāʾ: Dār al-Kalimah.
Maraqten M.
    1994. Typen altsüdarabischer Altäre. Pages 160–177 in N. Nebes (ed.), *Arabia Felix. Beiträge zur Sprache und Kultur des vorislamischen Arabien. Festschrift Walter W. Müller zum 60. Geburtstag.* Wiesbaden: Harrassowitz.

Mazzini G.
    2009. The ancient South Arabian root s²yṭ: Lexical and comparative remarks. *Egitto e Vicino Oriente* 32: 157–164.

Müller W.W.
    2010. *Sabäische Inschriften nach Ären datiert. Bibliographie, Texte und Glossar.* (Akademie der Wissenschaften und der Literatur Mainz. Veröffentlichungen der Orientalischen Kommission, 53). Wiesbaden: Harrassowitz.

Nashwān b. Saʿīd al-Ḥimyarī/ed. ʿA. b. I. al-Muʾayyad & I. b. A. al-Jurāfī.
    1958. *Mulūk Ḥimyar wa-aqyāl al-Yaman.* Al-Qāhira: Al-Salafiyya.

Nashwān b. Saʿīd al-Ḥimyarī/ed. Ḥ. al-ʿAmrī, M. al-Iryānī & Y. ʿAbdallāh.
    1999. *Shams al-ʿulūm wa-dawāʾ kalām al-ʿarab min al-kulūm.* (12 volumes). Dimashq: Dār al-Fikr.

Nöldeke T.
    1904. *Beiträge zur semitischen Sprachwissenschaft.* Strassburg: Trübner.

Orel V.E. & Stolbova O.V.
    1995. *Hamito-Semitic etymological dictionary. Materials for a reconstruction.* (Handbuch der Orientalistik. Erste Abteilung. Der Nahe und der Mittlere Osten, 18). Leiden: Brill.

Piamenta M.
    1990–1991. *Dictionary of post-classical Yemeni Arabic.* (2 volumes). Leiden: Brill.

Plinius Secundus/ed. and transl. R. König.
    1995. *Naturalis Historia. Naturkunde.* Book 18. *Botanik: Ackerbau.* Zürich: Artemis & Winkler.

Plinius Secundus/ed. and transl. K. Brodersen.
    1996. *Naturalis Historia. Naturkunde.* Book 6. *Geographie: Asien.* Zürich: Artemis & Winkler.

Rabin C.
    1984. On the probability of South Arabian influence on the Arabic vocabulary. *Jerusalem Studies in Arabic and Islam* 4: 125–134.

Ricks S.D.
    1989. *Lexicon of inscriptional Qatabanian.* (Studia Pohl, 14). Rome: Pontificio Istituto Biblico.

Rossi E.
    1939. *L'Arabo parlato a Ṣanʿāʾ. Grammatica-Testi-Lessico.* Rome: Istituto per l'Oriente.
    1940. Vocaboli sud-arabici nelle odierne parlate arabe del Yemen. *Rivista degli Studi Orientali* 18: 299–314.

Ryckmans J., Müller W.W. & Abdallah Y.M.
    1994. *Textes du Yémen antique inscrits sur bois.* (Publications de l'Institut Orientaliste de Louvain, 43). Louvain-la-Neuve: Institut Orientaliste.

Schopen A.
    1983. *Traditionelle Heilmittel in Jemen.* Wiesbaden: Steiner.

Al-Selwi I.
    1987. *Jemenitische Wörter in den Werken von al-Hamdānī und Našwān und ihre Parallelen in den semitischen Sprachen.* (Marburger Studien zur Afrika- und Asienkunde. Serie B: Asien, 10). Berlin: Reimer.

Sima A.
    2000. *Tiere, Pflanzen, Steine und Metalle in den altsüdarabischen Inschriften. Eine lexikalische und realienkundliche Untersuchung.* (Akademie der Wissenschaften und der Literatur Mainz. Veröffentlichungen der Orientalischen Kommission, 46). Wiesbaden: Harrassowitz.

Smith G.R.
    1978. *The Ayyūbids and Early Rasūlids in the Yemen.* ii. *Study of Ibn Ḥātim's Kitāb al-Simṭ including glossary, geographical und tribal indices and maps.* London: Luzac & Company.

Stein P.
    2003. *Untersuchungen zur Phonologie und Morphologie des Sabäischen.* (Epigraphische Forschungen auf der Arabischen Halbinsel, 3). Rahden/Westf.: Leidorf.
    2010. *Die altsüdarabischen Minuskelinschriften auf Holzstäbchen aus der Bayerischen Staatsbibliothek in München.* i. *Die Inschriften der mittel- und spätsabäischen Periode.* Part 1: *Text.* Part 2: *Verzeichnisse*

und *Tafeln*. (Epigraphische Forschungen auf der Arabischen Halbinsel, 5). Tübingen: Wasmuth.
2011. Ancient South Arabian. Pages 1042–1073 in S. Weninger (ed.) in collaboration with G. Khan, M.P. Streck & J.C.E. Watson, *The Semitic Languages. An International Handbook*. Berlin: De Gruyter.

Ullmann M.
1970. *Wörterbuch der Klassischen Arabischen Sprache*. i. *Kāf*. Wiesbaden: Harrassowitz.

Varisco D.M.
1994. *Medieval Agriculture and Islamic Science. The Almanac of a Yemeni Sultan*. (Publications on the Near East, 6). Seattle: University of Washington.
2004. Terminology for plough cultivation in Yemeni Arabic. *Journal of Semitic Studies* 49/1: 71–129.

Watson J.C.E.
2004. On the linguistic archaeology of Ṣanʿānī Arabic. *Proceedings of the Seminar for Arabian Studies* 34: 405–412.

Wellhausen J.
1897. *Reste arabischen Heidentums*. (Zweite Auflage). Berlin: Reimer.

Weninger S.
2001. Two sticks with Ancient South Arabian inscriptions. *Proceedings of the Seminar for Arabian Studies* 31: 241–248.

Author's address

Walter W. Müller, Centrum für Nah- und Mittelost-Studien, Phillips-Universität Marburg, Fachgebiet Semitistik, Deutschhausstraße 12, D-35032 Marburg, Germany.

e-mail: richterr@staff.uni-marburg.de

Towards a Ḥaḍramitic lexicon: lexical notes on terms relating to the formulary and rituals in expiatory inscriptions

ALESSIA PRIOLETTA

Summary

Although the corpus of Ḥaḍramitic inscriptions is highly fragmented both chronologically and geographically, its grammatical system and above all its lexicon display unique traits that make it of particular interest to scholars.

These traits are especially well defined in the textual genre of the expiatory inscriptions since they display a distinctive formulary and ritual lexicon compared to the textual counterparts in the other South Arabian kingdoms. The study focuses, in particular, on the lexical analysis of some key terms that appear in the fixed formulas within which these inscriptions are structured.

The lexicon of these texts is characterized by many unique features compared to the other ASA languages and, on a broader level, combines isoglosses with the Southern Semitic languages, archaisms that recall Akkadian, and a more typically Central Semitic lexicon.

These elements still await full analysis and systematic organization into a comparative Ḥaḍramitic lexicon that will allow scholars to pursue broader studies on the position of Ḥaḍramitic within the Ancient South Arabian and Semitic in general.

Keywords: South Arabia, Ḥaḍramawt, epigraphy, lexicon, comparative Semitics

Introduction

A complete lexicon of the Ḥaḍramitic language is still lacking in Ancient South Arabian (ASA) studies, but it represents an important project that needs to be undertaken.[1] There are, of course, objective difficulties with which the scholar has to reckon, arising primarily out of the fragmentary nature and exiguity of the available documentation, which often prevents a proper lexical analysis based on internal comparisons because of the lack of sufficient contexts of usage.[2] A further, and anything but minor, difficulty is the presence of a high number of Ancient South Arabian *hapaxes*, and the preference for roots that are rare or only poorly attested in the other Semitic languages.[3]

This paper will consider a small corpus of fewer than ten texts, which may be regarded as the Ḥaḍramitic version of the expiatory inscriptions, also referred to as the 'penitential' or 'confession' inscriptions. As is well known, the greatest number of texts belonging to this genre — written either in Minaic or Sabaic — originates from the region of al-Jawf.[4] The study focuses, in particular, on the lexical analysis of some key terms

---

[1] The other ASA languages have been the subject of a lexical study, although there is not, to date, any updated ASA dictionary. The last Sabaic dictionary dates back to 1982 (Beeston et al. 1982). For Qatabanic, one can refer to Ricks 1989; M. Arbach compiled a lexicon of the Minaic language that has never been published (1993). On the other hand, the ASA vocabulary has, in recent years, greatly increased thanks to the discovery and publication of hundreds of new inscriptions, especially those in minuscule script, for which the most complete reference is in Stein 2010a. The compilation of a Ḥaḍramitic lexicon is among the *desiderata* of Semitic Studies (Huehnergard 2005: 190−192).
[2] Among the ASA languages, the Ḥaḍramitic corpus is the smallest one in terms of the number of inscriptions. Of the approximately 900 texts published to date, only a few dozen are complete, of some length, and with relevant linguistic data.
[3] A first attempt of statistical analysis undertaken by S. Frantsouzoff (2003: 49) on the inscriptions from two temples at the site of Raybūn, those of dhat Ḥimyam dhat Raḥbān and Sin dhu-Mayfaʿān, has shown that approximately 32% of the terms have no parallels in Sabaic, Minaic, or Qatabanic, and that slightly less than 30% of these words are even unique in the rest of the Ḥaḍramitic documentation. With regard to the first point, however, this analysis should be checked today as a consequence of the huge amount of new epigraphic material that has recently come to light. For the second issue, we must not forget that this is also due to the lexical peculiarities of the textual genre, that of the expiatory inscriptions, which so far are only attested in Raybūn.
[4] The SAB expiatory inscriptions in the Amiritic dialect have been studied by Stein (2007). Two new examples of expiatory inscriptions originating from al-Jawf, written in Minaic and Sabaic respectively, were presented at the 2011 Seminar for Arabian Studies (Agostini 2012: 1−12; Prioletta 2012: 309−318).

that appear in the fixed formulas within which these inscriptions are structured.

The Ḥaḍramitic expiatory inscriptions are quite homogeneous in terms of their dating, provenance, and the deity to whom they are addressed, since all can be placed in the period between approximately the third and first centuries BC, in the town of Raybūn and, with rare exceptions, are addressed to the goddess dhat Ḥimyam.[5]

They were first published by the epigraphist of the Russian Mission to Ḥaḍramawt, S. Frantsouzoff (1995: 15–28), after being presented at the Seminar for Arabian Studies in 1994, followed by a more detailed analysis of some of the texts in two successive sessions of the same seminar (1997: 113–127; 1998: 61–67). Recently, in a communication delivered during the 2008 Seminar for Arabian Studies and in two articles published in 2010, A. Multhoff provided the results of her syntactic and semantic studies of some of the most significant texts in this series, drawing radically different conclusions from those of Frantsouzoff (Multhoff 2009: 295–302; 2010a: 19–69; 2010b: 7–40).

Today the general sense of these inscriptions appears clearer thanks to this new interpretation, which I share to a large extent. Nevertheless, there remain significant difficulties of interpretation in the sections describing the infringement committed, both from a semantic point of view in the understanding of some of the key terms, and on the syntactic level in the evaluation of the numerous prefixed verbal forms that follow one another in the more narrative sections.[6]

Examination of the textual model and lexical observations of some key terms

Firstly, it should be emphasized that the Ḥaḍramitic expiatory inscriptions differ completely in terms of their formulary from Minaic and Amiritic inscriptions, beginning with the fact that they are dedicatory texts.[7] In this sense they rather resemble the few examples of expiatory inscriptions written in Sabaic from Maʾrib and other areas of the central Sabaean region, which are also framed in the textual genre of the dedicatory text.[8] This peculiarity is of course important from a cultural point of view, because it testifies to the autonomy and maturity of the scribal school of Raybūn, which created an entirely original textual model that was at variance with those of other cultural centres, probably not only in the remainder of South Arabia but in Ḥaḍramawt itself. Nevertheless, the formulas of these inscriptions do not deviate from the standard composition of the South Arabian votive texts, whose fixed expressions, as was recognized by M. Höfner (1954: 314–341) and then studied in detail by Y. Gruntfest (1986: 1–34), refer to three temporal spheres: the neutral sphere of the present, the sphere of the past, and the sphere of the future.

The text of the Ḥaḍramitic expiatory inscriptions is usually divided into five main fixed formulas, although not all of them were compulsory: 'dedicatio' (verb s^1qny), 'ritual motivation' (verb $rḍw$), 'real motivation' (causal sentence), 'purpose period' (verb ys^3twr), and 'final invocation' (verb $tḏʾ$).[9] In this paper, I will limit myself to an examination of the first four formulas.[10]

1. Dedicatio: the BḤT

The nature of the ex-voto is formalized by the incipit, the formula of the *dedicatio*, containing the key verb of the textual genre, s^1qny, which formulates the dedication of the votive object. The deity being addressed is, as has been said, dhat Ḥimyam. The object dedicated to this goddess — like the other female deity of Raybūn, ʿAthtarum/ʿAśtarum — is always the *bḥt*. Apart from reservations expressed by a few scholars, and some alternative translations, such as that of 'stela' put forward by J. Pirenne (1979: 207), the translation of *bḥt* as 'votive *phallus*' proposed by Mahmud al-Ghūl in the late 1950s (1959: 2–4), became over time a *communis opinio* among scholars and was also accepted by Frantsouzoff (1995: 16 and pl. 2), who sought support for the hypothesis in somewhat forced interpretations of the archaeological

---

[5] Almost all the texts were found in the sanctuary of dhat Ḥimyam dhat Raḥbān (Raybūn I). There are, however, a few examples of expiatory inscriptions from other temples: Raybūn-Kafas/Naʿmān 148 (temple of Kafas/dhat Naʿman, at the site of Raybūn V) and some unpublished fragments from the temple of Sīn dhu-Mayfaʿān (Rb XIV/87 no. 29, Rb XIV/89 no. 65).
[6] It must be said that these inscriptions show such an exceptional degree of idiosyncrasy, with regard to both their syntax and lexicon, that they pose a particularly difficult challenge for the modern translator.
[7] The expiatory inscriptions from al-Jawf have a typical formula of the textual genre: $tḫy$ w-$tnḍrn$ (SAB) and $ntḫy$ w-$ntḏr$ (MIN), usually rendered as 'confessed and did penance'.

[8] See the beginning of Ja 720/1–6 (middle SAB): $^{1,3}grm$ w-$S^2rḫ^2m$ $ḏy$ $Ḏbyn$ $hqnyw$ $^3mrʾ$-hmy $ʾlmqhw$ ^4bʿl $ʾwm$ $ṣlmn$ $ḏ$-^5ṣrfn $tḏrm$ l-$qbly$ $ḏ$-$h^6ḫṭʾw$ b-$mrʾ$-hmw $ʾlmqhw$ $bʿl$ $ʾwm$ ^ʾgrm and $S^2rḫm$ those of $Ḏbyn$ dedicated to their lord Almaqah master of Awām this statue in silver, as a penance because they committed offence against their lord Almaqah'.
[9] Inscriptions also attest to the sporadic use of the oracle (*bhl*) formula, which is found after the *dedicatio* (e.g. Rb I/84 no. 178 etc.).
[10] The $tḏʾ$-formula that closes the dedicatory inscriptions has been studied in Multhoff 2010a: 60–65. See, however, Prioletta 2013: 101–102 for critical remarks.

evidence, such as the fact that some of the stone objects were phallic in shape. The translation of *baḥat* proposed by al-Ghūl was based on an entry in al-Qāmūs according to which the term, deriving from the root BWḤ, indicates the 'origin' from which springs the word for the male or female sexual organ.

A number of years ago, A. Sima (2000: 298–299) — while translating the term generically as 'votive object'[11] — had already highlighted the etymological weakness of this interpretation, pointing out how the passage in al-Qāmūs was considered problematic even by Arab lexicographers, and raised among them a protracted discussion. The word has been analysed in detail by Multhoff (2010*b*), according to whom the term *bḥt* has two principal meanings: in Sabaic and Ḥaḍramitic it generally indicates a surface that may bear an inscription or not, whereas in Minaic and Qatabanic, *bḥt* would be an object, namely a block or a stone slab, once again not necessarily inscribed. She linked this translation to the primary meaning of 'surface, area' in the sense of a delimited area, related etymologically to the Arabic *bāḥa* meaning 'court' (Lane 1968: 273).[12] This new interpretation seems indeed more satisfactory than the traditionally accepted reading of 'votive *phallus*' and is based on much more solid archaeological evidence.

It may be possible, however, to narrow even further the meaning of the term if we take the basic meaning of the root BWḤ. Aside from Arabic, the root in this form is attested only in Ethiopic among the Semitic languages. In both of these languages the meaning is 'to be seen, be revealed, become public'.[13] It is possible, then, that *bḥt* indicated an 'outer covering portion', constituting the floor, walls, or other structural parts of the temple. In the case of *baḥat* referring to a single limestone or bronze slab, even then one may think of the slabs affixed to the temple walls, intended to be clearly visible to all. From the point of view of lexicographic studies, it is important to stress that in this case the translation has only tenuous support in terms of its semantic etymology. In other words, the translation of the word is primarily based on a rigorous assessment of the epigraphic documentation, of the relationship between the referent and the material support used for the inscription, and of the archaeological evidence.

2. Ritual motivation: the verb RḌW

The formula that follows the *dedicatio* is the set expression that contains the verb *rḍw*. In the usual formulaic structure of dedicatory texts, this section communicates the 'ritual motivation', which is expressed through clauses conveying the command given by the deity, using verbs such as *wqh*, *ks³*, *ḥrg*;[14] or else it states the promise or request made by the dedicant to the deity, employing the verbs *s²ft*, *tkrb*, and so on.[15]

Syntactically, the verb appears in a relative clause that can be either asyndetic or introduced by the relative pronoun, and whose antecedent is the noun *bḥt*: (*s¹qny*) *bḥthn ḏt rḍwt ᶜlh-n-s¹* or (*s¹qny*) *bḥt rḍwt ᶜlh-n-s¹*. The subject of *rḍwt*, expressed in the feminine perfect, is the goddess. The clause is followed by a prepositional phrase with *ᶜlh-n* and the name of the dedicant or the suffix pronoun referring to him. The proposed translations of the clause, whose meaning can be easily understood, are only slightly different.[16]

P. Stein (2003: 231–238) has pointed out, however, that the preposition *ᶜlh-n* is parallel to the Sabaic *ᶜl-n*, which means 'from' and this in turn is semantically parallel to *bn*. The enclitic particle *-n* would then have an ablative function with a spatial connotation (meaning 'from' or 'away from') and would be interchangeable with *bn* itself.[17]

---

[11] This translation was also followed by Avanzini's edition of the QAT inscriptions (2004) and in the digital edition of the South Arabian inscriptions by the project CSAI — Corpus of South Arabian Inscriptions of the University of Pisa (http://csai.humnet.unipi.it/, replaced from October 2013 by DASI http://dasi.humnet.unipi.it/).

[12] This meaning of *bāḥatu d-dāri*, 'court of the house', was already listed in Lisān.

[13] Cf. Amharic *bäha* 'to be visible, be seen', *buh* 'that which is seen' (Leslau 1987: 155). Leslau also lists a second meaning of BWḤ that is attested in Ethiopic and Arabic, which has the meaning of 'to receive authority, permission', but this second meaning of the root BWḤ, which Leslau links to BḤT, 'to have power', does not seem to have a relation with the ASA *bḥt*.

[14] E.g. Rb XIV/87 no. 104/1–3 (HAD): *s¹q²ny S¹yn ḏ-Myfᶜn ms³n³[d]hn ḏ-ks³ʾ-h-s¹* '(NP) dedicated to Sīn dhu-Mayfaᶜān this inscription, which He ordered him'. It must be noted that the Ḥaḍramitic formulary only uses *ks³ʾ* as *verbum iubendi*, while in the other ASA languages it is found with another meaning and in different contexts. Qatabanic acts somehow similarly since it prefers almost exclusively the verb *ḥrg*; finally, *wqh* is mostly found in Sabaic.

[15] E.g. Rb XIV/90 no. 60/2–3 (HAD): *s¹q²ny S¹yn ḏ-Myfᶜn ms³ndhn ḏ-s²fᵗ-s¹ h-bnh-s¹ww* '(NP) dedicated to Sīn dhu-Mayfaᶜān this inscription, which he promised Him for his sons'.

[16] 'un phallus (votif) dont elle s'est contentée [or: agréé] à son bénéfice' (Frantsouzoff 2001*a*: 129–130; 2007: 191); 'the (votive) phallus, with which she was satisfied for his sake' (Frantsouzoff 1997: 114, 117, 122; 1998: 62, 64); 'the votive object [or: the inscription] of which she (the goddess) was pleased towards PN (the dedicant)' (CSAI); 'um derentwillen sie Gefallen an ihm fand' (Multhoff 2010*b*: 26).

[17] As Stein (2003: 235–236) noted, from the comparative point of view this function of the particle -*n* is also found in Ugaritic, while in the other North-west Semitic languages and in Arabic the preposition *mn* is used.

I would add that, if the use of the -*n* particle in Ḥaḍramitic were not a

In Ḥaḍramitic, an opposition exists in fact between ʿlhy (parallel to the Sabaic ʿly) and ʿlh-n (parallel to the Sabaic ʿl-n), as exemplified in the following sentence, attested in Raybūn-Ḥaḍrān 213/1–5: s$^{/2}$qnyt ʿs^{3}trm ḏt Ḥḍrn ^{3}| ms^{3}ndhn ḏ-rḍwt ʿs^{3}trm ^{4}| ʿlh-n ʾbrs^{2}d ʿlhy mr^{5}ḍ ʿyn-s^{3}yw. The sentence should therefore be translated: '[She dedicated] the inscription, with which ʿAśtarum was pleased by Abīrashad, with respect to the sickness of her eyes'.

When one examines the use of verbal derivatives of the root RḌW in ASA, it appears that in this formula rḍwt could be at first considered a 0_1 or base stem. The verb rḍw that has the god as its subject is a feature that the Ḥaḍramitic dedicatory texts share, although with slight differences, only with the Minaic dedicatory texts.

RḌW (0_1) 'to accept, be pleased with'
w-ʿrb ḫm^{9}s^{1}t mtʿyt Wd b-s^{1}m w-rḍw-s^{1}m fnwt 'and (he) made five offerings[18] to Wadd on behalf of them, and he [i.e. the god] was pleased with them publicly' (Shaqab 1/8–9, MIN).
tw yqhn mlkn ḏ-yrḍyn 'until the king gives orders he is pleased with' (Ry 507/9, late SAB).

As for the other ASA languages, Sabaic appears far more frequently, with the use of the h- and probably the 0_2 stems of RḌW.

RḌW (0_2) (?) 'to please, satisfy'
w-y^7[tʾ]wln mrʾy-hmw b-wfym w-ḥmdm w-b-ḏ-rḍw-hm^{8}w bn kl s^{1}bʾt w-tqdmt s^{1}bʾy w-tqdmn 'and so their two lords returned in safety and praise and with what gave them satisfaction from all the expeditions and battles they both carried out and made' (Ja 586/6–8, middle SAB).

HRḌW (h-) 'to please, satisfy'
w-yʾtyw ^{11}b-wfym w-mqḥm w-mngt ṣdqm ḏ-hrḍw mrʾ-h^{12}mw Wtrm Yhʾmn mlk S^{1}bʾ w-ḏ-Rydn 'and they returned in safety, with success and good luck, which pleased their lord Watarum Yuhaʾmin king of Sabaʾ and dhu-Raydān' (Ja 601/10–12, middle SAB).

On the other hand, it is striking to note that the root RḌW is completely unknown in Qatabanic, with the exception of sporadic occurrences in onomastics. The Ḥaḍramitic clause is therefore the only case in which the agent of the verb rḍw is expressed.

From a semantic point of view, the meaning of the verb rḍwt does not present particular problems. The root seems to belong only to Central Semitic (see Koehler & Baumgartner 1967–1995: 1195), since it is well attested in Ugaritic (rṣw/y 'to treat graciously', 'to consent to everything'), Arabic (raḍiya 'to accept'), Hebrew (raṣah 'to take pleasure in, be well disposed', 'to accept with pleasure'), and Aramaic (Old Aramaic rqy 'to appease, placate'),[19] whereas it is absent in Akkadian and in South Semitic with the exception of Modern South Arabian.[20] The context in which the verb is employed in all these languages may be very similar to the context of the Ḥaḍramitic inscriptions, since its subject is often the god.

It should, however, be underlined that in view of the position in the inscription that the formula is to be found in these texts, the meaning of rḍwt should not be simply understood as a 'satisfaction' that the deity has obtained. The fact that the goddess was pleased implies in fact that the author carried out her command satisfactorily in preparing the dedication. Moreover, as the example above has shown, although the formula is also used in 'normal', that is, 'not expiatory' dedicatory inscriptions addressed to the other female deity of Raybūn, ʿAthtarum/ʿAśtarum, in the context of the inscriptions dedicated to dhat Ḥimyam in expiation for a transgression we should not be too quick to discard a more forceful meaning of the verb rḍwt, as is indeed corroborated by the Semitic parallels. The verb might bear the meaning of 'to propitiate' or, as has been seen in Old Aramaic, 'to appease, placate', in which case the formula should be rendered: '(He dedicated) this baḥat, by which dhat Ḥimyam was propitiated [or appeased, pacified] by him'. In this case, rḍwt would probably be an internal passive of the 0_2 stem.[21]

---

loan from Sabaic, it would constitute an interesting isogloss between these two languages that excludes the other ASA languages — although, a more in-depth investigation is needed, in order to establish if a similar use of the -n particle is actually absent elsewhere in ASA. On the other hand, its occurrence in Ugaritic suggests that the -n particle is an archaism probably deriving from Proto-Central Semitic, which in ASA has been preserved in Sabaic and Ḥaḍramitic. At any rate, it puts Sabaic in contact with the rest of ASA, contrary to what Stein recently supported (see Stein 2012: 503–522; Kottsieper & Stein, this volume).
[18] It could also be 'the fifth offering', if we consider ḫms^{1}t as an ordinal and mtʿyt as a feminine singular.

[19] Attested either at the peʾal (G/0_1 stem) or paʾʾel (D/0_2 stem). The two stems are graphically identical, as in ASA.
[20] Müller (1962: 55) lists Soqotri riḍí 'to be pleased, agree' and Mehri rḍú.
[21] Müller (1962: 55–56) distinguished a second semantic field of the root RḌW/Y, which has the meaning of 'to pay' 'to remit a debt', and that he considered as a Hebraism from raṣah. There is, in fact, such a use of rḍy in ASA, where the noun is attested as 'good-quality coin' (Beeston et al. 1982: 115). As Stein (2010b: 329, n. 117) noted, however, except for Hebrew there is less evidence of a second root in Semitic with this meaning. Moreover, a semantic development from 'to please, satisfy' towards 'to pay a debt' is quite plausible.

3. The real motivation and the purpose period: some verbs of transgression

Despite the absence of the formulaic verbs 'to confess' and 'to do penance', the categorization of these texts as 'expiatory inscriptions' is based on the presence of two formulas that in fact express the concept of atonement.

The first formula is that of the 'real motivation', or the reason that led to the preparation of the offering to the deity. While in dedicatory texts this section describes the positive intervention of the deity in the life of the author,[22] in the case of expiatory texts the statement is negative in nature, describing the impious action committed by the author that he is required to expiate by making an offering to the deity.

The concept expressed in this part of the inscription is repeated later in what corresponds to the 'purpose or wish clause'. The temporal sphere of this later section is usually the future, and its quality can be positive or negative.[23] In this case, the author makes a vow not to repeat the same mistake and commit this particular transgression again. The structure of this part of the inscription can be resumed as follows:

I Clause (Real motivation): *b-ᶜbr ḏt* + verb → transgression committed (sphere of the past)
II Clause (Purpose period): *w-bn-mw* PN *ys³twr ḏ* + verb (often the same verb used above) → vow not to repeat the same mistake (sphere of the future).

Such an interpretation, which seems sound to me, was proposed by Multhoff on the basis of her new translation of the transposing verb *ys³twr* as 'to be far from' rather than 'to be absolved from, be remitted from', as originally proposed by Frantsouzoff (1995: 20).[24] The subordinate that follows, introduced by the pronoun *ḏ*, contains the verb at the prefix-conjugation, and would have a present/future signification.

These two clauses are certainly the most difficult in these texts, due to their convoluted syntax and unconventional lexical choices, the author employing terms that have rarely or never been found in South Arabian epigraphs, and which allow for few comparisons with the rest of the Semitic languages.

It is, however, these very sections that convey an idea, however confusing, of the relationship between the authors and the temple personnel who, quite interestingly, are almost always personified in the form of priestesses.[25] In other words, from the few examples available to us and despite the difficulties posed by the semantic analysis of these passages, it seems that the transgressions described in the Ḥaḍramitic expiatory inscriptions are connected with the faulty behaviour of the author towards the priestesses, or the failure to execute (or failure to execute correctly) the instructions prescribed by the temple.

Syntactically, the transgression may be expressed in one of two ways. In the first, the sentence is introduced by the conjunction *b-ᶜbr ḏt*, corresponding to the *b-ḏt* and *l-ḏt* used elsewhere in dedicatory inscriptions. Once again we find the wholly 'personal' lexical choice to form the causal conjunction with the preposition *b-ᶜbr*, which in the other ASA languages is only used as a preposition. Additionally, its root has particular force, being frequently used in legal contexts to signify 'to pass, transgress' (Beeston et al. 1982: 11).

(Ia) Transgression expressed by *b-ᶜbr ḏt* + verb:
b-ᶜbr ḏt tḥḏ wr⁶wtm bn mḥrm-s³ 'because he took[26] for himself a priestess from Her [i.e. the goddess's] temple' (Raybūn-Kafas/Naᶜmān 148/5–6);
b-ᶜbr ḏt s¹ᶜdw⁵-s³ ʾkrb ḏt Ḥmym w-rᶜbt-s³ 'because

---

[22] As Gruntfest (1986: 17–18) summarized, the positive intervention of the deity involves three main semantic spheres: complying with the author's petition (*hwfy*), granting of something or assisting the author in his activities (*ḥmr, s¹ᶜd, ṣdq, hwfy*), and assisting the author with a problem (*mtᶜ, hnᶜn*).
[23] A positive wish is the request to accomplish a favour; a negative wish is the request to prevent an evil occurrence (Gruntfest 1986: 24).
[24] The formula has been translated differently from the various authors: 'and from … may/must/let be remitted/removed that he did …' (S. Frantsouzoff in his various translations in English/French); 'may it be removed (the sin), he who did …' (http://csai.humnet.unipi.it/, accessed July 2013); 'may it be far that he will do …' (Multhoff 2009: 297, 298), 'und von PN wird (bzw. möge) es fern sein, daß er (fürderhin) … tut' (Multhoff 2010a: 54). The formula has been translated according to the new interpretation in the DASI database (http://dasi.humnet.unipi.it/, accessed April 2014).

[25] The texts do in fact reveal the important role of women in the relations between god and worshipper. In the temple of dhat Ḥimyam dhat Raḥbān, the priestesses of the goddess are mentioned (Rb I/84 no. 178etc/4: *ʾmh ḏt Ḥmym*; Raybūn-Kafas/Naᶜmān 148/5–6, Rb I/84 no. 197a–e/5: *wrwtm*, see below for both; Rb I/89 no. 291etc./5, 9, see below; Rb I/84 no. 196a–d+201a–b/6: *rᶜbt*). Also in this temple, a priestess interprets the oracle (Rb I/84 no. 197a–e/1–2: *bn² hy-ʾlrᶜd*), gives prescriptions to the community (Rb I/84 no. 198a–f: see below), and directs the repair work in the temple (Rb I/89 no. 306a–b). According to Frantsouzoff (2003: 62), the person referred to in the invocation *b-Qtm* (Rb XIV/89 no. 246/6–7) could be a priestess as well.
[26] Frantsouzoff believes *tḥḏ* derives from *ḥwz*, which is attested in MSA with the meaning of 'to deviate, move aside from'. The verb is, however, a derived verbal stem from the root with ʾḤD with assimilation of the first *alif* (a phenomenon recurring in the modern Arabic dialect of Ḥaḍramawt). See also Multhoff 2010a: 52–53.

ʾkrb rejected (?)²⁷ the help of the goddess and of her priestess' (Rb I/89 no. 291etc./4–5).

In the second variant the clause describing the transgression follows the clause containing the verb ys³twr, and is constructed with a personal pronoun in the frontal position, which places great emphasis on the subject and on the verb in the suffix-conjugation.

(Ib) Transgression expressed by w-s¹w + verb:

w-bn-mw Fṭnm l-s³twr ḏw ⁴yḥr ᶜm ʾs³tm 'and may it be far from Fṭnm that he lives with a woman'

w-s¹w-ḥwr ᶜm s²wᶜ⁵t-s¹ w-s³y wrwtm b-mḥrmhn 'and (i.e. 'because') he lived²⁸ with a woman, and she is a priestess in the temple' (Rb I/84 no. 197a–e/3–5);

w-bn-mw Qny[ʾl l-s³twr ḏw] ³ynṣf ḏ-yḍl ʾlrᶜd w[... ...]⁴m 'and may it be far from Qnyʾl that he may do²⁹ something that offends ʾlrᶜd and [... ...]m'

k-ḏʾl ʾlrᶜd 'as³⁰ he offended ʾlrᶜd'

w-⁵ḏw yngm bn fṭḥ tfṭḥ-s¹ ʾlrᶜd '(may it be far) that he may rebel against the orders ʾlrᶜd may order him'

w-s¹w ⁶ngm bn fṭḥ fṭḥt-s¹ ᶜm-s²wᶜt-s¹ 'and [i.e. 'because'] he rebelled against the orders she had ordered him with his wife' (Rb I/84 no. 198a–f/2–6).

It is worth dwelling in particular on this latest example that, although fragmentary in parts, uses key verbs that are quite interesting from a lexicographic standpoint. From the syntax, it is evident that the author has committed two reprehensible actions.

In the first passage the key word is ḏʾl.³¹ The verb has been translated as 'to offend'. The root has few parallels in Semitic. It is almost totally absent from Central Semitic, with the exception of Arabic where ḍaʾula bears the meaning 'to be or become small, ignominious' (Lane 1968: 1760). Frantsouzoff (1997: 121) subsequently discarded this comparison on the grounds of semantics and the intransitive nature of the root, which would not be appropriate in the context. The parallel suggested is therefore with the Ethiopic ṣaᶜala/ḍaᶜala meaning 'to rebuke, reprove, insult, offend', attested mainly with the second ᶜayn, but also with the second aleph (Leslau 1987: 543).³²

Despite the limited evidence available, we can say that this is definitely a common Semitic root because we also find it in the Old Akkadian ṣâlu meaning 'to fight, quarrel, object to' (Gelb et al. 1964: 89). There remains the question of the second etymological radical. Compared with the only other occurrence of ḏʾl in the other Ancient South Arabian languages, where it is attested in Minaic,³³ and given the preference in Akkadian for the spelling ṣâlu rather than ṣêlu,³⁴ I would lean toward the etymological aleph. This would be, therefore, an archaism that Ḥaḍramitic shares only with Ethiopic, while the Arabic meaning appears to be the result of a semantic evolution.³⁵ Because the meanings 'to blame', reproach' are hardly credible in the context of a fault committed by a believer toward his deity, the verb ḏʾl in the context in question would have the connotation of 'to offend' or 'to fight, object to', closer to Akkadian.

We finally come to the last term, which is one of the many *hapaxes* used in these inscriptions. The appearance of the root NĠM represents an extremely interesting lexical case. Not only is it unknown in Ancient South

---

²⁷ The verb s¹ᶜdw comes from the Semitic root ᶜDW whose basic meaning is 'to cross, pass over, transgress' (Leslau 1987: 56–57). Frantsouzoff (1995: 25) compares the verb, here at the causative stem, with the Sabaean ᶜdw 'to commit hostile action' and the Arabic ᶜadā 'to appear unfair to someone', and does not consider conform to the context in question the comparison with the sense of the Sabaic causative stem hᶜdw, which indicates, 'to remove, infringe boundary'. Multhoff (2010a: 55–56, n. 221) prefers to translate with a generic 'to push away', which is derived from the Sabaic meaning, and which could be likely. The semantic transition from the concrete meaning of 'to infringe a boundary' to the abstract 'to infringe a pact' is pretty obvious, however. This sense seems also characteristic of other derived stems such as the s¹t- stem — particularly in the Qatabanic legal inscriptions where the verb indicates 'to contravene, transgress' — and, probably, of the t- form, as in the Hadramitic example: w-⁵bn-mw Lbn ys³twr b-ḏ ytᶜdw mᶜd ⁶s²ym-s¹ 'and from Lbn may it be far that he will contravene the instructions of his patron' (Rb I/89 no. 65, unpublished inscription quoted in Frantsouzoff 2003: 50).

²⁸ From ḤWR 'to settle, establish'. In a few Semitic languages, as in Geʿez, the verb has the connotation of 'to have sexual intercourse' (Leslau 1987: 249–250).

²⁹ A. Multhoff (2010a: 52 and n. 200; 56 and n. 224) assumes the verb ynṣf may have the connotation of 'to order/be ordered', which could be likely as well.

³⁰ Despite the preceding lacuna, it seems that in this case the transgression is expressed with the conjunction k + verb at the suffix-conjugation.

³¹ Frantsouzoff assumes the verb yḍl (l. 3) stems from the root ḌLL and he translates it as 'to mislead'. In view of the parallel with the formula of Rb I/84 no. 197a–e, where the verb ḥwr is used twice and both at prefix and at suffix conjugation (ḥwr/yḥr), it seems reasonable that yḍl and ḏʾl originates from one same root ḎʾL as well, but the possibility that we have here two different verbs cannot be completely ruled out.

³² As is known, especially in North Ethiopic there are inconsistencies and interchanges in orthography between ʾ and ᶜ.

³³ Cf. Maʿīn 73/2, but the context is not clear.

³⁴ Since, in Akkadian, the pharyngals, conventionally transcribed with ʾ, may influence the change of the contigous a to e, if the middle radical were ᶜ, we would expect the spelling ṣêlu.

³⁵ On the other hand, if the hypothesis of a root ḌʾL is correct, the comparison made by Leslau with Syriac ṣaᶜlā 'soiled, defiled, impure' is probably incorrect. The comparison is in fact most probably with Arabic ṣaᶜala 'slender, small', which could be parallel to Akkadian ṣēlu 'rib, side'.

Arabian, it also seems to be absent in Semitic, with the exception of some Modern South Arabian languages. It is difficult to determine whether NĠM is a proto-Semitic root, given the presence of the velar fricative ġ, a phoneme that underwent orthographic and historical phonetic development in the various Semitic languages. The absence of NĠM in Akkadian and Ugaritic, however, the latter maintaining a distinguished sign for the phoneme ġayn, suggests that the root is a lexical innovation.

NĠM is therefore an isogloss of Ḥaḍramitic and Modern South Arabian; here it is found in Mehri, Jibbāli, and Ḥarsūsi with the meaning 'to be angry'. In these languages, the word seems to be used in particular in family contexts, for example in the relationship between husband and wife. The base form of the verb in this context would carry the meaning, for example, of 'to be angry and refuse her husband his conjugal rights' (e.g. Johnstone 1981: 185). Frantsouzoff's translation — 'he was taking part in a family quarrel' — takes precisely this meaning. Methodologically, however, it is risky to adopt such a narrow meaning for a lexeme from a cognate language, and one that constitutes the sole example attesting to this use, which would lead to the assertion that the same use of the word was carried from one culture to another. In addition, the absence of the root in Soqotri where there is also the tendency of velars to become pharyngeals, does not exclude the possibility that NĠM is a lexical borrowing from Ḥaḍramitic.

In this case, more than ever, given the difficulty of reconstructing the original meaning of the verbal root, we must necessarily resort to analysing syntagmatic relationships and the context of use. In the passage in question, nġm is followed by the preposition bn in an internal accusative construction in which the verb fth means 'to order' and has as its subject the priestess. The verb nġm would indicate something similar to 'to rebel against, object to'. Once again we see how the infringement involves a failure to obey the requirements of the temple.

Preliminary conclusions

This handful of examples is perhaps sufficient to convey an idea of the lexical variety of Ḥaḍramitic, which bears many unique features compared to the other ASA languages and, on a broader level, combines isoglosses with the Southern Semitic languages, archaisms that recall Akkadian, and a more typically Central Semitic lexicon.

Although lexical isoglosses are not useful for the purposes of classificatory linguistics, a systematic examination of the Ḥaḍramitic lexicon from a comparative perspective could tell us a great deal about this language, in addition to clarifying the occasionally obscure meaning of Ḥaḍramitic inscriptions.

Sigla and abbreviations

CSAI	Corpus of South Arabian Inscriptions, http://dasi.humnet.unipi.it/. See DASI.
DASI	Digital Archive for the Study of pre-Islamic Arabian Inscriptions, http://dasi.humnet.unipi.it/.
HAD	Ḥaḍramitic
Ja 586, 601, 720	Inscriptions in Jamme 1962.
Maʿīn 73	Inscription in Bron 1998.
MIN	Minaic
QAT	Qatabanic
Raybūn-Ḥaḍrān 213	Inscription in Frantsouzoff 2001a.
Raybūn-Kafas/Naʿmān 148	Inscription in Frantsouzoff 2007.
Rb I/84 no. 178 etc., Rb I/84 no. 196a–d +201a–b	Inscriptions in Frantsouzoff 1995.
Rb I/84 no. 197a–e, Rb I/84 no. 198a–f	Inscriptions in Frantsouzoff 1997.
Rb I/89 no. 291etc.	Inscription in Frantsouzoff 1995.
Rb I/89 no. 306a–b.	Inscription in Frantsouzoff 2001b.
Rb XIV/87 no. 29, Rb XIV/89 no. 65 (unpublished)	Cited in Frantsouzoff 2003.
Rb XIV/87 no. 104	Inscription in Frantsouzoff 2003.
Rb XIV/89 no. 246	Inscription in Frantsouzoff 2005.
Rb XIV/90 no. 60	Inscription in Frantsouzoff 2001c.
Ry 507	Inscription in Robin 2008.
SAB	Sabaic
Shaqab 1	Inscription in Gnoli 1993.

References

The complete references of the cited inscriptions can also be found on the DASI website.

Agostini A.
- 2012. New perspectives on Minaean expiatory texts. *Proceedings of the Seminar for Arabian Studies* 42: 1–12.

Arbach M.
- 1993. Le madhâbien: lexique, onomastique et grammaire d'une langue de l'Arabie méridionale préislamique. Thèse de doctorat, Université d'Aix-Marseille I. [Unpublished.]

Avanzini A.
- 2004. *Corpus of South Arabian Inscriptions I–III. Qatabanic, Marginal Qatabanic, Awsanite Inscriptions.* (Arabia Antica, 2). Pisa: Edizioni Plus–Università di Pisa.

Beeston A.F.L., al-Ghūl M.ᶜA., Müller W.W. & Ryckmans J.
- 1982. *Sabaic Dictionary (English–French–Arabic). Dictionnaire Sabéen (anglais–français–arabe)*. Louvain-la-Neuve: Éditions Peeters/Beirut: Libraire du Liban.

Bron F.
- 1998. *Maʿīn.* Fasc. A: *Les documents.* Fasc. B: *Les planches.* (Inventaire des inscriptions sudarabiques, 3). Paris: de Boccard/Rome: Herder.

Frantsouzoff S.A.
- 1995. The Inscriptions from the temples of Dhat Ḥimyam at Raybūn. With a Postscript by Alfred F.L. Beeston. *Proceedings of the Seminar for Arabian Studies* 25: 15–28.
- 1997. Regulation of conjugal relations in ancient Raybūn. *Proceedings of the Seminar for Arabian Studies* 27: 113–127.
- 1998. A Parallel to the Second Commandment in the inscriptions of Raybūn. *Proceedings of the Seminar for Arabian Studies* 28: 1998: 61–67.
- 2001*a*. *Raybūn, Ḥadrān, temple de la déesse ᶜAthtarum/ᶜAstarum.* Fasc. A: *Les documents.* Fasc. B: *Les planches.* (Inventaire des inscriptions sudarabiques, 5). Paris: de Boccard/Rome: Herder.
- 2001*b*. Le 'tailleur de pierre' (grby-n/-hn) dans les inscriptions sudarabiques. *Raydān* 7: 125–143.
- 2001*c*. Epigraphic evidence for the cult of the god Sīn at Raybūn and Shabwa. *Proceedings of the Seminar for Arabian Studies* 31: 59–67.
- 2003. En marge des inscriptions de Raybūn (remarques sur la grammaire, le lexique et le formulaire de la langue ḥaḍramoutique épigraphique). *Arabia. Revue de Sabéologie* 1: 39–58.
- 2005. Epigraphic documentation from Ḥaḍramawt. Pages 193–216 in A.V. Sedov, *Temples of Ancient Ḥaḍramawt* (Arabia Antica, 3). Pisa: Edizioni Plus–Pisa University Press.
- 2007. *Raybūn. Kafas Naᶜmān, temple de la déesse dhāt-Ḥimyam.* Fasc. A: *Les documents.* Fasc. B: *Les planches.* Avec une contribution archéologique de A.V. Sedov & J. Vinogradov. (Inventaire des inscriptions sudarabiques, 6). Paris: de Boccard/Rome: Herder.

Gelb I.J., Landsberger B. & Oppenheim A.L. (eds).
- 1956–. *The Assyrian Dictionary of the Oriental Institute of the University of Chicago.* Chicago: The Oriental Institute.

al-Ghūl M.
- 1959. New Qatabāni Inscriptions — [I]. *Bulletin of the School of Oriental and African Studies* 22: 1–22.

Gnoli G.
- 1993. *Shaqab al-Manaṣṣa. Con diciotto tavole fuori testo.* (Inventaire des inscriptions sudarabiques, 2). Paris: de Boccard/Rome: Herder.

Gruntfest Y.
- 1986. Language and style of the SA inscriptions: votive inscriptions from Marib. *Jerusalem Studies in Arabic and Islam* 7: 1–34.

Höfner M.
　1954. Das Sudarabische der Inschriften und der lebenden Mundarten. Pages 314–341 in B. Spuler (ed.), *Handbuch der Orientalistik.* iii. Leiden: Brill.

Huehnergard J.
　2005. Features of Central Semitic. Pages 155–203 in A. Gianto (ed.), *Biblical and Oriental essays in memory of William L. Moran.* (Biblica et Orientalia, 48). Rome: Loyola Press.

Jamme A.W.F.
　1962. Sabaean Inscriptions from Maḥram Bilqîs (Mârib). (Publications of the American Foundation for the Study of Man, 3). Baltimore: Johns Hopkins Press.

Johnstone T.M.
　1981. *Jibbāli Lexicon.* New York: Oxford University Press.

Koehler L. & Baumgartner W.
　1967–1995. *Hebräisches und aramäisches Lexikon zum Alten Testament.* Leiden: Brill.

Kottsieper I. & Stein P.
　(this volume). Sabaic and Aramaic — a common origin? *Supplement to the Proceedings of the Seminar for Arabian Studies* 44.

Lane E.W.
　1968. *An Arabic–English Lexicon. Derived from the best and most copious Eastern sources.* Beirut: Librairie du Liban.

Leslau W.
　1987. *Comparative Dictionary of Geʿez (Classical Ethiopic). Geʿez–English, English–Geʿez, with an Index of the Semitic Roots.* Wiesbaden: Harrassowitz.

Müller W.W.
　1962. Die Wurzeln mediae und tertiae Y/W im Altsüdarabischen. Eine etymologische und lexikographische Studie. Inaugural-Dissertation zur Erlangung des Doktorgrades einer Hohen Philosophischen Fakultät der Eberhard-Karls-Universität zu Tübingen, Weipert/Sudetenland. [Unpublished.]

Multhoff A.
　2009. 'A parallel to the Second Commandment...' revisited. *Proceedings of the Seminar for Arabian Studies* 39: 295–302.
　2010*a. tfʿl/ftʿl* — Die verbalen T-Stämme im Altsüdarabischen. *Folia Orientalia* 47: 19–69.
　2010*b.* Phalluskult und Bilderverbot? Beiträge zur ḥaḍramitischen Sprache und Kultur. *Zeitschrift der Deutschen Morgenländischen Gesellschaft* 160/11: 7–40.

Pirenne J.
　1979. L'apport des inscriptions à l'interprétation du temple de Bā-Quṭfah. *Raydān* 2: 203–241.

Prioletta A.
　2012. Evidence from a new inscription regarding the goddess ʿt(t)rm and some remarks on the gender of deities in South Arabia. *Proceedings of the Seminar for Arabian Studies* 42: 309–318.
　2013. Remarks on some processes of assimilation and innovation in the language and culture of Ḥaḍramawt during its ancient history. *Aula Orientalis* 31: 93–108.

Ricks S.D.
　1989. *Lexicon of inscriptional Qatabanian.* Rome: Editrice Pontificio Istituto Biblico.

Robin C.J.
　2008. Joseph, dernier roi de Ḥimyar (de 522 à 525, où une des années suivantes). *Jerusalem Studies in Arabic and Islam* 34: 1–125.

Sima A.
　2000. *Tiere, Pflanzen, Steine und Metalle in den altsüdarabischen Inschriften. Eine lexikalische und realienkundliche Untersuchung.* (Akademie der Wissenschaften und der Literatur. Veröffentlichungen der Orientalischen Kommission, 46). Wiesbaden: Harrassowitz.

Stein P.
- 2003. *Untersuchungen zur Phonologie und Morphologie des Sabäischen* (Epigraphische Forschungen auf der Arabischen Halbinsel, 3). Rahden Westfalen: Marie Leidorf GmbH.
- 2007. Materialien zur sabäischen Dialektologie: Das Problem des amiritischen ('haramischen') Dialektes. *Zeitschrift der Deutschen Morgenländischen Gesellschaft* 157: 13–47.
- 2010a. *Die altsüdarabischen Minuskelinschriften auf Holzstäbchen aus der Bayerischen Staatsbibliothek in München.* (Epigraphische Forschungen auf der Arabischen Halbinsel, 5). Tübingen: Wasmuth.
- 2010b. The monetary terminology of Ancient South Arabia in light of new epigraphic evidence. Pages 303–343 in M. Huth & P.G. van Alfen (eds), *Coinage of the Caravan Kingdoms. Studies in Ancient Arabian Monetization.* New York: American Numismatic Society/New York/Oxford: Oxbow.
- 2012. SABAICA — ARAMAICA (1). Pages 503–522 in T. Polański (ed.), *Studia Andreae Zaborski Dedicata.* (Folia Orientalia, 49). Cracow: Polish Academy of Sciences.

Author's address

Alessia Prioletta, Dipartimento di Civiltà e Forme del Sapere — University of Pisa, Via Galvani 1, 56126, Pisa, Italy.
e-mail a.prioletta@sta.unipi.it

The Minaeans beyond Maʿīn

IRENE ROSSI

Summary

In the first millennium BC, the South Arabian kingdom of Maʿīn was involved in trading activity along the trans-Arabian routes. Nearly seventy monumental inscriptions written in the Minaic language come from the oases of al-ʿUlā, Madāʾin Ṣāliḥ, and Qaryat al-Fāw (in modern Saudi Arabia), and from Egypt and Delos. This epigraphic corpus, labelled 'Marginal Minaic', is not merely the testimony of the economic relationships binding the South Arabian states with the rest of the Near East and the Mediterranean. The paper presents a comparative analysis of the cultural and textual features of these inscriptions. Similarities and divergences with respect to the documentation from the motherland, especially in textual models, lexicon, and formulae, are highlighted. The study enables the evaluation of the extent of language contact and cultural integration in different environments; at the same time, the role of the writing schools is appreciated in relation to the strategies enacted by the state or local communities in order to preserve their cultural identity and political cohesion in a foreign milieu.

Keywords: Maʿīn, trade, writing school, language contact, identity

The involvement of the South Arabian kingdom of Maʿīn in the trans-Arabian commerce in the first millennium BC is well known thanks to many internal and external sources.[1] The key testimonies of this trading activity are the nearly seventy Minaic monumental inscriptions that were found beyond the South Arabian borders of the kingdom, most of them in the oases of the Arabian Peninsula, but some even farther, in Egypt and in the Mediterranean.

The first publications of these texts go back to the end of the nineteenth century (Müller DH 1889; Mordtmann 1897) following the expeditions of Doughty, Hubert and Euting in northern Arabia. The best-documented edition of the Minaic monumental inscriptions and graffiti from North Arabia was published at the beginning of the twentieth century in the volumes of the *Mission Archéologique en Arabie* by Jaussen and Savignac (1909; 1914). Further expeditions by archaeologists and epigraphists, or the publication of inscriptions preserved in the museums, allowed the discovery and edition of new Ancient South Arabian texts found outside South Arabia (Fig. 1).[2]

The systematic publication of these texts in the *Répertoire d'Épigraphie Sémitique* basically includes the Ancient South Arabian inscriptions and graffiti from North Arabia edited by Jaussen and Savignac and G. Ryckmans, plus the Minaic inscriptions from Egypt (RES 3427 and RES 3571) and Delos (RES 3570) previously published in other contributions.[3] This edition was the basic reference for the collection of all the monumental texts in the Minaic language (therefore graffiti excluded) edited by Capuzzi under the supervision of Garbini in 1974; where possible,

---

[1] In the inscriptions from the Yemeni Jawf, long-distance commercial expeditions and their terminals are recorded in the texts M 152, M 247, Maʿīn 7, Maʿīn 10. Moreover, the stereotyped inscriptions traditionally called 'lists of hierodules' commemorated the marriage of local men with women from foreign localities (Maʿīn 93A–D to Maʿīn 98 and al-Saʿīd 2002/2009), providing a list of the places that constituted Maʿīn's commercial network.

[2] Texts from the Wādī Ramm and from the Ḥijāz (Ryckmans 1934: 590–591; 1965: 217–228), from the al-Jawf area in northern Arabia (Winnett & Reed 1970: 74), from southern Jordan (Graf 1983: 560–562), from the region of al-ʿUlā and Ḥegrā (Ryckmans 1921; Winnett & Reed 1970: 122; Jamme 1974; Naṣif 1988: 22–25; al-Theeb 1990: 21–22; Sima 1996: 279–286; 2000: 259–260). Note that Jamme's edition had little resonance, as eight years later the inscription Ja 2288 was published as a new text by Sayed (1982: 52–60) and welcomed as such by Beeston (1983: 1–2).

Regarding the inscriptions on seals and the graffiti, which are mostly onomastic texts, a Minaean origin of the authors can be ascertained only in the few cases when the family names are recorded or the personal names occur also in the Minaic texts from South Arabia. On this topic, see Avanzini 1979.

[3] RES 3427=M 338 in Derenbourg 1895 (for a list of the previous editions, see Derenbourg 1895: 7–8); RES 3571 in Green 1909: 253; RES 3570=M 349 in Clermont-Ganneau 1908. It should be mentioned that the seal RES 3927=M 376, preserved in the British Museum, was considered Minaic in the *Répertoire*, probably on the basis of G. Ryckmans's note that it was found in Petra (1927: 186). Besides not being sufficient to establish the cultural origin of the object, the provenance from Petra must be discarded because the catalogue of the British Museum records that the seal was donated by Major B.R. French in 1925, together with other objects from the wādī Bayḥan in Qataban (www.britishmuseum.org; accessed 30 October 2013).

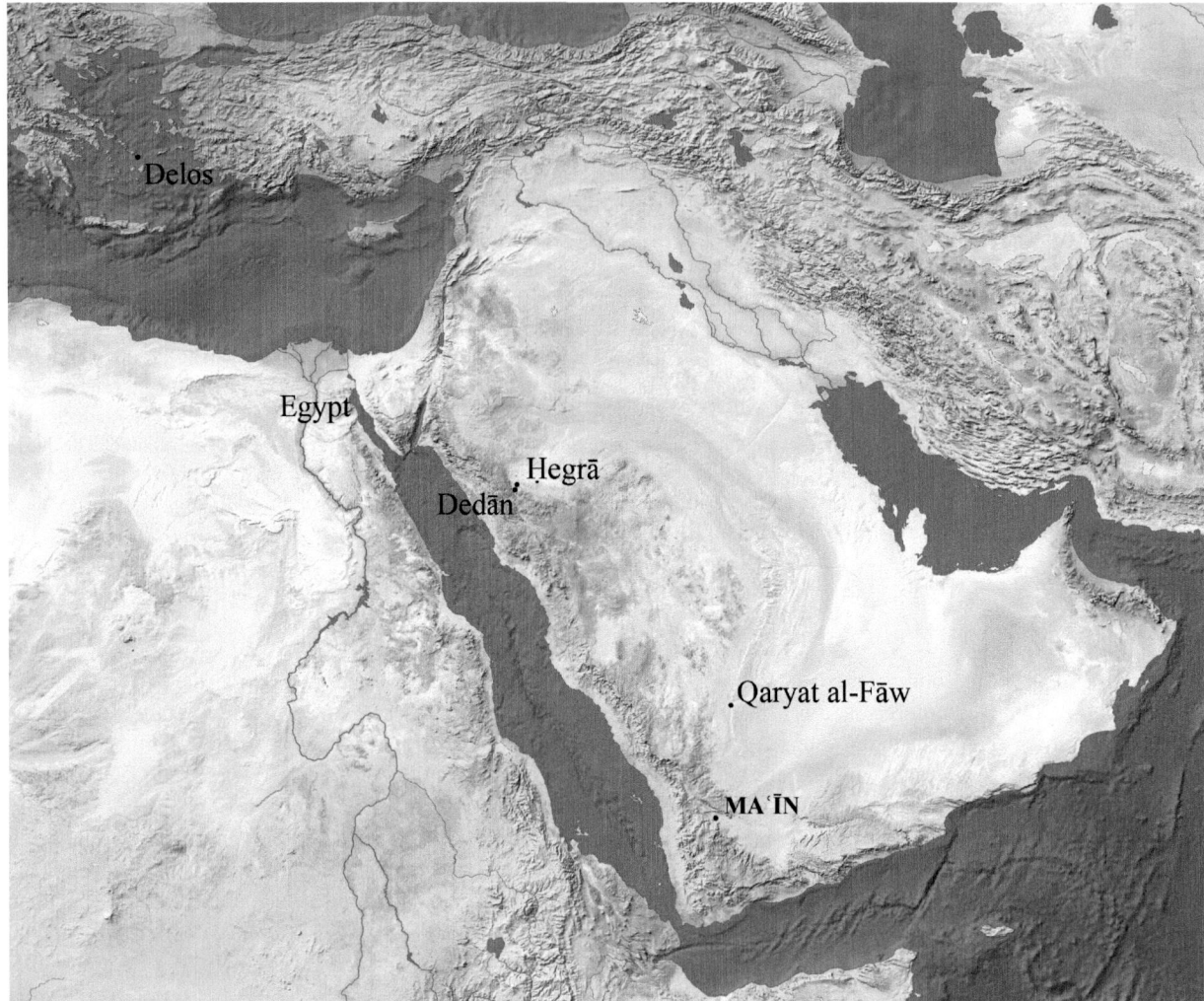

Figure 1. *The location of Maʿīn and distribution of the Minaic monumental texts outside South Arabia (made with Natural Earth).*

the inscriptions in the present contribution will be referred to using the siglum 'M' given in this collection.[4]

Recently, all the Minaic monumental texts from outside South Arabia were re-edited in the online *Digital Archive for the Study of pre-Islamic Arabian Inscriptions* project under the directorship of Prof. A. Avanzini at the University of Pisa (DASI; http://dasi.humnet.unipi.it)[5], where they have been collected in a distinct group of texts within the Minaic epigraphic corpus, under the label 'Marginal Minaic' inscriptions (MMIN). Although conventional, this label seeks to render not only the geographical but also the cultural and linguistic specificity of these texts with respect to the inscriptions from the homeland of the Minaean kingdom in South Arabia ('Central Minaic' — CMIN).

Through the analysis of the textual and cultural features of the corpus of the Marginal Minaic monumental texts, this paper aims to appraise the contribution that this documentation may make on the issue of the use of language and textual models as an element of identity or integration by the South Arabian communities settled abroad, and on the study of the relation between political power and writing schools.

---
[4] Unfortunately, from one edition to another, the copying produced some transcription errors, which show that neither the edition in the *Répertoire* nor that by Capuzzi (1974) is based on the autoptic reading of the images published by Jaussen and Savignac or in previous editions.
[5] Avanzini, Prioletta & Rossi, in press.

FIGURE 2. *The writing style of a MMIN inscription of the reign of ʾbkrb Ytʿ — M 358= RES 3697 (Jaussen & Savignac 1914: pls 76, 101/27).*

***

The most abundant group of MMIN texts was found in the oasis of al-ʿUlā (ancient Dadan) in north-west Arabia, where the Minaeans established a settlement on the trading route towards Taymāʾ, Gaza and Egypt.[6] Except for the rock texts, which are mostly graffiti, the nearly fifty monumental texts from Dadan are engraved on stone construction blocks, which were found reemployed in the houses of the modern village and are almost all fragmentary. Ten monumental inscriptions were also found in Madāʾin Ṣāliḥ, ancient Ḥegrā (nearly 15 km from Dadan). They suggest a presence of Minaeans in the site, although this cannot be proved since the inscriptions are not *in situ*.[7]

All the texts from the two sites are consistently Minaean. Well-known names of families are mentioned, most of which are referred to in the so-called 'list of hierodules' (see n. 1); four kings of Maʿīn are attested; the texts are dated by an eponymous *kbr* ('chief, superintendant'), who is once explicitly called the '*kbr* of Maʿīn in Dadan' (Ja 2288); the main gods of the Minaean

---

[6] The chronology of the Minaean presence in North Arabia is still vague. It plausibly coincided with the period of major trading expansion of the kingdom around the fifth and fourth centuries BC, but a broader time span cannot be excluded. The coexistence in Dadan, proved by some inscriptions, of the Minaean settlement with the local kingdom of Liḥyān does not help in defining the chronological frame: the reconstruction of Liḥyān's history is still debated and is mainly proposed on the basis of the history of the Minaeans' trade, thus creating a vicious circle (Rossi, in press).

[7] The expected publication of the inscriptions (including South Arabian ones) found along the newly identified Darb al-Bakra route (al-Ghabban 2007) will probably clarify if the Minaeans' presence in Ḥegra was related to the exploitation of this ancient itinerary, an alternative to the one leading north from Dadan.

FIGURE 3. *The writing style of a CMIN inscription of the reign of ʾbkrb Ytʿ — A-20-850 (photograph courtesy of the CASIS Project — University of Pisa).*

pantheon are evoked (*Wd*, *ʿttr ḏ-Qbḍ*, *Nkrḥ*, and the *ʾlʾlt Mʿn*). Although most of the inscriptions are fragmentary and the type of content is often difficult to identify, the pattern of the CMIN dedications is generally followed. At the same time, the recurrence of a juridical/economic lexicon (e.g. *fdy* 'purchase', *ʾhly* 'goods', *qny* 'property', *ṣʿq* and *ṣdq* 'claim rights', *wtq* 'guarantee', *ṣḥft* and *ṣlwt* 'written document') reveals a remarkable concern for property rights.

The texts are written in correct South Arabian script and all the distinctive Minaic grammatical features are present: the personal pronouns and the causative prefix are formed on the base *s¹*; demonstrative/relative pronouns are formed on the bases *ḏ* (singular) and *ʾhl* (plural); the *nomen regens* of the genitival construct displays the so-called 'parasitic *h*'; the nominal plural feminine ending is -*ht(n)*.

At the same time, the Minaic inscriptions from North Arabia display some divergences from the CMIN texts. Firstly, the writing style is more irregular (Figs 2 & 3). The oblique strokes of the letters (e.g. *n*, *ʾ*, *ḥ*) form very acute angles, the higher part of some signs is in many cases triangular, and the letter *w* is often wide and sometimes takes a rhombic shape. Secondly, some differences are apparent in the lexicon and the formulae. The frequent MMIN phrase *ʿnn ʿlyt ḏt ṣḥftn* (see Ja 2288/2; M 316/1; M 317/2; M 321/6; M 323/6; M 334/5; M 358/6), meaning 'on the basis of this document', never occurs in CMIN, neither does the compound preposition *ʿnn ʿlyt* occur on its own.[8] The singular feminine noun *ṣḥft* in CMIN is only attested with a different meaning, 'curtain wall' (referring to the part of the town walls between two towers); *ṣḥf* is the plural form (cf. *ʾhlt mḥfdtn w-ṣḥfn*, 'those towers and curtains' in M 239/2).[9]

A further example of formulaic discrepancy is the phrase *s¹brr w-s¹mtʿ* (probably meaning 'to release and save'), frequently attested in Dadan but absent from the CMIN texts (see M 319/3; M 350 A/6; M 351/1, 8; M 357/4; M 359/2; M 464/4; M 465/4), where the verb *mtʿ* occurs in one single inscription (M 247/2–3) and the verb *s¹brr* is widely used in a different expression, *b-krb s¹brr* 'as an obligation from which (the god) relieved (him/her)'.

The frequent formulae of commitment of goods to the protection of the divinities involve the use of the three verbs *s¹nkr*, *fʿy*, and *ms³r*, which list the calamities that the goods may undergo. In the texts from Dadan, however, this sequence is usually opened by the verb *ġrb* (see M 316/3; M 317/4; M 320/1, 2; M 325/2; M 326/5; M 334/6; M 351/2), which is absent from the CMIN corpus. The verb is related to the same semantic area as the other verbs of the phrase ('to remove, displace'), to be compared with Ar. *ġrb*, form II, 'to expel'.

Other MMIN words are never attested in CMIN, such as the verb *ṣʿq* 'to claim rights'[10] and the word *rytm/rtm*

---

[8] Of the only three cases of *ʿnn* in CMIN, two surely have to be interpreted as a preposition of place 'in front of': M 172 and Y.92.B.A 21+30 (although in the latter, *ʿnn* was considered by the editor as a name of family; see de Maigret & Robin 1993: 485–486).

[9] It seems that the two CMIN instances of *ṣḥf* with the meaning of 'document' are singular; but it cannot be excluded that, on the contrary, they are a plural of an unattested singular *ṣḥft* with the same meaning as in MMIN (Maʿīn 1/5: *b-ḥdyt ṣḥf ʾs¹mʿh-s¹*; as-Sawdāʾ 37/10: *b-ṣḥfh ʾs¹mʿh-s¹mn*). As for the few instances of the root in the other South Arabian languages, 'curtain' is always spelled *ṣḥft* (with plural *ṣḥf* and one instance of *ṣḥfw* in the Qatabanic CSAI I, 14). As for the meaning 'document', in Qatabanic the oscillation is evident between both the singular masculine and feminine forms e.g. CSAI I, 197 *ḏt ṣḥftn* vs. *ḏn ṣḥfn*.

[10] Mainly in the phrase *ys¹ṣʿq-s¹ ḏ-ʾdnh-s¹* ('he claims as belonging to him'); see M 325/3–4; M 326/4; M 333/6; M 464/3; M 465/2.

'decision, outstanding obligation' (see M 289/3–4; M 321/2; M 332/3–4; M 350 A/7; M 351/6; M 358/9; M 464/5). An interesting difference in lexicon is surely the word *lwʾ* (fem. *lwʾt*; see M 326/2; M 332/3; M 333/1, 2; M 351/3; M 358/3, 9; M 359/2) – presumably referring to the priestly class – which is absent from the South Arabian lexicon and also from the Dadanitic inscriptions known so far.[11]

Finally, it is known that the Minaic verbal causative prefix is *s¹*- (*s¹qny* 'to dedicate') as in Qatabanic and Hadramitic, yet the pattern of the derived substantives in CMIN conforms to the peculiar use of the Sabaic *h*-causative prefix (*hqnyt* 'dedication'; see e.g. M 247/4). By contrast, the MMIN texts maintain the *s¹*- prefix also in the pattern of the derived substantives, as is apparent in the word *s¹qnyt* (see Ja 2288/4; M 316/2; M 317/3; M 351/9) and in some occurrences of the noun *s¹brrt*.[12]

***

It is interesting to find this last feature also in the two published MMIN texts from Qaryat al-Fāw (Riyadh nos. 302F8 and 262F8; Robin in al-Ghabban et al. 2010: 324, cat. 135 and 136).[13] The archaeological excavations on this site in present-day Saudi Arabia have brought to light important religious, hydraulic, residential, and commercial structures, including an impressive market. The precious artefacts and the texts written in different languages and scripts of the Arabian Peninsula — including a significant number of Minaic and Sabaic inscriptions — clearly point to the key role of the oasis in the trade between southern, eastern and northern Arabia (al-Anṣari 2010).

Both texts, cast on bronze plaques, are consistently Minaic as regards grammar and textual pattern, as exemplified by the typical Minaic formula *s³lʾ w-s¹qny* 'dedicated and consecrated', but some peculiar features are apparent.

The inscription no. 262F8 provides the only certain notation of the verbal suffix conjugation dual ending -*y* in the Minaic corpus. The use of the causative prefix *s¹*- in the formation of derived substantives (e.g. *s¹qnyt*) is a shared feature with the MMIN inscriptions from Dadan. In text no. 302F8, the verbs *ns²* and *gbʾ* in the expression *b-hdyht w-ʾkrb ʾḥd ʾḥly-s¹m ns²-h k-Nhr ʿd S¹lky w-gbʾ-h ʿd Qryt w-Qrnw* are followed by an unusual ending -*h*, whose simplest interpretation — as suggested by the editor's translation — seems to be that of a suffix pronoun formed on the Sabaic base -*h* instead of the Minaic -*s¹*, which is actually used throughout the text: 'avec les dons et les taxes prélevés sur leurs marchandises, qu'ils ont emportées pour (le Pays de) Nahar (?) jusqu'à Séleucie et qu'ils ont rapportées à Qaryat et à Maʿīn' (Robin in al-Ghabban et al. 2010: 324). Moreover, the inscription contains the typical Hadramitic phrase *tʿs¹m ʾdn* ('the will (of the god) is great') (see Rb VI/04 s.w. no. 3/3–4; Rb XIV/87 no. 104/9; Rb XIV/87 no. 105/5–6; Rb XIV/87 nos. 110–111/6–7; Rb XIV/90 no. 60/5) and its graphic style is not typical at all of the Minaic epigraphic corpus but rather of the Sabaic and Qatabanic texts dated around the end of the first millennium BC.

In fact, the only Minaic inscription with a comparable writing style is the well-known text M 222 (Fig. 4), which celebrates some building activities on the walls of the Minaean town of Yathill in the Jawf 'at the time of *Wqhʾl Ytʿ* and his son *ʾlyfʿ Ys²r* kings of Maʿīn and *S²hr Ygl Yhrgb* king of Qataban', the three defined as 'lords' (*ʾmrʾ*) of the authors of the text. M 222 could be the case of a text written in the Jawf by Minaeans resident in Qataban or by Qatabanians working in the Minaean kingdom; indeed, the family of the authors of the text, *Ḍmrn*, is mentioned on a number of Qatabanian funerary stelae.[14]

It is interesting that M 222 proves a significant link between Qataban and Qaryat al-Fāw through Maʿīn; indeed, the authors of the text define themselves as *ʾdm Wdm S²hrn* 'servants of *Wdm S²hrn*', like the dedicants of the inscription from Qaryat al-Fāw no. 302F8. That *S²hrn* was the local epithet of *Wd* is proved by the fact that the god is among the divinities that receive the dedication of both the MMIN bronze plaques.[15]

***

It should be recalled that no Minaic inscription has been found so far in the other South Arabian kingdoms, even

---

[11] In CMIN, the priest is called *s³wʾ* or *rs²wʾ*; in Dadanitic, *s¹lḥ* and, more rarely, *qymh* or *ʾfkl* (Farès-Drappeau 2005: 89–90).
[12] The derived substantive from the root *BRR* is attested only in MMIN (M 319/1; M 325/5).
[13] The inscription no. 262F8 seems to be a complete copy of the fragmentary text on bronze from Qaryat al-Fāw, published by B. Jändl without a photograph (2009: 126). It remains unclear whether they are two different inscriptions.
[14] See BM 141583; CSAI I, 304, 306, 313, 579, 660, 665, 968 (plus the fragmentary occurrence in CSAI I, 173). In the Jawf, cf. only [......]*hl Ḍmr*[*n* ... ...] (al-Jawf 04.25). M 222 is a testimony of the long-lasting trading connection between Maʿīn and Qataban, which can be dated back to the rules defined for the Minaean traders in the Qatabanic decree on the Timnaʿ market stela (CSAI I, 205) and might be retraced in the wars waged against Maʿīn and Qataban by a Sabaean *mukarrib* at the end of the seventh century/ beginning of the sixth century BC (RES 3943).
[15] Other mentions of the god are found in the Early Sabaic text DhM 360 from al-Ḥadāʾ region and in the Central Middle Sabaic text CIH 30 from Ġaymān.

Figure 4. *The Qatabanian writing style of the Minaic inscription M 222 (courtesy of the Mission Archéologique Française en République Arabe du Yémen — Christian Robin).*

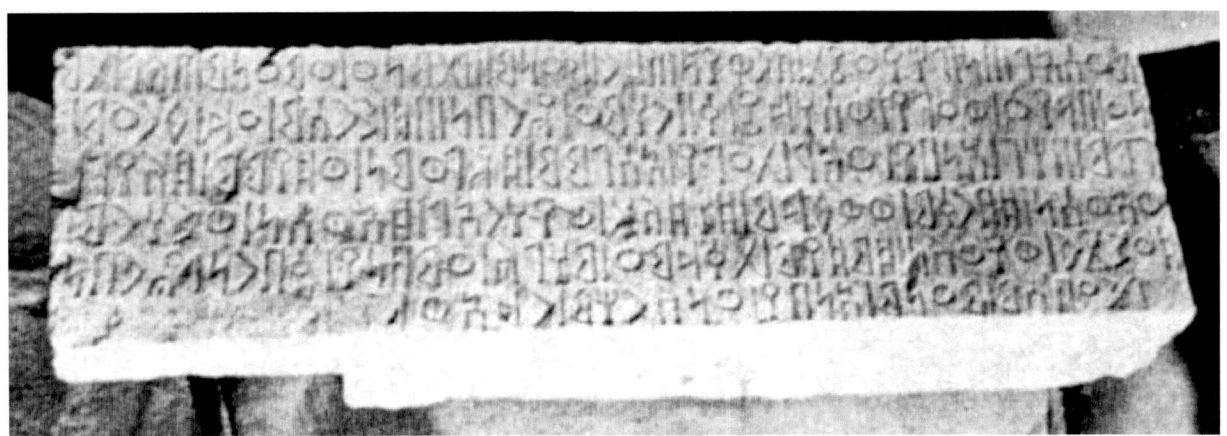

Figure 5. *The Minaean writing style of the Qatabanic inscription VL 9 = CSAI I, 72 (al-Ghūl 1959: pl. 1).*

where there are proofs of a stable Minaean presence. The inscription CSAI I, 72 (Fig. 5), which commemorates the construction of a tomb in the necropolis of the Qatabanian capital by some Minaean settlers, or the bronze inscription Lion 1 — dedicated by a Minaean woman at the time of her lords '*Wqhʾl Ytˤ* king of Maˤīn and *S²hr Hll* and his son *Hwfˤm Yhnˤm* the two kings of Qataban' (thus almost contemporarily to M 222)[16] — are written in Qatabanic, with some sporadic Minaic linguistic features. It is interesting, however, that the writing style of both

---

[16] Arbach suggests to date the inscription Lion 1 to the first century BC (Arbach 2005: 28–29; cf. Robin 1998: 180–186, dealing with M 222), while Avanzini dates it back to the end of the third century BC (Avanzini 2010: 186).

the inscriptions is rather Minaean; this feature recalls, inversely, the case of the Minaic text M 222, the writing style of which is definitely Qatabanian.

From the few examples at our disposal, therefore, it would seem that the inscriptions set up by Minaeans in other South Arabian kingdoms were written in the local language, while the writing style was maintained, as a marker of identity. The significant implication of this would be the presence of scribes following motherland models in the communities settled abroad.

The case of the Minaeans living beyond the South Arabian territories is remarkably different. As we have seen, the most significant textual evidence of the Minaeans abroad comes from northern Arabia. Here, the settlers were in contact with a local society which had its own script and language — the kingdom of Liḥyān. The fragmentary lines of text M 360 suggest that there were cases of mixed families, composed of Minaean women and men from Dadan. The interaction with the local culture is also evident in some texts by Minaeans written in the local (Dadanitic) language or script. A text by a member of a Minaean family is composed in the Dadanitic language and it is dated to the reign of a king of Liḥyān, but is carved in the Ancient South Arabian script (Abū al-Ḥasan 2005: 43–45). Two dedications to the Liḥyānite god ḏ-Ġbt are written in Dadanitic language and script by priests of the South Arabian god Wd: JSlih 49 by a ʾfkl of Wd (Fig. 6) and AḤ 199 by a slḥt of Wd from the Minaean family Yfʿn (Abū al-Ḥasan 2002: 43–45).

It is significant that the Minaean authors of these texts decided to write in a different language and/or script but at the same time the Minaic texts from the oasis do not show any Dadanitic influence on language, lexicon, or textual models, except — possibly — the isolated phonetic phenomenon of the writing s^1 instead of s^3 in the word ms^1r of M 317, which could reflect the absence of the third sibilant in Dadanitic.[17] The compliance to Minaic textual models and grammar by the Minaean community was the means to assert the identity of the residents and affirm the political control over their settlement. The formulaic, lexical, and palaeographical discrepancies already highlighted in the MMIN texts from North Arabia with respect to the texts from South Arabia might be due to the development of a local Minaean writing school.

As regards the inscriptions from Qaryat al-Fāw, only the availability of a wider group of texts and of chronological

FIGURE 6. *A Dadanitic inscription by a Minaean priest — JSLih 49 (Jaussen & Savignac 1914: pl. 82/49).*

data would enable the study on the peculiarities of MMIN texts from Qaryat al-Fāw with respect to the CMIN inscriptions and to the MMIN inscriptions from northern Arabia. At present, it seems that the formulae and the palaeography are somehow affected by the contact with other South Arabian languages in the site's international environment.

---

[17] According to A. Multhoff, this phenomenon rather recalls the Amiritic dialect, that is to say the language of the Amīr, a tribe living north of the Jawf, which — in its turn — is said to be strongly influenced by North Arabian structures (Stein 2011: 1047).

FIGURE 7. *A Minaic inscription on a sarcophagus from Egypt — M 338 (Derenbourg 1895).*

As for the Minaean presence in Egypt, a different situation is suggested by the MMIN inscription written on the sarcophagus of a Minaean merchant, who had been responsible for the import of aromatics for the temples of the Ptolemaic kingdom (M 338; Fig. 7).[18] A deep cultural integration of the man in the local society is reflected by the description of his Egyptian funerary ceremony and also in the lexicon of the text: some words are surely Egyptian loans (e.g. line 3: *bʾh-sʹ* 'his Bā', i.e. 'his person, his soul'), and others might be, as they have no comparison in the South Arabian languages.[19]

It is logical to suppose the presence of a Minaean community in the Ptolemaic kingdom for the management of trade with southern Arabia, which would have been organized differently from the settlements along the Arabian trading routes. These were commercial outposts established by the Minaean kingdom, which controlled the proceeds of the trade through religious structures: a temple of *Wd* has been uncovered by the excavations in Qaryat al-Fāw and the decree M 356 attests that the temple of the god in Dadan managed the flow of merchandise in the oasis.[20] Also in the CMIN texts there are hints of state control of the proceeds of the traffic, as the clans involved in trade participated in public construction activities and paid tithes to the gods.

Even on the Greek island of Delos, two Minaean merchants set up an altar (*nṣb mḏbḥ*) for '*Wd* and the gods of Maʿīn', writing the text in Minaic (M 349; Fig. 8).[21] From a linguistic point of view, in contrast to the inscriptions from Qaryat al-Fāw, the text keeps to the Minaic use of avoiding the notation of the dual ending -*y* in the suffix conjugation.[22] There is also what amounts to a gloss in Greek which reads simply 'of *Wd*, god of the Minaeans' and 'to *Wdʾ*', which was presumably added for the benefit of the local population and travellers who could not read Ancient South Arabian, but used Greek as their *lingua franca*.[23]

***

From the overview of the main textual features of the MMIN documentation, it is evident that the monumental inscriptions left by the Minaeans beyond the South Arabian territory of the kingdom provide far more than a simple attestation of the commercial activity of the kingdom. They show the strategies enacted by the state in order to manage this main source of revenue by establishing communities abroad, which were able to maintain their cultural and political identity in a foreign

---

[18] The object is preserved in the Egyptian Museum in Cairo. The chronology of this text is disputed. The dating to the 22nd year of 'Ptolemy son of Ptolemy' is far from being precise, due to the many homonym kings who reigned at least 22 years in the Ptolemaic dynasty. Robin considers the palaeography to be quite late, suggesting a date around the end of the second and the beginning of the first century BC (1994: 294–295). Even on a paleographical basis, however, an earlier dating cannot be excluded. For example, if the identification suggested by Walter W. Müller (1988: 627, n. f) of 'Ptolemy son of Ptolemy' with Ptolemy II Philadelphus (285–246 BC) proves to be correct, the text would interestingly be dated to around 263 BC, when Zeno's papyri record the trade of incense by Gerrhaeans and Minaeans in Syria-Palestine.

[19] See the commentaries given in the various editions of this text (for the bibliography, please refer to DASI — http://dasi.humnet.unipi.it).

[20] The decree set the taxes on the goods traded in the *byt Wd*; part of them is defined as property of the god (Beeston 1978: 142–143). The temple is also mentioned in M 315, where construction works in the building are recorded.

[21] It should be noted that this is the first explicit mention of the setting up of an altar in the whole Minaic corpus. The verb *nṣb* is never found in the CMIN inscriptions, where the root only forms an epithet of the god *Wd* in two inscriptions of the ancient period from Nashshān (as-Sawdāʾ 4 and YM 29827: *Wd ḏ-Nṣb*); a noun *nṣbn* is found only in the inscription M 355 from Dadan. Moreover, the noun *mḏbḥ* occurs possibly with the same concrete meaning only in two MMIN texts (M 315/4 and M 361/9, 12); its attestations in the CMIN corpus are limited to the inscription YM 10886 from Kamna (lines 5–7), where the noun surely points to the 'sacrifice' (otherwise *ḏbḥ*). On *mḏbḥ* and *nṣb*, see Robin 2012: 31 and 33–36.

[22] No dual verb form can be recognized in the texts from Dadan.

[23] The inscription has been dated to after 167 BC, when the island became of fundamental importance in international trade as a consequence of its annexation by Athens (Robin 1991–1993: 62). Clermont-Ganneau dated the Greek text to the second half of the second century BC and maintained that it was contemporary to the Minaic text (1908: 556 and 552).

FIGURE 8. *A Minaic inscription on an altar from Delos — M 349 (Clermont-Ganneau 1908: 547).*

and multicultural environment.

The use of language and script in monumental epigraphy emerges clearly as a primary element of this identity, proving the political significance of the scribal schools for the central power of the kingdom. On the other hand, the divergences of some MMIN textual features from the CMIN documentation reveal the capability and, possibly, the need of the communities settled abroad to re-elaborate the original canons, developing their own stylistic traits.

Acknowledgements

I am indebted to Prof. A. Avanzini and Mr M.C.A. Macdonald for their stimulating remarks and to Mr Samuel Howe and Ms Siobhan O'Neill for their friendly help in the revision of the paper.

The research leading to these results has received funding from the European Research Council under the European Union's Seventh Framework Programme (FP7/2007–2013)/ERC grant agreement no. 269774.

Sigla

Ancient South Arabian inscriptions[24]

BM 141583	Inscription in Bron 2006: 192–193, fig. 8.
CSAI I, 14, 72, 173, 197, 205, 304, 306, 313, 579, 660, 665, 968	Inscriptions in Avanzini 2004.
CIH 30	Inscription in *Corpus Inscriptionum Semiticarum*. iv. *Inscriptiones himyariticas et sabaeas continens*. Paris: Imprimerie nationale, 1889–1932.
DhM 360	Inscription in Prioletta 2013: 198–300, 309.
Ja 2288	Inscription in Jamme 1974: 67–68, pl. 17 ; Sayed 1982: 52–60, pls 1–2; Beeston 1983: 1–2
al-Jawf 04.25	Inscription in Arbach & Schiettecatte 2006: 39–40, pl. 9/26.
Lion 1	Arbach 2005: 22–24, 31, fig. 1.
M 152, 172, 222, 239, 247, 289, 315, 316, 317, 319, 320, 321, 323, 325, 326, 332, 333, 334, 338, 349, 350, 351, 355, 356, 357, 358, 359, 360, 361, 376, 464, 465	Inscriptions in Capuzzi 1974.
Maʿīn 1, 7, 10, 93 A–D, 94, 95, 96, 97, 98	Inscriptions in Bron 1998.
Rb VI/04 s.w. no. 3	Inscription in Sedov, Vinogradov & Frantsouzoff 2005: 397–399, pl. 10.
Rb XIV/87 no. 104	Inscription in Frantsouzoff 1999: 34–43, pl. I.
Rb XIV/87 no. 105	Inscription in Frantsouzoff 2003: 42, 53–54, pl. 7.
Rb XIV/87 nos. 110–111	Inscription in Frantsouzoff 2001: 63–64, figs 2a, 2b.
Rb XIV/90 no. 60	Inscription in Frantsouzoff 2001: 64–65, fig. 3.
RES 3571, 3943	Inscriptions in *Répertoire d'épigraphie sémitique*. v.–viii. Paris: Imprimerie nationale, 1929–1968.
Riyadh nos. 262F8, 302F8	Inscriptions in Al-Ghabban et al. 2010: 324.
al-Saʿīd 2002/2009	Inscription in Saʿīd 2002: 57–60, fig. 1; Saʿīd 2009: 100–105, fig. 44.
as-Sawdāʾ 4, 37	Inscriptions in Avanzini 1995.
Y.92.B.A 21+30	Inscription in de Maigret & Robin 1993: 485–486, fig. 22.
YM 10886	Inscription in Robin 2002: 197–201, fig. 8.
YM 29827	Inscription in Arbach & Audouin 2007: 26–27, cat. 15.

---

[24] The bibliographical references and the concordances of the inscriptions can be retrieved at http://dasi.humnet.unipi.it

Dadanitic inscriptions

JSlih 49	Inscription in Jaussen & Savignac 1914: 379–386, pl. 82/49.	AḤ 199	Inscription in Abū al-Ḥasan 2002: 43–45.

References

Abū al-Ḥasan H.
    2002. *Nuqūš liḥyāniyya min minṭaqat al-ʿUlā*. Riyadh: Wizārat al-maʿārif, wakālat al-wizāra li-l-ʾāṯār wa-l-matāṭif.
    2005. Analysis of a new Minaean inscription from al-ʿUlā. *Adumatu* 12: 29–38. [In Arabic.]

al-Anṣārī A.M. Al-Ṭayyib.
    2010. Qaryat al-Fâw. Pages 310–363 in A.I. al-Ghabban, B. André-Salvini, F. Demange, C. Juvin & M. Cotty (eds), *Routes d'Arabie. Archéologie et histoire du royaume d'Arabie Saoudite*. Catalogue de l'exposition du Musée du Louvre, 14 juillet–27 septembre 2010. Paris: Musée du Louvre.

Arbach M.
    2005. Un lion en bronze avec un nouveau synchronisme minéo-qatabānite. Pages 21–23 in A. Sholan, S. Antonini & M. Arbach (eds), *Sabaean Studies (Dirāsāt Sabaʾiyya). Archaeological, epigraphical and historical studies in honour of Yūsuf M. ʿAbdallāh, Alessandro de Maigret, Christian J. Robin on the occasion of their sixtieth birthdays*. Naples: Il Torcoliere/Università degli studi di Napoli 'L'Orientale'.

Arbach M. & Audouin R.
    2007. *Collection of Epigraphic and Archaeological Artifacts from al-Jawf Sites. Ṣanʿāʾ National Museum*. ii. Ṣanʿāʾ: UNESCO-SFD/National Museum.

Arbach M. & Schiettecatte J.
    2006. *Catalogue des pièces archéologiques et épigraphiques du Jawf au Musée National de Ṣanʿâʾ. Ṣanʿâʾ National Museum*. Ṣanʿāʾ: Centre français d'archéologie et de sciences sociales de Ṣanʿâʾ.

Avanzini A.
    1979. Alcune osservazioni sulla documentazione epigrafica preislamica dell'oasi di al-ʿUlā. *Egitto e Vicino Oriente* 2: 215–224.
    1995. *As-Sawdāʾ*. (Inventaire des inscriptions sudarabiques, 4). Paris: de Boccard/Rome: Herder. [Académie des inscriptions et belles-lettres; Istituto italiano per l'Africa e l'Oriente.]
    2004. *Corpus of South Arabian Inscriptions I-III. Qatabanic, Marginal Qatabanic, Awsanite Inscriptions*. (Arabia Antica, 2). Pisa: Edizioni Plus-Università di Pisa.
    2010. A reassessment of the chronology of the first millennium BC. *Aula Orientalis* 28: 181–192.

Avanzini A., Prioletta A. & Rossi I.
    (in press). The Digital Archive for the Study of Pre-Islamic Arabian Inscriptions: An ERC Project. *Proceedings of the Seminar for Arabian Studies* 44.

Beeston A.F.L.
    1978. A Minaean market code. *Bulletin of the School of Oriental and African Studies* 41: 142–145.
    1983. Minaean Raʾs-ṣidq. *Proceedings of the Seminar for Arabian Studies* 13: 1–2.

British Museum.
    Online catalogue. Accessed 30 October 2013. www.britishmuseum.org/research/collection_online/search.aspx

Bron F.
    1998. *Maʿīn*. (Inventaire des inscriptions sudarabiques, 3). Paris: de Boccard/Rome: Herder. [Académie des inscriptions et belles-lettres; Istituto italiano per l'Africa e l'Oriente.]

2006. Nouvelles antiquités qatabanites du British Museum. *Arabian Archaeology and Epigraphy* 17: 190–200.

Capuzzi A. (ed.).
 1974. *Iscrizioni sudarabiche. I. Iscrizioni minee.* (Istituto Universitario Orientale di Napoli, Ricerche 10). Naples: Università di Napoli, Istituto Universitario Orientale.

Clermont-Ganneau C.
 1908. Inscription bilingue minéo-grecque découverte à Délos. *Comptes rendus de l'Académie des inscriptions et belles-lettres*: 546–560.

DASI
 Digital Archive for the Study of pre-Islamic Arabian Inscriptions. Accessed 30 October 2013. http://dasi.humnet.unipi.it

de Maigret A. & Robin C.J.
 1993. Le temple de Nakraḥ à Yathill (aujourd'hui Barāqish), Yémen, résultats des deux premières campagnes de fouilles de la mission italienne. *Comptes rendus de l'Académie des inscriptions et belles-lettres*: 427–496.

Derenbourg H.
 1895. *Nouveau mémoire sur l'épitaphe minéenne d'Egypte inscrite sous Ptolémée, fils de Ptolémée.* (École Pratique des Hautes Études. Section des sciences religieuses). Paris: Imprimerie Nationale.

Farès-Drappeau S.
 2005. *Dédan et Liḥyân. Histoire des Arabes aux confins des pouvoirs perse et hellénistique (IVe–IIe s. avant l'ère chrétienne).* (Travaux de la Maison de l'Orient et de la Mediterranée, 42). Lyon: Maison de l'Orient et de la Méditerranée – Jean Pouilloux.

Frantsouzoff S.A.
 1999. Old Ḥaḍrāmi roots of an enigmatic Qurʾānic term. Pages 34–44 in M.N. Souvorov & M.A. Rodionov (eds). *Cultural Anthropology of Southern Arabia: Hadramawt Revisited.* St Petersburg: Museum of Anthropology and Ethnography.
 2001. Epigraphic evidence for the cult of the god Sīn at Raybūn and Shabwa. *Proceedings of the Seminar for Arabian Studies* 31: 59–67.
 2003. En marge des inscriptions de Raybūn (remarques sur la grammaire, le lexique et le formulaire de la langue ḥaḍramoutique épigraphique). *Arabia. Revue de Sabéologie* 1: 39–58.

al-Ghabban A.I.
 2007. Le Darb al-Bakra. Découverte d'une nouvelle branche sur la route commerciale antique, entre al-Ḥigr (Arabie Saʿūdite) et Pétra (Jordanie). *Comptes rendus de l'Académie des inscriptions et belles-lettres*: 9–23.

al-Ghabban A.I., André-Salvini B., Demange F., Juvin C. & Cotty M. (eds).
 2010. *Routes d'Arabie. Archéologie et histoire du royaume d'Arabie Saoudite.* Catalogue de l'exposition du Musée du Louvre, 14 juillet–27 septembre 2010. Paris: Musée du Louvre.

al-Ghūl M.ʿA.
 1959. New Qatabāni Inscriptions — II. *Bulletin of the School of Oriental and African Studies* 22: 419–438.

Graf D.F.
 1983. Dedanite and Minaean (South Arabian) inscriptions from the Ḥisma. *Annual of the Department of Antiquities of Jordan* 27: 555–569.

Green F.W.
 1909. Notes on some inscriptions in the Etbai district. *Proceedings of the Society of Biblical Archaeology* 31: 247–254.

Jamme A.
 1974. *Miscellanées d'ancient [sic] arabe.* vii. Washington. [Privately printed.]

Jändl B.
 2009. *Altsüdarabische Inschriften auf Metall.* (Epigraphische Forschungen auf der Arabischen Halbinsel, 4). Tübingen/Berlin: Wasmuth.

Jaussen A.J. & Savignac M.R.
- 1909. *Mission archéologique en Arabie. (Mars–mai 1907). De Jérusalem au Hedjaz Médâin-Saleḥ.* (Publications de la Société française des fouilles archéologiques, [1]). Paris: Librairie orientaliste Paul Geuthner.
- 1914. *Mission archéologique en Arabie. II. El-ᶜEla, d'Hégra à Teima, Harrah de Tebouk.* (Publications de la Société française des fouilles archéologiques, 2). Paris: Librairie orientaliste Paul Geuthner.

Mordtmann J.H.
- 1897. *Beiträge zur minäischen Epigrafik.* (Ergänzungshefte zur Zeitschrift für Assyriologie, 12. Semitistische Studien). Weimar: E. Felber.

Müller D.H.
- 1889. *Epigraphische Denkmäler aus Arabien.* (Kaiserlichen Akademie der Wissenschaften, Vienna). (Philosophisch-historische Klasse. Denkschriften, 37/2). Vienna: F. Tempsky.

Müller W.W.
- 1988. Altsüdarabische und frühnordarabische Grab-, Sarkophag-, Votiv- und Bauinschriften. Pages 621–640 in C. Butterweck (ed.), *Grab-, Sarg-, Votiv- und Bauinschriften. Religiöse Texte.* 4. Otto Kaiser (ed.), *Texte aus der Umwelt des Alten Testaments.* 2. Gütersloh: Gütersloher Verlagshaus Gerd Mohn.

Naṣif A.A.
- 1988. *Al-ᶜUlā. An historical and archaeological survey with special reference to its irrigation system.* Riyadh: King Saᶜūd University.

Prioletta A.
- 2013. *Inscriptions from the Southern Highlands of Yemen. The epigraphic collections of the Museums of Baynūn and Dhamār.* (Arabia Antica, 8). Rome: L''Erma' di Bretschneider.

Robin C.J.
- 1991–1993 [1992]. Quelques épisodes marquants de l'histoire sudarabique. Pages 55–70 in C.J. Robin (ed.), *L'Arabie antique de Karibʾîl à Mahomet. Nouvelles données sur l'histoire des Arabes grâces aux inscriptions.* (Revue du Monde Musulman et de la Mediterranée, 61). Aix-en-Provence: Édisud.
- 1994. L'Égypte dans les inscriptions de l'Arabie méridionale préislamique. Pages 285–301 in C. Berger, G. Clerc & N. Grimal (eds), *Hommages à Jean Leclant.* (Bibliothèque d'étude, 106). Cairo: Institut français d'archéologie orientale.
- 1998. La fin du Royaume de Maᶜīn. Pages 177–188 in Rika Gyselen (ed.), *Parfums d'Orient.* (Res Orientales, 11). Bures-sur-Yvette: Groupe pour l'étude de la civilisation du Moyen-Orient.
- 2002. Vers une meilleure connaissance de Kaminahū (Jawf du Yémen). Pages 191–213 in J.F. Healey & V. Porter (eds), *Studies on Arabia in honour of Professor G. Rex Smith.* (Journal of Semitic Studies. Supplement, 14). Oxford: Oxford University Press.
- 2012. Matériaux pour une typologie des divinités arabiques et de leurs représentations. Pages 7–118 in I. Sachet (ed.) en collaboration avec C.J. Robin, *Dieux et déesses d'Arabie. Images et représentations.* Actes de la table ronde tenue au Collège de France (Paris) les 1er et 2 octobre 2007. Paris: De Boccard.

Rossi I.
- (in press). Between the North and the South. The Minaic documentation from Dadān (al-ᶜUlā). In F. Briquel-Chatonnet, M. Debié & L. Nehmé (eds), *Le contexte de naissance de l'écriture arabe. Écrit et écritures araméennes et arabes au 1er millénaire après J.-C.* Actes du colloque international du projet ANR Syrab (Orientalia Lovaniensa Analecta). Louvain: Peeters.

Ryckmans G.
- 1921. Un sceau avec inscription sud-arabe. *Le Muséon* 34: 115.
- 1927. Inscriptions sud-arabes. Première série. *Le Muséon* 40: 161–200.
- 1934. Inscriptions minéennes de Ramm. *Revue Biblique* 43: 590–591.
- 1965. Graffites minéens relevés par H.St.J. Philby et R.G. Bogue dans Le Higâz septentrional. *Le Muséon* 78: 217–228.

Saᶜīd S.F.
- 2002. Zawǧāt al-maᶜīniyyīn al-aǧnabiyyāt fī ḍawʾ nuṣūṣ ǧadīdah. *Adūmātū* 5: 53–72.

2009. Les épouses étrangères des Minéens. Pages 93–114 in F. Briquel-Chatonnet (ed.), *Femmes, cultures et sociétés dans les civilisations méditerranéennes et proche-orientales de l'antiquité*. (Topoi Orient-Occident. Supplément, 10). Lyon: Maison de l'orient méditerranéen – Jean Pouilloux.

Sayed A.M.
1982. A new Minaean inscription from al-Ola. *Journal of the Faculty of Arts and Humanities*: 51–65.

Sedov A.V., Vinogradov J.A. & Frantsouzoff S.A.
2005. Novyj chram Sajina v Rajbunskom oazise (Raskopki 2004 g.). Pages 385–400 in A.V. Sedov & I.M. Smilyanskaya (eds), *Arabia Vitalis. Studies in honour of Vitaly V. Naumkin*. Moscow: Rossiskaya Akademiya Nauk.

Sima A.
1996. Drei neue minäische Inschriften aus al-ʿUḏayb (Saudi-Arabien). *Arabian Archaeology and Epigraphy* 7: 279–286.
2000. Neue Beiträge zur lihyanischen Epigraphik I. *Arabian Archaeology and Epigraphy* 11: 252–260.

Stein P.
2011. Ancient South Arabian. Pages 1042–1073 in S. Weninger et al. (ed.), *The Semitic Languages*. (Handbücher zur Sprach- und Kommunikationswissenschaft, 36). Berlin/Boston: Mouton.

al-Theeb A.
1990. A new Minaean inscription from North Arabia. *Arabian Archaeology and Epigraphy* 1: 20–23.

Winnett F.V. & Reed W.L.
1970. *Ancient Records from North Arabia*. With contributions by J.T. Milik and J. Starcky. (Near and Middle East series, 6). Toronto: University of Toronto Press.

Author's address

Irene Rossi, Scuola Normale Superiore di Pisa, P.za dei Cavalieri 7, 56126 Pisa (PI), Italy; Dipartimento di Civiltà e Forme del Sapere — Università di Pisa, c/o v. Galvani 1, 56126 Pisa (PI), Italy.
e-mail i.rossi@sta.unipi.it

A brief comparison of Mehri and Jibbali

Aaron D. Rubin

Summary
The exact relationship among the Modern South Arabian (MSA) languages has not been conclusively determined, in part because of the lack of data on some of the languages. This comparison of the two best-described languages, Mehri and Jibbali, can serve as a preliminary model for a more comprehensive study of the family. Despite a large number of similarities, Mehri and Jibbali show many interesting differences in phonology, morphology, and syntax. Some of these differences, if shown to be innovations, can serve in the internal classification of the languages, while others are purely of interest from the perspective of language change. Similarities between the languages aid in the reconstruction of Proto-MSA, a step that is necessary in order to determine the proper place of MSA within the greater Semitic family.

Keywords: Mehri, Jibbali, Modern South Arabian, Soqotri, Hobyot

Below is a tentative family tree model of the Modern South Arabian (MSA) languages, which serves to show the historical relationship between Mehri and Jibbali.

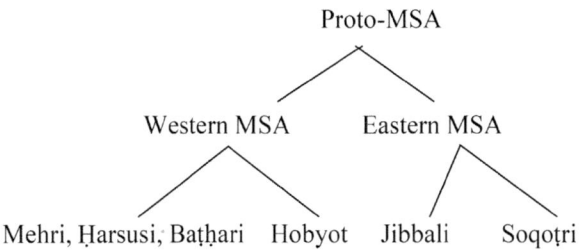

The exact relationship among the languages is not yet proven, but the following facts have support: Mehri, Ḥarsusi, and Baṭḥari can be called dialects of a single language; Hobyot shows numerous grammatical and lexical isoglosses with Mehri; and there are some morphological and lexical isoglosses that show a historical connection between Jibbali and Soqoṭri. Of course, geographically, Mehri and Jibbali are very close. Their territories in the Dhofar overlap, and there are a number of bilingual speakers. And even though Mehri and Jibbali probably do not share an immediate ancestor, the languages are still very similar in every way. For example, there is a large percentage of cognate words; they have very similar, if not identical, word order; the systems of verbal stems and tenses are nearly identical; the conjugation of verbs is quite similar; the numeral systems are very similar; the gender and number systems are the same, and so on. Speakers of the languages are not able to understand each other, however. One might suggest that the two languages are roughly equivalent to Spanish and Portuguese, or Italian and French, even if such a suggestion has no scientific value.

As with any pair of closely related languages, there are many more similarities than differences, but the differences are usually much more interesting to talk about. So this paper will mainly highlight some of the ways in which the languages differ, and point out some of the specific differences. It should first be stated that comparing the two languages is not always a simple matter of Mehri vs. Jibbali, since both languages have multiple dialects, and both show quite a bit of variation — both by location and by age — even within dialects. Thus there are times when Jibbali differs from just some Mehri dialects, or when Mehri differs from just some Jibbali dialects, as will be seen below.

Naturally, a comparison of Mehri and Jibbali could be made even more useful by also comparing Soqoṭri, Hobyot, Ḥarsusi, and Baṭḥari (the latter two of which are dialects of Mehri, from a purely linguistic point of view). Any such treatment of Modern South Arabian as a whole must include all of the languages, a feat which is probably not possible at this point, given the lack of data for some languages and dialects. This paper, then, serves primarily as a very preliminary comparative study of MSA, using the two best described — in fact, the only two well described — of the languages. It can also serve as a short introduction to the MSA group, for those readers not familiar with any of the languages.

1. Phonology

One of the most characteristic features of Jibbali is a rule by which the labials *b* and *m* are lost between vowels. In the case of *m*, the elision results in a nasalized vowel. Jibbali, therefore, has a series of nasalized vowels, unlike the other MSA languages, giving it a very distinctive sound. Below are some examples of this loss of *b* and *m*.

Loss of *b*:

ī 'father' < *ʾabī* (cf. Mehri ḥayb)
lūn 'white' < *labūn* (cf. Mehri əwbōn or əlbōn)
ḳɔ̄r 'he buried' < *ḳobór* (cf. Mehri ḳəbūr), imperf. *yəḳɔ̄r* < *yəḳóbər* (cf. Mehri yəḳáwbər)
yɔ̄k 'he weeps' < *yəbɔ́k* (cf. béké 'he wept'; Mehri bəkō 'he wept', yəbáyk 'he weeps')
ūt 'the house' < *ɛbūt* (cf. būt 'house'; Mehri bayt, def. abáyt)

Loss of *m* (with nasalization):

ũn 'Oman' < *ʿamún* (cf. Mehri (ʿ)āmōn)
xɔ̃š 'five (m.)' < *xamóš* (cf. Mehri xəm(m)ōh)
ʿɔ̃r 'he said' < *ʿamór* (cf. Mehri (ʿ)āmōr)[1]
yũlək 'he owns' < *yəmúlək* (cf. Mehri yəmūlək)
ĩndíḳ 'the rifle' < *ɛməndíḳ* (cf. məndíḳ 'rifle'; Mehri məndáwḳ, def. aməndáwḳ)

It can be seen that this rule is not merely historical but remains productive, with implications for the morphology. Thus, for example, *b* and *m* become weak root consonants in the verbal system. Besides the typical weak root consonants like *w*, *y*, and the guttural consonants, we can talk about II-*b* verbs or III-*m* verbs as being weak verbs in Jibbali. As for nouns and adjectives, when a word begins with *b* or *m*, it is elided after the prefixed definite article ɛ-. We therefore find forms like *ūt* 'the house' from indefinite *but* 'house'.

Another very characteristic difference between Mehri and Jibbali is the outcome of Proto-Semitic *s*.[2] In Mehri, *s* became *h*, while in Jibbali it became

š. This development does not have a big impact on the morphology but there is some, since in the Mehri verbal system the guttural consonant *h* is a weak root consonant. Still, this shift results in one of the most recognizable differences, especially in the pronominal system, as will be seen below. Some sample cognates are:

Mehri *ham* 'name' (cf. Jibbali šum, Hebrew שׁם šēm, Arabic اسم ism-)
Mehri *hōba* 'seven (f.)' (cf. Jibbali šōʿ, Heb. שׁבע šēbaʿ, Ar. سبع sabʿ-)
Mehri *hēxər* 'old man' (cf. Jibbali śáxər)
Mehri *ḥə-rōh* 'head' (cf. Jibbali reš, Heb. ראשׁ rōš, Ar. رأس raʾs-)
Mehri *hīma* 'he heard' < *sīmaʿ (cf. Jibbali šĩʿ, Heb. שׁמע šāmaʿ, Ar. سمع samiʿa)
Mehri *bəhēl* 'it was cooked, ready' (cf. Jibbali bɛ́šəl, Heb. בשׁל bāšēl, Geʿez basala)

Another very characteristic feature of Jibbali is the development of Semitic *w. Initial *w* is usually lost in Jibbali, unlike in Mehri. Some examples are:

ɔrx 'month' (root wrx; cf. Mehri warx)
(e)zúm 'he gave' < *wVzúm (Ga-Stem 3ms perf. of wzm; cf. Mehri wəzūm)
éṣəl 'he arrived' < *wéṣəl (Gb-Stem 3ms perf. of wṣl; cf. Mehri wīṣəl)

In the Jibbali verbal system, this means that I-w verbs are weak in all stems and tenses, while I-w verbs are often strong in Mehri. Thus, for example, Jibbali *ezum* (or *zum*) 'he gave' is weak in all forms, while the Mehri cognate *wəzūm* behaves like a strong verb in the perfect, imperfect, and future tenses. The same applies to the derived stems: *w* is often strong in Mehri, but always weak in Jibbali. A more unusual change is the shift of *w to b in Jibbali when it comes before a consonant (i.e. *wC > bC). This affects numerous lexical items, but also one of the internal plural patterns; where Mehri has an infixed *w*, Jibbali has an infixed *b*. Some examples are:

śɛ́br 'advice; plan' < *śawr (cf. Mehri śawr)
lɛ́bḳət 'bottle' < *láwḳət (cf. Mehri láwḳət)
ɛbḳáʿ 'he put' < *awḳáʿ (H-Stem 3ms perf. of wḳʿ; cf. Mehri həwḳā)
məkɛ́bṭər 'caravans' < *makáwṭər (sg. məkṭér)

---

[1] This root is I-ʿ throughout MSA, although I-ʾ elsewhere in Semitic.
[2] This PS phoneme has traditionally been reconstructed as *š, but there is very strong evidence from multiple ancient languages that it was actually *s, while the phoneme traditionally transcribed *s was actually an affricate *ts. See e.g. Faber 1981; 1985.

məlέbtəġ 'killed ones' < *məláwtəġ (sg. məltéġ)
b- 'and' < *w- (cf. Mehri w-)³

By far the most noticeable outcome of this shift is the final example above. The common Semitic conjunction *w- 'and' has become b-, at least for most Jibbali speakers,⁴ so the conjunction b- is homophonous with the common preposition b- 'in, at; with'.

2. Pronouns

In Figures 1 and 2, we see the forms of the independent pronouns in the two languages. One can see in the Mehri table (Fig. 1) that there are some variant forms. If we compare Jibbali with Omani Mehri, there is a structural difference, which is that while Jibbali distinguishes gender in the second person singular (masc. hɛt, fem. hit), Omani Mehri has just a single form hēt for both genders. If we move to Yemeni dialects, however, we find that most Yemeni dialects have a distinct feminine form hit (Watson 2012: 66).⁵ Thus here, Jibbali differs from its (partly) co-territorial Mehri dialect in Oman, but agrees with (nearly) neighbouring dialects from further away in Yemen. Also note that in the second and third person plural forms, gender is distinguished in Jibbali by both a vowel difference (u/ɛ) and a consonantal difference (m/n). In Mehri, the vowel has been levelled, as in Hebrew and Arabic.

	sing.	dual	plural
1c	hō	kay / kīh	nḥā
2m	hēt	ətay / tīh	ətēm / tām
2f	hēt (OM) / hīt (YM)		ətēn / tān
3m	hē	hay / hīh	hēm / hām
3f	sē		sēn / sān

FIGURE 1. *Mehri independent personal pronouns (with some variants).*

	sing.	dual	plural
1c	he	(ə)ši	nḥa(n)
2m	hɛt	(ə)ti	tum
2f	hit		tɛn
3m	šɛ	ši	šum
3f	sɛ		sɛn

FIGURE 2. *Jibbali independent personal pronouns.*

The third person ms, mp, and cd forms of the pronouns show the expected shift of PS *s to h in Mehri and to š in Jibbali, which was described above. Interestingly, all the MSA languages have retained Proto-Semitic *s in the third feminine singular pronoun, which is to say that the expected shift to h in Mehri and to š in Jibbali has been blocked in this form. This seems to have occurred in order to distinguish the masculine and feminine pronouns. This feature is also found in Ḥaḍramitic and therefore may reflect an areal phenomenon.⁶ Compare the Mehri and Jibbali 3sing. pronouns with those of some other Semitic languages in Figure 3.

	P-S	Akkadian	Hebrew	Arabic	Sabaic	Ḥaḍramitic	Mehri	Jibbali
3ms	*suʾa	šū	hū(ʾ)	huwa	h(w)ʾ	šV(s₁V)	**hē**	šɛ
3fs	*siʾa	šī	hī(ʾ)	hiya	h(y)ʾ	sV(s₃V)	**sē**	sɛ

FIGURE 3. *Third person singular independent personal pronouns in Semitic.*

Jibbali also exhibits another peculiarity pertaining to the third person pronouns. For all the third person pronouns in Mehri, the initial consonant of the independent form is identical with that of the suffixed form, as is the case in Arabic and most other Semitic languages. In Jibbali, however, the third person masculine plural independent pronoun is šum, with the expected š (< *s), but the suffixed form is -hum, which is unexpected and rather strange. Presumably, it reflects a borrowing.

---

³ I am assuming that, like the mono-consonantal prepositions b-, k-, and l-, the conjunction has no underlying vowel, since a b or m following w- or any of the aforementioned prepositions is not treated as intervocalic.
⁴ In Western Jibbali, the conjunction actually remains w-, although the shift *wC > bC occurs otherwise in this dialect. This is reminiscent (as John Huehnergard reminds me) of Northwest Semitic, where initial *w- shifts to y-, except for the conjunction w- 'and'.
⁵ At least the Western Yemeni dialect of the town of Qishn has forms equivalent to Omani Mehri; see Jahn 1905: 26; Bittner 1913: 7.

⁶ It is possible that in Ḥaḍramitic and/or in MSA the initial consonant of the 3fs pronoun was replaced (i.e. *s → *ʾs-) before the shift of *s > š or h. In that case, the 3fs s- in MSA would be the result not of a blocked sound change, but rather of the regular shift of PS *ʾs > s, and the spelling with s₃ in Ḥaḍramitic would be etymologically correct. I am assuming here that Ḥaḍramitic s₃ represents /s/. For further information on Ḥaḍramitic s₃, see Voigt 1998.

	3ms		3fs		3mp		3fp	
	Mehri	Jibbali	Mehri	Jibbali	Mehri	Jibbali	Mehri	Jibbali
indep.	hē	šɛ	sē	sɛ	hēm	**šum**	sēn	sɛn
suffixed	-h	-š	-s	-s	-həm	**-hum**	-sən	-sən

FIGURE 4. *Third person pronouns in Mehri and Jibbali.*

In Mehri the reflexive pronoun is ḥənōf- (pl. ḥənfáy-), while in Jibbali it is ɛnúf (pl. ɛnfɔ́f). Although the forms look a bit different and the plurals are built on different patterns, the two pronouns are cognate. Like the reflexive pronouns of the other MSA languages, they both derive from a base *nuf. However, even though the forms are cognate, they are used a bit differently. In Mehri, the reflexive pronouns always take pronominal suffixes (Bittner 1913: 57–58; Rubin 2010a: 49; Watson 2012: 77), but in Jibbali the reflexive is usually undeclined (Rubin 2014: §3.6). Thus Jibbali ɛnúf can mean 'myself', 'yourself', etc. depending on the context. Compare the following examples:

Mehri: kšēf ḥənáfk 'expose yourself!' (Stroomer 1999: text 24:40)
Jibbali: kšɛf ɛnúf 'expose yourself!' (Rubin 2014: text 17:40)

I found a few texts, however, from one speaker of an eastern Jibbali dialect, who used suffixes with the Jibbali forms, as in ōsəm ɛnúfš 'he identified himself' (Rubin 2014: text TJ4:85), so this is a case where Mehri and Jibbali differ only when it comes to some dialects of Jibbali. It should also be mentioned that there is a distinct dative form of the reflexive in Jibbali, ḥánúf (pl. ḥánfɔ́f) 'to oneself'. In Mehri, the equivalent *h-ḥənōf- is realized simply as ḥənōf because of a sound rule by which h- does not occur before ḥ (Rubin 2010a: 16–17).

3. Numbers

In general, the numeral systems are very similar in Mehri and Jibbali, both in the forms and in their use, that is, in things like gender and number agreement and word order. The forms of the cardinal numbers are very similar, as can be seen from the forms of the numbers 'one' through 'seven' given in Figure 5:

	Mehri (m/f)*	Jibbali (m/f)
1	ṭād / ṭayt	ṭad / ṭit
2	ṯroh / ṯrayt	ṯroh / ṯrut
3	śāṯayt / śhəlīṯ	śɔṯét / śhəlét
4	ərbōt / árbaʕ	ɛrbaʕɔ́t / órbaʕ
5	xəm(m)ōh / xáymah	xõš / xĩš
6	hətēt / hət	štet / šɛt
7	həbáyt / hóbaʕ	šəbʕét / šōʕ

*There are some minor dialectal variants in Mehri that are not included here; see Watson 2012: 110.

FIGURE 5. *Cardinal numbers 1–7.*

It should be noted that the numbers 'five', 'six', and 'seven' all reflect the sound change of *s to h or š, as discussed above.

Both languages also have a special set of numbers from 'three' to 'ten' that are used in conjunction with the word for 'day'. This is not something common to all MSA languages at present (viz. Soqoṭri, Baṭḥari, and probably Hobyot), although it still may be a proto-MSA feature. Examples can be seen in Figure 6.

	Mehri	Jibbali
1 day	nəhōr ṭayt	yum ṭit
2 days	nəhōri ṯrayt	yũ ṯrút (< *yúmi)
3 days	śēlət yūm	śélət ēm
4 days	rībaʕ yūm	rĩʕ ēm
5 days	xáymah yūm	xĩš ēm
6 days	šīdət yūm	šɛt ēm
7 days	šībaʕ yūm	šēʕ ēm

FIGURE 6. *1–7 days.*

It should be noted that in both languages, the number 'five' has no special form; the feminine cardinal is used instead. It should also be noted that in Mehri the forms used for 'six' and 'seven' unexpectedly show initial š-, rather than h- (< *s-), while the corresponding cardinals have the expected initial h-.

There are also some interesting differences in the numeral systems. For example, if we compare the forms of the 'teens' in Figure 7, we can see that Mehri joins the ten and the digit with the conjunction wə-, while Jibbali uses no conjunction.[7]

	Mehri (m)	Jibbali (m)
11	āśərīt wə-ṭād	ʿəśirét ṭad
12	āśərīt wə-ṯroh	ʿəśirét ṯroh
13	āśərīt wə-śāṯayt	ʿəśirét śɔtét
14	āśərīt wə-rbōt	ʿəśirét ɛrbəʿɔ́t
15	āśərīt wə-xəm(m)ōh	ʿəśirét xõš

FIGURE 7. *Teens 11–15.*

As for the 'tens', Mehri 'twenty' and above are all Arabic loans, while Jibbali retains the inherited forms for 'twenty' and 'thirty'. Jibbali 'twenty' is a dual form of 'ten', as it probably was in Proto-Semitic (Huehnergard 2005: 182–184, esp. n. 107; Rubin 2010b: 42–43), while 'thirty' seems to be broken plural of 'three'. Compare the forms in Figure 8.

	Mehri (m/f)	Jibbali (m/f)
10	āśərīt / ōśər	ʿəśirét / ʿɔ́śər
20	āšráyn	ʿáśəri
30	śəlāṯáyn	śħɛlɔ́ṯ
40	ərbaʿáyn	ərbaʿín
50	xamsáyn	xamsín

FIGURE 8. *Tens 10–50.*

In Figure 9 we see the masculine forms of the ordinal numbers in Mehri and Jibbali. Mehri has a full set of ordinals up to and including 'ten', with the ordinals 'three' to 'ten' mostly built on the same pattern. Jibbali has ordinals only up to and including the number 'three'. Beyond 'three', Jibbali uses the cardinal numbers wherever an ordinal is intended. In addition to this major difference, the words for 'first' come from different roots in the two languages, and some Mehri dialects use a different root (ṯny, probably borrowed from Arabic) for 'second'.

	Mehri (m)*	Jibbali (m)
1st	ḥāwəláy	ɛnfí
2nd	məśēgər/ṯōni	məšágər
3rd	śōləṯ	śōləṯ
4th	rōbaʾ	(=cardinal)
5th	xōməs/xōmah	(=cardinal)
6th	sōdəs	(=cardinal)
7th	sōbaʾ/hōbaʿ	(=cardinal)
8th	ṯōmən	(=cardinal)
9th	tōsa	(=cardinal)
10th	ōśər/áyśər	(=cardinal)

*For additional variant forms in Mehri, see Watson 2012: 110.

FIGURE 9. *Ordinals.*

It is important to note that in Mehri we find initial *s-* in the form for 'sixth' (where the cardinal has *h-* and the form used with 'days' has *š-*!); and also *s* in place of the expected *h* in some dialectal Mehri forms of 'fifth' and 'seventh'. The *s* in these forms is most likely a result of Arabic interference.

4. Nouns and adjectives

As one might expect, there a number of isoglosses among the more common nouns and adjectives. This is not unusual, even among closely related languages.[8] Some examples of nouns are:

Mehri ġiggēn (pl. əmbəráwtən) ~ Jibbali əmbérɛʾ (pl. ɛrśɔ́t) 'boy'
Mehri āgáwz ~ Jibbali šxarét 'old woman'
Mehri śxōf ~ Jibbali núśəb 'milk'
Mehri rəḥbēt ~ Jibbali ḥallɛ́t or s̃irɛ́t 'town'
Mehri nəhōr (pl. yūm) ~ Jibbali yum (pl. ɛ̃m) 'day'
Mehri k-sōbəḥ ~ Jibbali k-ḥáṣaf 'morning'
Mehri bəḳərēt ~ Jibbali léʾ 'cow'
Mehri fərháyn ~ Jibbali ḥáṣún 'horse'
Mehri ḳā 'land' (OM) / arẓ́ (YM) ~ Jibbali ɛrẓ́ 'land'

Naturally, lexemes can differ occasionally among Mehri dialects and, to a lesser extent, among Jibbali dialects.

There is also a difference in the declension of nouns in the two languages. In Mehri, there is a dual suffix *-i*, used

---

[7] For numbers above 'thirty', however, Jibbali does use the conjunction (Rubin 2014: §9.1.3). This was first pointed out to me by Janet Watson and confirmed by my own data.

[8] Compare, for example, the various words for 'boy' among the closely related Germanic languages (e.g. German *Junge*, English *boy*, Swedish *pojke*, Danish *dreng*, Norwegian *gutt*) or the Romance languages (e.g. French *garçon*, Italian *ragazzo*, Spanish *chico*, Portuguese *menino*, Occitan *dròlle*).

almost exclusively in conjunction with the number 'two' (Rubin 2010a: 61; Watson 2012: 58). That is, very few dual forms are used without the accompanying numeral, unlike in Arabic. In Jibbali, this dual suffix has been lost, with very few exceptions, with the result that the dual form of the noun looks identical to the singular, as can be seen from the following set of forms:

	Mehri	Jibbali
'one man'	ġayg ṭād	ġeyg ṭad
'two men'	ġaygi ṭroh	ġeyg ṭroh
'three men'	śāṭayt ġəyōg	śɔṭét ġag

Thus, synchronically speaking, the number 'two' is used in Jibbali with a singular noun. The only exceptions are when the noun ends in a labial *b* or *m*, in which case the final consonant is elided by the rule discussed above. An example can be found in Figure 6, where we see *yum ṭit* 'one day' vs. *yũ ṭrut* 'two days', with a distinct dual form *yũ* < **yúmi*.

The words for 'men', seen above in the phrase 'three men', illustrate another difference in noun declension. Even when there exist cognates forms, as Mehri *ġayg* 'man' and Jibbali *ġeyg* 'man' clearly are, the languages sometimes use different patterns to form the plural, as with Mehri *ġəyōg* and Jibbali *ġag* 'men'. Another example is the plural of 'thief' (Mehri *ḥērəḳ*, Jibbali *šerḳ*), which has the form *həráwḳət* in Omani Mehri, *hərwōḳ* in Yemeni Mehri, and *śírɛ́ḳ* in Jibbali. Differences in patterns can be found with singular nouns as well, as in Mehri *bayt*, Jibbali *but* 'house'.

Like nouns, Mehri and Jibbali cognate adjectives can be found in different patterns, and with different plural declensions. For example, one common adjectival pattern in Mehri (*CəCáyC* or *CəCíC*) normally has four forms, masculine and feminine singular, and masculine and feminine plural. There are other adjectives that have just three forms (masculine and feminine singular, and a common plural), and some with just two (common singular, common plural) or even one, but this particular pattern usually has four (Rubin 2010a: 78–79). In Jibbali, however, adjectives with the corresponding pattern *C(e)CíC* usually have just three forms (Rubin 2014: §5.2). Compare the following cognate adjectives:

Omani Mehri: ms *rəḥáym*, fs *rəḥáymət*, mp *rīḥōm*, fp *rəḥámtən* 'pretty; nice'[9]
Jibbali: ms *rəḥím*, fs *rəḥĩt*, cp *rəḥɛ̃t* 'pretty; nice; good'

An interesting feature of Jibbali is the development of the Semitic roots for 'father' and 'mother' into the adjectives for 'big', so we find *eb* 'big' used only with masculine nouns, and *um* 'big' used only with feminine nouns.[10] In Omani Mehri, there are likewise separate masculine and feminine words for 'big', but from different roots than the Jibbali words. Thus, we have masculine *śōx* 'big', but feminine *nōb*. In Eastern Yemeni Mehri, we find only the word *śōx* used for 'big', with both masculine and feminine forms, making this is an interesting case, where Jibbali and Omani Mehri share the same structure but use different roots, while the two types of Mehri share one of the roots, but have a different structure.[11] Following are the relevant forms:

Jibbali: *eb* (m. only; pl. *ētə*), *um* (f. only; pl. *emíti* or *ĩti*)
Omani Mehri: *śōx* (m. only; pl. *śīyəx*), *nōb* (f. only; pl. *nəyōb*)
Eastern Yemeni Mehri: *śōx* (pl. *śīyāx*), f. *śaxt* (pl. *śīyáxtən*)

5. Verbs

A large percentage of Mehri and Jibbali verbs are cognate, but there are a quite a number of differences in some of the most common verbs. Some examples are:

Mehri *səyūr* ~ Jibbali *aġád* 'go'[12]
Mehri *wīḳa* ~ Jibbali *kun* 'be'
Mehri *wəkūb* ~ Jibbali *égaḥ* 'enter'
Mehri *śxəwlūl* ~ Jibbali *skɔf* 'sit, stay'
Mehri *ġátri* ~ Jibbali *herɔ́g* 'speak'
Mehri *nūka* ~ Jibbali *zəḥám/nikaʿ* 'come'
Mehri *áymət* ~ Jibbali *šérék* 'do'
Mehri *səḥāṭ* ~ Jibbali *ḥez* 'slaughter'
Mehri *ḥōm* ~ Jibbali *ʿágəb* 'want'[13]
Mehri *mōt* ~ Jibbali *xarɔ́g/fɛ̄t* 'die'[14]

In many cases the roots do not exist in the other language, and in the cases where one does, it usually has a different meaning or a more limited use.

---

[9] The forms vary slightly in Yemeni Mehri; see Jahn 1905: 66; Watson 2012: 105.

[10] This development is an isogloss shared by Jibbali and Soqotri, as already recognized by Müller 1909.

[11] Western Yemeni Mehri, at least the Mehri of Qishn, patterns with Omani Mehri; see Bittner 1909: 87.

[12] There are several other verbs meaning 'go' in each language, some used only with reference to a specific time of day.

[13] Jibbali *ʿágəb* also means 'like, love'; cf. Mehri *áygəb* 'like, love'.

[14] In general, *xarɔ́g* is typically used for humans, while *fɛ̄t* is typically used for animals, but there are a number of examples of *fɛ̄t* used for humans in the texts included in Rubin 2014.

The systems of verbal tenses and their uses are nearly identical between the two languages, but one major difference is in the expression of the future tense. In fact, this development is a major innovation that we can use in classifying the MSA languages. In Mehri (like Ḥarsusi and Baṭḥari), the future tense derives from an original active participle with a suffixed *-ān, while in Jibbali the future is formed with the subjunctive verb plus a prefixed particle (dḥa-, ḥa-, or a-), which derives from an auxiliary verb that probably originally meant 'want'.[15] Examples are:

Mehri səyūr 'he went' → sīrōna 'he will go'
Jibbali aġád 'he went' → (d)ḥa-yġád 'he will go'

When it comes to the system of derived verbal stems, the uses of the stems themselves are nearly identical in the two languages. Thus, for example, the H-Stem (causative stem) has all the same functions in both languages, as do the T-Stems, Š-Stems, and so on. As for the forms, the patterns are for the most part very similar, as can be seen from Figure 10:

Stem	Language	3ms perf.	3ms imperf.	3ms subj.
Ga-Stem	Mehri	CəCūC	yəCōCəC	yəCCēC
	Jibbali	C(ɔ)Cɔ́C	yəCɔ́CəC	yɔ́CCəC
Gb-Stem	Mehri	CīCəC	yəCCōC	yəCCōC
	Jibbali	CéCəC	yəCéCɔ́C	yəCCɔ́C
D/L-Stem	Mehri	(a)CōCəC	yaCáCCən	yaCōCəC
	Jibbali	(ɛ)CóCəC	iCóCCən	yəCɔ́CəC
H-Stem	Mehri	(hə)CCūC	yəhəCCūC	yəháCCəC
	Jibbali	(ɛ)CCéC	iCéCɔ́C	yéCCəC
Š1-Stem	Mehri	šəCCūC	yəšəCCūC	yəšáCCəC
	Jibbali	šəCCéC	yəšCéCɔ́C	yəšéCCəC
Š2-Stem	Mehri	šəCēCəC	yəšCáCCən	yəšCēCəC
	Jibbali	šəCéCəC	yəšCéCCən	yəšCéCəC
T1-Stem	Mehri	CátCəC	yəCtəCūC	yəCtīCəC
	Jibbali	Cɔ́tCəC	yəCteCɔ́C	yəCtékəC
T2-Stem	Mehri	əCtəCūC	yəCtəCīCən	yəCtəCūC
	Jibbali	əCtəCéC	yəCtəCéCən	yəCtəCɔ́C

FIGURE 10. *Verbal stems.*

---

[15] On the development of the Mehri future, see Rubin 2007. On the Jibbali future, see Rubin 2012.

Some of the differences are the result of historical developments in the vowel systems. For example, the difference in the Š1-Stem perfects — Mehri *šəktūb* vs. Jibbali *šəktéb* — is probably just the result of vowel shifts. A bigger difference can be found in the Gb-Stem, which is the historical equivalent of the Arabic *faʿila* class. In Mehri, the Gb-Stem does not distinguish the imperfect and subjunctive, while Jibbali keeps these quite distinct. The loss of the prefixed/infixed *h* (< PS **s*) in Jibbali in the H-Stem, found also in the other MSA languages, is simply the result of erosion (cf. Arabic *ʾafʿala*, Aramaic *ʾapʿel*). There are also some interesting differences in the conjugation of some of the tenses, specifically with regard to the personal prefixes used. In the Jibbali D/L-Stem, H-Stem, Q-Stem, and the internal passives, the prefix *t-* is not used in the imperfect or subjunctive; in the subjunctive it is normally replaced by *l-*.[16] Thus we can compare, for example, the Mehri H-Stem 3fs (= 2ms) subjunctive *təhásḅəḥ* with Jibbali *l-éṣḅəḥ*.

As for verb conjugation, the forms are quite similar in the two languages. Below is a comparison of the G-Stem verb (Mehri *ḳədūr* and Jibbali *ḳɔdɔ́r* 'be able') in two of the three major tenses, along with the imperative. The missing tenses, namely the imperfect and conditional, are comparably similar, while the future tense is formed differently, as described above. Compare the forms in Figure 11:

Despite the obvious similarities, there are some important differences. For example, in the perfect, Mehri has a distinct third masculine plural form, distinguished either by ablaut or by a suffixed *-m*, depending both on the type of verb and on the dialect. In Jibbali, however, the third masculine singular and plural are always identical, as is the third feminine plural. The Mehri third feminine singular perfect suffix *-ūt* has the allomorph *-ēt*, used with certain verbal stems, while the Jibbali suffix is always *-ɔ́t* (pronounced *-út* in some environments). In the subjunctive, Mehri sometimes has a suffixed *-i* for the second feminine singular, while Jibbali has only ablaut. The same observation applies to the feminine singular imperative. In the masculine plural subjunctive and imperative forms, Mehri has a suffixed *-m*, which Jibbali never has; instead, Jibbali has ablaut again. Note also the placement of stress on the first syllable of the Jibbali subjunctive singular forms, as opposed to the Mehri forms that have stress on the vowel of the verbal base. Because of historical sound changes, the Jibbali imperative does not look like the subjunctive. Also in Jibbali, the first person plural subjunctive has a different base than the other forms, again because of sound changes. Thus, upon closer inspection there are a lot of interesting differences.

There are also differences in the conjugation of weak verb types that exist in both languages; differences in

	G-Stem Perfect:		Subjunctive:		Imperative:	
	Mehri	Jibbali	Mehri	Jibbali	Mehri	Jibbali
1cs	ḳədɔ́rk	ḳɔdɔ́rk	l-əkdēr	l-ɔ́kdər		
2ms	ḳədɔ́rk	ḳɔdɔ́rk	təkdēr	tɔ́kdər	ḳədēr	ḳədɛ́r
2fs	ḳədɔ́rš	ḳɔdɔ́rš	təkdēri	tíkdir	ḳədēri	ḳədír
3ms	ḳədūr	ḳɔdɔ́r	yəkdēr	yɔ́kdər		
3fs	ḳədərūt	ḳɔdɔrɔ́t	təkdēr	tɔ́kdər		
1cp	ḳədūrən	ḳɔdɔ́rən	nəkdēr	nəkdɛ́r		
2mp	ḳədɔ́rkəm	ḳɔdɔ́rkum	təkdērəm	təkdɔ́r	ḳədērəm	ḳədɔ́r
2fp	ḳədɔ́rkən	ḳɔdɔ́rkən	təkdērən	təkdɛ́rən	ḳədērən	ḳədɛ́rən
3mp	ḳədáwr/ ḳədūrəm	ḳɔdɔ́r	yəkdērəm	yɔkdɔ́r		
3fp	ḳədūr	ḳɔdɔ́r	təkdērən	təkdɛ́rən		

Figure 11. *Verb conjugation.*

---

[16] See further details on this complicated subject in Johnstone 1980; Rubin 2014: §6.2; §6.3; §7.1.2; §7.1.3; forthcoming.

the pronominal prefixes of some derived stems were mentioned above. It must also be mentioned that there are also differences in verb conjugation among the Mehri dialects. Among Jibbali dialects there are minor differences in some of the vowel patterns of certain types of verbs.

When it comes to quadriliteral verbs (Q-Stems), which are fairly rare in both languages, both languages have quadriliterals with and without a prefixed *n* (i.e. an NQ-Stem) (Rubin 2010a: 118–120; Rubin 2014: §6.6.2). Sometimes the NQ-Stem can function as a passive or an intransitive of a Q-Stem. There is more evidence for this in Jibbali, and it is not clear how productive this use is in either language, but examples are:

Jibbali: NQ *ənḵɛrbéṭ* 'be tied tightly' ~ Q *ɛḵɛrbéṭ* 'tie tightly'
Mehri: NQ *ənḵərbōṭ* 'be curled' ~ Q *aḵárbəṭ* 'curl'
Jibbali: NQ *ənšɛrxéf* 'slip away, sneak away (intrans.)' ~ Q *šerxéf* 'sneak s.t. to s.o.'
Mehri: NQ *ənšərxáwf* 'sneak away (intrans.)' ~ Q *šərxáwf* 'sneak s.t. secretly to s.o.'

There is also a difference in the usage of the NQ-Stem, however. For example, many of the verbs having to do with colour are NQ-Stems in Jibbali, but simple Q-Stems in Mehri. Examples are:

Jibbali *ənʕifirér* 'blush, become red' ~ Mehri *āfərūr* (root ʕfr)
Jibbali *ənḥīrér* 'become black' ~ Mehri *ḥəwīrūr* (root ḥwr)
Jibbali *ənlīnín* 'become white' ~ Mehri *əwbīnūn* (root lbn)
Jibbali *ənšəẓ́írér* 'become green/yellow' ~ Mehri *həẓ́īrūr* (root šẓ́r/ḥẓ́r)

Both Mehri and Jibbali, like the other MSA languages use the auxiliary **ber* (Mehri *bər/ber*, Jibbali *ber*), which has several functions. One common meaning is 'already', but it can also be used to indicate a perfect, such as 'have done' or 'had done', among other things.[17] Both languages use the word in the same ways, but the forms are quite different. In Mehri, as in Ḥarsusi and Hobyot, the word *bər* is best called a particle, and it is declined with the suffixes used for nouns, prepositions, and other particles. In Jibbali, however, as in Soqoṭri, *ber* has to be called a verb, since it conjugates like a verb in the perfect tense.

---

[17] See further in Rubin (2010a: 248–251; 2014: §7.2); Watson (2012: 125, 373).

Compare the forms in Figures 12 and 13.

	sing.	dual	plural
1c	bə́ri	bə́rki	bə́rən
2m	bərk	bə́rki	bə́rkəm
2f	bərš		bə́rkən
3m	bə́rəh	bə́rhi	bə́rhəm
3f	bərs		bə́rsən

Figure 12. *Mehri bər (particle).*

	sing.*	dual	plural
1c	bek	bérš̃i	bérən
2m	bek	bérš̃i	bérkum
2f	biš		bérkən
3m	ber	berɔ́	ber
3f	berɔ́t	bertɔ́	ber

*Note irregular bek < *berk and biš < *berš̃

Figure 13. *Jibbali ber (auxiliary verb).*

Each language, of course, has its own irregular and anomalous verbs, but there are some interesting examples where a verb is anomalous in one language, but totally regular in the other. Two examples are:

Jibbali *š̃éf* 'he slept' < **š̃š̃éf* < **š̃əš̃éf* < **š̃əwš̃éf* < Š1 **š̃əwkéf* (cf. Mehri Š1 *šəwkūf*)
Mehri *šfūḵ* 'they (f.) married'[18] < Š1 **šəhfūḵ* < **šəsfūḵ* (cf. Jibbali G *šfɔḵ* and Š1 *šəšféḵ*)

6. Syntax

A comparison of the many nuances of phrase and sentence construction in Mehri and Jibbali would be a lengthy exercise. Here we will just compare a handful of features. In general, the two languages exhibit very similar syntactic structures. For example, both express *have*-possession using the preposition *k-* 'with' (which has the form *š-* before pronominal suffixes in Mehri; *š̃-* in Jibbali). Thus, we find phrases such as Mehri *šay ḵəráwš* and Jibbali *š̃i ḵərɔ́š̃* 'I have money' (lit. 'with me [is] money'). When this construction is used with close family members, both languages require a pronominal

---

[18] This verb is used with feminine subjects only. Note also Hobyot *šəhfōḵ* (Nakano 2013: 104). The form *šəfhōḵ* (2013: 107) with metathesis, is either a variant or an error (or *šəhfōḵ* is an error). I am assuming *šəfhōḵ* is the error since forms with *hfḵ* occur in several other places in Nakano's lexicon (e.g. pp. 186, 283, 301).

suffix on the noun, so in order to say, for example, 'I have a daughter', one says literally 'I have my daughter': Mehri *šay ḥəbráyti*, Jibbali *ši ɛbríti*. Both languages can also use the possession construction to express environmental and physical conditions. Thus, for 'I'm cold', 'I'm hot', 'it's raining', they say literally 'I have heat', 'I have rain', and so on; compare Mehri *šay ḥəbūr* and Jibbali *ši ḫɔ́r* 'I'm cold' (lit. 'with me [is] cold').

Both languages can negate verbal and non-verbal sentences with two elements, as in the examples below:[19]

Omani Mehri: *hē əl sḥāṭ ḥaybə́təh lā* 'he didn't slaughter his camel' (Stroomer 1999: text 55:9)
Jibbali: *šɛ ɔl ḥez yitš lɔ* 'he didn't slaughter his camel' (Rubin 2014: text 2:9)

Both languages normally use the perfect tense following a conditional particle, even though the particles themselves differ between the languages and, in fact, among the Mehri dialects.[20] Examples are:

Omani Mehri: *hām kəsk* 'if I find...' (Stroomer 1999: text 45:11)
Jibbali: *her kisk* 'if I find...' (Rubin 2014: text 6:38)

Differences in syntax do exist, of course, but they are rather subtle. In other words, there are no major structural differences. For example, most (but not all) of the major prepositions in the languages are cognate, but they sometimes show differences in usage. This is true with regard both to the basic functions of a preposition as well as to idiomatic (lexical) usage with certain verbs. As an example of the latter, we can compare the following two sets of cognate verbs:

Mehri: *āmōr h-* 'say to'; *kəlūt l-* 'tell to'; *ġəlūḳ mən* 'look for'
Jibbali: *ᶜɔ̃r her* 'say to'; *kɔlɔ́t her* 'tell to'; *ġɔlɔ́ḳ her* 'look for'

The three Mehri verbs above are each followed by a different preposition. The corresponding Jibbali verbs, however, all take the preposition *her* 'to, for' (cognate with Mehri *h-* 'to, for'). This is despite the fact that the prepositions *l-* 'to, for' and *mən* 'from' are widely used in Jibbali, and with largely the same functions as in Mehri.

A difference in the basic use of a preposition can be found in the construction used for comparison of adjectives. The preposition used in this construction (corresponding to English 'than') is *mən* in Mehri, but *(ᶜ)ar* in Jibbali, despite the fact that *mən* has the basic meaning 'from' in both languages.

In Omani Mehri,[21] a negative non-verbal clause typically requires a pronoun, but in Jibbali a pronoun is not normally found. Compare the following sentences:

Mehri: *ḥalə́ts əl sē gīdət lā* 'its condition wasn't good' (Stroomer 1999: text 83:1)
Jibbali: *ḥalɔ́ts ɔl rəḥũt lɔ* 'its condition wasn't good' (Rubin 2014: text 83:1)

Mehri and Jibbali share some of the same subordinating particles, but cognate particles (like prepositions) may be used in different ways. For example, the particle *mət* in Mehri is used, like its Jibbali cognate *mit*, as a temporal conjunction 'when' with regard to a future context, as in:

Mehri: *mət aġáygəš ġátri šayš, xəzī* 'when your husband speaks with you, refuse!' (Stroomer 1999: text 94:6)
Jibbali: *mit aᶜáśəriš hérɔ́g šiš, ġalíb* 'when your husband speaks with you, refuse!' (Rubin: 2014, text 60:6)

Mehri also uses this particle, however, for a habitual or repeated action (English 'whenever'), while Jibbali uses the particle *her* in such contexts, as in:

Mehri: *mət ḥátrəf məkōn, yəśōni háləh yəbə́gdəh* 'whenever he moved places, he saw his shadow following him' (Stroomer 1999: text 95:4)
Jibbali: *her ḥɔ́trəf mukún yəśúnš yətɔ̃́ᶜš* 'whenever he moved places, he saw it following him' (Rubin 2014: text 39:4)

7. Conclusion

All the features discussed above are not merely curiosities, since many of them can be used for the purposes of classification and for reconstruction. There are also many other differences one could discuss, including the forms of the demonstrative pronouns; interrogative pronouns and adverbs; the use of object suffix pronouns, specifically the verb forms that can accept object suffixes, and the fact

---

[19] It is not uncommon in either language for the first element to be omitted (Rubin 2010*a*: 266; 2014: §13.2.3). Indeed, in Yemeni Mehri dialects it seems to be regularly omitted, at least in most contexts; see Watson 2012: 310–323.
[20] On the Mehri conditional particles, see Watson 2012: 396–399; Rubin 2010*a*: 279–284. On Jibbali, see Rubin 2014: §13.4.

[21] In Yemeni Mehri the pronoun seems to be optional (cf. Sima 2009: 212, texts 40:33 and 41:1), as also in Hobyot (cf. Nakano 2013: 272).

that Jibbali has no first person object pronouns attached to verbs; the usage of the direct object pronoun *t-*; nominal patterns, including broken plural patterns; and the conjugation of weak verbs. Of course, a comprehensive account must include all six languages in the MSA group. The features outlined in this article can serve as a starting point for such an undertaking.

The family tree shown at the beginning of this article will only be proven once a comprehensive comparison is made of all the MSA languages. And only when we are able to reconstruct the common features of MSA can we reliably establish the proper place of these languages within the Semitic family tree.

References

Bittner M.
    1909. *Studien zur Laut- und Formenlehre der Mehri-Sprache in Südarabien. I. Zum Nomen im engeren Sinne.* (Sitzungsberichte der Kaiserlichen Akademie der Wissenschaften in Wien. Philosophisch-Historische Klasse, 162/5). Vienna: Akademie der Wissenschaften.
    1913. *Studien zur Laut- und Formenlehre der Mehri-Sprache in Südarabien. III. Zum Pronomen und zum Numerale.* (Sitzungsberichte der Kaiserlichen Akademie der Wissenschaften in Wien. Philosophisch-Historische Klasse, 172/5). Vienna: Akademie der Wissenschaften.

Faber A.
    1981. Phonetic reconstruction. *Glossa* 15: 233–262.
    1985. Akkadian evidence for Proto-Semitic affricates. *Journal of Cuneiform Studies* 37: 101–107.

Huehnergard J.
    2005. Features of Central Semitic. Pages 155–203 in A. Gianto (ed.), *Biblical and Oriental Essays in Memory of William L. Moran*. Rome: Pontificio Istituto Biblico.

Jahn A.
    1905. *Grammatik der Mehri-Sprache in Südarabien.* (Sitzungsberichte der Kaiserlichen Akademie der Wissenschaften. Philosophisch-Historische Klasse, 150/6). Vienna: Akademie der Wissenschaften.

Johnstone T.M.
    1980. The non-occurrence of a *t*-prefix in certain Jibbāli verbal forms. *Bulletin of the School of Oriental and African Studies* 43: 466–470.

Müller D.H.
    1909. Soqoṭri-Glossen. *Wiener Zeitschrift für die Kunde des Morgenlandes* 23: 347–354.

Nakano A.
    2013. *Hōbyot (Oman) Vocabulary: With Example Texts*. (Ed. R. Ratcliffe). Tokyo: Research Institute for Languages and Cultures of Asia and Africa.

Rubin A.
    2007. The Mehri Participle: Form, function, and evolution. *Journal of the Royal Asiatic Society (Series 3)* 17: 381–388.
    2010a. *The Mehri Language of Oman*. Leiden: Brill.
    2010b. *A Brief Introduction to the Semitic Languages*. Piscataway, NJ: Gorgias.
    2012. Grammaticalization and the Jibbali future. Pages 193–203 in D. Eades (ed.), *Grammaticalization in Semitic*. Oxford: Oxford University Press.
    2014. *The Jibbali (Shaḥri) Language of Oman: Grammar and Texts*. Leiden: Brill.
(forthcoming). Recent developments in Jibbali. *Journal of Semitic Studies*.

Sima A.
    2009. *Mehri-Texte aus der jemenitischen Šarqīyah*. Annotated and edited by J.C.E. Watson and W. Arnold, and in collaboration with 'A.Ḥ. Sa'd. Wiesbaden: Harrassowitz.

Stroomer H. (ed.).
    1999. *Mehri Texts from Oman. Based on the Field Materials of T.M. Johnstone.* Wiesbaden: Harrassowitz.

Voigt R.
    1998. Der Lautwandel $s^3 > s^1$ und $s^1 > s^3$ im Altsüsarabischen. *Le Muséon* 111: 173–186.

Watson J.C.E.
    2012. *The Structure of Mehri.* Wiesbaden: Harrassowitz.

Author's address

Aaron D. Rubin, Penn State University, 108 Weaver Building, University Park, PA 16801, USA.

e-mail adr10@psu.edu

Traces of Arabian in Kumzari

CHRISTINA VAN DER WAL ANONBY

Summary

Kumzari is an endangered language spoken in the remote coastal villages of northern Oman. Described as the only Persian language indigenous to the Arabian Peninsula, Kumzari is related to both language families but intelligible to neither. Rather, it is a mixed language: its lexicon, phonology, and morpho-syntax are fundamentally rooted in both Arabian and Persian.

Kumzari's sound-system and grammatical retentions and innovations shared with northern Omani Arabic dialects and Modern South Arabian languages attest to potential historical links. Among these, lexically pervasive emphatic consonants, Semitic roots in core vocabulary, and prolific verb derivations are immediately conspicuous as Arabian traits. More subtle features that Kumzari holds in common with Modern South Arabian languages and local Arabic varieties are the participle-like functions of Semitic-root verbs, the relative morpheme, syntax distinguishing noun/pronoun objects, and multiply marked negation.

Beyond the language itself, Kumzari's historical context and geographical setting give credence to past connections and migrations across the Peninsula. Ancestors of the Kumzari people are traced to the Azd tribe, who migrated from Yemen in the third to fifth centuries AD and earlier, an era during which Oman was ruled and colonized by Sasanians. Invasions of north-central Arabians in the seventh century caused many to flee to Oman's northern mountains. Resemblances among the languages of the refugees may be a vestige of a time before the wars.

Keywords: Kumzari, mixed language, Iranian languages, Modern South Arabian, Oman

Kumzari is an endangered language spoken by approximately 5000 people in northern Oman (Fig. 1). Traditionally it has been grouped with the languages of Iran, but it is unintelligible to speakers of those languages, and Kumzaris' traditional history considers that they have dwelt in Oman for eighteen centuries, being descendants of the South Arabian sheikh Malik bin Fahm. They identify as ethnically Arab; Omanis from beyond Musandam view them as different. Their language is what is known as mixed, in which it is not possible to distinguish which of its linguistic ancestors is predominant: its lexicon, phonology, morphology, and syntax are fundamentally rooted in both Arabian and Persian. A strange situation has thus emerged: a mixed language and a debated ethnic identity.

Travelling in Oman in 1900, Samuel Zwemer described hearing about the Kumzaris:

> 'There is coffee-house babble in Eastern Oman concerning a mysterious race of light-complexioned people who live somewhere in the mountains, shun strangers, and speak a language of their own… At Khasab, near Ras Musandam, live a tribe whose speech is neither Persian, Arabic, nor Baluchi, but resembles the Himyaritic dialect of the Mahras… This language is used by them in talking to each other, although they speak Arabic with strangers' (Zwemer 1902: 57).

Thirty years after Zwemer, Bertram Thomas would disagree about their South Arabian origins, based on his sketch of the Kumzari language. Thomas disbelieved the Kumzaris' own accounts of their history in third-century migrations of Azd from Yemen (Thomas 1930: 785). The present author's own research on the language in recent years, however, has pointed to at least the possibility that that was indeed their origin. Thomas was probably swayed by his Omani informants, who referred to Kumzaris as 'Persians', essentially because they could not understand their language. If Thomas had asked the Persians on the other side of the Strait of Hormuz, they might have said — as they do now — that the Kumzaris speak Arabic, essentially because they do not understand them. Could both be true?

Since much has been made of the differences between Kumzari and Arabic, with reference to its Persian aspects, this paper focuses on the Arabian components of the language. It is worthwhile for the reader to keep in mind Holes's observation on languages spoken at the periphery of the Arabian Peninsula before the Muslim conquests: 'They spoke Arabic dialects that I will call "sedentary",

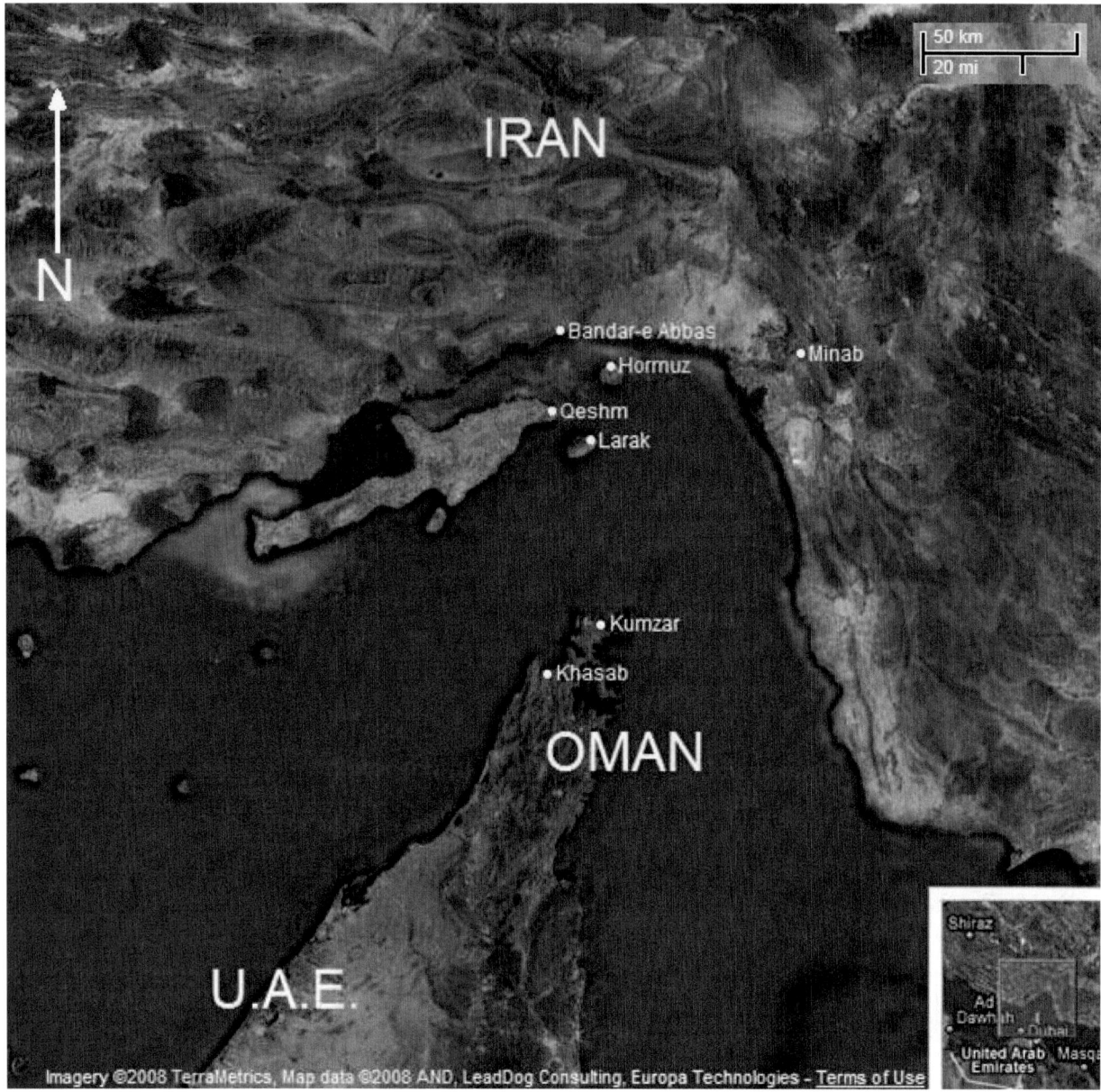

FIGURE 1. *A map of the Kumzari area.*

which shared certain features that distinguished them as a group from the dialects of the incomers [the incomers being speakers of Bedouin dialects, that is, Arabic of north-central Arabia]' (Holes 2006: 29).

1. Phonology and lexicon

Kumzari has a full set of the emphatic consonants well known in Arabian languages: pharyngealized alveolars *ḍ ḷ ṣ ṭ ẓ*, pharyngeal fricative *ḥ*, and uvular plosive *q* (Fig. 2). This may seem unremarkable from a Semitic point of view (see especially Watson & Bellem 2010), but Kumzari has traditionally been classified as a Western Iranian language (Skjærvø 1989). The full set of emphatics is something we would not expect if it were simply a Persian language that had borrowed Arabic vocabulary. In fact, a few of the Western Iranian languages use these sounds in careful pronunciation of vocabulary borrowed

	labial (-dental)	alveolar	emphatic alveolar	(alveo-)palatal	velar	uvular	pharyngeal	glottal
stop/affricate	p b	t d	ṭ ḍ	č j	k g	q		ʾ
fricative	f	s	ṣ ẓ	š		x ğ	ḥ	h
nasal	m	n						
approximant	w	l r	ḷ	y				

FIGURE 2. *Kumzari consonants.*

from Arabic, but in Kumzari the emphatic consonants are contrasting phonemes, and they are used not only in native Kumzari words, such as the following:

qāqum 'up (children's speech)'
būẓ 'chin'
qanḍaha 'rainbow'
xṣurg 'sister-in-law'
quḥḥū 'coughing'
ṭaʾr 'mountain ledge'
ṣanduḥ 'forehead'
ḥēriq 'hot/dry weather' (cf. Mehri *ḥark* 'hot' — Rubin 2009: 223)

but have even diffused to Kumzari lexical items of Persian origin:

čāẓ 'lunch'
ṣirx 'red'
ṭēẓ 'sharp'
pōṣṭ 'skin'
ẓardağ 'egg yolk'
ḥan 'iron'
ṭaẓağ 'fresh'
ṣawẓ 'green'

The *ẓāʾ* is an interesting case because in Kumzari it has no non-emphatic counterpart; all zeds are emphatic, even in Persian-origin words. This shows the equal likelihood that rather than being a Persian language that has borrowed words from Arabic, as has always been assumed, Kumzari may be an Arabian language that has borrowed words from Persian. The Persian-origin vocabulary in Kumzari was recognized even by Bertram Thomas (1930: 785) to be distinct from contemporary 'Ajami' borrowing in Gulf languages in the past century. Instead, most indications point to their origins in Middle Persian, even prior to the changes that took place in Iranian languages due to the seventh-century invasion of Fars by Arabic speakers.

Another part of the language in which traces of Arabian may be seen is the lexicon. In the author's 4500-item wordlist, 60% are of Arabic origin. Many basic Kumzari lexical items have cognates in Arabic, including words that are cross-linguistically unlikely to have been borrowed:

jism 'body'
šidrit 'tree'
bʾām 'thumb'
ṭēr 'bird'
ūmat 'sardine'
bukr 'firstborn'
ḥējub 'eyebrow'
ğbār 'dust'
nuxrit 'nose'

Forms such as borrowed sounds and words are interesting, but they are not proof of anything except possible language contact. Overlapping functions, however, — morphology and syntax — are more likely to be indicative of genetic relatedness between languages. This is because, as cross-linguistic typologies show, compared to borrowing phonology and lexicon, 'The diffusion of patterns is much less controllable' (Aikhenvald 2007: 40). Aspects of the language that are fully integrated and not obvious are more likely due to genetic inheritance rather than having been borrowed. Thus the following section presents evidence of shared grammar.

2. Verbs and verb phrase syntax

Aside from the emphatic consonants, the most obvious Semitic feature noticeable on hearing Kumzari is its ubiquitous Semitic verbal roots. These have a complex syntax, a much-simplified version of which will be presented here. Most are triliteral and correspond to their Arabic counterparts in meaning, taking the shape CVCVCV, with all vowels a short *a* in their basic form.

Semitic verbs in Kumzari

Arabic root: drs 'study, learn'
Kumzari verb: *darasa* 'learned, learning'

Arabic root: *fkr* 'think'
Kumzari verb: *fakara* 'thought, thinking'
Arabic root: *ḥrq* 'burn'
Kumzari verb: *ḥaraqa* 'burned, burning'

The Arabic-root verbs further derive through stem alternation or with the addition of affixes to form other word classes: nouns, adjectives, and adverbs.

Derived nouns take the shape C*a*CC*it* (with the suffix *-it*) to form a concrete, instantiable noun out of the Semitic verb, as in the following examples:

Nouns of the form C*a*CC*it* derived from Kumzari Semitic verbs

adaba (v.) 'irritated, irritating'
adbit (n.) 'irrita**tion**'
ḥaraqa (v.) 'burned, burning'
ḥarqit (n.) 'burning sensa**tion** (e.g. heartburn)'
baraẓa (v.) 'appeared, appearing'
barẓit (n.) 'appear**ance**'
rašawa (v.) 'bribed, bribing'
rašwit (n.) 'bribe, brib**ery**'
lawya (v.) 'wrapped, wrapping'
lawyit (n.) 'wrapp**er**'

This derivation is particularly interesting in light of Mehri using the *-t* suffix called a 'feminine' ending even on masculine words (Rubin 2010: 65), and of recent work on Mehri by Janet Watson showing that the *-t* suffix is used on nouns in all states, and that it is a salient feature distinguishing Himyaritic from Arabic (Watson 2011). We can also compare this form to one in dialects spoken by what Holes calls traditionally 'sedentary' people on the periphery of Arabia, with the 'syllable structure of 3rd person perf. verb CvCvCvC/CvCCvC, e.g. *katabat/kitbat* "she wrote"' (Holes 2006: 29) very much resembling the forms of the Kumzari verbs and their derived nouns, for example *kataba* > *katbit* 'writing'.

Derived adjectives have the shape C*a*CC, thus:

Adjectives of the form C*a*CC derived from Kumzari Semitic verbs

lawata (v.) 'shrivelling, weakened'
lawt (a.) 'shrivelled, weak'
qayama (v.) 'stood, standing'
qaym (a.) 'upright'
ğayaba (v.) 'finished, finishing'
ğayb (a.) 'absent'

xabaqa (v.) 'pierced, piercing'
xabq (a.) 'holey'

Derived adverbs are made with the addition of the suffix *-ītī* onto the form C*a*C*a*C:

Adverbs of the form C*a*C*a*C*ītī* derived from Kumzari Semitic verbs

axara (v.) 'delayed, delaying'
axarītī (adv.) 'late, after**ward**'
čaraxa (v.) 'straddled, straddling'
čaraxītī (adv.) [e.g. sitting]'**a**stride'

Words of these four classes may be further inflected and positioned according to the same morphology and syntax as their underived counterparts.

Kumzari verbs of Semitic roots defy categorization as a single word class, for reasons explained elsewhere (van der Wal Anonby, in press). The category that Kumzari Semitic verbs most satisfactorily compare with, however, is the Arabic verbal participle, especially that found in Omani dialects in which the active participle 'can function syntactically as a noun, verb, or attributive adjective' and the passive participle is 'used predicatively as quasiverbal adjective to indicate the result or present relevance of a completed action' (Holes 2004: 149–150). It is likely that the Kumzari Semitic verb and the Omani Arabic participle share or overlap in origins.

The Kumzari verb has taken the forms of other structures, the existential enclitic and light verb, to differentiate between the verb's roles as passive and active participle, as shown in the following examples:

Kumzari Semitic verbs in participial form

passive participle: *xasafaʾum* 'I am destroyed'
active participle: *xasafa tkum* 'I am destroying'
passive participle: *ḥarakaʾum* 'I am moved'
active participle: *ḥaraka tkum* 'I am moving'
passive participle: *qaffaʾum* 'I am stopped'
active participle: *qaffa tkum* 'I am stopping'

The Omani participial infix *-in(n)-* and the Kumzari relative particle *na*

In his *Dialect geography of Oman*, Holes analyses a feature common to all Omani dialects: 'an -/in(n)/- infix is obligatorily inserted in all Omani dialects between an active participle having verbal force and a following

	Arabic dialect	**Kumzari**
Khorāsānī	beneyt-**in** ḏēne 'a pretty girl'	ditk-ē mal-ē **na** 'a girl that is pretty'
Khorāsānī	lafd-**in** 'arabiyye 'an Arabic dialect'	majma arabītī **na** 'a dialect that is Arabic'
Khorāsānī	xalg-**in** minnah 'some of that group'	qādar pi šan **na** 'some of them'
Bahraini	māy-**in** bārda 'cold water'	aw sard **na** 'water that is cold'
Bahraini	bint-**in** zēna 'a good girl'	ditk-ē jwān **na** 'a girl that is good'
Bahraini	arāḍ-**in** šādda 'soils that hold together'	arḍ šadda **na** 'land that is disputed ('pulled')'
Omani	raǧǧāl-**in** 'āqil 'a clever man'	mardk-ē nādur **na** 'a man that is clever'
Omani	nāqt-**in** zēna 'a good female camel'	jāmal-ē jwān **na** 'a camel that is good'
Omani	'išrīn ǧamal, čill-**in** li s-sōk 'twenty camels, every one for the market'	bis-ta jāmal, ar tā-ē ba sōq-ō **na** 'twenty camels, every one for the market'

FIGURE 3. *The adnominal/relative morpheme in Arabic dialects and Kumzari.*

object pronoun… Some Omani speakers also insert the -/in/- infix between an imperfect verb and a suffixed object' (Holes 1989: 448). As Holes comments on this morpheme, 'More probable, given that morphological features are deeply embedded in language structure and, as a general rule, slower to change, is that the modern dialects which have the infix construction come historically from a group of cognate dialects in a confined geographical area… eastern and southeastern Arabia' (2011: 85). Indeed, this seems to be the case, for Bernabela (2011: 68) mentions this *inn* suffix in Šiḥḥī: it is obligatory after active participles with pronominal object suffixes. Eades also states that in the Šawāwi dialect of Oman, -*in(n)*- is obligatory after both participles and imperfects with object suffixes (2009: 89). Windfuhr (2005) notes that Central Asian Arabic has -*in(n)*- after active participles with pronominal object suffixes. There is an equivalent morpheme *na* 'of which' in Kumzari.

The relative enclitic *na* in Kumzari fulfills the same grammatical role of the Arabian suffix: it marks 'a verb, most often with a perfect-tense colouring, and its object pronoun' (Holes 2011: 81). Although the Kumzari morpheme's form and function are effectively the same as that in Arabian, it differs slightly in syntax: instead of following the imperfect or participial verb, the *na* clitic follows the verb phrase or relative clause, as can be seen in the following examples as compared to Shihhi:[1]

The object/relative morpheme in Shihhi and Kumzari

Shihhi: *šēyf* + *ham* > *šēyfinham* 'seeing/ having seen them'
Kumzari: *mēšē* + *šan* > *mēšē šan **na*** 'seeing/ having seen them'
Shihhi: *ḍērbih* + *hi* > *ḍērbitinhi* 'hitting/ having hit it'
Kumzari: *ḍaraba* + *yē* > *ḍaraba yē gisē **na*** 'hitting/ having hit it'
Shihhi: *kētb* + *u* > *kētbinnu* 'writing/ having written it'
Kumzari: *kataba* + *yē* > *kataba yē gisē **na*** 'writing/ having written it'

Holes notes similar geographical distribution for the 'adnominal linker' as it is termed in Khorāsānī, which also occurs in Bahraini (2011: 90): a suffix -*in* that attaches to a noun before a modifier, in the same context in which the -*na* clitic would be used in Kumzari (Fig. 3):[2]

It is to be noted that what has been called an 'infix' -*in(n)*- and what has been called a 'linker' -*in* are homophonic, as is the relative *na* enclitic in Kumzari pronounced the same in all contexts; as explained here, these morphemes have the same function, but as enclitics they can attach to the end of different parts of speech.

A candidate for a similarly functioning morpheme in Mehri is *ləhān*, translated as 'that which' or 'what' or 'all that' (Rubin 2010: 55): in all the examples listed in Rubin's grammar, this morpheme marks a relative clause or complement clause, that is, *ləhān* attaches to a clause that modifies or stands for the object of the verb (in the examples below the entire relative clause is highlighted). For all of these, the equivalent clause in Kumzari would be marked with the relative morpheme *na*.

---

[1] In all comparative data from the South Arabian languages and Arabic dialects, the authors' original orthographic conventions are retained; Shihhi data are from Bernabela 2011: 68; the Western Iranian language Luri has a similar enclitic *ne* to mark relative or object.

[2] Arabic dialectal data are from Holes 2011: 90.

The relative morpheme in Mehri[3]

wəzyēma tīk ləhān təḥōm 'they will give you **what you want**'

w-əlhān kəsk nxāsɛ hē ḏ-hō '**and that which** I find under it, it's mine'

šaxbərhəm ləhān ġatəryəm yəllō 'ask them **what they said last night**'

zəgdəm həbɛr əlhān kūsəm 'they seized the camels **that they found**'

śētəm amrawkəb w-əlhān bərkīhəm 'he bought the vessels and **what was in them**'

śītəm ləhān šəh 'he bought **what he had**'

kəlūṯ ḥābū bə-ləhān həmayh 'he told the people **what he had heard**'

The other similar morpheme in Mehri is the suffix *-ān* (which becomes *-ōna*[4]) on the Semitic active participle verb base C*a*CC (Rubin 2007: 385).[5] Rubin (2007: 385) suggests that the Mehri suffix evolved out of the agentive-noun-forming suffix *-ān*, a suffix which also occurs in Akkadian, Syriac, and Kumzari, and overlaps in this meaning with the south-eastern Arabic dialectal suffix (Holes 2011: 75) discussed above.

Both of the contexts indicated for the relative enclitic *na* correspond to those in Arabian dialects but differ from them in syntactic position. There is, however, syntactic resemblance on another point between the Kumzari verb phrase and its Arabian counterpart. Holes (2011: 81) notes that the *-in(n)-* infix occurs with a verb and its object pronoun 'and never occurs if the object is a full noun.' In Kumzari, verb phrases display differential word order for pronouns and full nouns as the direct object. In a verb phrase, the direct object of a verb precedes the verb when it is in the form of a full noun, and follows the verb when it is in the form of a pronoun:

Kumzari differential word order for direct object as noun or pronoun

deverb: *fakka* 'opening' + light verb: *tka* 'do'

dōr-ō	fakka	t-k-a.
door-the	opening	IMPF-do-3s

'He opens **the door**.'

fakka	**yē**	t-k-a.
opening	3s	IMPF-do-3s

'He opens **it**.'

Such alignment would indicate that in its morphosyntactic discrimination of noun- vs. pronoun- objects, the Kumzari Semitic-root verb is functionally equivalent to the active participle in some Arabian languages and dialects.

In this context it is unsurprising that Mehri too has differential word order for subjects that are nouns or pronouns in negation (Rubin 2010: 265). Mehri has two negation particles, *əl* and *lā*. If the subject of a non-verbal clause is in the form of a pronoun, the negative particle *əl* comes before the item, and if the subject is in the form of a noun, the negative particle *əl* falls after it. 'The result is that the nominal subject is essentially fronted.' (Rubin 2010: 265):

aġəlēt əl hē mənay lā. '**The fault is not** mine.'
əl hō hērəḵ lā. '**I am not** a thief.'

It is evident that these languages — Mehri, Kumzari, and Omani Arabic dialects — use a distinct syntax that is contingent on the form of a full noun or a pronoun.

3. Post-constituent negation

In a discussion of negation and word order, it is important to note that on this point Kumzari aligns again in its morphosyntax not with Persian or Arabic languages, but with South Arabian and Shihhi: it has negation following the verb or negated constituent.

Is post-negation a shared innovation or a shared retention? Watson and Eades (2012: 3) note that 'The MSAL (excepting Soqoṭri) are the only Semitic languages in which the negative particle follows the negated term.' They state that post-negation is 'an issue of typological interest for research on grammaticalization and negation.' 'Lucas (2009) and Watson (in press) suggest this word order is an innovation' (Watson & Eades 2012: 3).

Kumzari, despite Middle Persian being one of its ancestor languages, does not resemble other Western Iranian languages in this respect; even closely related Iranian languages use pre-verbal negation. Although Shihhi, which geographically surrounds Kumzari on the Musandam peninsula, is called an Arabic dialect and not a South Arabian language, it also has post-constituent negation. Simeone-Senelle (1997: 406) points out that the

---
[3] Mehri data are from Rubin 2010.
[4] The *-a* at the end of the Mehri participle is called a 'participial marker' (Rubin 2007: 385); it appears to be parallel to the object marker in Šiḥḥī, Central Asian Arabic, Šawāwī, and other Omani dialects of Arabic.
[5] The Mehri participle has the feminine dual suffix *ēti*, resembling the Kumzari suffix *-ītī*, which transforms Semitic-root verbs into adverbs: Mehri *məsfərēti* 'travelling' Kumzari *safarūtī* 'travelling'; Mehri *məġtəryēti* 'speaking' Kumzari *majmūtī* 'speaking'; Mehri *āmərāwti* 'saying' Kumzari *amarūtī* 'sealing, finishing'; Mehri *sīrāwti* 'going' Kumzari *sīyarūtī* 'going by car' (Rubin 2007: 384).

Kumzari	Mehri	Gloss
qaḥwē xor **na**.	tgirā ḳaḥwēt **lá**ʾ.	'**Don't** drink coffee.'
Kumzari	**Bathari**	**Gloss**
dūr **na**.	raḥak **lā**.	'It is **not** far.'
Kumzari	**Shihhi**	**Gloss**
kištiš šan **na**.	qatalhám **lu**.	'He did **not** kill them.'
ba yē **na**	lih **lu**	'**not** for him'
wā-yē **na**	maʔu **lu**	'**not** with him'
muǧ šan tēmišī **na**.	tšūf **lu** nxīlham.	'You do**n't** see their date palms.'
čum **na**.	ʔamši **lu**.	'I do**n't** go.'
dānum **na**.	ʔadri **lu**.	'I do**n't** know.'
yē ṭalbē **na**.	hōh ṭōláb **lu**.	'He is **not** a student.'
yē xaffa **na**.	hōh xabīl **lu**.	'He is **not** crazy.'
ṭarb dariš yē **na**.	ḍarabu **lu**.	'He did **not** hurt/hit him.'

FIGURE 4. *Negation in Kumzari, Shihhi, and South Arabian languages.*

Kumzari	Mehri	Gloss
tō ḥakmēt-ō **na**.	wə-hēt əl hēt ḥōkəm **lā**.	'You are not the ruler.'
tō bētarī **na** pē mā **na**.	hēt əl hēt axayr mənīn **lā**.	'You are not better than us.'
dānud **na** či xujmū ka **na**.	əl wīda hešən mən məḥnēt yāmōl **lā**.	'He didn't know what kind of work he might do.'
Kumzari	**Jibbali**	**Gloss**
hazza yē kin **na**.	ɔl égbəḍəš lɔʔ?	'Don't anger him!'

FIGURE 5. *Double-marked negation in Kumzari and South Arabian languages.*

South Arabian languages differ from Arabic syntactically as well (Fig. 4).[6]

Some of the South Arabian languages have doubly marked negation in some cases (Fig. 5):[7]

In Kumzari, negation is doubly marked on arguments following a negated verb. In the MSAL languages where double negation is attested, it is less clear why sometimes there is doubly marked negation and sometimes it is marked only once (Fig. 6):[8]

---

[6] Mehri and Bathari data are from Simeone-Senelle 1997: 407; Shihhi data are from Bernabela 2011: 53, 56, 87.
[7] Mehri data are from Rubin 2010: 32, 129, 134; Jibbali data are from Simeone-Senelle 1997: 406–407.
[8] Mehri data are from Rubin 2010: 32, 134; Hobyot data are from Simeone-Senelle 1997: 406–407; Shihhi data are from Bernabela 2011.

Kumzari	Mehri	Gloss
amma kin **na**.	təḵtəlōb **lā**.	'**Don't** worry.'
amma kin **na** ba yē **na**.	əl təḵtəlōb bəh **lā**.	'**Don't** worry about it.'
Kumzari	**Hobyot**	**Gloss**
tāta **na** čāʾī xōra **na**.	əl ixóm yəʾnśoz šēhi **lá**ʾ.	'He does **not** want to drink tea.'
tarum **na** majma tkum **na**	əkhōl əǵətér **laʔ**.	'I ca**nnot** speak.'
Kumzari	**Shihhi**	**Gloss**
rāyim **na**.	niqdar **lu**.	'We ca**nnot**.'

FIGURE 6. *Single- and double-marked negation in Kumzari, Shihhi, and South Arabian languages.*

Other morpho-syntactic similarities between Kumzari and South Arabian languages exist, but limitations of space necessitate that these are deferred for another occasion. Instead, the region's history will be examined to facilitate an explanation of how resemblances came to be. Specifically, it will give further validation to the suggestion, regarding features observed in Gulf Arabic dialects, that 'these might possibly be the vestiges of ancient non-Arabic but Semitic substrate language(s)' (Holes 2002: 271).

In order to circumvent a very long history, this paper will focus on a key figure at a key moment in Kumzari history: a person named Laqīt bin Malik Dhū al-Taj, a place named Dibba, and a time, the seventh century.

By the time the Arabic-speaking Muslim armies arrived from northern Arabia in the seventh century, Persians had been living in Oman for over a millennium, and South Arabians from Yemen had been living there for at least five centuries. The history of Kumzari centres on the northern Omani town of Dibba, which was a grand market in the early seventh century. At least twice before that time, Omanis had attempted to expel the Persians from Oman. Once was in the early third century, when the South Arabian Azd tribe had already migrated to Oman under Malik bin Fahm, whom Kumzari traditions assert is their ancestor. The Azd fought against the Persians near Nizwa and won; under the terms of a truce the Persians were supposed to leave Oman and go to Fars. It is known, however, that between that time and the seventh century, Sasanian maritime trade flourished through the market towns all along the south-eastern coast of Arabia including Dibba, so it appears that the Persians did not all leave (Ulrich 2011: 381). Yet they did adapt their operations to the newcomers from Yemen, because we find that there were several levels of Sasanian imperial

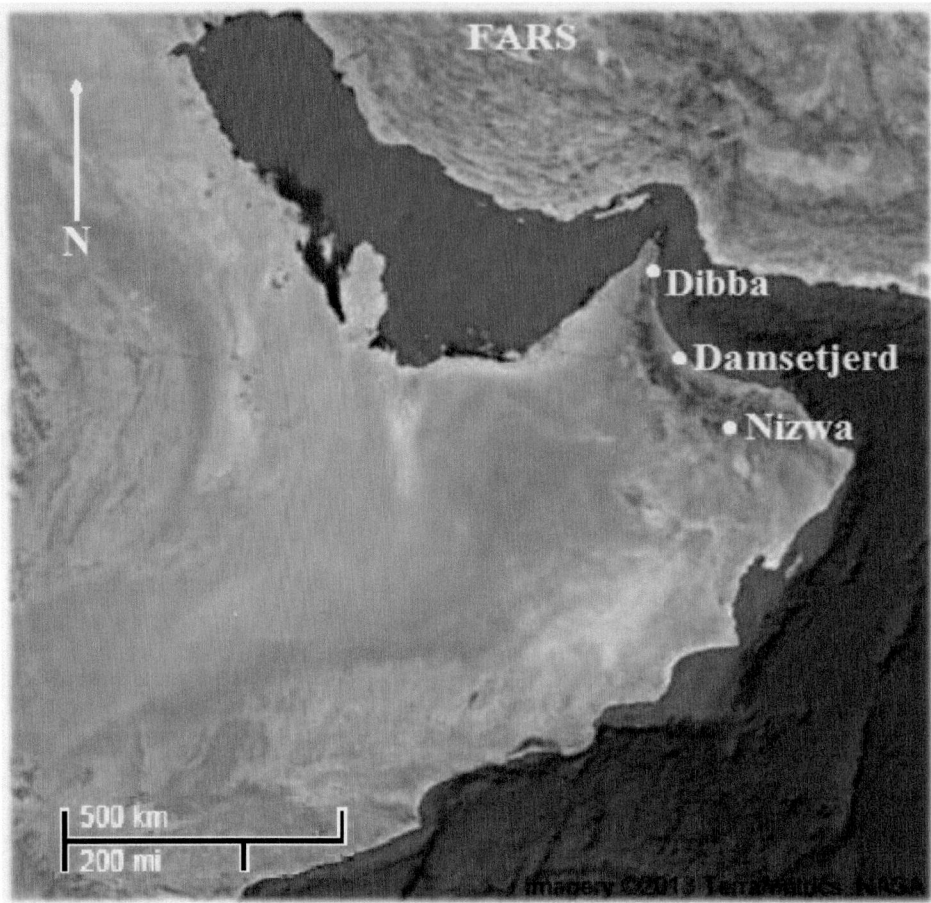

FIGURE 7. *Places in Kumzari history.*

administration in Yemen and Oman during that time. In sixth-century Yemen, the *muluk* (sg. *malik*) were a ruling class brought about by Persian occupation; also known as *abnāʾ*, they were the offspring of Persian fathers and Arab mothers (Shoufani 1973: 35). The title of *malik* became a powerful position responsible for guarding wealthy Persian caravans, and *muluk* were drawn from South Arabian tribal chiefs at the Sasanian empire's borderlands (1973: 28, 36). It was these South Arabian tribes who would later clash with the Arabic-speaking armies from Medina. Persians also enlisted administrators called Julanda as their agents in Oman, responsible for collecting taxes from market towns including Dibba.

The Sasanians appointed a South Arabian sheikh named Laqīt bin Malik as *Dhū al-Taj* 'crowned one' in Oman (Wilkinson 2010: 85). To the north Arabians, seeing the *malik* title and the crown of pearls that went with it symbolized subjugation to Sasanian state power. This fuelled an ongoing dispute between the North and South Arabians regarding the role of kingship (Lecker 2003: 58–59). In this context, when Sasanian power began to wane in the early seventh century, the Julanda switched allegiances and fought for the Muslim armies from Medina against the Azd under Laqīt bin Malik. In AD 630, the Julanda and northern Arabians fought against the Persians near Sohar; the Persians were expelled a second time, and again were told to go north to Fars. At that point their appointee *malik* Laqīt had regained control over the whole of Oman, as the Azd were fighting against the Julanda and Muslim forces. The battle intensified in AD 633 when the Dibbans heard that Muslim armies had attacked their South Arabian relatives in Yemen (al-Rawas 2000: 44). They rallied the Azd with the battle cry of *Ya al-Malik!* The South Arabians, probably with Sasanian Persians alongside them, fought and lost the battle of Dibba, which became famous as the last battle of the Muslim conquest of Arabia. In that battle thousands died, thousands were taken prisoner, and thousands fled to the mountains of Musandam. Northern Arabs who settled in Dibba after the wars called the people who fled the battle of Dibba *šiḥḥī*, because they had refused to pay taxes to the Muslim armies (Dostal 1972: 2; Lancaster & Lancaster 2011: 492, 546). The Shihhi today claim heritage from those who fled Dibba, and Dibba's descendants speak either Shihhi or Kumzari.

The context of history explains how Kumzaris can be culturally Shihhi yet speak their own language, and why their language is infused with both Middle Persian and Arabian features.

Much more research remains to be done comparing these varieties, which have obviously influenced each other, although perhaps over many centuries and in the distant past. Analysing Kumzari grammar leads the author to agree with Watson (2011) that 'Arabic may not have replaced all the ancient languages of the Peninsula, and that we may be witnessing the rediscovery of descendants of the ancient languages.' Indeed, such a comparative-historical investigation would reveal much about the intersection of cultures in south-eastern Arabia.

References

Aikhenvald A.Y.
    2007. Grammars in contact: A cross-linguistic perspective. Pages 1–66 in A.Y. Aikhenvald & R.M.W. Dixon (eds), *Grammars in contact: A cross-linguistic typology*. Oxford: Oxford University Press.

Bernabela R.S.
    2011. *A phonology and morphology sketch of the Šiḥḥi Arabic dialect of əlǦēdih (Oman)*. Leiden: Leiden University.

Dostal W.
    1972. The Shihuh of northern Oman: A contribution to cultural ecology. *The Geographical Journal* 138: 1–7.

Eades D.
    2009. The Arabic dialect of a Šawāwī community of northern Oman. Pages 77–98 in E. Al-Wer & R. de Jong (eds), *Arabic dialectology: In honour of Clive Holes on the occasion of his sixtieth birthday*. Leiden: Brill.

Holes C.
    1989. Towards a dialect geography of Oman. *Bulletin of the School of Oriental and African Studies* 52/3: 446–462.
    2002. Non-Arabic Semitic elements in the Arabic dialects of eastern Arabia. Pages 269–280 in W. Arnold & H. Bobzin (eds), *Sprich doch mit deinen Knechten aramäisch, wir verstehen es! 60 Beiträge zur Semitistik. Festschrift für Otto Jastrow zum 60. Geburtstag*. Wiesbaden: Harrassowitz.
    2004. *Modern Arabic: Structures, functions, and varieties*. Washington, DC: Georgetown University Press.
    2006. The Arabic dialects of Arabia. *Proceedings of the Seminar for Arabian Studies* 36: 25–34.
    2011. A participial infix construction of eastern Arabia — an ancient pre-diasporic feature? *Jerusalem Studies in Arabic and Islam* 38: 75–98.

Lancaster W.O. & Lancaster F.C.
    2011. *Honour is in contentment: Life before oil in Ras al-Khaimah (UAE) and some neighbouring regions*. Berlin: de Gruyter.

Lecker M.
    2003. King Ibn Ubayy and the Quṣṣāṣ. Pages 29–72 in H. Berg (ed.), *Method and theory in the study of Islamic origins*. Leiden: Brill.

Lucas C.
    2009. The development of negation in Arabic and Afro-Asiatic. PhD thesis, Emmanuel College, University of Cambridge. [Unpublished].

al-Rawas I.
    2000. *Oman in early Islamic history*. Reading: Garnet & Ithaca Press.

Rubin A.D.
- 2007. The Mehri participle: Form, function, and evolution. *Journal of the Royal Asiatic Society*, 3rd series, 17/4: 381–388.
- 2009. The functions of the preposition *k-* in Mehri. *Journal of Semitic Studies* 54/1: 221–226.
- 2010. *The Mehri language of Oman*. Leiden: Brill.

Shoufani E.
- 1973. *Al-Riddah and the Muslim conquest of Arabia*. Toronto: University of Toronto Press.

Simeone-Senelle M-C.
- 1997. Modern South Arabian languages. Pages 378–423 in R. Hetzron (ed.), *The Semitic Languages*. London: Routledge.

Skjærvø P.O.
- 1989. Languages of southeast Iran: Lārestānī, Kumzārī, Baškardī. Pages 363–369 in R. Schmitt (ed.), *Compendium Linguarum Iranicarum*. Wiesbaden: Ludwig Reichart Verlag.

Thomas B.
- 1930. The Kumzari dialect of the Shihuh tribe (Musandam), Arabia, and a vocabulary. *Journal of the Royal Asiatic Society* 62/4: 785–854.

Ulrich B.
- 2011. Oman and Bahrain in late antiquity: The Sasanians' Arabian periphery. *Proceedings of the Seminar for Arabian Studies* 41: 377–386.

van der Wal Anonby C.
- (in press). *A Grammar of Kumzari, a language of Oman*. Leiden: Leiden University.

Watson J.C.E.
- 2011. South Arabian and Yemeni dialects. *Salford Working Papers in Linguistics and Applied Linguistics* 1: 27–40.
- (in press). Translation, mistranslation and the seasons in Mahrah. *Wiener Zeitschrift der Kunde des Morgenlandes*.

Watson J.C.E. & Bellem A.
- 2010. A detective story: Emphatics in Mehri. *Proceedings of the Seminar for Arabian Studies* 40: 345–356.

Watson J.C.E. & Eades D.
- 2012. Documentation and ethnolinguistic analysis of the Modern South Arabian languages. Leverhulme Trust Project Grant outline. Accessed 16 February 2013. [Unpublished.]

Wilkinson J.C.
- 2010. *Ibâḍism: Origins and early development in Oman*. Oxford: Oxford University Press.

Windfuhr G.L.
- 2005. Central Asian Arabic: The Irano-Arabic dynamics of a New Perfect. Pages 111–123 in É.Á. Csató, B. Isaksson & C. Jahani (eds.), *Linguistic Convergence and Areal Diffusion: Case studies from Iranian, Semitic, and Turkic*. London: Routledge Curzon.

Zwemer S.M.
- 1902. Three journeys in northern Oman. *The Geographical Journal* 19/1: 54–64.

Author's address

Christina van der Wal Anonby, Leiden University, Department of Languages and Cultures of the Middle East, Witte Singel 25, M. de Vrieshof 4, 2311 BZ, Leiden, The Netherlands.

e-mail cvanonby@gmail.com

Southern Semitic and Arabic dialects of the south-western Arabian Peninsula

JANET C.E. WATSON

Summary

In this paper I examine a selection of key phonetic, phonological, and morphological commonalities exhibited by Ancient South Arabian (ASA), Modern South Arabian (MSAL), and Arabic varieties spoken in western Yemen, south-western Saudi Arabia, and Oman, drawing relevant comparisons with Ethio-Semitic. This study shows a wide range of shared and overlapping features between the so-called southern Arabic varieties examined and the non-Arabic varieties, suggesting a need to realign the position of southern Arabic in the Semitic language family.

Keywords: Modern South Arabian, Ancient South Arabian, Yemeni Arabic, Ethio-Semitic, language inheritance

1. Phonetics and phonology

In this section, I consider the realization of emphatics in Modern South Arabian, the presence of lateral emphatics and affricate reflexes of emphatics, and voiceless plain sibilants. I also examine total assimilation of nasals to following obstruents in Sabaic, Modern South Arabian, and Rāziḥīt, the Yemeni variety spoken in Jabal Rāziḥ.

1.1. Emphatics

Since 1970 and until recently, it was claimed that the main phonetic correlate of emphasis in the Modern South Arabian languages was glottalization, as in Ethio-Semitic, which exhibits glottalized emphatics, and in contrast to Arabic, which exhibits backed emphatics. Acoustic and impressionistic work conducted on Mehri by Watson (in Sima 2009; Watson 2012) and Watson and Bellem (2011), however, has since shown that several emphatics exhibit no glottalization, and that those that do may fail to exhibit glottalization in weak prosodic environments (in particular, Naïm & Watson 2013). This is supported by impressionistic observations by Kogan, Naumkin, and others on Soqotri (Leonid Kogan, personal communication). The main characteristic of the MSAL emphatics, in contrast to that of Ethio-Semitic emphatics, is one of backing or pharyngealization. Thus, while /ḳ/ is usually glottalized and released as an ejective [k'], and /ṣ/ in strong prosodic positions (syllable initial, foot initial) may be released as an ejective, the emphatics /ṣ́/, /ṣ̌/, /ṭ/ are realized as ejectives only in pre-pausal position (as a result of pre-pausal glottalization, Watson & Bellem 2011), and /ḍ/ ~ /ṭ/ is never realized as an ejective. Even in cases where emphatics are realised as ejectives, they are accompanied by backing which spreads to adjacent vowels, as in Arabic varieties and in contrast to Ethio-Semitic. In Mehri, the emphatics together with pharyngeals diphthongize adjacent stressed high long vowels, and back adjacent low vowels. Consider the following examples from eastern Yemeni Mehri:

> *bīṣ́ayt* 'egg' v. *rēśīt* 'snake"
> *ṣalḥayt* 'fat f.s.' v. *xaṭmīt* 'thin f.s.'
> *ḳadḳayd* [type of fish] v. *harhēr* [type of fish]
> *malḥawt* 'salt' v. *barwūt* 'she gave birth'
> *ṭād* 'one m.' v. *tēṭ* 'woman'

The combined backing effects and ejective realization in strong prosodic environments implies, as we have stated elsewhere (e.g. Watson & Bellem 2011; Watson 2012), that the Modern South Arabian emphatics occupy a stage in the development of Semitic consonants between Ethio-Semitic and Arabic.

1.2. Lateral emphatics and affricate reflexes of emphatics

Lateral obstruents feature in many varieties of the south-west Peninsula. The Modern South Arabian languages exhibit plain and emphatic lateral sibilants, and distinguish between the cognates of Arabic *ḍ and *ḏ̣. On the basis of lateral cognates in Biblical Hebrew and Modern South Arabian, it is considered probable that Ancient South Arabian s² had a lateral articulation (cf. Steiner 1977; Beeston 1984; Sima 2001). Until recently the reflex of *ḍ was a voiceless lateral affricate in Rāziḥīt[1] in traditional words.[2]

There are indications that non-stop emphatics may originally have been realized as affricates in some Semitic languages (Steiner 1982). Beside the lateral affricate reflex of *ḍ in Rāziḥīt, a non-pharyngealized /st/ reflex of the emphatic sibilant is attested in a number of north Yemeni dialects — *stadīgin* 'friend', *stabrin* 'patience' (Behnstedt 1987a; 1987b; 1998) — and in Faifi spoken north of the current Yemen-Saudi border — for example *stayfin* 'summer' (Abdullah al-Faifi, personal communication). On the basis of frequent similar sound changes in Egyptian Arabic, Biblical Hebrew, and Syriac, Behnstedt (1987a: 8–9; 1998: 7; see also Steiner 1982) suggests that /st/ may have originally been an affricate *ts which was subject to metathesis, making affrication in these varieties the phonetic correlate of emphasis.

The cognate of *ḏ̣ is generally believed to have been an emphatic lateralized fricative in Proto-Semitic (Kogan 2011). Lateral fricative and lateral sonorant realizations of *ḏ̣ are still found today in dialects within the regions of Rijāl Almaʿ and al-Rubūʿah in south-west Saudi Arabia (Watson & Al-Azraqi 2011; Heselwood et al. 2013), in Ġaylḥabbān in the Hadramawt (Habtour 1988), and in the dialect spoken by Bait Kathīr in western Oman. A number of dialects spoken in the south-west of Saudi Arabia continue to make a phonological distinction between *ḍ and *ḏ̣ (Watson & Al-Azraqi 2011; Heselwood et al. 2013).

1.3. Voiceless sibilants

Within the phonology, Modern South Arabian is unique among extant Semitic languages in exhibiting a three-way distinction in the voiceless sibilant series, a distinction shown in Ancient South Arabian. The third sibilant in the series is lateral, as believed to have been the case for s² in Ancient South Arabian. Sabaic and Mehri cognates involving the three plain voiceless sibilants are given below:

Sabaic: s¹nt, Mehri: *šnēt* 'sleep'
Sabaic: ʿs²r, Mehri: *ʿōśar* 'ten'
Sabaic: ʾks³wt, Mehri: *kiswēt* 'clothes'

Śḥerēt exhibits a four-way contrast among the voiceless sibilants: in addition to /s/, /š/, /ś/, a labialized alveo-palatal sibilant /šʷ/. The contrast between /s/, /š/, and /šʷ/ can be seen in the minimal triplet below:

ibrit-š 'his daughter' v. *ibrit-šʷ* 'your f.s. daughter', v. *ibrit-s* 'her daughter'

In other extant languages of the region, there is only a two-way distinction in the plain voiceless sibilant series; the laterality of *š allegedly attested in early Arabic (e.g. Steiner 1977), however, is still found among older speakers in Rāziḥīt spoken in Jabal Rāziḥ (Watson et al. 2006a).

1.4. Nasal assimilation

Total anticipatory assimilation of /n/ was a regular occurrence in mid-Sabaic and late Sabaic, as evidenced by the frequent defective spellings of certain words, such as: ʾfs < ʾnfs, bt < bnt, ʾtt < ʾntt (Stein 2003: 19; see also Beeston 1984: 11). A comparative frequency count of defective versus full spellings in the mid- and late Sabaic inscriptions indicates that /n/ assimilation became an increasingly common process in the language, particularly around Mārib and the central Yemeni highlands (Stein 2003: 20).

Total assimilation of /n/ to a following non-guttural consonant is a productive phonological process in northern Yemeni Rāziḥīt, as exemplified in: *našar — yiššur* 'to go out in the afternoon', *nagal — yiggul* 'to extract', *iṯnēn — ṯaṯṯē* 'two m., f.' (Sab. tty) (cf. *ssān* 'man' *ssānih* 'woman', etymologically related to *ʾinsān, cf. Behnstedt 1987a: 98), but *anḥaʾ* 'we'. Assimilation of /n/ is now historical in Modern South Arabian,[3] with evidence of assimilation in lexicalized

---

[1] Behnstedt (1987a), on the basis of information from one informant in an-Naḍīr [sic], describes the reflexes of *š and *ḍ as retroflex. According to Bonnie Glover Stalls (personal communication), who spent several months conducting linguistic fieldwork in in-Naḍīr, , these sounds are more lateral than retroflex, although the laterality of *š is slight today, and may now be historical. An electropalatographic investigation of this variety would be useful at this point — with the palatograms showing the place of articulation, and the linguograms providing information about the tongue shape, including degree of laterality.

[2] Behnstedt (1987a: 136) notes 160 forms with the pan-Yemeni voiced pharyngealized interdental fricative as opposed to seventy forms with the retroflex /ɖ/. The voiceless lateral affricate reflex of *ḍād* is present within the phonological memory of some present speakers but is no longer in current usage (Bonnie Glover Stalls, personal communication).

[3] Unless otherwise noted, Mehri data from eastern Yemen (Mahriyōt) is taken from my own recordings and the sound files published on the Semitic Sound Archive, University of Heidelberg (www.semarch.uni-hd.de/index.php43?LD_ID=5&RG_ID=3&lang=en). Mehri data from western Oman (Mehreyyet) is taken from Watson 2012 and my own

forms only, as in Mehri: *k'annūn ~ k'annawn* 'small m.s.', *k'annitt* (<*k'annan-t*) 'small f.s.'; *tēṭ* 'woman' is pronounced without initial /n/, and the /n/ reappears in the plural form *īnēṭ* 'women'. In Śḥerēt, /n/ of the prepositions *min* 'from' and *ʕan* 'from, by' assimilates totally to the consonants of the singular, but not the plural, pronoun suffixes, as in: *mɛk* 'from you m.s.', *mɛšʷ* 'from you f.s.', *mɛš* 'from him', *mɛs* 'from her', but *munkum* 'from you m.pl.' and *munhum* 'from them m.'; /n/ is absent in the singular of words relating to woman, e.g. *tɛṭ* 'woman', *tyɛṭ* 'newly married woman', but returns, as it does in Mehri, in the plural: *īnɛṭ* 'women', *nṭiniʕtī* 'newly married women'.

Total assimilation of /n/ to a following sonorant is common in the languages of the world, including dialects of Arabic (cf. Watson 2002; Elramli 2012). Total assimilation of /n/ to a following obstruent, however, is not. The occasional results of assimilation of /n/ in Andalusian, with examples such as /att/ 'you m.s.' < *anta and /kittará/ 'you would see' < *kint tara Corriente (1989: 97) considers to be due to South Arabian influence. The result of total assimilation of /n/ to a following obstruent is found in a very few lexicalized forms in various Arabic dialects (Elramli 2012) — notably in the words *bint > *bitt* 'girl' and *kunt > *kutt* 'I/you m.s. was/were' (Egyptian) and *kunta > *kutta* 'I/you m.s. was/were' (Sudanese), but interestingly the trigger of assimilation in these cases shares with /n/ both the articulation feature (coronal), and the manner feature (non-continuant). Toll (1983: 11) notes a few instances of /n/ assimilation to coronal and non-coronal obstruents in the Ḥijāzī dialect of Ghāmid: assimilation to /z/ in the word *manzal > *mazzal* 'house', and assimilation to /x/, /š/, and /t/ apparently involving the preposition /min/ 'from'. Elsewhere, /n/ assimilates only in terms of place (e.g. *jambīya* 'dagger', *zumbil* 'basket', *muŋ kull* 'of all').

2. Morphology

In this section, I consider *kaškašah*, the *k*-suffix conjugation for 1s and 2 persons, the *-t* feminine ending, the 3fpl prefix conjugation verb, and the non-assimilating definite article.

2.1. *Kaškašah*

The realization of the 2fs object and possessive pronoun as *-iš* or *-ic*, known in the Arabic literature as *kaškašah*, is characteristic of southern Ethio-Semitic (but not northern) and Modern South Arabian, and is widely attested in Arabic varieties spoken in Yemen, Asir, southern Najd, al-Hasa, Oman, and the ʕAjman of Kuwait (Holes 1991). Consider the following examples:

San'ani (Yemen): *aḥibb-iš* 'I love you f.s.', *ibn-iš* 'your f.s. son', *fawg-iš* 'on you f.s.'
Rāziḥīt: *fihmū-c* 'they m. understood you f.s.', *bēt-ic* 'your f.s. house', *naḥā-c* 'at your f.s. house; with you f.s.'
Amharic: *näggärä-š* 'he told you f.s.', *wəšša-š* 'your f.s. dog'
Harari: *sabar-ēš* 'he broke you f.s.'
Mehri: *aġarb-aš* 'I know you f.s.', *śīnk tē-š* 'I/you m.s. saw you f.s.', *hnī-š* 'at your f.s. house', *ḥabrit-š* 'your f.s. daughter'
Śḥerēt: *śinkto-šʷ* 'I/you m.s. saw you f.s.', *ʕa-šʷ* 'from you f.s.', *ī-šʷ* 'your f.s. father'

Kaškašah was mentioned by the early Arab grammarians for dialects of Arabic. There are indications, however, that it is a relatively recent phenomenon in the history of Semitic, as neither Ancient South Arabian nor Ancient Ethio-Semitic exhibit *kaškašah*.

2.2. The *k*-suffix conjugation 1s and 2

The realization of the first singular and second person subject suffixes in suffix conjugation verbs as *-k-*, rather than *-t-*, is a feature of Yemeni dialects throughout the western mountain range (Behnstedt 1985; 1987*a*; 1987*b*) up to Jabal Rāziḥ and the region around Sa'dah in the north, in southern Yemeni Yāfiʕ (Vanhove 1995*a*; 1995*b*), Modern South Arabian (Simeone-Senelle 1997; 2011), Sabaic, Minaean (Stein 2011), Himyaritic (Robin 1991), and the ancient and modern languages of Ethio-Semitic. It is not attested in the south-west Saudi Arabian varieties of Faifi or Rijāl Almaᶜ, and indeed, from the information we have to hand including recent fieldwork conducted by Al-Azraqi, Watson and Naïm in south-west Saudi Arabia, does not appear to feature north of the present-day Yemeni-Saudi border. An interesting difference between the k-dialects of Yemen and the languages of Ethio-Semitic, on the one hand, and Modern South Arabian, on the other, is that the former distinguish between 1s and 2ms, while the latter do not. Compare the following:

---

recordings, some of which are available on the Semitic Sound Archive (www.semarch.uni-hd.de/index.php43?LD_ID=1&RG_ID=6&lang=en). The translations are my own.

Amharic: *qom-k* 'you m.s. got up', *qom-ku* 'I got up', *säbbär-ku* 'I broke'
Rāziḥīt: *sarḥ-uk* 'I went before noon', *sarḥ-ik* 'you m.s. went before noon'
Ibbi (Yemen): *ištarō-k* 'I bought', *ištarē-k* 'you m.s. bought'
Mehri: *haṣbaḥ-k* 'I/you m.s. got up in the morning', *syar-k* 'I/you m.s. went'
Śḥerēt: *ḳhab-k* 'I/you m.s. came at midday', *nfoś-k* 'I/you m.s. went in the afternoon'

In the varieties which exhibit both k-perfect endings and *kaškašah*, both the 2fs suffix conjugation subject pronoun and the 2fs object or possessive pronoun are realized as *-š* or *-c* (see also Behnstedt 1985: 82, 118):

Amharic: *säbbär-š* 'you f.s. broke', *näbbär-š* 'you f.s. were'
Rāziḥīt: *jī-c* 'you f.s. came', *rē-c* 'you f.s. saw', *katb-ic* 'you f.s. wrote'
Mehri: *śīn-aš* 'you f.s. saw', *syar-š* 'you f.s. went'
Śḥerēt: *ḳhab-šʷ* 'you f.s. came at midday', *ġsom-šʷ* 'you f.s. went early morning'

2.3. The *-t* feminine ending

The *-t* nominal feminine ending is attested for many nouns in Rāziḥīt, always in the definite and construct states but, as in Modern South Arabian, Sabaic, and Ethio-Semitic, also in the absolute state in many basic nouns. Consider the examples below:

Rāziḥīt: *jahwit* 'small room on lower floor for animals', *dēmit* 'kitchen', *šōfit* '(married) woman', *iḥ-ḥalgit* 'the series', *ik-kaḏbit* 'the lie' (Watson et al. 2006a; 2006b)
Amharic: *gärmän-awi* 'a male German' > *gärmän-awi-t* 'a female German' (Meyer 2011: 1190)
Mehri: *salfat* 'story f.', *ʕaydīt ~ aydīt* 'sardine f.'
Śḥerēt: *yit* 'camel mare'; *šʷabdat* 'liver f.'

In the adjective class, Rāziḥīt marks most non-participle adjectives by final *-īt* in all three states — absolute, definite, and construct. Adjectives that take final *-īt* include all the relational (*nisbah*) adjectives and a small set of non-*nisbah* adjectives:

Rāziḥīt: *bunnīt* 'brown', *aṣlīt* 'original', *gudēmīt* 'old', *lahjah rāziḥīt* 'Rāziḥīt dialect' (Watson et al. 2006a; 2006b)
cp. Eastern Yemeni Mehri: *lbōn — labnīt* 'white m., f.', *rḥīm — rḥīmat* 'beautiful m., f.'; Omani Mehri: *ūbōn — ūbanīt* 'white m., f.', *dwayl — dwaylat* 'old m., f.'

The *-t* feminine ending in all states is said to have distinguished the ancient Arabian languages from Arabic: the King of Himyar is legendarily said to have expressed the absence of Arabic in his language with the words: *laysa ʕindanā ʕarabiyyat* 'there is no Arabic among us' where it is explained that, unlike in Arabic, *-t* is not dropped in pause (Rabin 1951: 34).

2.4. The 3fpl prefix conjugation verb

The 3fpl prefix conjugation verb in Modern South Arabian is expressed by the circumfix *ta-...-an*, in common with Sabaic (t-fʕl-n(n)), but in contrast to Arabic and the other Semitic languages:

Mehri: *t-baky-an* 'they f. cry', *t-katb-an* 'they f. write'
Śḥerēt: *t-ḳodar-an* 'they f. are able'
Sabaic: t-fʕl-n(n)

Compare these forms with the following for Classical Arabic, Sanʕani Arabic, and Old Ethiopic:

Classical Arabic: *ya-fʕal-na* 'they f. do'
Sanʕani Arabic: *yi-saww-ayn* 'they f. do'
Old Ethiopic: *yə-ḳettəl-ā* 'they f. kill' (Weninger 2011)

2.5. The definite article

Many Arabic dialects in the south-west of the Arabian Peninsula do not exhibit the /l/ definite article often cited as typical of Arabic. The nasal definite article, hn-/h-/0 in Ancient North Arabian (Macdonald 2000; Stein 2003: 85) and *n-* or *m-* in Himyaritic (al-Hamdāni 1884–1891; Robin 1991: 204; 2007: 259, 260), said to distinguish non-Arabic Semitic languages of the Peninsula from Arabic (Macdonald 2000), is attested today throughout the Yemeni and Saudi Tihāmah (cf. Greenman 1979; Asiri 2009), and in the mountain area of far northern Yemen (Behnstedt 1985; 1987a: 85–6; 2007).[4] In many dialects of northern and coastal Yemen and south-western Saudi Arabia, it is realized as invariable *m-* or *n-*, depending on dialect, as in: *am-safar* 'the journey', *am-qamar* 'the moon'. Several dialects in northern Yemen exhibit an /n/ definite article, which again shows no complete assimilation to any following consonant, as in northern Yemeni Majz *in-ṣaʕbah* 'the female donkey foal', *in-šams* 'the sun'.

In addition, several Arabic dialects throughout the

---
[4] An interesting observation made by Behnstedt (2007: 54) for dialects spoken within the political borders of Yemen is that the *m*-definite article never occurs in a *k*-dialect variety.

western Yemeni mountain range exhibit an article which involves gemination of the nominal-initial consonant, irrespective of its identity, as in: *ab-bēt* 'the house', *ag-gamar* 'the moon', *ih-hōd* 'the wedding' as, for example, in Rāziḥīt, Jiblah, Ghamar, and Khawlān (see Behnstedt 1987*a*: 85). This geminate reflex of the definite article is exhibited optionally in several varieties of the mainland Modern South Arabian languages spoken in Oman, where the initial consonant of the nominal is neither emphatic nor voiced, in particular after prefixes or conjunctions. Thus, Omani Mehri shows the following forms:

kansīd 'shoulder' v. *w-akkansaydī* 'and my shoulder'
xīl 'maternal uncle' v. *axxaylī* 'my maternal uncle'
farahayn 'horse' v. *āgōb bi-ffarahayn* 'I like the horse'

In other cases, definiteness in Mehri is expressed by *ha-* or *ḥa-* in some lexically marked plurals, as in: *bōni* 'sons' > *ḥabūn* 'the sons'; by *ḥa-* in a few nominals with initial etymological glottal stop, as in: *bar* 'son' > *ḥabrī* 'my son'; or by *a-* where the initial nominal consonant is either voiced or emphatic, as in: *bayt* 'house' > *abayt* 'the house'. This *a-* allomorph is shown, according to Domenyk Eades (personal communication), in the Arabic spoken in the Wahiba Sands of Oman before nominals with initial labials or /g/ (< *q),[5] as in:

a-fār 'the mouse', *a-fxīḏa* 'the clan'
a-gabīla 'the tribe'
a-baḥar 'the sea', *a-bint* 'the girl'
a-madīna 'the cemetery', *a-midnī* 'the pregnant camel'

---

[5] The definite article is realized as *l-* before guttural fricatives (/ḥ/, /ʕ/, /ġ/, /x/), and in all other cases as gemination of the initial C.

3. Conclusion

In my presentation during the Seminar, I considered a number of additional features shared across languages of the southern Peninsula. Within the morphology, these included dual pronouns and verb forms attested in many dialects of the MSAL and ASA; the invariable clausal definite article *ḏ-* found in several Yemeni Arabic dialects, Sabaic, and Mehri; and the number-variable clausal definite article: *ḏ-* (singular), *l-* (plural) in the MSAL, and the number/gender-variable clausal definite article *ḏ-*, *t-*, *l-* attested in late Sabaic and the Arabic of Rijāl Almaʕ. Within syntax, I considered the tens + unit structure of the numerals above 10 in the MSAL and Ethiopic, as opposed to the unit + tens structure of ASA and Arabic.

The presence of dual pronouns and verb forms, the three-way plain voiceless sibilant distinction, and the *ta-...-n* 3fpl prefix conjugation affixes shared only between Sabaic and MSAL suggest that the MSAL may be the oldest continuously spoken Semitic sub-family today. The complex matrix of shared grammatical features between many varieties of Arabic in Yemen and south-west Saudi Arabia, MSAL, ASA, and Ethio-Semitic: the *k-* suffix for first and second person in the suffix conjugation, *kaškašah*, the *-t* nominal feminine ending, the non-*l* definite article and, in Rijāl Almaʕ, the variable clausal definite article, suggest that many of these so-called Arabic varieties are closer to southern Arabian than they are to northern Arabic dialects. Future research in this area may provide more conclusive evidence for claims researchers have made elsewhere (e.g. Retsö 2000; Watson 2011) that many of these so-called Arabic dialects are not Arabic at all, but rather continuations of the ancient languages of the Peninsula.

References

Asiri Y.
    2009. Aspects of the phonology and morphology of Rijal Alma' (south-west Saudi Arabia). PhD thesis, University of Salford. [Unpublished.]

Beeston A.F.L.
    1984. *Sabaic Grammar*. (Journal of Semitic Studies. Monograph, 6). Manchester: University of Manchester.

Behnstedt P.
    1985. *Die nord-jemenitischen Dialekte. Teil 1: Atlas*. Wiesbaden: Dr Ludwig Reichert.
    1987*a*. *Die Dialekte der Gegend von Ṣaʕdah (Nord Jemen)*. Wiesbaden: Harrassowitz.
    1987*b*. Anmerkungen zu den Dialekten der Gegend von Ṣaʕdah (Nord-Jemen). *Zeitschrift für Arabische Linguistik* 16: 93–107.

1998. Anmerkungen zum Jemenitisch-Arabischen. Pages 5–18 in *Aktualisierte Beiträge zum 1. Internationalen Symposium Südarabien Interdisziplinär*. Graz.

2007. Zum bestimmten Artikel und zur Ortsnamenkunde im Jemen. *Zeitschrift für Arabische Linguistik* 47: 50–59.

Corriente F.
1989. South Arabian features in Andalusi Arabic. Pages 94–103 in P. Wexler, A. Borg & S. Somekh (eds), *Studia Linguistica et Orientalia Memoriae Haim Blanc Dedicata*. Wiesbaden: Harrassowitz.

Elramli Y.
2012. Assimilation in the Phonology of a Libyan Arabic Dialect: A Constraint-based Approach. PhD thesis, University of Newcastle. [Unpublished.]

Greenman J.
1979. A sketch of the Arabic dialect of the Central Yamani Tihāmah. *Zeitschrift für Arabische Linguistik* 3: 47–61.

Habtour M.
1988. L'arabe parlé à Ġaylḥabbān: Phonologie et morphologie. PhD thesis, University of the Sorbonne, Paris. [Unpublished.]

al-Hamdānī, Abū Muḥammad al-Ḥasan b. Aḥmad/ed. D.H. Müller.
1884–1891. *Ṣifat jazīrat al-ʿarab. Al-Hamdânî's Geographie der Arabischen Halbinsel*. (2 volumes). Leiden: Brill.

Heselwood B., Watson J.C.E., Al-Azraqi M. & Naïm S.
2013. Lateral reflexes of Proto-Semitic *ḍ and *ḏ̣ in Al-Rubūʕah dialect, south-west Saudi Arabia: Electropalatographic and acoustic evidence. Pages 135–144 in R. Kuty, U. Seeger & S. Talay (eds), *Nicht nur mit Engelszungen: Beiträge zu semitischen Dialektologie: Festschrift für Werner Arnold zum 60. Geburtstag*. Wiesbaden: Harrassowitz.

Holes C.D.
1991. *Kashkasha* and the fronting of the velar stops revisited: a contribution to the historical phonology of the peninsular Arabic dialects. Pages 652–678 in A. Kaye (ed.), *Semitic Studies in Honor of Wolf Leslau*. i. Wiesbaden: Harrassowitz.

Kogan L.
2011. Proto-Semitic phonetics and phonology. Pages 54–150 in S. Weninger et al. (eds), *The Semitic Languages: An international handbook*. Berlin: Mouton.

Macdonald M.C.A.
2000. Reflections on the linguistic map of pre-Islamic Arabia. *Arabian Archaeology and Epigraphy* 11: 28–79.

Meyer R.
2011. Amharic. Pages 1178–1212 in S. Weninger et al. (eds), *The Semitic Languages: An international handbook*. Berlin: Mouton.

Naïm S. & Watson J.C.E.
2013. La corrélation occlusive laryngovélaire dans des variétés néo-arabes et sud-arabiques. Pages 133–151 in J.L. Léonard & S. Naïm (eds), *Base articulatoire arrière: Backing and Backness*. Munich: Lincom.

Rabin C.
1951. *Ancient west Arabian*. London: Taylor's Foreign Press.

Retsö J.
2000. Kaškaša, *t*-passives and the ancient dialects in Arabia. Pages 111–118 in L. Bettini (ed.), *Oriente Moderno: Studi di dialettologia Arabe*. Rome: Istituto per l'Oriente.

Robin C.
1991. Les langues de la péninsule arabique. Pages 89–111 in *L'Arabie antique de Karib 'îl à Mahomet: Nouvelles données sur l'histoire des Arabes grâce aux inscriptions*. Aix-en-Provence: Edisud.

2007. Himyaritic. Pages 256–261 in K. Versteegh et al. (eds), *Encyclopedia of Arabic Language and Linguistics 2*. Leiden: Brill.

Sima A.
- 2001. Der Lautwandel s³> s¹ und s¹> s³ im Sabäischen. *Zeitschrift der Deutschen Morgenländischen Gesellschaft* 151: 251–262.
- 2009. *Mehri-Texte aus der jemenitischen Sharqīyah: Transkribiert unter Mitwirkung von Askari Hugayran Saad*, edited, annotated and introduced by J.C.E. Watson & W. Arnold. Harrassowitz: Wiesbaden.

Simeone-Senelle M-C.
- 1997. The Modern South Arabian languages. Pages 378–423 in R. Hetzron (ed.), *The Semitic Languages*. London: Routledge.
- 2011. Modern South Arabian. Pages 1073–1113 in S. Weninger et al. (eds), *The Semitic Languages: An international handbook*. Berlin: Mouton.

Stein P.
- 2003. *Untersuchungen zur Phonologie und Morphologie des Sabäischen*. Rahden/Westf.: Leidorf.
- 2011. Ancient South Arabian. Pages 1042–1073 in S. Weninger et al. (eds), *The Semitic Languages: An international handbook*. Berlin: Mouton.

Steiner R.C.
- 1977. *The Case for Fricative-Laterals in Proto-Semitic*. New Haven, CT: American Oriental Society.
- 1982. *Affricated Ṣade in the Semitic Languages*. New York: American Academy for Jewish Research.

Toll C.
- 1983. *Notes on Ḥiǧāzī Dialects: Ġāmidī*. Copenhagen: C.A. Reitzel.

Vanhove M.
- 1995*a*. Notes on the Arabic dialectal area of Yāfiʕ (Yemen). *Proceedings of the Seminar for Arabian Studies* 25: 141–152.
- 1995*b*. À propos du verbe dans les dialectes arabes de Yāfiʕ (Yémen). Pages 257–269 in T. Harviainen & H. Halen (eds), *Dialectologia Arabica — A collection of articles in honour of the sixtieth birthday of Professor Heikki Palva*. Helsinki: Studia Orientalia.

Watson J.C.E.
- 2002. *The Phonology and Morphology of Arabic*. Oxford: Oxford University Press.
- 2011. South Arabian and Yemeni dialects. Pages 27–40 in G. Howley (ed.), *Salford Working Papers in Linguistics & Applied Linguistics* I.
- 2012. *The Structure of Mehri*. Wiesbaden: Harrassowitz.

Watson J.C.E. & al-Azraqi M.
- 2011. Lateral fricatives and lateral emphatics in southern Saudi Arabia and Mehri. *Proceedings of the Seminar for Arabian Studies* 41: 425–432.

Watson J.C.E. & Bellem A.
- 2011. Glottalisation and neutralisation in Yemeni Arabic and Mehri: An acoustic study. Pages 235–256 in B. Heselwood & Z. Hassan (eds), *Arabic Instrumental Phonetics.* Amsterdam: Benjamins.

Watson J.C.E., Glover Stalls B., Al-Razihi Kh. & Weir S.
- 2006*a*. Two texts from Jabal Rāziḥ. Pages 40–63 in L. Edzard & J. Retsö (eds), *Current Issues in the Analysis of Semitic Grammar and Lexicon II*. Wiesbaden: Harrassowitz.
- 2006*b*. The language of Jabal Rāziḥ. Arabic or something else? *Proceedings of the Seminar for Arabian Studies* 36: 35–41.

Weninger S.
- 2011. Old Ethiopic. Pages 1124–1142 in S. Weninger et al. (eds), *The Semitic Languages: An international handbook*. Berlin: Mouton.

Author's address

Janet C.E. Watson, School of Modern Languages and Cultures, University of Leeds, Leeds LS2 9JT, UK.
e-mail j.c.e.watson@leeds.ac.uk

Papers read in the Special Session of the Seminar for Arabian Studies on 27 July 2013

SEMANTICS & LEXIS

W.W. Müller	Sabaic lexical survivals in the Arabic language and dialects of Yemen
O. Elmaz	A South Arabian Journey through Early and Classical Arabic literature
A. Prioletta	Toward a Ḥaḍramitic lexicon: lexical notes on terms relating to the formulary and rituals in expiatory inscriptions
S. Naïm	L'expression des émotions dans une perspective comparative (dialectes de la Péninsule arabique): la variation intra-langue

PHONOLOGY & PHONETICS

J.C.E. Watson	MSAL, ASA and Yemeni dialects of the south-western Arabian Peninsula
L. Kogan	The Vowels of Soqoṭrī as a phonological system
R. Gravina	The vowel system of Jibbali in its historical context

CULTURE & LANGUAGE

S. Liebhaber	Intersections of Mahri oral poetry and Arabic nabaṭi poetry: The case for shared cultural inheritance
I. Rossi	The Minaeans' documentation beyond Maʿīn
P. Stein & I. Kottsieper	Sabaic and Aramaic: A common origin?

MORPHOLOGY & SYNTAX

A. Bellem & G.R. Smith	"Middle Arabic"? Morpho-syntactic features of clashing grammars in a 13th-century Arabian text
A. Avanzini	From the inscriptions to the grammar: notes on the non-Sabaic languages of South Arabia
D. Eades	Syncretism in the verbal morphology of Ḥarsūsī, a MSAL of central Oman
A. Rubin	A comparison of Mehri and Jibbali morphology